AMERICAN COURTS

AMERICAN COURTS

PROCESS AND POLICY

Sixth Edition

Lawrence Baum

The Ohio State University

HOUGHTON MIFFLIN COMPANY   Boston   New York

*To Bill Jenkins, Scott Jennings, Sam Shepherd,
Mike Simmons, and John Stewart*

Publisher: Suzanne Jeans
Senior Sponsoring Editor: Traci Mueller
Marketing Manager: Edwin Hill
Senior Development Editor: Jeffrey Greene
Senior Project Editor: Fred Burns
Senior Art and Design Coordinator: Jill Haber Atkins
Cover Design Director: Tony Saizon
Senior Composition Buyer: Chuck Dutton
New Title Project Manager: Susan Peltier
Editorial Assistant: Jason McDonald
Marketing Assistant: Erin Timm
Editorial Assistant: Jill Clark

Cover credit: Getty Images/Digital Vision/Jim Arbogast

Printed in the U.S.A.

Library of Congress Control Number: 2007924276

Instructor's examination copy:
ISBN-13: 978-0-618-73102-2
ISBN-10: 0-618-73102-4

For orders, use student text ISBNs:
ISBN-13: 978-0-618-52284-2
ISBN-10: 0-618-52284-0

3 4 5 6 7 8 9—CRS—11 10 09 08

CONTENTS

Chapter 4   **The Selection of Judges**   **93**

Chapter 6   **Trial Courts: Criminal Cases**   **150**

Chapter 8   **Appellate Courts: The Process**   **243**

PREFACE

The United States has a bewildering array of courts in more than fifty separate court systems. What those courts do ranges from the routine handling of traffic offenses in local trial courts to the resolution of broad legal issues in the Supreme Court. Courts use complex procedures to do their work, and judges write opinions in a specialized and technical language. For all these reasons, the courts are difficult to understand.

Courts are the subject of considerable attention in television shows, movies, newspapers, and books. Ideally, that coverage would teach us a good deal about what the courts do and how they function. But the picture of the courts that is presented in those forums often diverges a good deal from reality. A dedicated viewer who never missed a television show about the courts would gain a fairly distorted picture of what goes on in the third branch of government.

Because it is so difficult to comprehend the courts, people could hardly be faulted if they gave up trying. And yet there is good reason to keep trying. While there is considerable disagreement about the power of the courts to shape American life, it is clear that they play a significant role. They shape national policy on issues such as federalism, abortion, and the death penalty. Court decisions on crime and personal injuries, to take two examples, directly affect the lives of millions of people. This book is an effort to help make sense of the judicial branch, to provide a better understanding of the courts as part of American government and society.

One goal of this book is descriptive—to show how courts operate and what they do. I look closely at the work of the various types of courts in the United States. I also examine the people and institutions that help to shape the courts' activities, including lawyers, litigants, and policy makers in the other branches of government.

A second goal of the book is to explain what courts do and how they relate to the rest of the political system. To take one example, it is important to know that a high proportion of criminal cases are resolved through plea bargains, but it is also important to understand the forces that make plea bargaining so common. Throughout this book, I consider explanations for matters such as the president's choices of federal judges and the positions that Supreme Court justices take in the cases they decide.

The mass media, the general public, and policy makers elsewhere in government constantly evaluate the courts. Much of that evaluation is negative. One consequence is an array of proposals to remedy what people perceive as the courts' failings. This book examines many of these proposals and shows that reforms often fail to achieve the positive effects that were sought. A third goal of the book is to help readers make informed judgments in evaluating both the current state of the courts and proposals for change.

FEATURES OF THIS REVISION

The courts constantly change. This sixth edition of the book reflects the changes that have occurred in the time since the fifth edition was published. Among the developments covered in this edition are President George W. Bush's appointments of judges to the federal courts and their impact on judicial policy (Chapter 4), the Supreme Court's decisions striking down federal and state systems of sentencing guidelines (Chapter 6), and the role of the courts in the government's efforts to deal with terrorism (Chapters 8 and 9).

New developments in the courts are also reflected in the book's illustrative material. This edition has more case studies set off in exhibits than did prior editions. Most of the exhibits are new, and most of the others are extensively revised. The new exhibits cover a range of subjects. Among them are a state supreme court justice who sued his colleagues over the right to become chief justice (2.9), the efforts of lawyers to appeal to potential clients through the Yellow Pages (3.6), the plea bargain in the prosecution of the "American Taliban" (6.6), and the heated legal battles between two major corporations (7.4).

New research and writing by scholars and journalists continue to expand our understanding of the courts. This work is incorporated throughout the book, and major new books are included in the bibliographies at the end of each chapter.

CONTENTS OF THE SIXTH EDITION

The book is divided into nine chapters. Chapter 1 introduces the courts and the perspectives that I take in examining them. Chapter 2 describes the organization of the federal and state courts, including both the structure and administration of court systems. It also shows that the organization of courts affects what they do, sometimes leading to heated debates over seemingly routine issues of court organization. Chapter 3 focuses on lawyers, who shape both the courts and the larger legal system. The chapter begins by examining the law as a profession and then discusses the availability of lawyers to potential clients and the relationships between lawyers and clients.

Chapters 4 and 5 deal with judges. Chapter 4 examines the selection of federal and state judges. The chapter gives attention to the formal rules used for selection of judges, including debates about their desirability and their impact on the courts. It also examines the processes by which judges are elected and appointed in practice. Chapter 5 discusses judges themselves. It begins by looking at the political activities, career experiences, and social circumstances of people who become judges and at how those elements of judges' backgrounds affect them. It then turns to judges' activities on the bench. Finally, it probes the quality of judges' work and considers means to strengthen their performance.

Chapters 6 and 7 cover the work of trial courts. Chapter 6 examines criminal cases, focusing on the most important stages in the criminal process: decisions to prosecute suspects, plea bargaining, trials, and sentencing decisions. The chapter discusses the impact of two types of proposals for change in the courts' work, those designed to limit plea bargaining and those designed to reduce judges' discretion in sentencing. Chapter 7 looks at civil cases, focusing on decisions to initiate cases, the processing of cases in court, and patterns of outcomes in cases. One of the questions considered is the accuracy of the common image of Americans as quite eager to take their grievances to the courts.

Chapters 8 and 9 turn to appellate courts. Chapter 8 examines the processes that occur in appellate courts, including choices to appeal unfavorable decisions, screening of cases by the courts themselves, and the process of reaching decisions. In its discussion of decision making, the chapter focuses on the forces that shape the decisions of the Supreme Court and other appellate courts. Chapter 9 considers appellate courts as policy makers. Its discussion of the policies made by appellate courts gives attention to "judicial activism," the subject of considerable debate. It then explores the impact of judicial decisions on public policy and American society.

WEBSITE

Websites have become increasingly valuable sources of information about the courts, and the new website for the book lists relevant websites on the courts. The website also contains ACE questions (test questions for student practice), Flashcards to review glossary terms, Web links, and a Judicial Process Simulation. To see the website, go to: **college.hmco.com/pic/baum6e.**

ACKNOWLEDGMENTS

This sixth edition continues to reflect the help of a great many people in my writing of prior editions. I would like to thank those who assisted in this revision. Several scholars provided valuable suggestions for improving the book: Jeffrey Davis, University of Maryland; Ashlyn Kuersten, Western Michigan University; Samuel T. Shelton, Troy University; and Paul Wahlbeck, George Washington University. A number of people helped by providing information about the courts for use in this edition: Stephen Burbank, Rachel Caufield, Brett Curry, Mark Hurwitz, Herbert Kritzer, Peter Nagler, Kate Sampson, Kevin Scott, Wendy Watson, and especially Ruth Baum. I appreciate all the help I received from people who work for and with Houghton Mifflin. I owe special thanks to Fred Burns, Jeff Greene, and Leslie Kauffman.

L. B.

1

An Overview of the Courts

As a nation, Americans have a fascination with the courts. Newspapers frequently devote headlines to Supreme Court decisions and sensational cases, and each year a large stack of books about courts and judges is published. "Reality" shows starring judges are a staple of daytime television, and prosecutors and judges regularly appear in prime-time entertainment shows. A whole cable channel is devoted to the courts. Blogs analyze courts in general, particular aspects of their work, and even individual judges. When politicians and political commentators vent their wrath, courts are often the target.

One source of this fascination is a widespread recognition that courts are important. Each year, courts in the United States affect the lives of millions of people in cases that involve them directly—as criminal defendants and victims of crime, as people who seek compensation for injuries, as contestants for custody of children. Courts address national issues such as the power of the states to regulate abortion and the balance between national security and personal freedom. In the past forty years judicial decisions have led to the resignation of one president (Richard Nixon) from office, made possible the impeachment of another (Bill Clinton), and ensured the election of a third (George W. Bush).[1]

American courts are large in number and complex in their operation. As a result, even among people with a strong interest in the courts, most have a limited sense of what courts do and why they do it. Because the courts are important, it is important that we understand them. This book is an effort to help provide that understanding. It has three related goals: to lay out a clear description of courts and their activities; to suggest explanations of the behavior of people in and around the courts; and to offer perspectives from which to evaluate the work that courts do.

In this introductory chapter, I provide an overview of the courts, outlining some ways of thinking about them. Starting with the relationship between courts and law, the chapter then moves on to examine courts as institutions and their roles in government and society. I also discuss perspectives from which court processes and outcomes can be explained as well as the task of evaluating courts. Many of the topics discussed in this chapter will be examined more closely in the chapters that follow; the brief discussions here provide some background with which to begin.

COURTS AND LAW

Courts deal with law. The concept of law is complex, but it can be defined simply as authoritative rules made by government.[2] The rules are authoritative in the sense that they are intended to bind government itself, people and institutions outside government, or both. Courts have the task of interpreting laws that are made elsewhere; in doing so, courts make law themselves.

Sources of Law

Law has multiple sources. As Exhibit 1.1 illustrates, the body of law dealing with an issue such as discrimination has many sources.

The highest form of law is the content of *constitutions.* State constitutions are superior to any other state laws. The federal constitution is superior both to other federal laws and to state laws—including state constitutions. The federal and state constitutions establish basic rules about the powers of government and the procedures by which government is to operate. State constitutions also contain a great many rules about the substance of government policy that one might not expect to find in a constitution. The Kentucky Constitution, for instance, includes a provision dealing with intersections of tracks belonging to different railroad companies.[3]

Second in the hierarchy are *statutes*, laws enacted by legislatures. (Laws passed by local legislative bodies are usually called *ordinances.*) Legislatures are free to enact statutes of any type, so long as those statutes do not conflict with provisions of the federal constitution and, in the case of state statutes and local ordinances, the relevant state constitution. While constitutions deal primarily with what government can do, statutes generally are directed at society as a whole. Statutes often prohibit a form of conduct, such as damage to the environment, or provide benefits, such as medical care.

Statutes typically are written in broad terms—in effect, outlining the law. An administrative agency that is responsible for carrying out a statute often fills in the outline by adopting more detailed legal rules, called *rules* or *regulations.* For Title VII of the Civil Rights Act of 1964, the statute on discrimination in employment that is excerpted in Exhibit 1.1, the regulations defining discrimination more precisely go on for many pages.

Executive orders, laws made by chief executives such as presidents and governors, occupy two different positions in the legal hierarchy. Some executive orders are based on statutes, so they are similar to administrative regulations. Other executive orders are based on the powers that the federal or state constitution gives the chief executive, so they are similar to statutes.

Court decisions occupy an ambiguous place in the hierarchy. Courts interpret constitutions, statutes, and executive orders, and they are bound by the language of the laws they interpret. In that sense, their rulings are subordinate to all those forms of law. But courts have power to enforce the hierarchy of law when they determine whether an administrative regulation is consistent with the statute it interprets or whether a statute is "unconstitutional" because it conflicts with a relevant constitutional provision. And in offering their interpretations of the law, courts in effect create new law. In giving more specific meaning to the constitutional requirement that states provide "the equal

EXHIBIT 1.1   Examples of Language in Various Types of Federal Laws Dealing with Discrimination

---

Constitution

"No State shall . . . deny to any person within its jurisdiction the equal protection of the laws."

— U.S. Constitution, Amendment XIV, Section 1

Statute

"It shall be an unlawful employment practice for an employer—

(1) to fail or refuse to hire or to discharge any individual, or otherwise to discriminate against any individual with respect to his compensation, terms, conditions, or privileges of employment, because of such individual's race, color, religion, sex, or national origin. . . ."

— *United States Code,* Title 42, sec. 2000e-2 (a) (2006) (Title VII of the Civil Rights Act of 1964)

Regulation

"A recipient [of federal money] may administer or assist in the administration of scholarships, fellowships, or other forms of financial assistance established pursuant to domestic or foreign wills, trusts, bequests, or similar legal instruments or by acts of a foreign government which requires that awards be made to members of a particular sex specified therein; *Provided,* That the overall effect of the award of such sex-restricted scholarships, fellowships, and other forms of financial assistance does not discriminate on the basis of sex."

— *Code of Federal Regulations,* Title 34, sec. 106.37(b)(1) (2006) (regulations for Title IX of the Education Amendments of 1972)

Executive Order

"Except in contracts exempted in accordance with Section 204 of this Order, all Government contracting agencies shall include in every Government contract hereafter entered into the following provisions:

'During the performance of this contract, the contractor agrees as follows:

'(1) The contractor will not discriminate against any employee or applicant for employment because of race, color, religion, sex, or national origin. . . .'"

— Executive Order 11246, sec. 202 (issued Sept. 24, 1965), as amended by Executive Order 11375 (issued Oct. 13, 1967)

Court Decision

Title VII of the Civil Rights Act of 1964 "forbids an employer from 'discriminat[ing] against' an employee or job applicant because that individual 'opposed any practice' made unlawful by Title VII or 'made a charge, testified, assisted, or participated in' a Title VII proceeding or investigation. . . . We conclude that the anti-retaliation provision does not confine the actions and harms it forbids to those that are related to employment or occur at the workplace."

— Decision of U.S. Supreme Court in *Burlington Northern & Santa Fe Railway Co. v. White* 165 L. Ed. 2d 345, 352–353 (2006) protection of the laws" or in resolving an ambiguity in the Civil Rights Act of 1964, courts add to the law on discrimination.

In some fields of law, such as contracts and torts (which deals mostly with personal injuries), English and American courts first developed rules of law on their own rather than by interpreting laws from other sources. Even today, much of the law in those fields is contained in court decisions that were established independent of statutes. Such independent, judge-made law is often called the *common law*, though that term has other meanings as well.

The courts' interpretations of the law can be overridden by rewriting the law in question—that is, by amending the state or federal constitution or by enacting a new statute. Rulings about the common law can also be overridden through statutes. To the extent that the other branches of government undertake such overrides, courts do not have the final word on the law. But most court decisions stand undisturbed by the other branches, and this fact makes the courts an important source of law.

Categories of Law

The body of law established by government policymakers ranges widely in its subject matter. Several distinctions can be made among categories of law, and a few are especially important for an understanding of courts.

One distinction is between *public* and *private* law. Public law has been defined in different ways, but basically it involves the government acting as government rather than in other roles, such as property owner. Public law includes such matters as taxation, regulation of business practices, public welfare programs, foreign policy, and criminal justice. Law that does not involve government as government is private. Some common kinds of private law cases are those concerning marriage and personal injuries.

Another distinction is between *criminal* and *civil* law. Criminal law prohibits certain conduct and threatens punishment for the prohibited conduct. In criminal cases people (and occasionally corporations) are prosecuted by government for alleged violations of criminal laws. Everything else can be called civil, though civil law sometimes has a narrower meaning. Much of the civil law also prohibits conduct, but here the consequences of a violation ordinarily do not involve punishment as such. Most often, violators are required to compensate those who suffered losses as a result of the prohibited conduct. A specific situation may bring both criminal and civil law into play. After the collapse of the Enron corporation, former executives Kenneth Lay and Jeffrey Skilling were prosecuted for criminal offenses in federal courts, and they were also the defendants in lawsuits brought by people who had suffered losses in the company's collapse.

Within these broad categories, law is subdivided further. Criminal statutes deal with *felonies*, the more serious offenses, and with *misdemeanors*. Civil law covers a variety of fields, such as *contracts, property*, and *domestic relations*.

UNDERSTANDING COURTS AS INSTITUTIONS

The judicial branch of government is composed of trial and appellate courts in both the federal system and the fifty state systems—altogether, thousands of courts. As institutions, these courts share some important traits. Most fundamentally, all courts interpret and apply the law in individual cases. To take another example, judges and lawyers play the central parts in nearly every court. Because of these shared traits and because courts are all in the judicial branch, people usually think of courts as a distinct set of institutions.

Yet this view of courts obscures two important realities: courts differ from each other in fundamental ways, and they have similarities with institutions other than courts. Both of these realities require some elaboration.

Differences among courts can be illustrated by comparing the U.S. Supreme Court with municipal courts, which exist in most states as trial courts for cases with relatively small stakes. (In those and other states, there are courts with different names that carry out the same function.) This comparison highlights some important ways in which courts differ:

1. The municipal court is a *trial court* and the Supreme Court is an *appellate court*. Cases are heard first in trial courts. When cases go to trial, the emphasis is usually on ascertaining facts, chiefly through the testimony of witnesses. Appellate courts review lower court decisions. They hear arguments that deal primarily with the application of the law to the facts that were already ascertained at trial. A single judge presides in a trial court, and either the judge or a jury makes a decision. In appellate courts, cases are heard and decided by multiple judges. (Members of the Supreme Court and of state supreme courts are usually called justices rather than judges.) The differences between trial and appellate courts are so great that the two sets of courts will be examined separately in the last four chapters of the book.

2. Public proceedings in the two courts look quite different. Municipal court sessions typically involve action on large numbers of cases, which are often handled informally and speedily. Someone who walks into a courtroom may find it difficult to follow the action, and the overall impression is likely to be one of chaos. In contrast, the Supreme Court conducts its public sessions with considerable formality in a rather majestic setting. To the observer, the difference between the Supreme Court and a municipal court may seem like the difference between a well-staged show and a three-ring circus.

3. To continue the metaphor, the casts of characters in the two courts are also different. Lawyers who appear before the Supreme Court are likely to work in the most prestigious segments of the legal profession, while lawyers from those segments of the profession seldom appear in municipal courts. Similarly, most Supreme Court justices come from legal and political elite groups, but judges typically reach municipal courts from lower levels of the legal and political systems.

4. The two courts hear different kinds of cases. Municipal courts handle criminal and civil cases with relatively small stakes under state statutes and local ordinances. Common types of municipal court cases include small claims and misdemeanors (including traffic and parking violations, which are generally classified as misdemeanors in most states). The Supreme Court hears cases raising broad legal issues under the U.S. Constitution and federal statutes. Most of these cases concern civil liberties and government regulation of the economy. Nearly all cases heard by

the Supreme Court were originally decided by some trial court, and occasionally a case that began in a municipal court is later decided by the Supreme Court. Even in such a case, however, the central issues generally change so much—from narrow factual questions to broad questions of legal interpretation—that the Supreme Court in effect decides a different case from the one that was heard in municipal court.

Taken together, these characteristics show basic distinctions between municipal courts and the Supreme Court. The more general lesson should be clear: courts are not a homogeneous set of institutions.

A second and related point is that courts share attributes with institutions other than courts. Indeed, a great many nonjudicial institutions are similar to courts in their functions, their operation, or both.[4] Many of these institutions are in the executive branch of government, often called administrative courts or tribunals. One example is the immigration courts within the Department of Justice that deal with issues such as applications for asylum and deportations for criminal conduct. There are also court-like institutions in the private sector. An example is arbitration, in which two parties present their cases to an arbitrator for a decision. Arbitration has become increasingly common as a mechanism to resolve legal disputes. Some religious and ethnic groups use their own courts to resolve disagreements within their communities.

More broadly, some institutions that do not look or act like courts share important attributes with them. Indeed, both the Supreme Court and municipal courts have similarities with seemingly very different institutions in other branches of government. The Supreme Court is similar to Congress in many respects. Both set their agendas by selecting issues for consideration from a much larger body of requests. Both reach decisions through a series of group processes. Each establishes general policies on national issues, policies that must be put into effect by other people and institutions.

For their part, municipal courts have much in common with bureaucratic agencies that apply the law by processing large numbers of cases involving individuals, such as the Social Security Administration and state motor vehicle bureaus. The bureaucrats who deal with those individual cases are required to follow a set of rules for their decisions, rules that are often highly detailed. But in practice bureaucrats may have considerable discretion in acting on cases, and they often operate under time pressures that make it difficult to follow prescribed procedures. These generalizations apply well to judges on municipal courts. For instance, they usually have a wide range of options in setting bail for criminal defendants, and they generally lack the time and information with which to make careful choices among those options.

Thus it can be misleading to think of courts as a single unique category of institutions. The differences among courts and their similarities to other institutions are noted throughout the book.

THE ROLES OF COURTS: FUNCTIONS AND IMPACT

A central goal of this book is to discern the roles that courts play in American government and society. In the process, two related questions are explored: what do courts do, and what impact do they have? In the chapters that follow, these questions are addressed in specific contexts; here I discuss them in more general terms.

The Functions of Courts

Courts engage in a variety of activities. One way to think about these activities is in terms of their functions for government and society. A few of the courts' functions stand out as especially important.

The first is *dispute resolution.* Civil cases explicitly involve disputes between at least one plaintiff (the party that brings the case) and defendant (the party against whom the case is brought). A great many criminal cases also arise from disputes between a complainant and the defendant. (A complainant is someone who calls a possible criminal case to the attention of the police or the prosecutor.) Thus courts provide a forum for ventilating and resolving disputes. In the great majority of civil cases, the parties themselves agree on a settlement prior to trial. Similarly, in most criminal cases, the defendant pleads guilty and thus settles a key issue in the case. In other cases, of course, courts themselves determine how disputes are resolved by reaching decisions.

By establishing courts as a forum for dispute resolution, the government provides an important service for its residents. People are better off if they can bring lawsuits to deal with conflicts that otherwise might be difficult to resolve. At the same time, government serves its own goal of preventing conflicts from disrupting social relations and the operation of the economy.

Government has an interest not only in resolving conflicts but in helping to set the terms for their resolution. This interest leads to a second function, *behavior modification.* Courts reward certain kinds of behavior and penalize others, with the goal of encouraging what is rewarded and discouraging what is penalized. This function is clearest on the criminal side of the law. Courts are part of a system for enforcement of the criminal laws, a system designed to reduce the incidence of certain actions by threatening serious penalties for those actions.

Similar purposes underlie the civil side of the law. Here the government allows lawsuits for damages against people who engage in certain types of behavior, hoping thereby to discourage such behavior. A negligent driver may face a lawsuit brought by someone who has suffered an injury through the driver's actions, and the prospect of such suits may induce people to drive more carefully. In this sense, private individuals or groups who bring civil cases act unintentionally as agents of government.

This function is illustrated by the False Claims Act, adopted in 1863 and strengthened in 1986 as a means to deter false monetary claims against the federal government. Under the act, individuals can bring lawsuits in the name of the federal government against people who allegedly have made false claims. The Justice Department can take over those suits; if not, the original plaintiff can carry the suit forward. In either case the person who brought the suit can recover a portion of the proceeds, as much as 25 percent.[5] The government's incentive works. By an incomplete count, individuals have brought more than five thousand cases since the law was strengthened in 1986. More than nine billion dollars have been won in court judgments or settlements, and the people who brought the cases have received more than 1.6 billion dollars as their share.[6]

A third function of courts, one that flows from the first two, is the *allocation of gains and losses.* In criminal cases, courts impose penalties on defendants in the form of monetary fines, imprisonment, and even death sentences. In civil cases, courts often order transfers of money (or decide not to order such transfers) from one party to another. They also determine such matters as the status of marriages and the control of corporations. In this process, civil courts often make one person or organization better off and another worse off.

This allocation function, of course, has direct effects on individual litigants. Through their actions as an aggregate, courts also allocate gains and losses between groups in American society, such as creditors and debtors in contract cases or insurance companies and injured people in accident cases. In doing so, courts may benefit some groups systematically at the expense of others.

A fourth function of courts, *policymaking,* is implicit in the first three. Policymaking can have many different definitions; here I mean the creation and application of authoritative rules—that is, law. In itself, the distinction between creating new legal rules and applying existing rules seems clear, but in practice the distinction can be fuzzy. In particular, what seems like the routine application of rules often has elements of rule creation. A judge who regularly imposes the maximum allowable sentence on individuals who are convicted of burglary is thereby helping to shape the law of burglary.

Of course, the legislative and executive branches also engage in policymaking. Indeed, judicial policymaking is sometimes regarded as an illegitimate intrusion into the domain of the other branches. But policymaking is inherent in the task of deciding cases. Even the creation of new rules can be unavoidable when courts confront legal issues that have not yet been resolved. Still, judges make choices that enhance or limit their roles in policymaking, choices that relate to the long and often heated debate over "judicial activism."

Of these four functions, the first three are dominated by trial courts. This is because the great majority of court cases are terminated at the trial level—through a settlement, through a choice by the initiating party to drop the case, or through acceptance of the court decision by all the parties. Thus, most of what courts do in resolving disputes, modifying behavior, and allocating gains and losses is done by trial courts. Appellate courts hear a small proportion of all cases, so they have less to do with these functions. But appellate judges, who adopt interpretations of the law that are applied by other policymakers, probably have greater impact as policymakers than do their counterparts in trial courts.

The Impact of Courts

The impact of what courts do is difficult to ascertain. It is clear that courts help to shape American society, but there is considerable disagreement about the extent of that impact. Some scholars and commentators emphasize the forces that limit courts' impact. In contrast, others depict the courts as a dominant force, often a force for harm. According to one commentator in 2003, "federal courts and judges in America today are to be more feared than al-Qaida."[7] Where does the reality lie?

In exploring this issue, it is useful to distinguish between trial courts and appellate courts, which are important in somewhat different ways. Trial courts gain their impact chiefly through the large numbers of decisions they make in individual cases. Each year millions of individuals are subject to court action involving such matters as criminal offenses, divorces, auto accidents, and traffic and parking violations. Decisions about matters such as child custody or imprisonment have an enormous impact on people's lives. And what courts do in these cases affects still more people—those who resolve matters out of court—because predictions of what a court would decide help to determine the bargaining positions of people who settle a dispute through negotiation.

Appellate courts exert influence primarily through the broad impact of the legal rules they proclaim. This impact follows from the doctrine that a court's interpretation of the law is binding on courts below it in the judicial hierarchy. Thus a state supreme court ruling on the obligations of landlords to tenants can affect decisions on landlord-tenant relationships in every court in the state. A ruling by the U.S. Supreme Court on the acceptability of religious observances in public schools under the Constitution affects every state or federal judge who decides a school religion case. A Supreme Court decision on school religious observances can also affect the language that legislatures put into statutes and the practices of individual schools.

Important as these effects are, they should not be exaggerated. For one thing, courts are only part of the set of institutions that make government policy in an area. Even when court decisions determine what happens to individuals, those decisions usually reflect actions by legislators and administrative officials. In deciding a criminal case, for instance, a trial court is applying rules that the legislature established, and the case came to court because of decisions by police officers and prosecutors. Whether a judge grants a divorce and how much a divorced parent pays in child support may be largely dictated by state statutes.

Nor does a court necessarily have the last word on an issue. The impact of appellate court decisions depends heavily on the actions of other policymakers. A Supreme Court decision on religious exercises in public schools or on the questioning of suspects by the police must be interpreted and applied by lower courts. Ultimately, administrators—such as school principals and police officers—determine the effect of such a decision in practice. Indeed, on both school religion and police questioning, actual practice deviates a good deal from what the Supreme Court has ruled. And Congress or a state legislature might limit the impact of a decision or even overturn it altogether.

Further, courts do not play a major part in all the areas of government policy. Most notably, foreign policy is almost entirely the province of Congress and the executive branch. This is especially true of international conflicts in which the United States is involved. In Iraq, as in past wars, courts have had only marginal effects on what the government does.

A second limitation on the impact of courts applies to government in general. Government is only one of many forces that shape society, and it is not necessarily the most powerful. Important nongovernmental forces—including the family, the mass media, and the economy—have major effects on conditions such as racial equality and free speech. Those effects are likely to be more fundamental than the impact of court decisions.

I emphasize limitations on the impact of courts because those limitations are sometimes given insufficient attention. But we should not lose sight of the impact that courts do have. Courts affect the lives of many people in significant ways and shape national policy on major issues. Thus they merit the attention that we give them, and nobody can understand American government and society without understanding the courts.

EXPLAINING COURT PROCESSES AND OUTCOMES

One of my goals is to help explain the processes by which courts operate and the outcomes of cases that are brought to court. Thus I will discuss explanations for such matters as the prevalence of plea bargaining in criminal cases, the pattern of outcomes in automobile accident cases, and disagreements among judges in appellate court decisions. Ultimately, such explanations must rest on the choices of the individuals involved in the courts—litigants, lawyers, judges, and others. Those choices seldom have simple explanations, and our ability to explain them is often limited by insufficient information.

It is difficult to explain what courts do in general terms because different aspects of their work are best explained in different ways. But we can begin by thinking about broad categories of explanations for court processes and outcomes: the legal, the environmental, and the personal.

The Legal Perspective

Courts work within a legal framework. In making decisions, judges and juries apply legal rules to the facts of specific cases. These rules are found in the federal and state constitutions, in the statutes adopted by legislatures, and in past court decisions.

Judges, lawyers, and observers of courts disagree sharply about the importance of this legal framework in shaping what the courts do. Some people, including many judges, argue that courts do little more than follow the law. At the other extreme, some critics argue that the law is primarily a way for judges to rationalize decisions they actually make on other bases, such as their attitudes about the policy issues involved in cases. The reality, I think, is somewhere between these two views.

The law is important in courts chiefly because judges and lawyers believe that they are in the business of applying the law. To a degree, this belief is embedded in American culture, with its strong emphasis on the rule of law. And lawyers undergo intensive law school training in legal reasoning, training that is reinforced by their later experience in the legal system.

For these reasons, courts generally are pervaded by an atmosphere in which people speak and think in terms of legal principles. As a result, the law channels and constrains activity in courts. Lawyers seek to win cases by showing that their clients' positions are consistent with the best interpretation of the law. In turn, judges consider and decide cases within a legal framework. The Kansas legislature adopted a statute in 2002 that allowed for an increased sentence based on prior offenses if a criminal defendant was convicted of involuntary manslaughter "while driving under the influence of alcohol and drugs." Undoubtedly, the legislators who enacted the statute meant "alcohol *or* drugs." But two years later the state supreme court held that the statute had to be read as it was written. "We assume the legislature meant what it passed."[8] And when an Ohio appellate court had to "determine whether a cow is an uninsured motor vehicle under appellants' insurance policy," the judges did not simply say that it made no sense to treat a cow as a motor vehicle. Rather, they cited a dictionary definition of a motor vehicle (the cow met three of the four criteria in the definition but lacked the wheels required by the fourth criterion) and two prior decisions of Ohio courts to reach that result.[9]

The impact of the law is most apparent when it moves judges away from decisions they would prefer to reach. It is not always easy to ascertain when that happens, because judges often say that they simply followed the law even when they reach a result that they find desirable on other grounds. But sometimes judges say explicitly that the law required them to reach a result they did not want, and they do so in a way that seems credible. Two examples are described in Exhibit 1.2.

Yet the law is an incomplete explanation of what courts do, for two fundamental reasons. First, in contrast with the cases described in Exhibit 1.2, the law frequently leaves considerable discretion to judges and juries. In some instances, legislatures create this discretion deliberately. For example, statutory criteria for decisions on child custody are typically quite broad so that judges can make what they regard as the appropriate decision in light of all the relevant facts.

More often, discretion results from ambiguities in the law and its application. Jurors are asked to apply the law to the facts of a particular case. But if there are two or more plausible readings of the facts, conscientious jurors may reach different conclusions. Similarly, many provisions of constitutions and statutes contain vague language, such as "due process of law," which requires judges to choose among credible alternative interpretations.

The other reason that the law fails to explain court activities fully is that the motivations of people in the courts go beyond simply trying to follow the law. Undoubtedly, most judges strongly believe that they *should* follow the law in deciding cases and supervising court proceedings. But judges also hold preferences about public policy issues and feel external pressures to handle cases in certain ways. These factors affect the behavior of judges, even of judges who try to apply legal rules faithfully. In *Bush v. Gore* (2000), the Supreme Court's decision halted the recount of votes in Florida and thereby ensured the election of George W. Bush as president. The five justices in the majority can all be characterized as conservatives, while the four dissenting justices who favored Al Gore's position were the most liberal members of the Court. It may well be that all the justices sought only to interpret federal law as well as they could. But their readings of the law inevitably were affected by their rooting interests in the election result, and the lineup of justices in the final decision could hardly be coincidence.

The limitations of the law as an explanation of court behavior are highlighted by disagreements among judges and among jurors. On the Supreme Court, whose nine members apply the same body of law to the same case, only a minority of decisions are unanimous—38 percent in the 2004–2005 term. There are so many legal issues on which two or more lower federal courts have reached differing conclusions that the Supreme Court can resolve only a portion of them. And when the Court does resolve them, not surprisingly, the justices often disagree among themselves. Such disagreements reflect both the ambiguity of the law and the influence of other motivations on the judges who decide cases.

EXHIBIT 1.2   Federal Judges Decide Two Immigration Cases

A federal statute allows illegal immigrants to remain in the United States if they have lived in the U.S. continuously for at least the last seven years, and an absence of up to ninety days during that period is allowed. Fernando Mendiola-Sanchez and his son met the seven-year criterion, but what the father had intended as a short trip to Mexico went beyond three months when both his parents were injured and he—joined by his son—stayed to take care of them. A few years later, both father and son were ordered to be deported.

When the decision was appealed to the federal court of appeals for the Ninth Circuit, Chief Judge Mary Schroeder wrote the court's 2004 opinion upholding the deportation. But Judge Schroeder, speaking for two colleagues in the case, expressed her considerable unhappiness with the decision. "Although we deny the petition for review because that is the proper conclusion under the relevant statutes, we pause in recognition of the injustice of this result." "This result," she added, "is harmful to an entire family." The opinion suggested that officials in the executive branch could still prevent deportation. "Our immigration laws severely limit the power of courts, but when we are confronted with injustice we must urge those who do have discretion to exercise it wisely."

A year later, Judge Donovan Frank of the federal district court for Minnesota decided another deportation case. Cynthia Lamah, a citizen of Cameroon living in Germany, had a husband and child in the United States when she entered the country illegally in 2003; the child was born with sickle-cell anemia and required frequent medical treatment. After her application for asylum was denied, she was ordered to turn herself in for deportation. She did so, was jailed pending deportation, and suffered a miscarriage in jail. After she was denied an emergency stay of removal, she went to federal court.

Judge Frank concluded that "the law clearly does not allow this Court jurisdiction" over the case. But he also said that "this is a case where the law and human decency have diverged." And he added that "this is a sad day for those who believe that when a judge adheres even-handedly to his or her oath of office, justice will prevail and the public interest will be served."

Sources: Mendiola-Sanchez v. Ashcroft, 381 F.3d 937 (9th Cir. 2004); *Lamah v. Department of Homeland Security*, 2005 U.S. Dist. LEXIS 18181 (D. Minn. 2005). The quotations are from *Mendiola-Sanchez*, at 941–942, and *Lamah*, at 11–12.

It is worth reiterating that legal rules offer a good guide to much of what courts do. Without a legal perspective, it is impossible to understand what happens in courts, and the law is often the best starting point for an explanation of court behavior. But it is only a starting point, and other perspectives are needed to gain a more comprehensive understanding of courts.

The Personal Perspective

In its strongest form, the legal perspective assumes that people who make decisions in courts act only on their commitment to the law. In contrast, what might be called the personal perspective allows for a broader range of motivations that can influence behavior. Judges, for instance, may make choices on the basis of their own values or self-interest. Indeed, their personality traits can influence what they do. Thus the personal perspective shifts the focus from the law to the individuals who work in the legal system.

A focus on individuals has proved very useful in the study of Supreme Court decision making. Many scholars view the Court's decisions mostly as reflections of one motivation, the justices' desire to make what they see as good policy. According to this view, divisions on the Court can be explained by differences in policy preferences, and the Court's collective position results from the sum of the nine justices' conceptions of good policy.

The terms *liberal* and *conservative* are used regularly to describe judges' personal policy preferences and court policies. These labels require some discussion. On most issues that courts decide, the competing positions generally are given one label or the other; Exhibit 1.3 summarizes what are usually considered to be the liberal and conservative positions on some major judicial issues. One common thread binding

EXHIBIT 1.3   Liberal and Conservative Positions on Some Common Judicial Issues

Issue Area	Liberal Position	Conservative Position
Criminal cases	Relatively sympathetic toward defendants and their procedural rights	Gives greater emphasis to the effectiveness of the criminal justice system in fighting crime
Personal liberties	More supportive of liberties such as freedom of speech and right to privacy	More supportive of values that may conflict with these liberties, such as public order and national security
Disadvantaged groups	More strongly supports expanded rights and improved status for groups such as African Americans, women, and the poor	Gives relatively great weight to the costs of these expansions and improvements, such as the monetary costs of public welfare
Regulation of business	More favorable to government regulation on behalf of such goals as protection of the environment	More protective of the autonomy of businesses
Businesses vs. individuals	In economic conflicts, such as disputes between insurance companies and injured drivers, more likely to support the individual	Less likely to support the individual; more favorable to business

Note: Positions of liberals and conservatives should be read in relation to each other; for instance, liberals are more likely to support individuals in disputes with businesses than are conservatives.

together positions on different issues is that the liberal position on most issues is the one more favorable to equality rather than to competing values such as the autonomy of businesses. In part because of this common thread, people tend to be consistent in their ideological positions. In other words, a judge with liberal views on one issue is likely to have liberal views on most other issues. For this reason it is possible to characterize most judges on the basis of where they stand on the spectrum from very liberal to very conservative.

A different motivation, self-interest, is highlighted by the plea bargaining that takes place in criminal courts. In plea bargaining, lawyers, defendants, and judges resolve cases through negotiation rather than through trials. Plea bargaining is prevalent chiefly because it offers important advantages to each group. Among other benefits, prosecutors avoid the risk of an acquittal at trial, defendants and their attorneys limit the severity of the sentence, and judges save the time and effort that trials would require. Initiatives to eliminate plea bargaining nearly always fail because of this mutual self-interest in maintaining it.

An implication of the personal perspective is that courts should be understood as institutions with their own dynamics. All the participants bring their motivations to court, and court processes and case outcomes emerge from the interaction of these motivations. One result is that legal mandates can be distorted. Legislatures may establish a mandatory minimum sentence for an offense, only to discover that judges and prosecutors who disagree with that requirement have found ways to avoid imposing it.

Another implication is that it often makes considerable difference who participates in the courts generally and in particular cases. This reality is illustrated very well by the Supreme Court. President Bush's appointments of John Roberts and Samuel Alito to the Court have made the Court somewhat more conservative. If John Kerry had been elected in 2004 and the same two vacancies had appeared on the Court, the shift would have been in a liberal direction. As a result, some significant cases over the next several years would have been decided differently.

Another illustration is the impact of having a case decided by one judge (or set of judges) rather than another. Lawyers and litigants routinely engage in "judge-shopping," maneuvering to get their cases before judges whom they perceive as favorably inclined. Indeed, lawyers often work to have a case heard in one county or state rather than another because of their perceptions of judges in the two places. In the federal courts of appeals, where the three-judge panels that hear cases are chosen randomly from all the judges in a circuit, the luck of the draw can make considerable difference for the chances that a criminal defendant or someone with a civil rights case will prevail.

The personal perspective can go far toward explaining what happens in the courts. But this perspective is incomplete, for two reasons. The first is that it does not take into account the impact of law that was discussed earlier.

Second, a narrow concentration on people within the courts can obscure the broad forces that affect the courts. A focus on individuals helps a great deal in understanding why a Supreme Court justice has selected the more liberal position of the two that are debated in a particular case. It is less useful in identifying a position that no justice has considered because it lacks sufficient support outside the Court. For example, since the mid-1990s the Supreme Court has interpreted the Constitution to limit the power of Congress to regulate certain state and private activities.[10] But no matter what the justices' views are, they can go only so far in this direction. A ruling that Congress cannot establish a minimum wage is exceedingly unlikely, because such a ruling and its broader implications would be unacceptable to too many people in and out of government. Nor does the focus on individuals take into account the social forces and political currents that help produce a liberal or a conservative Court in any given period. These considerations point to the need for a broader perspective on court behavior.

The Environmental Perspective

The environmental perspective views courts in relation to the government and society of which they are part. Courts are influenced by their environments in several ways. The experiences of lawyers and judges within American society shape their values and perceptions. The other branches of government influence courts by writing the laws that judges interpret and selecting the judges themselves. Interest groups bring cases to court and make arguments that influence judges' perceptions of the issues in those cases. The state of the economy and social trends help determine what kinds of cases go to court and how judges and jurors think about those cases.

For all these reasons, there is a tendency for courts to mirror American society. But what exactly do they mirror? To some degree, they reflect the pattern of social values and attitudes in the United States. For one thing, lawyers and judges are likely to share these attitudes. For another, attitudes that are widely shared and strongly held among the public are likely to exert at least a subtle influence on people in the courts. For both reasons, to take one example, widespread concern about illegal drugs since the 1980s has had considerable effects on the courts. One effect is the tendency for courts to interpret civil liberties narrowly when those liberties seem to conflict with efforts to attack the drug problem. The Supreme Court, for instance, has upheld most of the government drug testing programs that it has reviewed.[11]

Courts also tend to reflect the distribution of economic and political power in society. Those segments of the population that have the most power are generally in the best position to influence what courts do. Most lawyers and judges come from higher-status backgrounds. Individuals and organizations with the greatest economic resources are the most capable of bringing cases to court and presenting them effectively. This does not guarantee that courts serve the interests of business corporations more diligently than the interests of individuals with low incomes, but it makes that outcome likely.

Courts sometimes respond to more direct pressures from their environments. Pressure from the local news media can influence prosecutors' decisions whether to bring charges in a case. Most judges would prefer to avoid criticism, and elected judges have a strong incentive to retain public support. The impact of this concern is most easily seen today in decisions on the death penalty. Some appellate judges have lost their positions because of charges that they were unwilling to uphold death sentences, and judges sometimes vote in favor of death sentences as a means to avoid similar fates.[12]

Powerful as these influences are, their impact is limited by the degree of autonomy that courts enjoy. Mechanisms such as the life terms of federal judges and norms that restrict direct lobbying of judges and juries give courts some insulation from external pressures. This insulation helps to explain the willingness of some judges to make highly unpopular decisions, such as rulings that allow flag burning and prohibit religious obser-vances in public schools. It is difficult to imagine legislatures taking similar positions.

Thus, courts reflect society imperfectly. Strong currents of thought and power in American society inevitably affect courts, but other influences and motives also shape what happens in the courts.

General Implications

The discussion so far has pointed out several different perspectives from which one can explain the behavior of courts. It has also indicated that court processes and the results of court cases are shaped by a good many forces, so that few significant court phenomena can be explained in simple terms.

The examination of courts in this book reflects these lessons. I give primary em-phasis to the personal perspective and thus the motives of judges and other people in the courts, but the book employs the other perspectives as well. External influences on court processes and on the outcomes of cases receive considerable attention. And I take into account the legal framework within which courts work.

EVALUATING COURTS

People constantly evaluate the courts. Indeed, it is almost impossible to write about the Supreme Court or criminal courts without assessing the performance of those courts. This book contains a good deal of evaluation, addressing such issues as the quality of judges and the effectiveness of trials in discovering the truth. More often than not, however, my evaluations are tentative rather than firm. This reflects my feeling that there are fundamental difficulties in reaching conclusive judgments about the courts.

One difficulty is that there are many criteria by which the courts can be evaluated. The work of trial courts in criminal cases is an example. We might assess that work in terms of the quality of the representation that prosecutors and defense attorneys provide for their clients, the fairness with which judges preside over proceedings, the ability of juries to reach verdicts that are consistent with the evidence, the consistency with which judges apply sentences to convicted defendants, or the court's success in avoiding long delays in resolving cases—to cite a few of all the possibilities. A court that does well on one criterion might be quite unsuccessful on another.

It is important, then, to be clear about one's criteria for evaluating courts and to recognize that alternative criteria might lead to quite different conclusions. People who disagree in their evaluations often are talking past each other because they have based their judgments on different premises.

Agreement on criteria does not end the difficulties of evaluation, because the ap-plication of these criteria to a particular situation is often problematic as well. This is especially true when we assess courts in terms of the outcomes of cases. What is the "right" pattern of outcomes? A pattern of criminal sentencing that seems appropriate to one observer may seem unduly lenient to another. Businesses that come to court to col-lect debts from individuals are generally quite successful. Is that a good result? Starting with one set of premises, we may view the success of businesses as appropriate, on the ground that courts are properly requiring people to pay their debts. Starting with different premises, we may view this success as undesirable, on the ground that it allows an advantaged segment of society to exploit those who are often economically vulnerable.

It would seem much easier to evaluate a court according to how well it interprets the law, but that is not the case. What is a good interpretation of the Constitution when the relevant constitutional language is vague and several conflicting methods of interpretation are available? Judges on appellate courts, facing the same issues in the same cases, frequently disagree sharply about the best interpretation of the law. The case described in Exhibit 1.4 is an example. Such differences reflect the difficulty of many legal questions and the inevitable impact of judges' own values in shaping their interpretations.

EXHIBIT 1.4   A Disagreement Over the Proper Reading of the Constitution

When a defendant is convicted of first-degree murder and the prosecutor seeks the death penalty, the jury is asked to consider "aggravating" circumstances that support a death sentence and "mitigating" circumstances that support a lesser sentence. Under Kansas law, if a jury finds that the aggravating and mitigating circumstances have equal weight, the death penalty is to be imposed. In *Kansas v. Marsh* (2006), the Supreme Court decided by a 5–4 vote that this rule did not violate the constitutional prohibition of cruel and unusual punishment in the Eighth and Fourteenth Amendments. For both the justices in the majority and those who dissented, the appropriate interpretation of the Constitution was self-evident:

—From Justice David Souter's dissenting opinion:

> In Kansas, when a jury applies the State's own standards of relative culpability and cannot decide that a defendant is among the most culpable, the state law says that equivocal evidence is good enough and the defendant must die. A law that requires execution when the case for aggravation has failed to convince the sentencing jury is morally absurd, and the Court's holding that the Constitution tolerates this moral irrationality defies decades of precedent aimed at eliminating freakish capital sentencing in the United States.

—From Justice Clarence Thomas's majority opinion:

> The dissent's general criticisms against the death penalty are ultimately a call for resolving all legal disputes in capital cases by adopting the outcome that makes the death penalty more difficult to impose. While such a bright-line rule may be easily applied, it has no basis in law. Indeed, the logical consequence of the dissent's argument is that the death penalty can only be just in a system that does not permit error. Because the criminal justice system does not operate perfectly, abolition of the death penalty is the only answer to the moral dilemma the dissent poses. This Court, however, does not sit as a moral authority. Our precedents do not prohibit the States from authorizing the death penalty, even in our imperfect system. And those precedents do not empower this Court to chip away at the States' prerogatives to do so on the grounds the dissent invokes today.

Source: Kansas v. Marsh, 165 L. Ed. 2d 429 (2006). The excerpt from Justice Souter's opinion is at 462–463; the excerpt from Justice Thomas's opinion is at 446–447.

Often a lack of information increases the difficulty of evaluation. People in the legal profession probably could reach partial agreement on what constitutes competence in a trial lawyer. But there are so many trial lawyers across the country that it is impossible to make a definitive judgment about how competent they actually are as a group.

Even more problematic is evaluation of court decisions on the basis of their intended impact. Many people feel that the primary goal of criminal sentencing should be to limit the future incidence of crime, and one purpose of court decisions in personal injury law is to reduce the frequency of accidents. But at this point we know too little to determine what kinds of sentences or personal injury rules will best achieve these goals.

Despite all these difficulties, we should not be deterred from evaluating courts; their work is too important not to be assessed. But these evaluations must proceed with considerable caution and modesty. To offer a definitive assessment of court actions has little value when both the appropriate criteria and their application are uncertain.

This is also true of efforts to describe and explain court processes and the outcomes of court cases, for there is a great deal that we do not know about courts. Caution is always appropriate in examining the courts. But our knowledge is considerable, and it is growing. The remaining chapters of this book lay out what we do know about these institutions that play so central a part in American life.

Online Study Center **Go to college.hmco.com/PIC/baum6e for ACE practice test questions and additional resources.**

NOTES

1. On Nixon, the decision that led most directly to the president's resignation was *United States v. Nixon*, 418 U.S. 683 (1974). This decision and the district court decisions that preceded it are discussed in Theodore H. White, *Breach of Faith: The Fall of Richard Nixon* (New York: Atheneum, 1975). On Clinton, the key decision was *Clinton v. Jones*, 520 U.S. 681 (1997). On Bush, the Supreme Court decision that settled the election was *Bush v. Gore*, 531 U.S. 98 (2000).

   In citations of court decisions, the first number is the volume of the court reports in which the decision and accompanying opinions are found. The abbreviated designation of the court reports follows that number. "U.S." refers to the United States Reports, the official reporter of Supreme Court decisions. The second number is the page on which the decision and opinions begin: "1326, 1330–1331" would indicate that the decision began on page 1326 and that relevant material is on pages 1330–1331. The number in parentheses, of course, is the year of decision. (LEXIS citations differ in form, in that the second number is the number assigned to that decision rather than a page number.) If a reporter covers multiple courts, a citation will include within the parentheses, before the year of the decision, an abbreviation for the specific court issuing a decision. For instance, "F. Supp." is the Federal Supplement, which includes decisions of all federal district courts; "D.D.C." indicates that the district court in the District of Columbia decided the case.
2. This definition is adapted from Herbert Jacob, *Law and Politics in the United States* (Boston: Little, Brown, 1986), 6–7.
3. *Kentucky Constitution*, sec. 216 (*Ky. Revised Statutes Annotated*, 2005 ed.).
4. See Martin Shapiro, *Courts: A Comparative and Political Analysis* (Chicago: University of Chicago Press, 1981), ch. 1.

5. 31 *United States Code*, sec. 3730 (2006 ed.).
6. Civil Division, U.S. Department of Justice, "Fraud Statistics—Overview, October 1, 1986–September 30, 2005," posted at the website of Taxpayers Against Fraud (http://www.taf.org/).
7. Michael Savage, *The Enemy Within: Saving America from the Liberal Assaults on Our Schools, Faith, and Military* (Nashville: WND Books, 2003), 25.
8. *State v. Manbeck*, 83 P.3d 190, 194 (Kansas 2004).
9. *Mayor v. Wedding*, 2003 Ohio App. LEXIS 5947, at 1 (Ohio Ct. App. 2003).
10. Examples include *United States v. Morrison,* 529 U.S. 598 (2000), and *Board of Trustees v. Garrett*, 531 U.S. 356 (2001).
11. Examples include *Skinner v. Railway Labor Executives' Association,* 498 U.S. 602 (1989), and *Board of Education v. Earls*, 536 U.S. 822 (2002).
12. Melinda Gann Hall, "Justices as Representatives: Elections and Judicial Politics in the American States," *American Politics Quarterly* 23 (October 1995), 485–503; Richard R. W. Brooks and Steven Raphael, "Life Terms or Death Sentences: The Uneasy Relationship Between Judicial Elections and Capital Punishment," *Journal of Criminal Law and Criminology* 92 (2002), 609–639.

2

Court Organization

The federal court system is divided into circuits, each with a court of appeals. From time to time, with growth in population and caseloads, a circuit has been divided in two. For more than three decades, Congress has considered dividing the Ninth Circuit in the West into two or even three circuits. The fact that division has not yet occurred points to an important lesson about the organization of courts.[1]

There would seem to be an excellent case for splitting the Ninth Circuit. It contains nine states and two territories, stretching from Alaska to Arizona and from Montana to Guam, making it by far the largest of the federal judicial circuits in area. Its population is also considerably larger than that of any other circuit. Sixteen thousand cases were filed in the court of appeals for the Ninth Circuit in 2005, nearly as many as the number filed in any two other circuits. The court of appeals has twenty-eight judges scattered across the circuit, and in 2005 nineteen senior (semi-retired) judges also heard cases. The geographic size of the circuit, its caseload, and the number of judges all make its operation more difficult.

There is a practical problem in dividing the circuit. About two-thirds of the circuit's cases come from California, and it would be undesirable to divide California between two circuits. But California and a few other states and territories could be made into one circuit, quite large in population and caseload but not as unwieldy as the current Ninth Circuit.

In any event, this practical problem is not the primary reason for the failure of proposals to divide the circuit. Rather, the main source of opposition to these proposals is also a major source of support: political ideology. For many years, the Ninth Circuit Court of Appeals has been the most liberal of all the courts of appeals. Conservatives in the Northwest disapprove of the court's liberalism, especially on environmental issues, because of what they see as damage to timber and other industries in their region. To a considerable degree they identify this liberalism with judges from California. Thus, a proposal to put California in one circuit and the Northwest in another is appealing to them. Conservatives throughout the country disapprove of the Ninth Circuit's liberal decisions on a wide range of issues. Because a new circuit without California probably would be less liberal, those conservatives see a split as attractive.

Some proponents of a circuit split openly express their ideological motives, but others argue that they seek only to improve the quality of judicial administration. Alex Kozinski, a Ninth Circuit judge who opposes division of the circuit, has responded that "you'd have to believe in the tooth fairy to say that this has nothing to do with politics."[2] Acting on their own ideological views, liberals have strongly opposed division of the circuit. At least thus far, the strong opposition of liberals and Democrats, combined with the opposition of most Ninth Circuit judges, has been sufficient to prevent enactment of any circuit division proposal.

The lesson of this episode should be clear. A judicial system needs to have a structure of courts, and the system and its courts need to be administered. Decisions about court structure and administration would appear to be neutral matters, so that any debates about them would involve only issues of efficiency. But the reality is very different. Court organization is *not* neutral, because decisions about organization give an advantage to some individuals, groups, and policies over others. For this reason even the most seemingly innocuous issues—whether to combine small courts, which judges are assigned to which types of cases—can become the subject of great controversy. If politics is about conflict between competing interests, court organization is very political.

This chapter examines the organization of courts in the United States. I give close attention to the mechanics of court organization. But I also consider the politics of court organization: the debates that arise over organizational arrangements and the impact of those arrangements. The first section of the chapter discusses general principles of court organization; the second section focuses on the organization of the federal court system; and the third examines regularities and variation in state court systems.

GENERAL PRINCIPLES OF COURT ORGANIZATION

Before looking at the specifics of court organization, we need to consider two broader subjects: the relationship between the federal and state court systems and general patterns in the organization of court systems.

Federal and State Court Systems

Perhaps the most important feature of court organization in the United States is the existence of multiple court systems. There is a separate court system in each of the fifty states, the territories, and the District of Columbia, and the federal government has its own court system.

Separation of Court Systems   Of course, the state systems are divided from each other by geography. In contrast, the federal and state systems overlap geographically. Indeed, many cities have both federal and state courts. But the two sets of courts are in separate and distinct organizations.

Cases ordinarily stay within a single system. A case brought to a federal court almost always remains in the federal courts. It is uncommon but not rare for a case to begin in a state court system and then move to the federal courts. Some cases go from a state supreme court to the U.S. Supreme Court, and some cases are "removed" from state trial courts to federal court.

Each system is organized and managed by its own government. The constitution and statutes of Minnesota determine the form of the Minnesota court system. As a result, the Minnesota system need not take the same form as that of other states or of the federal court system. Indeed, court systems vary considerably in such characteristics as the structure of trial courts and the methods used to select judges. Of course, the laws that courts carry out also differ from one system to another. In part for these reasons, each court system develops its own distinctive ways of operating.

Federal and State Court Jurisdiction   The concept of *jurisdiction* refers to a court's power to hear cases; that concept is central to the organization of court systems. Rules of jurisdiction, set primarily by state and federal constitutions and statutes, determine what kinds of cases each court can hear. By doing so, they also indicate which court or courts are appropriate forums for any specific case. Jurisdiction may be based on several characteristics of a case, including its subject matter (criminal versus civil, for instance), the parties (for example, whether the federal government is a party), and its geography (where the parties reside and the location of the events from which a case stems). Jurisdiction can be considered a characteristic both of court systems as a whole and of individual courts. The jurisdiction of the Oregon court system is the sum of the jurisdiction of all the individual state courts in Oregon.

The dividing line between the work of federal and state courts is based on the jurisdiction of the federal court system. Federal courts may hear only those classes of cases that federal law puts within their jurisdiction. Everything else is within the jurisdiction of state courts. The U.S. Constitution outlines the scope of federal court jurisdiction, which is developed in more detail in federal statutes. Although the rules of federal jurisdiction are complex, nearly all the cases they admit to federal courts fall into three categories.

1. *Federal question jurisdiction* is based on the subject matter of cases. Federal courts are entitled to hear all civil and criminal cases that are based on the U.S. Constitution, on treaties with other nations, and on federal statutes.
2. *Federal party jurisdiction* consists of cases in which the federal government is a party. Nearly all cases brought by or against the federal government, a federal agency, or a federal officer can be heard in federal court.
3. *Diversity jurisdiction* is based on geography. Federal courts can hear cases in which there is a diversity of citizenship between the parties (if they are citizens of different states or if one is a citizen of a foreign nation), as long as the suit is for more than seventy-five thousand dollars.

Jurisdiction over a particular class of cases may be exclusive to a particular court, or it may be concurrent (shared by two or more courts). This distinction can also be applied to court systems as a whole. With some exceptions, the jurisdiction of federal courts is concurrent with that of state courts. Thus, for example, most kinds of civil cases brought by the federal government can be heard in either state or federal courts. Criminal cases based on federal statutes can be brought only in federal court, but many offenses could be charged under either federal or state statutes. Because penalties for federal crimes are typically more severe than penalties for the equivalent state crimes, law enforcement agencies sometimes seek to have their cases prosecuted in the federal courts.[3]

Cases based on diversity of citizenship illustrate the workings of concurrent jurisdiction. When citizens of different states become involved in a controversy involving more than seventy-five thousand dollars, the plaintiff has the option of filing a case in either federal or state court. But if the plaintiff chooses state court, the defendant can have the case removed to federal court. Thus either party can take an appropriate case to federal court.

Diversity cases also illustrate the politics of jurisdiction.[4] Congress first established diversity jurisdiction in 1789 as a protection against state bias; it was feared that state courts would favor their own citizens against those of other states. Since the late nineteenth century, there have been proposals to eliminate the diversity jurisdiction or to curtail it substantially. In part, these proposals reflected the belief that bias against out-of-state litigants was no longer a problem. But many of the proposals resulted from dissatisfaction with the policies of the federal courts, first from political liberals and later from conservatives. In recent years, many federal judges have seen diversity cases as a burden that they would prefer to eliminate.

Despite these efforts, the most sweeping proposals have all failed. Over the years, Congress has raised the minimum amount of money for diversity cases several times, and it has cut back the diversity jurisdiction in limited ways. But diversity cases are still large in number and a large share of the federal courts' work. There have always been enough supporters of diversity jurisdiction to maintain it. Today, the most important of these supporters are lawyers who like the choice between federal and state courts because it allows them to engage in "forum shopping" by choosing the court system whose judges seem more likely to favor their clients.

Most cases that fall under federal jurisdiction do end up in federal court. Yet only a small proportion of all court cases go to federal court, simply because the great majority of cases fit under no category of federal jurisdiction and thus go to the state courts by default. Every year, the largest set of cases results from traffic and parking violations, and almost all of these fall under state law. Criminal law is primarily a state matter, and people charged with common crimes such as burglary and assault ordinarily are tried under state law. Similarly, most common types of civil cases, such as those that arise from personal injuries or contract disputes, are based on state law and involve citizens of the same state.

On the other hand, a disproportionate number of cases that raise major policy questions come to federal court: many of these cases arise under the U.S. Constitution or federal statutes, and only a federal court—the Supreme Court—can lay down legal rules that apply to the country as a whole. As a result, the federal courts are a good deal more important than the numbers of their cases alone would indicate.

General Patterns of Court Organization

Although American court systems are diverse, there are some general patterns in the structure of courts within systems and in the administration of courts.

Court Structure   The jurisdiction of a court system must be divided among courts within that system. At the federal level and within each state, constitutional provisions and statutes create a set of courts and establish the jurisdiction of each. Such jurisdiction is always divided along two lines, vertical and horizontal.

Vertically, some courts are primarily trial courts, others primarily appellate courts. Most systems in the United States make a further distinction: between first-level appellate courts, which hear appeals from trial court decisions, and second-level appellate courts, which hear primarily cases brought from first-level appellate courts. A strong hierarchical element exists in every system. Higher courts review the decisions of the courts below them. Their judgeships are also more prestigious (and, in most systems, better paying) than those on lower courts.

Horizontally, jurisdiction may be divided among different sets of courts at the same level. Such a division occurs primarily at the trial level. In most states, one set of courts is designated to try cases with larger stakes, while other courts try cases with smaller stakes. Certain courts may be given relatively narrow responsibilities, such as tax cases or domestic relations cases. Sometimes two or more sets of courts in a system hold concurrent jurisdiction over a particular type of case.

Related to horizontal jurisdiction is *venue*, which concerns the place and court in which a case may be brought. At the trial level, there are usually multiple courts of the same type that sit in different places. For instance, there are ninety-four federal district courts spread across the United States. Venue rules are complex, but generally the place in which a case may be brought depends on the location of the parties' residences and of the actions from which the case stems. Although venue seems like a technical matter, courts take it quite seriously. In 2004, for instance, a federal court of appeals overturned guilty verdicts on dozens of counts in an insider trading case on the ground that the defendants had been prosecuted in the wrong district.[5]

Sometimes a case can be brought in only a single place, sometimes in two or more places. In the latter situation, as in cases that could go to either a state or a federal court, the litigant can engage in forum shopping. Lawyers who file large-scale personal injury cases favor districts in which they think jurors are sympathetic toward injured plaintiffs. Sometimes litigants maneuver to put potential cases in particular places. The federal government has moved suspected enemy combatants to a navy brig in South Carolina so that any lawsuits involving those individuals would be heard in the federal Fourth Circuit, whose court of appeals is relatively favorable to the government's positions in criminal justice.[6]

A special case of forum shopping involves motions for a "change of venue," which can be made in either criminal or civil cases. Perhaps the most common use of these motions is by criminal defendants who point to possible prejudice against them in the place where the alleged offense took place. Such motions seldom are granted. Former Enron executives Kenneth Lay and Jeffrey Skilling sought to have their trial moved out of Houston because of negative attitudes toward them in their home city. Skilling's lawyers cited the results of a survey they commissioned in which local residents referred to Skilling with such terms as "evil," "liar," "thief," "despicable," and "Darth Vader."[7] But in another case that garnered massive publicity, described in Exhibit 2.1, a judge did change the venue of a criminal prosecution—though only the first time that the defense asked for a change.

Court Administration   The operation of individual courts and court systems is called court administration. Power and responsibility for court administration are divided between courts and the other branches of government. Legislatures establish some rules for the operation of courts, but for the most part courts administer themselves. Administration takes place in both individual courts and court systems.

EXHIBIT 2.1   Change of Venue in the Scott Peterson Case

In December 2002, a young pregnant wife disappeared from her home in Modesto, a medium-sized city in the Central Valley of California. Four months later Laci Peterson's body was discovered, and her husband Scott Peterson was arrested for murder. The case had garnered enormous media coverage and public attention from the start, and Scott Peterson was widely judged to be guilty of murder. The trial judge to whom the case was assigned granted Peterson's motion for a change of venue, citing the high level of publicity. He then decided that the trial should be held seventy miles away in a suburban county south of San Francisco.

Because of the massive news coverage that they anticipated, "tourism officials in San Mateo County cheered wildly" when their county was chosen. Indeed, the news coverage was as heavy as expected, and during jury selection Peterson's lawyer cited evidence of prejudice on the part of potential jurors in asking for a second change of venue to Los Angeles. The trial judge turned down the motion on the ground that the problems cited by the defense would exist in Los Angeles as well.

Peterson was convicted of first-degree murder. His lawyers asked for a change of venue for the phase of the trial to determine whether Peterson would be sentenced to death. The trial judge said that the only way to avoid the effects of publicity about the case would be to "hold the trial on Mars—and that might not even be far enough." The state supreme court upheld his decision to keep the case in San Mateo County, and Peterson was sentenced to death.

Sources: Newspaper reports. The quotations are from, respectively, Dean E. Murphy, "Judge Chooses San Mateo County as Site of Murder Trial," *New York Times*, January 21, 2004, A10; and Stacy Finz and Diana Walsh, "Lawyer Asks for Second Jury," *San Francisco Chronicle*, November 18, 2004, B2.

Conflicts over court administration often arise from disagreements about control. Most individual judges prize their autonomy, so they resist efforts at control by chief judges and administrators within their own court and in their court system. And people in the courts try to limit external control by the other branches of government.

The most powerful force in court administration is growth in court caseloads. As the numbers of cases grow, traditional ways of managing courts—which often mean letting individual judges do things in their own ways—increasingly seem inadequate. Judicial budgets have not kept up with the growth in caseloads, giving greater urgency to administrative change. Efforts to cope with caseload pressures can affect not only the management of courts but what happens to cases that come to court. One recurring theme of this book is the impact of caseload pressures on court processes and outcomes.

THE FEDERAL COURTS

The basic structure of the federal court system is relatively simple. The organization chart in Figure 2.1 shows a bewildering array of courts, but the bulk of the system's work

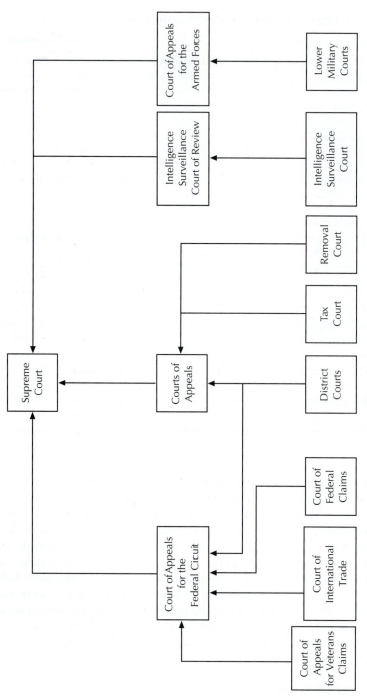

FIGURE 2.1   Organization Chart of the Federal Court System

Note: The lines and arrows show the routes of cases through appeals and Supreme Court grants of hearings. A few uncommon routes have been omitted.

is done by the three sets of courts in the center of the figure. The district courts serve as the primary trial courts of the system and the courts of appeals as the primary first-level appellate courts. The Supreme Court is the only second-level appellate court.

Paralleling the district courts and courts of appeals are several other courts that are specialized by subject matter. Taken together, these courts are also a significant part of the system.

Federal District Courts

For the great majority of cases, the district courts are the point of entry into the federal judicial system. Most cases go no further. Thus these courts are the primary center of activity in the federal system.[8]

Geography and Personnel   There are ninety-four federal district courts, one in each judicial district.[9] These districts cover the fifty states, the District of Columbia, and some of the U.S. territories. Every state has at least one district of its own. Twenty-six states have a single district. The rest of the states are divided into two or more districts, with three states (New York, Texas, and California) having four districts each. Many districts are divided into divisions, in each of which the court holds proceedings.

In federal district courts, as in other trial courts, cases are generally tried before a single judge, with or without a jury. Each district is staffed by at least one district judge, with a total of 678 judgeships authorized for the ninety-four districts. A few districts have only one or two judges, while others have many. Twenty-eight judges are authorized for the Southern District of New York, which includes Manhattan. The districts in which Los Angeles, Chicago, and Philadelphia are located all have more than twenty judges.

District courts also make frequent use of visiting judges from other federal courts, most often senior (semi-retired) judges from that district and from other courts. The continued participation of senior judges in cases has helped courts to keep up with growing caseloads, a problem aggravated when the president and Senate are slow to fill vacancies created by retirements—as they have been in recent years.

In addition to district judges, each district employs two other kinds of judges, bankruptcy judges and magistrate judges. These three sets of judges are assisted by staff members, such as law clerks, secretaries, and probation officers. In the district courts, as in other courts, law clerks play important roles through their work on cases. One litigant who was unhappy with the denial of his motions by a North Carolina district judge actually sued the judge's two law clerks, complaining that the clerks were "usurping the function of an Article III federal judge" and seeking an injunction to prevent them "from authoring, ghostwriting, or even participating in *anything* to do with" the litigant's case.[10] In numbers, district judges are overshadowed by the several thousand people who serve their courts in other positions. With these other personnel, the larger district courts are organizations of considerable size.

Jurisdiction and Business   Federal district courts have jurisdiction to hear all types of cases that go to federal courts, except for the few categories that are heard solely by specialized courts. As a result, the great majority of federal cases are tried in the district courts, and their business is quite diverse.

Exhibit 2.2 shows the distribution by subject matter of cases brought to the district courts in 2005. The data in the exhibit indicate that each of the three major categories of federal jurisdiction accounts for a significant number of cases but that federal question cases predominate. It also demonstrates that district court cases span a broad

EXHIBIT 2.2   Composition of Cases Filed in Federal District Courts in 2005 and Total Cases Filed in Selected Years

	2005 Cases	
Type of Case	**Number**	**Percentage**
By source of jurisdiction		
Federal party cases	52,386	16.2
Federal question cases	208,271	64.5
Diversity cases	62,191	19.3
By subject matter		
Criminal prosecutions	69,575	21.6
Prisoner petitions	61,238	19.0
Civil rights	36,096	11.2
Labor laws	18,322	5.7
Social Security laws	15,487	4.8
Torts	51,335	15.9
Contracts	28,020	8.7
Other	42,775	13.2

	Total Cases Filed	
Year	**Number**	**% Change**
2005	322,848	0
2000	322,262	+10
1995	294,121	+10
1990	266,783	−14
1985	311,915	+58

Note: The actual periods covered are fiscal years. Cases handled by bankruptcy judges and petty criminal offenses handled by magistrates are not included. Criminal cases are included in the federal question category. Figures given under "% Change" indicate change in the total number of cases over the preceding five years.

Sources: Administrative Office of the United States Courts, *Judicial Business of the United States Courts: Report of the Director* (2005) (Washington, D.C.: Administrative Office of the United States Courts, n.d.), 158–160, 213; *Annual Report of the Administrative Office of the United States Courts* (Washington, D.C.: Administrative Office of the U.S. Courts) for earlier years.

range of legal and policy areas. As the exhibit shows, the caseloads of the district courts have remained moderately stable over the past two decades, following a period of rapid growth.

As caseloads grew over the years, federal judges and others sought increases in the numbers of district judgeships. Congress sometimes added substantial numbers of judgeships, typically when the same party controlled Congress and the presidency. But since 1990 Congress has expanded the district courts only once, adding eight judgeships in 2002. The absence of larger increases seems to reflect the leveling off of caseloads, the monetary costs of new judgeships, and frictions between Congress and the judiciary.

Magistrate Judges and Bankruptcy Judges   In 1998, California deregulated its electricity market. Two years later, actions by energy companies and other events produced power shortages and rapid increases in electricity prices. In April 2001, these price increases led the state's largest public utility, Pacific Gas and Electric, to file for bankruptcy. For the next three years Dennis Montali, the federal judge who supervised the bankruptcy, made a series of rulings that shaped the company's future, limited the power of the state public utility commission, and allocated substantial costs to consumers.

Judge Montali is a bankruptcy judge. Of all the work that district courts do in the cases that come before them, a large share is carried out not by district judges but by other sets of judges who are attached to the district courts, magistrate judges and bankruptcy judges. As the Pacific Gas and Electric case illustrates, these two sets of judges sometimes deal with matters of considerable importance.

As of fall 2005, there were positions for 503 full-time and 48 part-time magistrate judges in the various federal districts. Full-time magistrates serve for eight-year terms, part-time magistrates for four years. Magistrate judges may conduct many types of pre-trial proceedings, rule on matters such as petitions challenging prison conditions, and (with the consent of the parties in most instances) try and decide civil cases and criminal misdemeanor cases. Depending on the type of case and other circumstances, a magistrate judge's decision can be appealed either to a district judge or to the court of appeals.

For the most part, the judges in a particular district determine which duties are actually given to magistrate judges, and there is great variation in their work from district to district. Across the country as a whole, magistrates have come to perform a large part of the district courts' work, including a substantial number of trials. With this growth in responsibilities, the position is sufficiently attractive that some state judges have become magistrate judges.

In 2005 there were 352 bankruptcy judgeships. Bankruptcy judges are appointed for fourteen-year terms by the courts of appeals. In a continuing case that resulted from a decision not to give a bankruptcy judge a new term, the Court of Federal Claims has held that bankruptcy judges are entitled to reappointment unless their performance is deficient.[11] Bankruptcy judges are attached to the district courts. Their decisions can be appealed to either the district court or to a panel of bankruptcy judges, depending on the district and circuit.

Bankruptcy judges handle far more cases than district judges, an average of more than 1.5 million per year from 2001 through 2005, though that number may decline considerably under a 2005 statute that makes it more difficult and less attractive for individuals to seek bankruptcy. The overwhelming majority of bankruptcy cases are filed by individuals, but the tens of thousands filed by businesses often have broad impact on stockholders, employees, and the structure of industries. Some airline companies have used bankruptcy proceedings to gain reduced salaries for their employees. Corporate executives often engage in forum shopping in bankruptcy cases, going to districts in which judges are likely to impose terms that favor the executives' interests.[12]

District judges have been happy to give significant responsibilities to magistrate judges, thereby reducing their own workloads. The same is true of bankruptcy cases, which district judges found burdensome, but with a complication. Bankruptcy judges want greater job security and recognition as full judges, while district judges do not want their own status diminished by the designation of bankruptcy judges as their equals or near-equals. Congress has refereed these conflicts, and the current law represents a compromise between the two sides.

Three-Judge District Courts   A three-judge district court, ordinarily consisting of two district judges and a court of appeals judge, is set up to hear a single case. An appeal from the court's decision goes directly to the Supreme Court.

From 1903 on, Congress enacted a series of statutes requiring that certain kinds of cases go to three-judge courts. The primary goal was to take decisions of great importance out of the hands of single district judges. As such statutes accumulated, three-judge courts became increasingly common. In 1973, they heard 320 cases.

But with such frequent use, three-judge courts also became a burden on the federal court system. Not only did each case require that three judges from two levels of courts find the time to meet, but the provision for a direct appeal of their decision to the Supreme Court added to that court's workload. These burdens seemed to outweigh the original purposes of three-judge courts. In response, Congress eliminated most of the grounds for convening them in 1976, restricting them largely to suits that challenge the drawing of legislative districts and to certain civil rights cases.

Since then, Congress occasionally has required three-judge courts for additional types of cases. One example was the McCain-Feingold Act of 2002 that regulates election campaign finance, which required that constitutional challenges to the law go to three-judge courts. Members of Congress wanted to expedite the resolution of constitutional questions to reduce the period of uncertainty about what candidates and political groups could do. Indeed, despite the complexity of the issues, the three-judge district court and then the Supreme Court had ruled on challenges to the law by the end of 2003.[13] Even with such additions to their jurisdiction, three-judge courts now hear only about ten cases a year, except for the bulge that occurs early in a decade after states draw new district lines for legislative seats.

Federal Courts of Appeals

If the district courts are the primary location of activity in the federal court system, the courts of appeals rank second. Most appeals from federal trial courts go to the courts of appeals. Because the Supreme Court accepts so few cases, these courts also represent the end of the line for nearly all litigation that reaches them. As a result, the courts of appeals are policymakers of considerable importance.

Geographic Division: Circuits   The basic geographic unit at this level is the circuit, and each circuit has a court of appeals. The twelve circuits are shown in Figure 2.2 on page 32. The District of Columbia is a circuit in itself. The states and territories are divided into eleven numbered circuits, each of which contains three or more states. The number of court of appeals judgeships in the circuits ranges from 6 in the First Circuit (New England and Puerto Rico) to 28 in the Ninth Circuit (the Pacific), with a total of 167 in the twelve circuits.

There have been two major controversies over division of circuits in the last few decades. The current controversy over the Ninth Circuit was discussed at the beginning of the chapter. The other controversy, involving the Fifth Circuit in the Deep South, raged during the 1960s and 1970s.[14] The court of appeals had a majority that was sympathetic to claims of racial discrimination, and anti–civil rights senators favored a split because the proposed southeastern circuit seemed likely to be dominated by judges who were more conservative on civil rights issues. Pro–civil rights judges in the Fifth Circuit and their allies fought successfully against the division proposal for more than a decade; the court finally was divided in 1980, after concerns about civil rights had lessened.

Ordinarily, cases in the courts of appeals are decided by panels of three judges, which are not permanent but rather are rotated for each set of cases. Along with active judges from the circuit, these panels often include visiting judges (primarily district judges from the same circuit) and retired judges. By majority vote, a court of appeals can hear or rehear a case *en banc*, a term that in most circuits means participation by the court's full membership of judges. However, this procedure is used in only a small proportion of cases, primarily those perceived as especially important and those involving issues that have divided the court.

Geographic arrangements vary by circuit, with some courts sitting in a single city and others dividing their time among several cities. In most circuits, the judges themselves reside in different cities, complicating the task of scheduling hearings and conferences. In 2005, for example, the judges on the Ninth Circuit Court of Appeals worked in more than a dozen cities, including Phoenix, San Francisco, Seattle, Boise, and Honolulu.

Like district courts, the courts of appeals employ a great many people other than judges. Each judge has three law clerks. Each court of appeals also has a central legal staff whose members have become subordinate judges in fact if not in name. The staff screens appeals and helps to decide those that it designates as routine. The growth in personnel in the courts of appeals—and in courts in general—is illustrated by the Ninth Circuit Court of Appeals. In 1975, there were 48 members of the support staff for the court as a whole. In 2005, there were 287.[15]

Jurisdiction and Business   The courts of appeals have jurisdiction primarily over district court decisions. A dissatisfied litigant may appeal to the court of appeals after nearly any final district court decision and after some preliminary decisions in a case. Appeals from the decisions of three-judge district courts go directly to the Supreme Court, and appeals in patent cases go to the Court of Appeals for the Federal Circuit. The general rule is that litigants have the right to appeal district court decisions to some court. The only important exception is the rule that the federal government as criminal prosecutor may not appeal acquittals. Such an appeal is regarded as violating

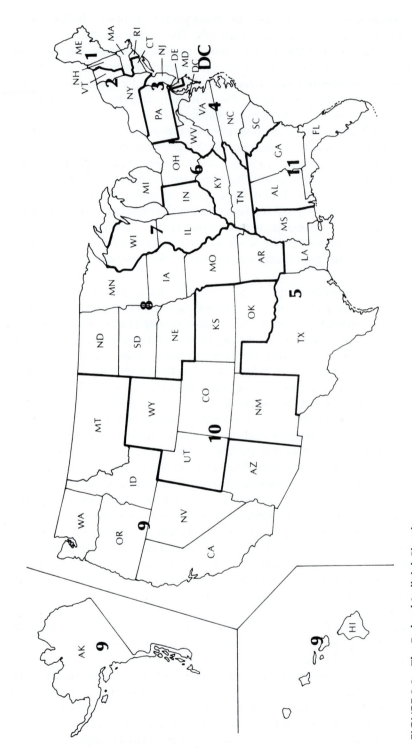

FIGURE 2.2   The Federal Judicial Circuits

Note: Not shown are Puerto Rico (First Circuit), Virgin Islands (Third Circuit), and Guam and the Northern Mariana Islands (Ninth Circuit).

the constitutional prohibition against double jeopardy (putting a person in jeopardy of criminal punishment twice for the same offense).

The courts of appeals have two other sources of cases. First, they hear appeals from decisions of the Tax Court, which acts as a trial court for some tax cases. More important, orders of certain federal administrative agencies may be appealed directly to the courts of appeals without going first to the district courts. In 2005, such administrative appeals constituted 20 percent of all the cases brought to the courts of appeals. Ninety percent of these cases were appeals from the Board of Immigration Appeals in the Justice Department, which had increased sevenfold in four years.[16]

Caseloads of the courts of appeals have grown even faster than those of the district courts, tripling between 1975 and 1995 before leveling off. Like the district courts, the courts of appeals have obtained congressional help in the form of additional personnel. Legislation between 1978 and 1990 increased the total number of judges from 97 to 167. And, as noted earlier, the courts of appeals have given their central legal staffs substantial responsibilities for decisions in some cases.

The Supreme Court

The Supreme Court is a single national court that decides cases with its full membership. The Court's size is determined by Congress, and the number of justices was changed several times in the nineteenth century. Some of these changes were motivated by the desire to affect the Court's policies. But there have been nine justices since 1869, and that number is unlikely to change. In contrast, the Court's staff has grown considerably and now includes about four hundred fifty people. The most important of these staff members are the justices' law clerks. The justices generally have four clerks, who perform such tasks as drafting opinions and screening requests to hear cases.

The Supreme Court's jurisdiction is almost entirely appellate. Cases come to the Court from several sets of lower courts. The two primary sources of cases are the federal courts of appeals and state supreme courts, but a case can be brought from a state system to the Supreme Court only if it contains an issue of federal law. A case that is initiated in a state court on the basis of state law sometimes develops a federal law issue, such as the procedural rights of a criminal defendant under the Constitution. Such cases are eligible for Supreme Court consideration, although they must go through the full set of appeals in state courts before the Supreme Court has jurisdiction to hear them.

With one minor exception—cases decided by three-judge district courts—the Supreme Court's appellate jurisdiction is discretionary. Thus, nearly all cases come to the Court not as appeals but as petitions for writs of certiorari. If the Court grants such a writ, this means that it calls up the case from the lower court for its consideration. If the Court denies the writ, as it does in the overwhelming majority of cases, the lower court decision is left standing.

The Constitution also gives the Supreme Court original (trial) jurisdiction over some cases involving states as parties and cases involving foreign diplomatic personnel; these cases are uncommon. When the Court does hear a case as a trial court, it delegates the task of gathering evidence and reaching a proposed decision to a special master, often a retired judge, who has been selected for that purpose.

Because the Supreme Court screens cases, and because its cases come from many sources, its agenda looks somewhat different from those of the lower federal courts. A large share of its decisions involve issues arising under the Constitution, and in the past quarter century it has concentrated heavily on civil liberties.

Like other federal courts, the Supreme Court has faced a growing caseload. The number of cases brought to the Court each term did not reach two thousand until 1961, but each year since 1999, the Court has received more than seven thousand cases.

After several years of urging by the justices, Congress in 1988 eliminated nearly all of the Court's mandatory jurisdiction. As a result, the Court gained almost complete freedom to reject cases that the justices do not wish to decide. The Court itself has acted to lessen its workload by accepting fewer cases for full decisions. In recent years, even as the number of petitions for hearings kept growing, the Court reduced considerably the number of cases that it accepted. In its 1984–1987 terms, the Court accepted an average of 180 cases per term. In the 2001–2005 terms, the average was less than 80, a drop of more than 50 percent, despite a continuing increase in the number of petitions for hearings.[17]

Specialized Courts

The district courts, courts of appeals, and Supreme Court can all be considered generalists in that they deal with a broad range of cases. The federal system also includes specialized courts, which have narrower jurisdiction. The characteristics and responsibilities of these courts are summarized in Exhibit 2.3. As the exhibit shows, there are two distinctions among them. First, some courts have their own permanent judges, while others borrow judges from the generalist courts. "Borrowed" judges are assigned to the specialized court for a limited period and serve on that court in addition to their regular duties on a district court or a court of appeals. The second distinction among the specialized courts is that some with their own judges are, like the generalist courts, established under Article III of the Constitution. Judges on Article III courts have lifetime appointments, and their salaries may not be reduced. Other specialized courts with their own judges are called legislative courts because they are established under Article I (which deals with the legislative branch); their judges lack these protections.

The specialized courts are hybrid institutions. In most respects they resemble generalist courts. But their focus on a relatively narrow set of issues also gives them characteristics that are more typical of administrative agencies. Such agencies frequently develop a strong point of view on the policy issues that they address. One reason is that agency officials with specialized responsibilities often develop narrow and parochial perspectives. Another reason is the special opportunity for influence that an interest group gains when an agency deals continuously with that group's area of concern. Specialization can have similar effects on courts. Indeed, according to one scholar, courts that are not generalists thereby "lose the one quality that clearly distinguishes them from administrative lawmakers."[18]

Partly for this reason, Congress has rejected a good many proposals to create specialized courts. But some proposals have been accepted, largely because they seemed to offer important advantages: the expertise of judges who specialize in a technical field such as tax law, the opportunity for a single court in a field to avoid the legal conflicts

EXHIBIT 2.3   Selected Characteristics of Specialized Federal Courts

Court	Type of Judge	Level	Status Under the Constitution	Areas of Activity
Tax Court	Permanent	Trial	Article I	Federal taxes
Court of Federal Claims	Permanent	Trial	Article I	Claims against the federal government
Court of Appeals for Veterans Claims	Permanent	Trial	Article I	Veterans' benefits
Court of International Trade	Permanent	Trial	Article III	International trade issues
Court of Appeals for the Federal Circuit	Permanent	Appellate	Article III	Patents, trademarks, international trade, claims against the federal government
Foreign Intelligence Surveillance Court	Borrowed	Trial	—	Foreign intelligence surveillance warrants
Foreign Intelligence Surveillance Court of Review	Borrowed	Appellate	—	Foreign intelligence surveillance warrants
Removal Court	Borrowed	Trial	—	Deportation of suspected terrorists

Note: Military courts and some minor courts are not included.

that develop among multiple courts, and reduced caseloads for generalist courts. And officials in the federal government and groups in the private sector sometimes seek the creation of a specialized court because they anticipate that the proposed court would rule more favorably toward them than would the district courts or courts of appeals. The cumulative result has been to make specialized courts a major part of the federal judicial system, handling issues as important as patent rights and international trade.

Some of these courts have made a mark with their policies. The Court of Appeals for the Federal Circuit, created in 1982, hears all appeals from the district courts in patent cases. One reason for its creation was to establish more lenient standards for the legal validity of patents than the courts of appeals had adopted. Indeed this has occurred, cheering those who think that lenient standards foster innovation but disturbing those who think that such standards make it too easy for companies to create monopolies over innovations. Critics have argued that the Federal Circuit's rulings help to foster an atmosphere in which patents unduly restrict what can be done in fields such as medical research.[19] A very different kind of court is the Foreign Intelligence Surveillance Court, discussed in Exhibit 2.4.

Federal Court Administration

The federal court system has a tradition of independence for individual courts and even individual judges. But the system also has a substantial and growing set of administrative structures.[20]

Administration of Individual Courts   Individual federal courts have chief judges (called the chief justice in the Supreme Court). When a chief justice leaves the Supreme Court, the president makes an appointment to fill the vacancy, either elevating a sitting justice to that position (as was the case with William Rehnquist) or selecting a chief justice from outside the Court (as with John Roberts). In lower courts, with some exceptions, the chief judge is simply the judge who has served on the court the longest.

A chief judge has general administrative responsibility for a court. This responsibility covers such matters as assigning judges and panels to cases, supervising nonjudicial personnel, and budgeting. Administrative actions by a chief judge occasionally become a matter of controversy. One controversy is described in Exhibit 2.5. Supervision of nonjudicial personnel has gained importance with growth in the number of people who work in the federal courts—from about one thousand in 1925 to thirty-four thousand in 2003.[21] This growth has required chief judges and other judges to spend more time on personnel management.

Formal powers aside, the leadership of chief judges can affect the workings of their courts. A skillful chief judge can foster harmony on a contentious court, but some chief judges have created conflict with their administrative styles. In a few instances, chiefs have engaged in long-standing battles with colleagues.

Administration of the System as a Whole   The routine administration of the federal judicial system is done by a body called the Administrative Office of the United States Courts. The Administrative Office deals with matters such as personnel and finances. General administrative policies are established by organizations of judges, the Judicial Councils of the circuits and the Judicial Conference.

EXHIBIT 2.4   The Foreign Intelligence Surveillance Court

The Foreign Intelligence Surveillance Court was created in 1978. The court consists of eleven district judges chosen by the chief justice. If the federal government seeks to engage in a search or wiretap within the United States for foreign intelligence purposes, one of the judges hears the request. The judge does so in a secret proceeding in a room at a Justice Department building, with an attorney representing the federal government but none representing the party for whom the wiretap is intended.

The decisions of the Surveillance Court are also secret. But annual reports indicated that as of 2001 the court had not denied any applications for warrants except in one case where its jurisdiction was in question. Thus the government had won thousands of cases and lost only that one, which was not really a loss. Perhaps the government's record would have been as successful if these cases were heard by a wide array of district judges in their own courts, but the use of a specialized court probably reinforced the government's advantage. Warren Burger and William Rehnquist, the chief justices who had selected judges for the court, were conservatives who seemed inclined to choose judges with basically favorable attitudes toward the warrant program. Further, the frequent involvement of judges in surveillance cases is likely to make them sympathetic toward the federal officials with whom they interact in these cases.

After the terrorist attacks in 2001, two statutes expanded the government's ability to obtain and use warrants from the Surveillance Court. Ironically, the court became a bit less favorable to the government. Its judges continued to grant nearly all the government's requests for warrants, but in 2003 and 2004 they modified a much higher proportion of warrant requests than in the past. And in 2002 the court ruled that the Justice Department had given too broad an interpretation to its powers relating to foreign intelligence searches. The government appealed to the Foreign Intelligence Surveillance Court of Review, three court of appeals judges who had never had to meet because the government had never had a reason to appeal. The review court ruled in favor of the Justice Department.

In 2005 President Bush acknowledged that since 2002 his administration had frequently bypassed the Surveillance Court and engaged in electronic surveillance without warrants. Federal officials argued that the procedure for obtaining warrants was unwieldy and the legal standard too high. One member of the court resigned from it in protest, and the Justice Department held a briefing for the remaining judges to discuss and defend its position. Thus a court that long seemed highly supportive of the government's interest in surveillance for national security had created some difficulties for the administration. The role of the court became one issue in a continuing debate over the administration's use of electronic surveillance.

Sources: Stewart M. Powell, "Secret Court Modified Wiretap Requests," *Seattle Post-Intelligencer*, December 24, 2005; Eric Lichtblau, "Judges and Justice Dept. Meet Over Eavesdropping Program," *New York Times*, January 10, 2006, A14; other newspaper articles; *In re All Matters Submitted to the Foreign Intelligence Surveillance Court* (Foreign Intelligence Surveillance Court 2002); *In re Sealed Case No. 02-001* (Foreign Intelligence Surveillance Court of Review 2002).

EXHIBIT 2.5   A Court of Appeals Battles Over Its Chief Judge

In 1978 the Supreme Court upheld certain types of affirmative action programs in college admissions. After the Court became more conservative, the Center for Individual Rights undertook a litigation campaign aimed at changing the Court's position on this issue. One of the cases the Center brought concerned the University of Michigan law school. In 2002 the federal court of appeals for the Sixth Circuit, sitting en banc, reversed a district court decision and upheld the law school's admissions program.

   The Sixth Circuit's decision was by a 5–4 vote, and the majority and dissenters presented strong arguments about the merits of the case. But one of the dissenting opinions also included a "procedural appendix" that charged the case had been handled in an inappropriate way. The key element of the charge was that Chief Judge Boyce Martin had caused a delay in consideration of a petition for en banc hearing, thereby causing the case to be considered without two conservative members who had become senior judges. The charge was answered in strong terms by two concurring opinions that defended the court's procedures.

   The next year an interest group, Judicial Watch, brought a complaint of judicial misconduct against Chief Judge Martin, based on his actions in this case and a case involving a stay of execution. The complaint was considered by Acting Chief Judge Alice Batchelder, whose dissent in the affirmative action case had endorsed the charges against the chief judge. Batchelder held that the chief judge had behaved improperly but concluded the case on the ground that further action was unnecessary because the court had changed its procedures in the preceding year. Five of the court's judges then signed a letter arguing that Batchelder's conclusions about the chief judge were unjustified. Both Martin and the interest group asked the circuit council to consider the case, and the council upheld Batchelder's conclusion of the case.

Sources: Grutter v. Bollinger, 288 F.3d 732 (6th Cir. 2002); *In re Complaint of Judicial Misconduct* (Judicial Council of the 6th Circuit, July 30, 2003); newspaper reports.

   The Judicial Conference is made up of the chief judges of the courts of appeals and one district judge from each circuit. The chief justice of the Supreme Court presides. The conference develops rules of practice and procedure for federal courts, subject to Supreme Court approval. To take one example, in 2006 the Supreme Court approved a new rule of appellate procedure allowing lawyers to cite decisions that are not officially published. The conference also takes positions on legislative proposals affecting the courts, and it puts together the proposed budget for the federal courts.

   On the whole, these national-level organizations have only limited impact on individual judges, who enjoy considerable autonomy. And judges collectively are in a strong position to fight control by administrators. In an unusual public conflict in 2001, judges who cited privacy concerns forced the Administrative Office to back off from monitoring of computer use by judges and other court employees.[22]

   The Judicial Councils for the circuits, usually called circuit councils, are composed of judges from the court of appeals and district courts in the circuit; the chief judge of the court of appeals presides. By statute, each council has sweeping authority to "make all necessary and appropriate orders for the effective and expeditious administration of justice within its circuit."[23]

The circuit councils also have some more specific powers. Their most controversial power involves the disciplining of judges within the circuit. According to the statute, a council may investigate a complaint of misconduct against a judge if the chief judge of the court of appeals thinks that investigation is merited. If that complaint is found to be justified, the council can take any appropriate action short of removing a judge from office. That action can include a temporary order that no further cases be assigned to a particular judge. Such an order was issued in a complex set of proceedings involving Texas district judge John McBryde. The circuit council for the Fifth Circuit publicly reprimanded McBryde and ordered that no new cases be assigned to him for a year. McBryde then brought a lawsuit in the federal district court in Washing-

EXHIBIT 2.6   The Inquiries into Judge Real's Conduct

In 1999 a defendant pled guilty in Los Angeles to federal charges of loan fraud and making false statements. District judge Manuel Real sentenced her to probation and, as was his practice, supervised her probation directly. Later that year she was threatened with eviction from her home, but she delayed the eviction proceedings by filing for bankruptcy. Judge Real took over the bankruptcy case from a federal bankruptcy judge, and he issued an order blocking the eviction. Judge Real continued to prevent eviction until 2002, when a panel of the Ninth Circuit ruled that he had improperly taken over the bankruptcy case.

Stephen Yagman, a lawyer who was unconnected to the case but who had been involved in an earlier conflict with Judge Real, made a misconduct complaint about the judge's handling of this case. Ninth Circuit Chief Judge Mary Schroeder dismissed the complaint. Yagman then asked the Ninth Circuit Judicial Council to consider the case. The council ruled by a 6–4 vote that the complaint should not have been dismissed and asked the chief judge to reconsider it. She did so and dismissed the case once again. This time, in 2005, the circuit council affirmed the dismissal by a 7–3 vote.

One of the dissenters issued a long opinion that emphasized what he saw as severe misconduct by Judge Real, and the actions of the circuit council and Chief Judge Schroeder received criticism from outside the court. A review committee of the Federal Judicial Conference held by a 3–2 vote that it could not review the circuit council decision but said that Schroeder should have set up a special committee to review the complaint against Real. In response, the chief judge did set up a special committee. Meanwhile, the chair of the House Judiciary Committee introduced a resolution to consider impeachment of Judge Real, and the Judiciary Committee held hearings on the resolution in September 2006. By the end of that year impeachment seemed unlikely, but the committee's inquiry still represented a rebuke of the federal courts for their handling of complaints against judges.

Sources: In re Canter, 299 F.3d 1150 (9th Cir. 2002); *In re Complaint of Judicial Misconduct*, 425 F.3d 1179 (Jud. Council of 9th Cir. 2005); Judicial Conduct and Disability Act Study Committee, *Implementation of the Judicial Conduct and Disability Act of 1980: A Report to the Chief Justice*, September 2006, 80–85; articles in the *Los Angeles Times* and other newspapers.

ton, D.C., arguing that the sanctions against him went beyond the power of the circuit council under federal law and that the law itself was unconstitutional, but the district court and court of appeals ruled against him and thereby affirmed the powers of the circuit councils.[24] A circuit council can recommend that Congress consider impeachment of a judge, as the council for the Eleventh Circuit did in the case of Florida district judge Alcee Hastings. Congress removed Hastings in 1989. Three years later, he was elected to the House of Representatives, where he still sat in 2007.

In 2006 a study committee headed by Supreme Court justice Stephen Breyer concluded that the chief judges and circuit councils had generally handled complaints about judges' misconduct effectively, but it said that they had not done as well in "high-visibility cases."[25] Exhibit 2.6 discusses one of the high-visibility cases in which the study committee found problems.

Congress retains ultimate administrative authority over the federal courts. It can alter the structure of administration as its members see fit. It can also intervene in specific administrative matters through such means as disapproving new rules of procedure and changing rules unilaterally, as it increasingly has done since the 1970s.[26] Most important, Congress provides funding for the federal courts. Judges usually feel that the courts are underfunded, and that feeling has grown in recent years. The most visible effect of funding problems has been staff cuts. One source of these problems is the rent the executive branch charges the judiciary for courthouses, a level of rent that Chief Justice Roberts called "unfair."[27] With concerns about the budget deficit and continuing frictions between Congress and the courts, it seems unlikely that funding for the federal courts will grow dramatically in the near future.

THE STATE COURT SYSTEMS

The structures of the fifty state governments show a good deal of similarity. This similarity is not surprising, because the states borrow ideas from each other and because they have been subject to common influences. Yet there are significant differences in structure from state to state, differences that reflect each state's freedom to design its own institutions. All this is true of state court organization. The states vary a good deal in their structures of courts; there are nearly as many different structures as there are states. But the basic patterns of organization differ far less than they might.

For the past century, both the structure and administration of state court systems have been shaped by a movement for "court unification."[28] That movement continues today. The main prescriptions of the movement have been consolidation of trial courts into one or two sets of courts and centralization of court administration under professionals supervised by the state supreme court. These prescriptions are seen as promoting efficiency and, in the case of court administration, the independence of courts from undue control. The court unification movement has achieved considerable success, but opposition from various sources has slowed the consolidation and centralization of court systems. Exhibit 2.7 illustrates the sources and effects of this opposition. Differences in the success of the unification movement have helped to create the differences in court systems across states.

The impact of these differences in court consolidation and centralization should not be exaggerated. For one thing, it is not certain that unification actually produces all

EXHIBIT 2.7   Mayor's Courts in Ohio

The justice of the peace is an old American tradition that refuses to die. Eight states retain justice courts, and a few others have something approximating justice courts. One example is the mayor's courts of Ohio. Mayor's courts can operate in any municipality that has at least one hundred residents and that does not have a municipal court. In 2004, there were 333 mayor's courts in Ohio. The mayor's courts can hear cases involving misdemeanors and traffic cases, and across the state they resolved more than three hundred thousand cases in 2004.

The mayor's courts have long been viewed with suspicion, primarily because they are thought to be devices for the collection of revenue rather than impartial courts. In 1927 the Supreme Court struck down a practice in which a mayor received part of the fine paid by defendants, on the ground that the mayor had a direct financial incentive to rule against defendants. In 1972 the Court held that it also violated defendants' due process rights when the fines that a mayor imposed represented a large proportion of a local government's revenue. Most local governments with mayor's courts then hired magistrates to run them, a kind of minimal compliance with the Supreme Court's decision.

The Court's ruling underlined why some local governments wanted to maintain mayor's courts: they liked the money they gained from fines, money that would otherwise go to counties. For some, such as a village that had a quarter mile of interstate highway within its borders, traffic fines were a bonanza. And collectively, they had sufficient political power to prevent the state legislature from abolishing mayor's courts. In response to a series of scandals in one small village that took in a large volume of money from passing motorists, the legislature in 2003 adopted the current rule that prohibits mayor's courts in villages with fewer than one hundred residents. But the prospects for eliminating all mayor's courts seemed slim, despite the support of the state's chief justice for that step. Whatever might be the value of a tighter court structure, economic considerations and the political pressures that resulted from them worked against change.

Sources: Newspaper stories; *Mayor's Courts: 2004 Summary* (Columbus: Supreme Court of Ohio, n.d.). The Supreme Court's decisions were *Tumey v. Ohio*, 273 U.S. 510 (1927), and *Ward v. Village of Monroeville*, 409 U.S. 57 (1972).

the benefits that have been ascribed to it. Consolidating courts and centralizing authority do not necessarily improve the capacity of a judicial system to process and dispose of cases. More fundamentally, factors other than court structure have considerable impact on aspects of court performance such as the ability to process cases efficiently. In any event, the actual effects of unification are very difficult to measure, so we have only a limited understanding of the difference that it makes.

State Court Structure: An Overview

State courts fit into four general categories, two at the trial level and two at the appellate level.[29] Trial courts may be classified as *major* and *minor* courts, and appellate courts include *intermediate* appellate courts and *supreme* courts.

Major Trial Courts   For current advocates of court unification, the ideal trial court structure is a single type of court that handles all cases. Only five states fit that model. Other states retain multiple sets of trial courts, ranging in number from two to ten. Thus the movement toward consolidation of trial courts is hardly complete.

Where multiple courts exist, they are usually divided into two categories. Sometimes these categories are labeled *general jurisdiction* and *limited jurisdiction*, but those terms are misleading since most courts in both groups are limited in the kinds of cases they can hear. The terms *major* and *minor courts* are imperfect but preferable, because the chief distinction between the two types of courts is in the seriousness of the cases brought before them.

Most states now have a single set of major trial courts, commonly known as district courts, superior courts, or circuit courts. About a dozen states retain multiple sets of major trial courts, with the jurisdiction of each based on geography and subject matter. Most often, one court with broad jurisdiction sits alongside another that hears a specific type of case, such as those involving taxes or probate.

The formal structure of state trial courts is misleading in an important sense: what appears to be a single court often is divided into specialized divisions, with judges serving permanently or temporarily in a particular division. This system is especially common in courts serving populous areas, which have enough judicial business and enough judges to allow such specialization. In practice, then, major trial courts are not quite as consolidated as they appear to be in organization charts. Indeed, in recent years there has been a burgeoning of specialized court units, ranging from business courts to drug courts.

Major trial courts typically conduct trials involving criminal offenses for which the most severe penalties are possible (felonies rather than misdemeanors) and civil cases involving relatively large sums of money. In many states, some special categories of cases are also heard in major trial courts: juvenile criminal offenses; domestic relations cases (primarily divorces); and probate cases (primarily the handling of wills).

In most states, major trial courts also have appellate functions, hearing appeals in at least some types of cases that are tried in minor trial courts. In many states, these appeals are *de novo*, meaning that the case is actually retried in the major court. As a result, a party who is unhappy with what may be a relatively informal trial in the minor court can go to the major court for a trial with a fuller set of procedural rights, such as a trial by jury.

Like federal district courts, major state trial courts are geographically dispersed. In some states, each county has its own court. In others the counties are grouped into circuits. In that system, each circuit typically has a set of judges who serve the whole area, traveling from county to county to hear cases.

Major trial courts have a great deal of business: in 2003, about 33 million cases were filed in these courts across the country. This number is enormous compared with the number of cases filed in federal district courts.

As Exhibit 2.8 shows, the cases that come to major trial courts range widely. More than one-third involve traffic and parking violations. Among the other cases, most are civil rather than criminal.

Minor Trial Courts   Below their major trial courts, most states still have minor courts, which handle less serious civil and criminal cases. These courts may also have jurisdiction over special categories of cases, such as juvenile criminal offenses. In

EXHIBIT 2.8   Subject Matter of Cases Filed in Major and Minor State Trial Courts in 2003

Subject	Major Courts		Minor Courts	
	Number (millions)	Percentage of Total	Number (millions)	Percentage of Total
General civil	7.6	23%	9.4	14%
Domestic (civil)	4.1	12%	1.6	2%
General criminal	6.2	19%	14.4	22%
Juvenile (mostly criminal)	1.4	4%	0.8	1%
Traffic and parking	14.0	42%	40.6	61%
Total	33.3	100%	66.8	100%

Note: "Major Courts" includes the single set of trial courts in the five states that have consolidated major and minor courts.

Source: Richard Y. Schauffler, Robert C. LaFountain, Neal B. Kauder, and Shauna M. Strickland, eds., *Examining the Work of State Courts, 2004: A National Perspective from the Court Statistics Project* (Williamsburg, Va.: National Center for State Courts, n.d.), 14.

several states the minor courts handle the preliminary stages of felony cases as well. As a result, cases routinely move from one court to another before trial.

State systems became most fragmented at this level. The fragmentation of minor trial courts has been reduced a good deal over time, but only about a dozen states have a single set of minor courts. Other states retain multiple courts, sometimes a great many.

There are two common lines of division among sets of minor courts. The first is geographic, with urban areas often served by municipal courts and rural areas by county courts or justices of the peace. The second line of division is functional, with separate courts handling different types of cases. Jurisdictional lines are often confusing. Seemingly parallel courts, such as municipal and county courts, may differ in their jurisdiction. And in some states the jurisdiction of different courts overlaps.

In most states, minor trial courts are highly decentralized. It is common for every city of moderate population to have its own municipal court. In states that have retained justices of the peace, there are sometimes several hundred separate justice courts. As a result, in 2004 there were about thirteen thousand separate minor trial courts alongside more than two thousand major trial courts.[30]

The division of jurisdiction between major and minor trial courts varies among the states, but minor courts generally have more business. As Exhibit 2.8 shows, in 2003 minor trial courts received twice as many cases as major courts, even though five states (including California, the most populous) lack minor courts. But the work of minor courts is dominated by cases with relatively small stakes, especially traffic and parking offenses. The volume and composition of the business in minor trial courts make their operation distinctive. Because most cases involve small stakes and few are really contested, cases are typically handled in routine fashion. Often cases are processed and disposed of by administrative personnel rather than by judges. Even when judges handle cases, they may do so quite rapidly and informally.

Intermediate Appellate Courts   A century ago, state systems generally included only a single appellate court, the supreme court. But growth in the volume of appeals gradually caused state policymakers to create one or more intermediate appellate courts below the supreme court level. Today, thirty-nine states have intermediate courts as first-level appellate courts, most of them called courts of appeals or something similar. The eleven states without intermediate courts, such as South Dakota and Vermont, are all low in population.

The structures of intermediate appellate courts vary in several respects.[31] While most states have only a single court, one-third follow the federal model and provide separate courts for different regions. In a few states, one court hears criminal appeals and another hears civil appeals. In most states, intermediate courts sit in panels, either with judges permanently assigned to a particular panel or with rotating panel membership.

The jurisdiction of intermediate courts also varies. All share the function of hearing appeals from the decisions of major trial courts, although certain kinds of cases may go directly to the state supreme court. In some states, some or all appeals from minor trial courts go to the intermediate appellate court rather than to the major trial courts. In many states, appeals from at least some administrative agencies are heard by intermediate courts. In general, the jurisdiction of intermediate appellate courts is mandatory because of the doctrine that the parties to a case are entitled to one appeal. But the Virginia Court of Appeals has discretionary jurisdiction over criminal cases, and many other courts have discretion over narrower categories of cases.

Despite the mandatory jurisdiction of most intermediate courts, only a small fraction of the cases handled by trial courts reach them. In 2005, to take one example, state trial courts in Michigan received more than four million cases, while the state's intermediate court received about eight thousand.[32] Of course, the cases that do come to appellate courts generally have much larger stakes than average. Courts that can hear both civil and criminal cases receive substantial numbers of both, with the balance between civil and criminal business varying by state.

Supreme Courts   Every state has a court that serves as its supreme court. With a few exceptions, this court is actually called the supreme court or some variant of that name. In effect, Oklahoma and Texas each have two supreme courts; their supreme courts hear only civil cases, while their courts of criminal appeals serve as the final courts for criminal cases.

Supreme courts have between five and nine justices. Even the larger courts generally sit en banc rather than in divisions or panels. Some courts hear cases not only in the state capital but in other cities as well.

A state supreme court, like its federal counterpart, is the final appellate court within its system. The functions of this court depend largely on the presence or absence of an intermediate state appellate court. Where that court exists, the supreme court is a second-level appellate court. As such, it receives most cases from the intermediate court and has discretionary jurisdiction over most of those cases. Typically, some classes of cases come from the intermediate court on a mandatory basis. Others bypass the intermediate court altogether, going directly from trial courts to the supreme court.

Because of their discretionary jurisdiction, these courts have considerable control over their agendas. Indeed, in many states the supreme court is highly selective in choosing cases to hear, granting hearings in less than 10 percent of the discretionary cases it considers. Even so, because the range of state cases is so broad, a supreme court is likely to deal with a diverse set of legal issues in any given year.

In states without an intermediate appellate court, the functions and business of the supreme court resemble those of an intermediate court. Most cases come to such a supreme court from trial courts on a mandatory rather than a discretionary basis. But most of the jurisdiction of the West Virginia Supreme Court is discretionary, and the New Hampshire Supreme Court has adopted a rule under which it can refuse to hear cases. Thus these two states deviate the furthest from the general principle that litigants are entitled to one appeal.

Two Examples of State Court Structure

Two examples provide a clearer sense of state court structure. The states chosen, Illinois and New York, are both populous ones, with a great deal of judicial business. But they also represent two extremes of court organization. Illinois was the first state to consolidate all its trial courts, and only three other states have adopted the same fully consolidated structure. In contrast, New York is one of six states whose courts are at the lowest level of consolidation according to one set of criteria.[33]

Illinois   The simplicity of the Illinois court system, resulting from a full consolidation of trial courts in 1962, is obvious from the diagram in Figure 2.3.[34] The highest court is the supreme court, which sits in Springfield, the state capital, and in Chicago. Cases come to the supreme court primarily from the intermediate appellate

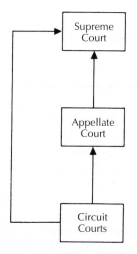

FIGURE 2.3   Organization Chart of the Illinois Court System

court, and its jurisdiction is mainly discretionary. The supreme court also hears appeals directly from trial courts in some types of cases, such as those with death sentences.

The intermediate appellate court, known in Illinois as the Appellate Court, hears all other appeals from trial courts. It also hears appeals from several administrative bodies, such as the Pollution Control Board and three boards dealing with labor relations. This court is split into five divisions on a geographic basis.

The most noteworthy aspect of the Illinois system is the single set of trial courts, the twenty-two circuit courts, which handle the functions of both major and minor trial courts. The trial court structure is not quite as simple as it seems, however, because the circuit courts may be subdivided. In Cook County (Chicago), which has about four hundred judges, the subdivision is quite detailed: the circuit court includes a county department with six specialized divisions for functions such as probate and domestic relations, a juvenile justice and child protection department with two divisions, and a municipal department with six districts. Within these subdivisions, judges are assigned to hear particular categories of cases in a given time period. Some courtrooms are devoted to very specific types of cases. Thus the Illinois courts match the prescription of court unification advocates for a single trial court, but in Chicago that single court is an umbrella for a large number of court units and a good deal of specialization.

New York   As Figure 2.4 shows, the New York court system is exceedingly complex.[35] In 1961, it underwent a partial consolidation, but a large number of separate courts and multitudinous routes for appeals were left standing. Efforts at further consolidation have been made from time to time but so far have not succeeded.

While the organization of Illinois courts can be described rather easily, any attempt to trace the position and functions of each New York court produces great confusion. Only at the top of the system, where the state's court of appeals is equivalent to the supreme court in most other states, is there much clarity. The court of appeals primarily hears cases brought from the intermediate appellate courts, but it also hears appeals from trial courts in cases involving only the constitutionality of a statute. Its jurisdiction is partly mandatory and partly discretionary.

At the intermediate appellate level, the structure begins to become complicated. Here jurisdiction is divided among the county courts and the appellate divisions and appellate terms of the supreme court. The county courts and the supreme court are also trial courts. (It is symbolic of the confusing structure of New York courts that the state has a lower court called the Supreme Court, and a supreme court called the Court of Appeals.) Where an appeal goes depends on the trial court from which it came, its subject matter, and the region of the state in which it was tried.

The New York supreme court is one major trial court, divided into eleven districts. It has unlimited trial jurisdiction, but it generally hears cases outside the jurisdiction of other courts. The county court, which is the other major state trial court, exists in each county outside the city of New York.

Minor trial courts are the most numerous, with hundreds of city, town, and village courts scattered throughout the state. Two Long Island counties also have district courts, and the city of New York has its own civil court and criminal court. Special courts exist for matters related to children (Family Court), for probate (Surrogates' Court), and for claims against the state (Court of Claims).

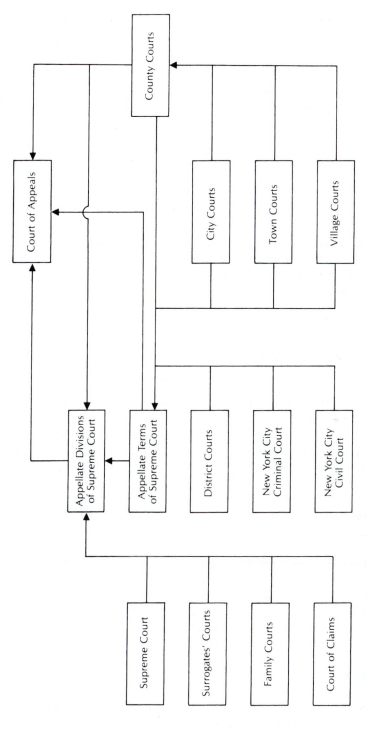

FIGURE 2.4   Organization Chart of the New York Court System

Note: Some of the routes of cases shown in the chart are uncommon, but very rare routes are not shown.

Sources: New York Unified Court System, "Court Structure" (www.courts.state.ny.us/courts/structure.shtml); League of Women Voters of New York State, *The Judicial Maze: The Court System in New York State* (New York: League of Women Voters, 1988), 7.

The contrast between this complex structure of minor trial courts and the simpler system in Illinois, where such courts are absent altogether, underlines the extent of the differences among the court systems of the various states.

Administration of State Courts

Like court structure, the administration of state courts today reflects changes spurred by the movement for court unification. The efforts of that movement to modify court administration have been reinforced by the need to respond to caseload pressures. But traditional patterns of administration have resisted efforts at change.

Individual Courts   Within state courts, responsibility for administration is divided in two respects. One, similar to the federal courts, is division between individual judges and chief judges. In most courts each judge has a good deal of autonomy, but chief judges hold real power over the operation of their courts and the work situations of their fellow judges. Especially important, where it exists, is the power to assign judges to particular kinds of cases or to particular locations. In 2004, for instance, Chicago judge Daniel Locallo displeased a presiding judge in another court division with a lampoon of her slowness in disposing of a case. The offended judge complained to the court's chief judge, who punished Locallo with assignment to a suburban courthouse, an assignment that Locallo likened to "work-release."[36]

These powers sometimes lead to tensions between a chief judge and other judges on a court. Because the position of chief justice carries both power and prestige, there are occasional battles over the right to that position. One example is the lawsuit between a member of the Oklahoma Supreme Court and his colleagues that is described in Exhibit 2.9.

The other line of division in administration is between judges and clerks. As people who do much of the day-to-day work of court administration, court clerks and their staffs inevitably play important roles. Even if they seek only to follow judges' lead, they shape the functioning of the courts and court systems for which they work. One reporter called Stephen Townsend, Clerk of a state supreme court, "the most influential lawyer in New Jersey that no one knows."[37] In the forty states that elect trial court clerks, clerks and their employees are largely independent of the judges in their courts. This independence often results in frictions between judges and clerks, such as a battle in Ohio over control of a court's computer network.[38]

Few judges or elected court clerks are trained in administration, and some of the administrative problems that arise in courts may reflect this "amateur" status. Professional administrators have become common at the appellate level, less so in trial courts. In any event, the strains that result from growing caseloads in many courts would be difficult to handle no matter who was responsible for court administration.

State Court Systems   Historically, the administration of state courts was fragmented along several lines. Individual courts operated independently of each other for the most part and with a minimum of control from the state supreme court. Legislative responsibility for the courts was divided between state and local governments, a division of authority reflected in the common practice of referring to

EXHIBIT 2.9   Suing to Become Chief Justice

Under the Oklahoma Constitution, the nine members of the state supreme court select their chief justice. The court's internal rules created a system in which the position rotated among the justices. Those rules apparently would have made Justice Marian Opala the chief justice early in 2005. But two months earlier, the justices changed the rules and gave the sitting chief justice a second term.

Opala did not accept this result; instead, he sued his eight colleagues in federal court. Eighty-three years old, he argued that the court's action represented age discrimination in violation of the equal protection clause of the Fourteenth Amendment as well as a violation of his due process rights under that amendment. In 2005 a federal district judge denied a motion by the defendants to dismiss the case prior to trial. But a year later the court of appeals for the Tenth Circuit reversed that decision and ordered that the case be dismissed on the ground that the federal courts lacked jurisdiction over the issue.

A lawsuit between one justice and his colleagues would seem likely to create a degree of tension on the court, but a few weeks after Opala filed his case he reported that there was no problem. "I think we are civilized and interact professionally, in a civilized way. . . . We just have a disagreement about the law."

Sources: Newspaper stories; *Opala v. Watt*, 393 F. Supp. 2d 1154 (W. D. Okla. 2005), 454 F.3d 1154 (10th Cir. 2006). The quotation is from Janice Francis-Smith, "Okla. Supreme Court Justice Marian Opala Talks About His Suit Against Fellow Justices," *Oklahoma City Journal Record*, January 24, 2005.

state trial courts as "local courts." Finally, authority for the governance of courts was split between the courts themselves and the other branches.

Supporters of court unification have sought to centralize administrative control and responsibility for court systems, primarily in the state supreme courts.[39] Such centralization would shift power from lower courts to the supreme court, from local governments to the state government, and from the other branches to the courts. Largely because of opposition from those who would lose power, administrative centralization is far from complete across the country as a whole. Not surprisingly, the degree of centralization differs a great deal from state to state and from one area of court governance to another.

One area in which considerable centralization has occurred involves supreme court authority over lower courts. Nearly every state now has professional court administrators under supreme court control, and in most states these administrators have substantial power over the management of lower courts. In every state but California (where the legislature holds some of the power), the supreme court now has power to establish procedural rules for trial and appellate courts. These powers have been employed to differing degrees across the states, but they are used enough to bring about a considerable increase in centralized control over the courts.

Perhaps the most significant manifestation of supreme court authority has been the use of formal rules as means to speed the processing of cases in trial courts. Rising caseloads, funding shortages, and inefficiencies often combine to create long backlogs

of cases to resolve. Mechanisms such as recommended time standards for the processing of cases are now common, and state chief justices sometimes engage in informal
campaigns to encourage administrative innovations and other means of attacking case
backlogs. Vermont Chief Justice Jeffrey Amestoy spurred trial courts to reduce their
backlogs of criminal cases by promising his bobblehead doll of U.S. Chief Justice William Rehnquist to the court that achieved the greatest success in the next six months.[40]
At least in some states, incentives to reduce backlogs have brought about shorter average times to dispose of cases. But under some conditions that benefit may be offset by
reduced care in the handling of cases.

Another area of significant change concerns the funding of trial courts, traditionally the responsibility of local governments. Most state governments now provide
substantial funding for trial courts, though few supply all of their funds. Like their
federal counterparts, state judges and court administrators often complain of inadequate resources to do their work effectively. Those complaints have a real basis: in
many states, court budgets have failed to keep up with growing caseloads. In some
years in some states, appropriations for the courts have been cut substantially from
prior levels.[41]

But administrative problems in the state courts are not entirely the result of funding deficiencies. A 2003 report on management of the Massachusetts courts noted that
funding of the state's trial courts had grown by 79 percent between 1994 and 2002,
a period in which the number of cases filed in court was essentially unchanged. Yet
the report concluded that the state's courts were "mired in managerial confusion."
The report cited both the courts and the legislature as sources of these bad results.[42]
The 2003 report was only the most recent of a series of reports on court administration in Massachusetts, and it was uncertain that the report would have much effect.
The long-standing pattern of legislative intervention in court administration to serve
members' political purposes remained highly evident two years later.[43]

Leaving aside the specific forms that legislative intervention takes in Massachusetts, the broader issue of control by the other branches illustrates the disagreements
that may arise over court unification. Advocates of unification argue that it is desirable that the courts have broad autonomy to run themselves. Others see it as appropriate
that the legislature and governor shape matters of administrative policy that affect the
outputs of courts and the interests they best serve. In any event, some intervention by
the other branches is inevitable.

CONCLUSIONS

It is important to understand the ways that courts are organized, simply as a means to
follow what goes on in them. But the organization of courts has broader implications,
and this chapter points to two important lessons.

First, organizational arrangements affect what happens in the courts. Specialized
courts may resolve policy issues differently from generalist courts, so the creation of a
new specialized court can be a consequential decision. Consolidation of scattered local
courts into a single court in a county seat is likely to change the ways in which cases
are handled and resolved.

Second, because court organization makes a difference, it is the subject of political conflicts rather than simply technical judgments. People who have a stake in what the courts do fight for the arrangements they think will serve their interests best. Thus, battles over such matters as division of a federal circuit in two can go on for many years, and contention over court unification in the states is not going to end soon. One effect is to slow the pace of change in courts and court systems even when there is a widespread feeling that change is desirable.

FOR FURTHER READING

Barrow, Deborah J., and Thomas G. Walker. *A Court Divided: The Fifth Circuit Court of Appeals and the Politics of Judicial Reform.* New Haven, Conn.: Yale University Press, 1988.

Hays, Steven W., and Cole Blease Graham, Jr., eds. *Handbook of Court Administration and Management.* New York: Marcel Dekker, 1993.

Hellman, Arthur D., ed. *Restructuring Justice: The Innovations of the Ninth Circuit and the Future of the Federal Courts.* Ithaca, N.Y.: Cornell University Press, 1990.

LoPucki, Lynn M. *Courting Failure: How Competition for Big Cases Is Corrupting the Bankruptcy Courts.* Ann Arbor: University of Michigan Press, 2005.

Nolan, James L., Jr., ed. *Drug Courts in Theory and in Practice.* New York: Aldine de Gruyter, 2002.

Posner, Richard A. *The Federal Courts: Challenge and Reform.* Cambridge, Mass.: Harvard University Press, 1996.

Smith, Christopher E. *United States Magistrates in the Federal Courts: Subordinate Judges.* New York: Praeger, 1990.

Online Study Center Go to college.hmco.com/PIC/baum6e for ACE practice test questions and additional resources.

NOTES

1. The discussion of the proposed Ninth Circuit split is based primarily on newspaper articles. The arguments for and against a split are summarized in two articles by judges on the Ninth Circuit: Diarmud O'Scannlain, "Ten Reasons Why the Ninth Circuit Should be Split," *Engage* 6 (October 2005), 58–64, and Mary M. Schroeder et al., "A Court United: A Statement of a Number of Ninth Circuit Judges," *Engage* 7 (March 2006), 63–66. *Engage*, a journal of the Federalist Society for Law and Public Policy Studies, can be found at www.fed-soc.org/Publications/Engage/Engage.htm.
2. Joel Connelly, "Right Wing Goes After 9th Circuit Court," *Seattle Post-Intelligencer*, May 15, 2006.
3. Lisa L. Miller and James Eisenstein, "The Federal/State Criminal Prosecution Nexus: A Case Study in Cooperation and Discretion," *Law & Social Inquiry* 2005, 239–268.
4. This discussion is based largely on Brett William Curry, "The Courts, Congress, and the Politics of Federal Jurisdiction," Ph.D. dissertation, Ohio State University, 2005, chs. 4–5.

5. *United States v. Geibel*, 369 F.3d 682 (2d Cir. 2004).

6. Laura Sullivan, "4th Circuit's Reputation is Polite, Conservative," *Baltimore Sun*, November 18, 2003.

7. "Texas Barbecue," *Harper's Magazine*, May 2006, 29.

8. Data on the work of the district courts and courts of appeals in this section of the chapter are taken primarily from Administrative Office of the United States Courts, *Judicial Business of the United States Courts: Report of the Director (2005)* (Washington, D.C.: Administrative Office of the U.S. Courts, n.d.).

9. The evolution of the federal judicial districts and circuits is shown in Russell R. Wheeler and Cynthia Harrison, *Creating the Federal Judicial System*, 3d ed. (Washington, D.C.: Federal Judicial Center, 2005).

10. *Stewart v. Thomas*, CA-02-57-3-WLO, Complaint for Fraud Upon the Court (W.D.N.C. 2002), 1, 7 (emphasis in original). The case was dismissed. See *Stewart v. Thomas*, 50 Fed. Appx. 184 (4th Cir. 2002).

11. *Scholl v. United States*, 54 Fed. Cl. 640 (Ct. Fed. Claims 2002).

12. Lynn M. LoPucki, *Courting Failure: How Competition for Big Cases Is Corrupting the Bankruptcy Courts* (Ann Arbor: University of Michigan Press, 2005).

13. *McConnell v. Federal Election Commission*, 540 U.S. 93 (2003).

14. Deborah J. Barrow and Thomas G. Walker, *A Court Divided: The Fifth Circuit Court of Appeals and the Politics of Judicial Reform* (New Haven, Conn.: Yale University Press, 1988).

15. Cathy Catterson, "Changes in Appellate Caseload and Its Processing," *Arizona Law Review* 48 (2006), 293.

16. Administrative Office of the U.S. Courts, *Judicial Business (2005)*, 114.

17. These figures were calculated from data collected by the Supreme Court and published annually by *United States Law Week*.

18. Martin Shapiro, *The Supreme Court and Administrative Agencies* (New York: Free Press, 1968), 53.

19. Adam B. Jaffe and Josh Lerner, *Innovation and Its Discontents* (Princeton, N.J.: Princeton University Press, 2004).

20. The structures for administration of the federal courts are summarized in Russell Wheeler, *A New Judge's Introduction to Federal Judicial Administration* (Washington, D.C.: Federal Judicial Center, 2003).

21. U.S. Bureau of the Census, *Statistical Abstract of the United States: 2006* (Washington, D.C.: U.S. Government Printing Office, 2006), 330.

22. Neil A. Lewis, "Plan for Web Monitoring in Courts Dropped," *New York Times*, September 9, 2001, sec. 1, 34.

23. 28 *United States Code,* sec. 332 (d) (2006 ed.).

24. *In re: John H. McBryde, U.S. District Judge*, 117 F.3d 208 (5th Cir. 1997); *McBryde v. Committee to Review Circuit Council Conduct and Disability Orders,* 264 F.3d 52 (D.C. Cir. 2002).

25. Judicial Conduct and Disability Act Study Committee, *Implementation of the Judicial Conduct and Disability Act of 1980: A Report to the Chief Justice*, September 2006, 5.

26. Lori A. Johnson, "Creating Rules of Procedure for Federal Courts: Administrative Prerogative or Legislative Policymaking?" *Justice System Journal* 24 (2003), 23–42.

27. John G. Roberts, Jr., "2005 Year-End Report on the Federal Judiciary," *The Third Branch*, 38 (January 2006). See Pamela A. MacLean, "Judges Rip the Rent," *National Law Journal*, July 11, 2005, 1, 23.

28. The court unification movement is discussed in Robert W. Tobin, *Creating the Judicial Branch: The Unfinished Reform* (Williamsburg, Va.: National Center for State Courts, 1999), ch. 7.

29. This discussion of state court organization is based in part on Shauna M. Strickland, comp., *State Court Caseload Statistics, 2004* (Williamsburg, Va.: National Center for State Courts, n.d.), for information on the structure of court systems; and Richard Y. Schauffler, Robert C. LaFountain, Neal B. Kauder, and Shauna M. Strickland, eds., *Examining the*

Work of State Courts, 2004: A National Perspective from the Court Statistics Project (Williamsburg, Va.: National Center for State Courts, n.d.), for information on court business.

30. Calculated from data in Strickland, *State Court Caseload Statistics 2004*, 7–59. *Court* can be defined in different ways, so these totals should be regarded as approximate.

31. State intermediate appellate courts are discussed in a set of articles in *Justice System Journal* 26 (2005), 91–104.

32. *Michigan Supreme Court Annual Report 2005* (Lansing: Michigan Supreme Court, n.d.), 19, 64.

33. Victor E. Flango and David B. Rottman, "Research Note: Measuring Trial Court Consolidation," *Justice System Journal* 16 (1992), 68–69.

34. This discussion of the Illinois court system is based in part on Administrative Office of the Illinois Courts, *Annual Report of the Illinois Courts: Administrative Summary 2004* (Springfield: Administrative Office of the Illinois Courts, n.d.).

35. The structure of the New York court system is depicted at the website of the system (www .courts.state.ny.us/courts/structure.shtml). See also League of Women Voters of New York State, *The Judicial Maze: The Court System in New York State* (New York: League of Women Voters, 1988).

36. Steve Bogira, *Courtroom 302: A Year Behind the Scenes in an American Criminal Courthouse* (New York: Alfred A. Knopf, 2005), 347.

37. Kate Coscarelli, "Behind the Bench, He Calls the Shots," *Newark Star-Ledger*, January 3, 2005.

38. Jim Woods, "Judges Say They'll Take Control from Reluctant Clerk," *Columbus Dispatch*, May 15, 2001, B4.

39. See Tobin, *Creating the Judicial Branch*, ch. 8.

40. Alan J. Keays, "Rutland Court Wins Noddin' Noggin Award," *Rutland Herald*, September 10, 2004.

41. Leonard Post, "Lean Times for State Courts Get Leaner Still," *National Law Journal*, December 6, 2004, 1, 25.

42. Visiting Committee on Management in the Courts, *Report to Chief Justice Margaret Marshall* (March 2003). The quotation is from p. 2 of the report.

43. Frank Phillips, "Budget Shifts Judicial Power," *Boston Globe*, June 27, 2005, B1. See Mark C. Miller, "Court-Legislative Conflict in Massachusetts," *Judicature* 88 (September–October 2004), 97–99.

3

Lawyers

In the United States, lawyers are highly visible, perhaps more visible than the members of any other occupation. To a degree, their visibility is a product of their numbers: in 2006, 1.1 million people were licensed to practice law.[1] But more important are the roles they play. They are well represented at the highest levels in government, business, and education. And collectively, the lawyers who have not achieved high positions have enormous impact simply by serving as lawyers. In acting on behalf of clients they shape individual lives and national policy. For these reasons, which individuals and organizations are represented by lawyers and *how* they are represented have powerful effects.

This chapter focuses on the work of lawyers in the legal system. The first section discusses law as a profession. The second considers access to the services of lawyers. The final section explores relationships between lawyers and their clients.

THE LEGAL PROFESSION

To understand law as a profession, it is necessary to look at several aspects of the profession. The place to start is with the work that lawyers do.

Lawyers' Work

Of all the things that lawyers do, the most visible is litigation, handling cases in court and preparing for court appearances.[2] Understandably, television and movie portrayals of lawyers emphasize litigation. But litigation is only a small part of most attorneys' work, and many lawyers seldom or never go to court.

Similar to litigation is representation of clients—most often businesses—in the other branches of government. For example, lawyers represent clients in formal administrative proceedings before such agencies as the Environmental Protection Agency and state public utilities commissions and in informal contacts with those agencies.[3] Lawyers also lobby for clients in legislatures, seeking results such as a favorable provision in federal tax law or an exemption from local zoning rules.

A third activity is negotiation, aimed at working out an agreement between a client and another party. Some negotiation occurs in the context of litigation, as lawyers seek to resolve cases prior to trial. Most serious criminal cases are resolved by the prosecutor and defense attorney through a plea bargain, and the preponderance of serious civil cases are settled by an agreement between lawyers representing the two parties. Lawyers frequently negotiate to avoid lawsuits altogether, helping clients settle disputes at an early point or preventing the development of disputes in the first place.

Lawyers also engage in what can be called securing, providing security through the writing of documents. Contracts are central to the functioning of the economy. Wills allow people to designate how their assets will be allocated after death. Wills illustrate the importance of securing, in that a properly written will can ensure that an estate will be settled with minimal delay and in the way that the writer wished.

The final activity of lawyers, counseling, involves helping clients to find the most favorable course of action in a particular situation. Every area of law entails a good deal of counseling. Antitrust lawyers, for example, advise companies about whether certain decisions might lead to federal antitrust investigations or lawsuits by other companies. Tax lawyers provide advice on the tax consequences of different activities. Counseling is linked to everything else that lawyers do.

Lawyers and Other Alternatives

Someone who could employ a lawyer to carry out any of the activities I have described might instead obtain the help of someone other than a lawyer. This option is severely limited by state statutes that restrict the practice of law to licensed attorneys. One statute says simply that "no person shall practice law in California unless the person is an active member of the State Bar."[4] In most states, the "unauthorized practice of law" is a criminal offense.

If "practice of law" is defined broadly, it might cover the full range of activities in which lawyers engage. In reality, nonlawyers frequently engage in some of these activities. For instance, groups such as accountants and insurance agents provide a good deal of legal advice to clients. Indeed, states have authorized nonlawyers to carry out some activities that involve the law. For instance, most states allow land title and escrow companies to handle the settlement of real estate transactions.

It appears that what might be called legal work by non-lawyers has grown considerably in the past decade, in part because those services can be provided over the internet. As in the past, individual lawyers and bar associations have made some efforts to enforce prohibitions on unauthorized practice against these activities. In 2005, for instance, a lawyer's complaint led the disciplinary counsel of the Ohio Supreme Court to investigate a nurse's talk at a church about living wills and related documents, ultimately ruling that the nurse had not violated any rules.[5]

People who might hire lawyers always have another option, simply acting on their own. In the array of situations in which a lawyer's expertise might be helpful, only a small minority of people actually hire a lawyer. Even among people who go to court, it is common to act "pro se," without a lawyer. Only a minority of divorce cases have lawyers representing both sides.[6] Not surprisingly, the great majority of cases brought to federal court by prisoners are filed pro se. But it is also the case that more than one quarter of the other civil cases brought to the federal courts of appeals are pro se.[7] It appears to be increasingly common for people to handle serious legal matters on their own. One reason is the financial costs of attorneys. Finances aside, many people fear or distrust lawyers, or they may not know how to find an appropriate lawyer. The growing availability of information about the law and legal procedure also plays a part in this trend. Indeed, as pro se cases have become more common, courts themselves are doing more to help people navigate the legal system.

Litigants who act without lawyers would seem to be at a substantial disadvantage in legal proceedings. The difficulties they face are symbolized by the opening statement of John Muhammad, defending himself against the charge that he was one of the two snipers who killed ten people in the Washington, D.C., area in 2002. Muhammad told the jury that the prosecutors weren't at the scene of the crimes. "I was. I know what happened, and I know what didn't happen."[8] Even though lawyers represented Muhammad later in his trial, they could not do much to overcome his inadvertent admission. On the other hand, people sometimes represent themselves very well. In 2004, for instance, a Seattle woman argued and won a complex case involving insurance law in the Washington Supreme Court.[9] It is not clear that people who represent themselves, taken as a group, do substantially worse in court than they would if they had been represented by attorneys.[10] Whatever may be the success rate for self-represented litigants, the growth in their numbers makes them an important feature of the legal system.

Entry into the Legal Profession

Licensing of attorneys is handled by the states. Each state adopts its own rules to determine who can become an attorney. Licensing, like regulation of other aspects of legal practice, is supervised by state supreme courts but administered primarily by boards of lawyers.

Law School Training   In the great majority of states, the first step required for licensing as an attorney is achieving a law degree. The traditional method of legal education in the United States was apprenticeship with a practicing attorney, but today only seven states authorize apprenticeship as a substitute for some or all of the standard three years in law school.[11] Even where these options exist, few prospective attorneys use them. In 2005, thirty-seven people took a bar examination after following the apprenticeship route, and only five of them passed.[12] Among the small number of people who have taken this route are a justice on the Vermont Supreme Court and a law professor at UCLA, who noted that "the first time I was ever in a law classroom, I was teaching law."[13]

Most states require not only that applicants graduate from law school but also that their school be accredited by the American Bar Association (ABA). The ABA's requirements for accreditation are highly detailed. One standard holds that "a student may not be employed more than 20 hours per week in any week in which the student is enrolled in more than twelve class hours."[14] Another standard mandates that law students complete a set of courses "of not fewer than 58,000 minutes of instruction time, except as otherwise provided. At least 45,000 of these minutes shall be by attendance in regularly scheduled class sessions at the law school."[15]

In other states, students from unaccredited schools in the United States or in other countries are eligible to practice under certain circumstances. Of the students who took a bar examination in 2005, nearly 10 percent took one of these routes. Although these groups of students have a lower passing rate than those from accredited schools, about nineteen hundred were successful in 2005.[16] The great majority of exam-takers from non-U.S. law schools were in New York state. The largest number of exam-takers from schools that the ABA has not accredited was in California, which has nineteen law schools accredited only by the state and twenty-eight law schools with no accreditation.[17]

The number of law schools has grown considerably over the years, and that growth continues today. Because ABA accreditation is so important to survival and success, the administrators of most new law schools work hard to obtain accreditation—several law schools have even hired deans who had served on the ABA's accreditation committee—and nine were successful between 2002 and 2006.[18] Schools operated for a profit have become more common since the ABA began allowing such schools to win accreditation.

Many of the newer law schools have distinctive attributes as a reflection of their founders' goals or as a means to attract students. Some long-standing law schools also have distinctive traits. Several emphasize particular fields of law, and some adhere to certain religious or philosophical principles. But on the whole, law schools resemble each other in the general type of legal training they provide. The heart of their curricula is a series of classes on various areas of the law, such as contracts, property, criminal procedure, and constitutional law. The primary texts are the opinions of the appellate courts, which are intended to help students understand the substance of the law and to train them in legal analysis.

The content of law school education has been criticized a good deal. The main complaint is that a focus on appellate court opinions does not give students much of the practical knowledge they need to practice law. Many new lawyers find that their education is just beginning when they leave school. In response to this complaint, law schools have established clinical programs, in which students work with actual legal matters in order to gain such practical skills as interviewing clients and conducting negotiations over cases. As part of some programs, students may even make supervised appearances in court. But clinical programs still constitute only a small portion of the law school curriculum, and both faculty and students tend to view them as peripheral to the mainstream of a legal education.

Law schools have always differed considerably in prestige. The most widely respected, such as Michigan, Yale, Stanford, and Harvard, can be the most selective in choosing their students. In turn, because of their reputations and the abilities of their students, these schools provide the widest opportunities for graduates. Large law firms recruit disproportionately from the most prestigious schools, which are also the source of most Supreme Court law clerks. Ultimately, graduates of these schools are the most likely to achieve eminence, such as positions on the Supreme Court itself. Naturally, prospective law students are attracted to prestigious schools, and the rankings of law schools by *U.S. News & World Report* appear to have considerable impact on students' decisions where to apply and to enroll. In turn, law schools devote considerable effort to gaining the best possible scores on the criteria that *U.S. News* uses to rank schools. At some schools, it appears, a drop in the rankings has played a part in a dean's losing that position.[19]

Law school is expensive, and the costs have risen rapidly. Not surprisingly, about 80 percent of law-school students take on some debts to finance their education, and the average debt accumulated is high: $51,000 for graduates of public law schools in 2004–2005, $79,000 for private school graduates.[20] Accumulating loans reinforce the desire of most law students to find high-paying jobs after education. Those in lower-paying positions are often in difficult financial straits—difficult enough that some have taken second jobs to cope with loan repayments.[21] In response to this problem, a growing number of law schools have established programs to help pay off debts of students who take low-income jobs in government or nonprofit organizations.[22] And some law schools have established programs to save students one year of schooling and thus considerable money by allowing them to go through law school in less than three years or to complete undergraduate and law school in a total of six years.[23]

Other Licensing Requirements   Beyond the requirement of law school, the most important requirement for licensing as an attorney is passing the state's bar examination. With some exceptions in Wisconsin, every prospective attorney must submit to a two- or three-day examination.[24] This test includes essay questions on the laws of the state, and several national-level components may be added. These include the Multistate Bar Examination, a multiple-choice test used by all but two states; the Multistate Professional Responsibility Examination, dealing with ethical issues, used by all but three states; and two recent options, the Multistate Performance Test and the Multistate Essay Examination. In nearly all states, the examination is offered in February and July.

Typically, about two-thirds of the applicants across the country pass the bar examination, 64 percent in 2005. But success rates vary among the states—in 2005, from 86 percent in Utah to 46 percent in California.[25] To a degree, the low pass rate in California reflects the large number of students from unaccredited law schools who take the examination. But the examination is difficult, and in 2005 one of the people who failed it was Kathleen Sullivan, a distinguished legal scholar who had been dean of the Stanford law school. That result could be explained by her work schedule, which did not allow her to engage in concerted preparation for the exam.[26] Most applicants take special "bar review" courses to provide that preparation. For those who fail, there is another chance: every state allows people to retake the bar examination at least once, and most allow unlimited retries. Professor Sullivan passed on her second attempt. One applicant passed the California bar examination on his forty-eighth try.[27]

Nearly all states require that applicants for law licenses have a good character. Few applicants are denied admission because of that criterion, which creates difficulties primarily for people who have been convicted of serious crimes. A few states prohibit the admission of people who have been convicted of felonies. In other states felony convictions typically are viewed as creating a presumption against an applicant, but a presumption that can be overcome.[28] In a 2005 case the Arizona Supreme Court refused to admit an applicant who had been convicted of first-degree murder, but the court considered an array of evidence about the applicant's conduct since his release from prison rather than barring him automatically on the basis of his conviction.[29]

Attorneys who are licensed to practice in one state do not automatically gain the right to practice in other states. Indeed, in nearly half of the states, outsiders must pass all or part of the bar examination before doing business in the new state. In the others, a lawyer can be admitted to the bar on the basis of some period of experience in another state, most often five years. However, courts usually allow an attorney who is a resident of another state to participate in a single case.

Federal courts also establish their own requirements for the right to practice before them. In most instances, a lawyer need only be licensed in the state in which the federal court sits, but some courts have set up more stringent requirements. In several federal districts, attorneys must pass a written examination or have a certain amount of trial experience before they can try federal cases. Like state courts, federal courts usually allow an attorney who is not admitted to practice in that court to participate in a single case. But a New Jersey district judge upheld a magistrate judge's barring of one such attorney whose "past behavior has been uncivilized and unprofessional and has resulted in reprimands, mistrials, and wasted judicial time."[30]

The Size and Composition of the Legal Profession   It is hardly a secret that the number of lawyers has grown enormously. That growth is documented in Figure 3.1. Not all lawyers actually engage in the practice of law, but the number who do practice has also grown at a rapid rate.

The growth in the size of the legal profession reflects several spurts in the number of students enrolling in law school since the early 1960s, and in the first half of that period there was a substantial increase in the proportion of law students who completed their degrees. Forty-two thousand law degrees were awarded in 2005, nearly four times the number in 1965.[31]

Growth in law school enrollments and law degrees reflects several forces. Population growth has expanded the pool of potential law students. A breakdown of barriers to the profession for women and members of racial minority groups has also expanded the pool. Growth in population and economic activity has created more work for lawyers to do. It also appears that there was a growing awareness of the impact that lawyers can have on society. Inevitably, this growth in the legal profession affects lawyers. It intensifies economic competition, which helps to explain the more aggressive marketing of legal services in recent years. The job market for new lawyers has also tightened.

Until a few decades ago, almost all lawyers were white and male. In 1963, fewer than 3 percent of practicing attorneys were female, and in 1970, about 1 percent were black.[32] This pattern stemmed in part from restrictive practices by law schools and law firms. For example, few southern and border state law schools admitted black students until the 1950s, and many law schools throughout the country were equally restrictive for women. Until 1950, Harvard did not accept women as law students. Columbia had the same policy in 1922, when its dean (future Supreme Court chief justice Harlan Stone) justified the refusal to admit women by saying, "We don't because we don't."[33] Until at least the 1960s, most law firms were unwilling to hire women or members of racial minority groups.

As barriers have been broken and aspirations have risen, more women and non-whites have entered law school; the growth has been more substantial for women. Of the first-year students in the 2005–2006 academic year, 47 percent were women and

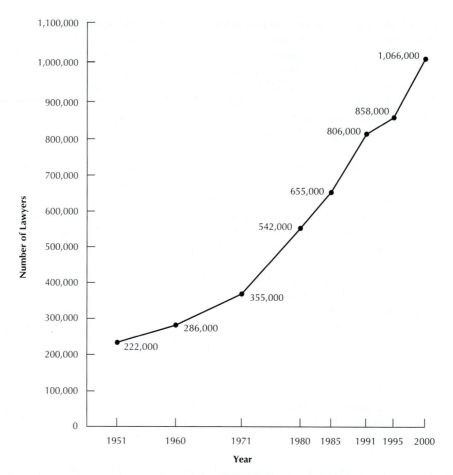

FIGURE 3.1   Growth in the Number of Lawyers in the United States

Source: Clara N. Carson, *The Lawyer Statistical Report: The U.S. Legal Profession in 2000* (Chicago: American Bar Foundation, 2004), 1.

22 percent were minority group members.[34] Exhibit 3.1 shows the change that has occurred in the demographics of law school enrollments since the 1960s.

This trend has already produced substantial increases in the proportion of lawyers who are not white men—by 2000, 27 percent of all lawyers were women[35]—and guarantees further increases in the future. Women and members of racial minority groups are also occupying important legal positions in greater numbers. But both women and minority group members continue to face discrimination within the legal profession at every stage from law school to appearances in court. The extent of discrimination against women has been documented in several studies.[36]

Lawyers come primarily from families with higher than average economic status. Aside from other factors, the cost of a college and law school education makes it easier for people to become lawyers if their parents are well-off.

EXHIBIT 3.1   Enrollments of Women and Members of Racial Minority Groups in Law Schools

Year	Women		Minority Groups	
	Number	%	Number	%
1965–66	2,374	4.3	—	—
1975–76	26,020	23.4	8,703	7.8
1985–86	47,486	40.0	12,357	10.4
1995–96	56,961	44.0	25,554	19.7
2005–06	66,613	47.5	29,768	21.2

Note: Enrollments are in programs leading to the J.D. degree, in law schools approved by the American Bar Association. Percentages are enrollments of students in that group as a percentage of all students. Data on minority group enrollment are not available for 1965–1966. A few schools do not report minority group enrollment, so the numbers and percentages are slight underestimates.

Source: American Bar Association, "First Year and Total J.D. Enrollment by Gender 1947–2005" and "Total Minority J.D. Enrollment, 1971–2005" (www.abanet.org/legaled/statistics/stats.html).

Where Lawyers Work

Lawyers perform their activities in several different settings. Most are in private practice, but a significant and growing minority work in the business sector or for the government.

Private Practice   In 2000, 78 percent of all active attorneys were engaged in private practice.[37] Although less dominant than it once was, private practice remains the primary form of work for lawyers.

Lawyers in private practice are members of a profession who are also engaged in a business. At least ideally, they do their work in accord with the standards of the legal profession. But they must also obtain enough work from clients and make a sufficient profit from that work to maintain a successful practice.

The private practice of law follows no single model. Some lawyers specialize narrowly, while others deal with a broad range of legal matters. Strategies to attract clients differ considerably. One important difference, linked to most others, is the size of the firms in which lawyers work.

As of 2000, 52 percent of all lawyers in private practice were involved in some kind of cooperative arrangement with other attorneys.[38] Such arrangements can range from a simple sharing of office facilities by two attorneys to a highly structured firm employing several hundred lawyers. The proportion of solo practitioners, lawyers who work entirely on their own, declined for a long time. But that decline has halted in recent years, perhaps because the growing number of new lawyers has outpaced the ability of law firms to absorb them. It is striking that even today, solo practitioners and those who have only loose cooperative arrangements with other lawyers constitute a majority of those in private practice. These kinds of practice predominate in rural areas, and they are relatively common in medium-sized cities, but they are not rare even in large cities.

Still, the long-term trend toward multi-lawyer firms is a key trend in the profession, one that reflects their efficiency: groups of lawyers can pool both the costs of a law practice and their personal expertise. It is also much easier for an inexperienced attorney to join an established group of lawyers than to start out alone, bearing all the costs of a legal practice and searching out sources of business. The advantages of practicing with other lawyers are reflected in incomes: lawyers practicing in large firms do far better than solo practitioners, with lawyers in small firms falling in between. In 1995, solo lawyers in Chicago earned a mean of $80,000, while those in firms of three hundred lawyers or more earned a mean of $272,000.[39]

Large Law Firms   A rapidly growing minority of lawyers practice in firms of substantial size. If we define large firms as those with more than fifty attorneys, there has been massive growth in both the number and size of large firms. Part of that trend, illustrated by Exhibit 3.2, is the spread of large firms from New York City to other large and medium-sized cities. Even in the current era, large firms hardly dominate the practice of law; of all the lawyers in private practice in 2000, 18 percent were in the 737 firms with more than fifty lawyers. But this segment of the profession has a significance far beyond its share of lawyers. Moreover, most characteristics of large firms are more extreme versions of those found in medium-sized firms.

Large firms are significant because of their clienteles: they primarily represent business corporations, with an emphasis on the largest companies. To corporate deci-

EXHIBIT 3.2   Selected Large Law Firms, 2006

Rank	Firm	Major City	Number of Lawyers
1	Baker & McKenzie	Chicago	3,535
5	Skadden, Arps, Slate, Meagher & Flom	New York	1,915
10	Morgan, Lewis & Bockius	Philadelphia	1,315
20	Reed Smith	Pittsburgh	1,038
50	Paul, Weiss, Rifkind, Wharton & Garrison	New York	679
100	Steptoe & Johnson	Washington	413
200	Fredrikson & Byron	Minneapolis	209

Note: "Major city" is the one in which a firm has its largest office in the United States (Baker & McKenzie's largest office is in London).

Source: "The NLJ 250," *National Law Journal*, November 13, 2006, S18–S36. Reprinted with permission.

sion makers, the collective resources of a large law firm make it seem like the best and safest choice to deal with significant legal problems. So major corporations flock to large law firms—in 2005, one firm represented more than forty of the 250 largest companies in the country[40]—and their business allows large firms to maintain themselves and often to grow. The clients of large firms are able to afford high fees, and fees have become high indeed: in 2005, partners' time at the largest firms was nearly always billed at more than $200 an hour, in many firms the highest-priced lawyers charged more than $500 an hour, and at least one lawyer charged as much as $1,000 an hour for some of his work.[41]

Through their legal actions and their advice, on both legal and nonlegal matters, large law firms affect the fortunes of the businesses they represent. Inevitably, they also have a broader impact on society. This impact is accentuated by the political work of large law firms. All of the twenty-five largest firms in 2006 had offices with at least seventy-five lawyers in Washington, D.C.[42] because their clients want to influence decisions in the legislative and executive branches. The importance of political work to large firms is reflected in their frequent hirings of prominent politicians.

Among the lawyers in large law firms, as in their smaller counterparts, the primary status distinction is between partners and associates. Attorneys at the beginning of their careers enter firms as associates. If they remain with a firm for some period of time, typically five to ten years, they are considered for promotion to partnership status. That status ordinarily gives lawyers a permanent position in the firm and a share in its profits, although some firms now have salaried partners. Associates who are denied partnerships usually must leave the firm. But firms increasingly retain some lawyers who do not become partners, giving them titles such as "counsel" or "staff attorney."

Large firms seek to recruit the top-ranked graduates of the most prestigious schools. To attract these lawyers, firms offer high salaries to new associates. In 2006, the median base salary for first-year associates in firms with more than five hundred lawyers was $135,000, and substantial bonuses are common.[43] Large firms can also offer extensive support services and some freedom from the difficult task of finding business.

In exchange for these benefits, associates typically work long hours under considerable pressure. In 2002, associates in firms with more than 250 lawyers reported that they had worked a median of fifty hours the previous week, and one-third had worked more than sixty hours.[44] Despite their credentials and salaries, associates often do uninteresting work that involves little independent responsibility.

Many associates leave large firms before they reach the point of being considered for partnerships. A 2005 study indicated that 78 percent of associates in law firms had left by their fifth year.[45] One reason is that some associates dislike their work or working conditions. Another is that the odds against becoming a partner in most large firms are high and becoming higher. Exaggerating for effect, a legal recruiting firm captured that development in an advertisement aimed at lawyers who had been denied partnerships: "So they promised to put you on the fast track, huh? That you'd make partner six years out of law school? Yeah, right. The last time someone made partner at your firm, Reagan was president."[46] This situation reflects the economics of law firms: even with their high salaries, associates generate substantial profits for firms, while every new full partner means that firm profits have to be divided by a larger number.

The world of large law firms has changed considerably in recent years. A few decades ago practice in large firms was somewhat genteel, with limited competition among firms and a relatively relaxed pace for partners. It was also an exclusive world, with highly restrictive hiring along lines of race, religion, gender, and class.

The exclusiveness has broken down to a degree, because of social changes and the need to attract the most skilled attorneys—although women and members of racial minority groups often face special difficulties once they enter a firm.[47] More fundamentally, the world of large firms has become less stable. For firms, the lack of stability stems largely from greater competition for legal business. Corporate clients increasingly shop around among law firms rather than maintain stable long-term relationships with firms, and they give more of their legal work to their own salaried lawyers.

One result is more aggressive marketing of services by firms. Another is the growing frequency of mergers between firms and hiring of partners from other firms, largely in an effort to add lawyers who can bring and attract business. Through this process, some firms have grown rapidly, and most large firms have become increasingly dispersed geographically. Other firms have difficulty competing and fall behind or fail altogether. For instance, a long-standing San Francisco firm that had more than nine hundred lawyers in 2000 disbanded three years later.[48]

Instability for firms has brought changes for their lawyers as well. Partners were never equal in income and power—seniority and the ability to attract clients made a difference—but inequalities have become sharper. Partners who do not bring in substantial business may find their incomes reduced, and partnership no longer guarantees a lifetime job: firms increasingly fire partners. One story of firings, described in Exhibit 3.3, illustrates the changes in large firms. Lawyers are more likely to move from one firm to another, some because their ability to attract business makes them prized "free agents," others because they have been fired or their firms have closed. These changes have served some lawyers well. In part, they are responsible for the high levels of income enjoyed by lawyers in some firms: in 2005, ten firms had at least $2 million in profits per partner sharing in those profits.[49] But the changes have had negative effects on other lawyers. And life in large firms is certainly less relaxed than it once was.

Business   In 2000, 9 percent of all active lawyers worked directly for businesses. This sector has grown as more businesses establish their own legal departments and these departments employ more "in-house" counsel. In 2005, eighty-six legal departments had at least one hundred attorneys. Citigroup, a financial services company, employed fifteen hundred lawyers.[50]

This growth has several sources. For one thing, businesses have more legal needs than in the past. Further, business executives see advantages to the use of in-house counsel. In general, legal work done within a company is less expensive than the same work done by outside law firms. And companies can exert greater control over the legal work done by their own employees. As a result, corporations assign more of their legal work to their own employees than they did in the past.

The content of the work done by in-house counsel has also changed. Traditionally, in-house counsel concentrated on a company's routine and recurring legal work, and companies turned to outside law firms for less routine work such as litigation.

EXHIBIT 3.3   Turmoil in a Large Law Firm

The New York law firm Cadwalader, Wickersham & Taft traces its origins to 1792. Of the three people in the firm's name, one had been a U.S. attorney general, another an assistant secretary of state, and the third was a president's brother. Like other long-standing firms, it had something of a genteel image.

But according to an account by Joseph Goulden, the firm became less genteel as the practice of law changed. In the early 1990s, some of the younger partners became dissatisfied with the division of profits among the partners. As they saw it, relatively unproductive older partners were receiving more than their work merited; they wanted more money for themselves, and they worried that a failure to reallocate profits would damage the firm by causing some highly productive lawyers to leave. After considerable intrigue and conflict, the dissatisfied partners won out: seventeen of the 105 partners were pushed out of the firm, and a Florida office with fifteen lawyers was closed.

Some of the purged partners did not go quietly, and the firm spent millions of dollars to pay damages in lawsuits and associated legal costs. But the lawyers who had removed some of their partners from the firm still came out ahead, as firm profits and their shares of those profits increased. They have continued to do well. In 2005, Cadwalader ranked third among all law firms in profits per partner, at $2.55 million.

Sources: Joseph C. Goulden, *The Money Lawyers* (New York: Truman Talley Books, 2006), ch. 6; Anthony Lin, "Ten Firms Hit $2M Per Partner in Profits in '05," *National Law Journal*, May 8, 2006, 10.

Now, as one study reported, "many in-house counsel report they now keep the most exciting, strategically important work for themselves, and farm out the routine or overflow work to their outside counsel."[51] Even more than outside counsel, in-house lawyers are likely to participate in decision making on nonlegal issues such as corporate acquisitions and labor negotiations, and their legal services often blend with nonlegal work.[52]

The dominant image of in-house legal departments contrasts strongly with that of large law firms: legal departments hire young lawyers with less impressive credentials and pay them less but give them greater security and shorter work hours. This image does not fit reality as much as it once did, but it still has some validity. In 2002, second-year lawyers in corporate legal departments worked a median of forty-eight hours a week, only two fewer than those in large firms; on the other hand, they were much less likely to work sixty hours or more. Average salaries for second-year lawyers were higher than those of lawyers who had solo practices or who worked in small firms but considerably lower than those in large firms. The same was true of the average prestige level of the law schools that these lawyers attended.[53]

Not all attorneys in the business world actually work as lawyers. Many can be found in fields such as banking and real estate, where their legal knowledge provides an advantage even if they are not practicing law as such. It appears that the proportion of lawyers in this category has grown as the market for legal jobs has become tighter.

Government   Eleven percent of all active attorneys worked for government in some capacity in 2000. Of these, about one-third were in the federal government, while the other two-thirds were scattered among the state and local governments. A small proportion worked in legislatures, and one-quarter were in the judicial branch. In this discussion, I focus on those who serve in the executive branch.

The federal government employs about thirty thousand attorneys. A substantial number of the federal government's lawyers work in the Department of Justice, either in the United States Attorneys' offices in the ninety-four federal judicial districts or in specialized divisions such as Antitrust and Civil Rights. U.S. Attorneys and their assistants represent the government in criminal prosecutions and civil litigation in the district courts.[54] The specialized divisions handle some civil litigation at the trial level and take over cases from U.S. Attorneys at the appellate level. The Office of the Solicitor General within the Justice Department must approve most federal government appeals to the courts of appeals and nearly all government appeals or petitions to the Supreme Court. The office itself handles litigation in the Supreme Court. Every other executive branch agency of significant size has a legal staff, and some of these staffs—particularly the corps of lawyers in the Department of Defense—are quite large.

Much of what government lawyers do is litigate. Governments are parties in a high proportion of all court cases, both as a criminal prosecutor and as a plaintiff or defendant in civil cases. A considerable volume of "internal litigation" also occurs within government agencies, such as the Internal Revenue Service and the Social Security Administration, and lawyers represent the agency's position or serve as judges in these cases.

At the state and local level, the largest concentration of lawyers is in the office of the state attorney general. That office aside, government legal services within the states are highly decentralized. Most lawyers work for local governments in prosecutors' offices, city attorneys' offices, and other organizations. Some of these organizations have several hundred attorneys.

Like in-house counsel, government attorneys are important decision makers. Through the litigation process, they help to shape government policy. For instance, prosecutors who give a high priority to white-collar crime have the effect of enhancing legal sanctions against that category of offenses. Lawyers also exert an impact through their advice on legal issues. In the George W. Bush administration, lawyers in the White House and the Justice Department have played key roles in developing and justifying administration policy on legal questions involved in the effort to fight terrorism, including the treatment of people who are detained as suspected terrorists. For both reasons, the positions of attorney general (held by John Ashcroft and then Alberto Gonzales in the Bush administration) and White House counsel (held by Gonzales, Harriet Miers, and Fred Fielding) are among the most powerful in the federal government. Ashcroft put his stamp on government policy in several areas, and he played an important part in shaping the Bush administration's efforts to prevent further terrorist attacks after 2001.[55]

Because presidents appoint the lawyers who serve in high positions, they can expect those lawyers to follow their lead on most matters. On matters related to terrorism, lawyers in the Bush administration have generally provided legal support for the president's goal of strengthening his powers.[56] The situation is different at the state level. In most states the attorney general and heads of prosecuting agencies are elected, so they are more likely to differ in their views from officials in the other branches and have greater freedom to follow their own course. Indeed, they sometimes get into serious conflicts with policymakers in the other branches. After San Diego elected a reformist city attorney in 2004, a joke circulating in city government had him introducing himself to other officials: "Hi, I'm Mike Aguirre. As city attorney I represent you, and I just wanted to let you know: You have the right to remain silent."[57]

This freedom allows some state attorneys general to become highly visible policymakers in recent years, and that has become increasingly true in the past two decades. New York attorney general Eliot Spitzer (1999–2007), discussed in Exhibit 3.4, used

EXHIBIT 3.4   A Government Lawyer and the Corporate World

Eliot Spitzer was elected attorney general of New York in 1998 and re-elected in 2002. In his eight years in that office, he took an active role in attacking what he saw as corporate wrongdoing. He charged one investment firm with adjusting its ratings of companies' stocks to win the banking business of those companies. He charged other investment firms with allowing favored customers to engage in illegal transactions in stocks, to the disadvantage of their other customers. He charged a pharmaceutical company with failure to disclose unfavorable information about the safety of a popular drug it sold. He sued the former chair of the New York Stock Exchange, charging that he had obtained his very large compensation in inappropriate ways and demanding that he repay more than $100 million. He charged several employers with violation of minimum wage laws. He sued companies that owned power plants whose discharges reached New York for failing to comply with the federal Clean Air Act.

Spitzer was less interested in prosecuting individual wrongdoers than in securing changes in corporate behavior. He sought and won settlements in which companies promised to stop engaging in questionable practices. His successes stemmed in part from the fact that even the announcement of an investigation could depress the value of a company's stock and create other problems for the company; executives sought to avoid or limit that damage. Spitzer's record included significant losses alongside his victories, but his investigations and lawsuits had considerable impact—especially on the financial industry. And he served as an example for attorneys general in other states.

Spitzer took advantage of the broad powers of his office, which included an old and little-noticed state law that gave him a great deal of freedom of investigate and prosecute business activities. To a degree, he also took advantage of a void created by the limited enforcement of some federal regulatory laws. Opponents charged that Spitzer was motivated chiefly by ambition. One commentator said that he was "temperamentally unable to stay out of the headlines for more than 72 hours," and he was elected New York governor in 2006. Whatever his motives, Spitzer demonstrated that a state legal official could achieve a substantial impact on the corporate world.

Sources: Newspaper and magazine articles; Brooke A. Masters, *Spoiling for a Fight: The Rise of Eliot Spitzer* (New York: Times Books, 2006). The quotation is from Daniel Gross, "Eliot Spitzer: How New York's Attorney General Became the Most Powerful Man on Wall Street," *Slate Magazine* (www.slate.com), October 21, 2004.

his position to attack a range of practices in the business world. One development is cooperation across states to undertake coordinated legal actions. The most prominent example is the multistate lawsuit to recover damages from tobacco companies for the health costs incurred by the states because of cigarette smoking. That lawsuit, initiated by Mississippi attorney general Michael Moore and joined by nearly all his colleagues in other states, resulted in a massive 1997 settlement in which the companies agreed to pay the states 368 billion dollars. Since then, attorneys general have worked together on issues such as mortgage lending practices and pricing of prescription drugs.[58]

One common image of government lawyers below the top levels is that they are young and inexperienced people who work with the government briefly before moving on to the private sector to make more money. There is considerable truth to this image. The salaries of government lawyers are relatively low, especially at the state and local level. And law school graduates who take jobs in a federal agency or a prosecutor's office are likely to leave for private firms after a few years, trading on the experience they have gained in government.

But this does not necessarily mean that government agencies provide low-quality legal services. For one thing, there are advantages to government work that compensate for low pay: opportunities to take on major responsibilities much earlier than associates can do in most law firms, the chance to participate in making public policy, and often high job security. These advantages attract lawyers to government service and keep some of them from leaving. And lawyers can gain considerable expertise in an area such as criminal prosecution within a short time, so even short-time government attorneys can serve their clients well.

Some lawyers work for the government on a part-time basis. In less populous areas, many lawyers divide their time between local government positions and private practice. State attorneys general often hire private lawyers for specific jobs, a practice that allows some to reward campaign contributors.

Specialization in the Practice of Law

Lawyers are often thought of as generalists, as professionals who handle any kind of legal task for any client who comes to them. This image is largely and increasingly inaccurate: most lawyers specialize to a considerable extent. This specialization occurs along three lines.

The first is by type of activity. Lawyers differ considerably in how they allocate time to the various activities described at the beginning of the chapter. Most striking is variation in their involvement in litigation. A small proportion of attorneys are primarily litigators. In contrast, many other lawyers seldom, if ever, go to court.

The second form of specialization is by type of legal issue. In a complex legal system, no attorney can be an expert on everything. Largely for this reason, most lawyers devote themselves to a few fields or even to a single one. In a sample of Chicago lawyers, 33 percent practiced exclusively in one field.[59] Common specialties include tax law, criminal law, personal injuries, and real estate.

Finally, lawyers can specialize by type of client. Some lawyers serve the various legal needs of corporations. Others combine client specialization with legal specialization. Examples include lawyers who represent primarily personal injury plaintiffs (sometimes called trial lawyers) and those who represent criminal defendants. This combination helps produce some relatively narrow specialties, such as defense of white-collar criminal defendants or class-action suits by stockholders against corporations.

Patterns of specialization are influenced by social and legal developments, which are reflected in the needs of current and potential clients. For example, the growth in corporate bankruptcies in recent years has attracted more lawyers to that field. Some lawyers choose their specialties quite consciously. Others develop specialties largely by chance, based on such circumstances as the tasks they are given as associates in law firms.

The degree of specialization varies according to the setting in which lawyers practice. Lawyers in big cities are the most specialized, those in rural areas the least.[60] Lawyers who practice alone are less specialized than those in large firms, partly because those firms can combine specialists in different fields to offer a broad range of services.

Because lawyers specialize, their perspectives and their self-interest differ. These differences often come to the surface on public issues. Today, for instance, lawyers who represent manufacturers strongly support proposals to limit legal liability for injuries caused by defective products, while lawyers who represent personal injury plaintiffs fight hard against these proposals. Because of differing needs and interests, most lawyers orient themselves primarily toward their own group of specialists rather than toward the legal profession as a whole.

The Two Hemispheres

The discussion of lawyers so far has referred to several kinds of distinctions among them. These distinctions are not random. Rather, to a considerable degree lawyers cluster into what John Heinz and Edward Laumann called "the two hemispheres of the profession."[61]

These hemispheres are defined primarily by the kinds of clients that lawyers represent. Lawyers in one hemisphere serve primarily large organizations, especially corporations. Those in the other hemisphere represent mainly individuals and small businesses. A smaller number do substantial work for both types of clients.

As Exhibit 3.5 shows, this distinction between the "corporate" and the "personal" sectors is related to other important distinctions. Lawyers in the two sectors tend to specialize in different kinds of legal issues. Lawyers in the corporate sector are also far more likely to work in large firms (or, of course, for businesses themselves) rather than in solo practice or small firms. Lawyers in the corporate sector tend to serve a small number of clients over long periods of time, while those in the personal sector tend to serve a succession of clients on single matters. As I discuss later, one result is that attorneys in the corporate sector are generally subject to greater control by their clients.

Another difference is that lawyers in the corporate sector are higher in status than those in the personal sector. One aspect of this status differential is lawyers' backgrounds: the economic status of the families they grew up in and the prestige of the

EXHIBIT 3.5   A Comparison of Legal Practice on Behalf of Corporations and Individuals

	Primary Clients	
	Corporations	Individuals and Small Businesses
Socioeconomic background of lawyers	Higher status	Relatively lower status
Law school attended	Relatively high percentage from elite schools	Primarily nonelite schools
Type of practice	Large firm or business legal department	Small firm or solo practice
Typical number of clients each year	Fewer	More
Control by clients	Higher	Lower
Prestige within profession	Higher	Lower
Income	Higher	Lower

Sources: John P. Heinz and Edward O. Laumann, *Chicago Lawyers: The Social Structure of the Bar* (New York: Russell Sage Foundation, 1982); John P. Heinz, Robert L. Nelson, Rebecca L. Sandefur, and Edward O. Laumann, *Urban Lawyers: The New Social Structure of the Bar* (Chicago: University of Chicago Press, 2005).

law schools they attended. More important, they enjoy higher incomes and greater prestige as lawyers. The difference in income between lawyers in the two sectors and the difference between solo practitioners and lawyers with large firms grew between the 1970s and the 1990s.[62]

The distinctions between the two hemispheres should not be exaggerated. For one thing, the sectors are not completely separate from each other. And like specialization by field, the separation between the corporate and personal sectors is sharpest in large cities and more blurred in smaller cities and rural areas.

But real distinctions do exist, and they have important consequences. In the words of John Heinz, the two hemispheres make up "two systems of justice, 'separate and unequal.'"[63] At least in large cities, they are increasingly unequal in size; in 1995, more than twice as much of Chicago lawyers' work was in the corporate sector as in the personal sector, a much larger difference than in 1975.[64]

It also appears that the two sectors differ in the quality of lawyering. Because work in the corporate sector typically is better paying and more comfortable, that sector probably includes a disproportionate share of the most skilled lawyers. Further, the good support services and other attributes of practice in the corporate sector are more conducive to effective legal work. For both reasons, the legal services provided in the corporate sector almost surely are superior on the whole to those provided in the personal sector.

Organization and Regulation of Lawyers

As noted earlier, regulation of the legal profession is done almost entirely by state governments. For the most part, state legislatures have given their supreme courts the power to regulate lawyers, including licensing and disciplinary action. Most of the actual regulation is performed by lawyers themselves, under the supreme court's direction. About two-thirds of the states have an integrated bar, which means that all lawyers must belong to the state bar association; these associations are then given the primary role in regulating the profession.

The legal profession has a great deal of other organized activity. The most important single group is the American Bar Association (ABA), which had more than 400,000 members in 2006.[65] The ABA is divided into a number of sections, some based on specialized areas of practice. Both the ABA and its sections engage in a variety of activities. These include meetings and publications intended to improve the skills of members, as well as work in government on behalf of ABA positions on legal issues. The ABA also seeks to influence the selection of federal judges by rating potential or actual nominees.

The state bar associations, whether compulsory or voluntary in membership, generally resemble the ABA in organization and activities. There are also many city and county bar associations. In addition, each legal specialization has its own separate associations, some of which play significant roles within the profession and in politics. For example, the Association of Trial Lawyers of America, an organization of about 55,000 lawyers[66] who represent plaintiffs in personal injury cases, exerts considerable impact on law and policy in its area of specialization. Perhaps most important, in recent years the association has fought against tort law "reform," a movement to change major legal rules about compensation for personal injuries in ways that favor defendants. For many lawyers, these specialized groups are more important than those that are open to all lawyers because they more fully represent their members' interests and serve their professional needs.

Lawyers' Lives[67]

As a group, lawyers would seem to have good reason to be unhappy about their careers. The growing number of lawyers and increasing economic competition within the profession put more pressure on lawyers and suppress their incomes. Lawyers typically work longer hours than the average worker, often under considerable stress. The legal profession is among the most unpopular segments of American society, and criticism of lawyers has been unusually intense in recent years.

The evidence on lawyers' actual happiness or unhappiness with their work is mixed. Some surveys and studies of the physical and mental state of lawyers suggest that they are not doing very well. Drawing from this research, one law professor concluded that the legal profession was "one of the most unhappy and unhealthy on the face of the earth."[68] On the other hand, some surveys suggest a reasonably high level of satisfaction with professional life. For instance, a survey of Chicago lawyers in 1995 found that 84 percent were satisfied with their jobs, 10 percent neutral, and 6 percent dissatisfied.[69] And in a 2002 survey of lawyers who were two years into their careers—a stage at which the difficulties of legal practice are especially great—80 percent expressed satisfaction with their decision to become a lawyer.[70]

Whatever may be the general level of satisfaction in the legal profession, there appears to be considerable variation. Because of the enormous differences among lawyers in what they do and the conditions under which they work, that variation is not surprising. The Chicago study found that lawyers' income levels had greater impact on their satisfaction than any other single factor.[71]

ACCESS TO LEGAL SERVICES

There are many reasons why people might not hire attorneys to help them with legal problems, but the most significant barrier to their use is monetary cost. Most people who consider going to a lawyer lack a clear sense of how much a lawyer's help will cost them, but they often perceive that the cost will be more than they can afford or feel comfortable in paying. Indeed, standard rates for lawyers' services can make those services quite expensive.

If there were no mechanisms to overcome this monetary barrier, the use of legal services by nonwealthy individuals would be quite limited and their use by people with low incomes virtually nonexistent. In turn, most individuals would have little ability to make effective use of the legal system and the courts; in practice, whatever legal rights they had would mean little. But some mechanisms to address the problem of legal costs *have* developed, and they have grown considerably in number and scope over the last thirty years. After these mechanisms are considered, the impact of costs on access to lawyers can be assessed.

Overcoming the Cost Barriers to Legal Services

The types of mechanisms that allow litigants to avoid the usual costs of legal services fall into two general categories. One consists of programs, primarily governmental, to meet the legal needs of the poor. The other includes an array of developments in the private sector that may reduce cost barriers for the population as a whole.

Criminal Defense Services for the Poor   There is a long history of efforts to provide free legal services to indigent criminal defendants, but until the 1960s these efforts were limited and unsystematic. Although low-income defendants in federal court and in most states had a legal right to free services, this right was not implemented very effectively.

The primary impetus for strengthening this right was *Gideon v. Wainwright* (1963), in which the Supreme Court held that indigent criminal defendants in serious state cases must be provided with free counsel for their trials.[72] Although the Court's decision did not change the law in most states, it underlined the obligation to provide meaningful access to counsel. Other Supreme Court decisions extended the right to counsel to some misdemeanor cases and to other stages of the court process. Spending on counsel for the indigent increased dramatically at all levels of government, to $3.3 billion in 2002.[73] Attorneys from programs for low-income people now represent most defendants in felony cases. In 1998, two-thirds of the felony defendants in federal court and more than 80 percent in the seventy-five largest U.S. counties had lawyers provided by government.[74]

Across the country, three systems are used for defense of the poor.[75] The first is the public defender system, in which public employees (sometimes part-time) represent defendants. The second is the assigned counsel system. In this system, judges appoint private attorneys, usually from a list of volunteers, on a case-by-case basis to represent defendants. The third is a system in which a government unit contracts with lawyers or organizations such as bar associations to represent indigent defendants on a continuing basis. A growing minority of the states have statewide public defender systems. Most other states employ both public defenders and one or both of the other systems. In these states public defenders' offices are used primarily in urban counties, which have enough cases to make them practical.

Despite the great increase in financial support for defense of the poor, all of these systems suffer from serious monetary problems. These problems reflect the large and growing numbers of criminal cases, the periodic fiscal problems of state and local governments, and the general unpopularity of criminal defendants. In the assigned counsel system, the problem lies in low hourly fees and limits on the maximum amounts allowed per case, both of which are quite widespread. In 2004, for instance, lawyers who represented the indigent in Illinois were paid $30 to $40 per hour, with a maximum of $1,250 no matter how many hours they worked on a case.[76] Low fees and maximums per case discourage lawyers from taking cases, and in some places assigned counsel systems have broken down because lawyers are unavailable. In 2005 the Louisiana Supreme Court ruled that judges could prevent prosecutions from going forward if there were insufficient funds to pay a lawyer for the defense. A year earlier, the Massachusetts Supreme Court required dismissal of cases if lawyers were unavailable to represent defendants; the court cited the low fees paid to assigned counsel in the state.[77] These low fees, as well as lump-sum payments to lawyers who contract to take cases for the indigent, can also limit the effort that lawyers give to each case they take. In public defender systems, the funding provided to offices tends to be insufficient for them to meet their responsibilities effectively, so that individual lawyers are often burdened with large numbers of cases at any given time.

Inevitably, these financial problems weaken the quality of legal assistance that indigent defendants receive. In 2006 a commission set up by the chief judge in New York State concluded that the system of defense for low-income people in the state was highly inadequate, primarily because of limited funding.[78] The weakness of legal assistance programs is most visible in death penalty cases, in which attorneys are often ill-equipped to represent their clients effectively. In other cases lawyers sometimes have minimal contact with their clients, meeting them only on the day of the court hearing and urging them to plead guilty. According to one lawyer, "this sort of meet 'em and plead 'em is a pretty prevalent practice throughout the state of Georgia."[79]

Yet the quality of representation offered by lawyers for the indigent is not always low. In particular, some public defenders and defenders' offices do very good work despite caseload pressures. One Chicago defendant paid his public defender what an observer called "the highest compliment a PD can receive," praising his work and asking him why he hadn't "become a real lawyer."[80] As a study of Texas concluded, there can be enormous variation in the quality of this work even within a single state.[81] And if indigent defendants typically receive representation that is well short of the ideal, the same is true of many defendants who are not indigent. Working-class and middle-class people, the primary users of privately hired attorneys in criminal cases, are also limited in the quantity and quality of services they can obtain. In any event, the evidence we have indicates that the outcomes for defendants with public defenders are about the same as those for defendants who hire their own lawyers.[82]

Civil Representation for the Poor   The great majority of legal problems faced by low-income people are civil rather than criminal, and many of these problems are quite significant to the people involved. In a 1981 decision, however, the Supreme Court indicated that seldom if ever do the indigent have a constitutional right to be provided lawyers in civil cases,[83] and it has not departed from that position. But some mechanisms have been developed to supply legal services to low-income people in civil matters.

The most important is the Legal Services Corporation (LSC), created by Congress in 1974 as a successor to one of President Johnson's War on Poverty programs. LSC operates as an administrator of grants to more than one hundred local agencies that provide assistance directly to the indigent, agencies that together cover every county in the country. About three-fifths of all legal aid attorneys who provide services to the poor in civil matters work for LSC-funded agencies.[84] Most of these agencies set up law offices to which clients can come for help. These offices handle approximately one million legal matters each year, encompassing a wide variety of problems that reflect the situations of the poor—family, housing, income maintenance, health, consumer, and personal finance.

Most of the business of local agencies funded by LSC is fairly routine and is resolved without litigation. But LSC-funded attorneys have used lawsuits and other actions for the broader purpose of shaping the law, sometimes through challenges to the legality of government practices. This activity has aroused opposition to the LSC in Congress. That opposition is reflected in a set of restrictions on the kinds of cases that LSC-funded agencies can handle with federal money, enacted in 1996 and maintained since then. In 2001, the Supreme Court struck down one of those restrictions, a prohibition on challenges to welfare laws, on the ground that it violated the First Amendment.[85] But there remain other specific restrictions and general prohibitions on activities that might have a broad impact on public policy. Unhappiness with some of the LSC's activities helps to explain the slow growth of its budget. In 2006 the LSC received $327 million, a bit under one-half of its 1980 budget when inflation is taken into account.[86]

A quite different program is IOLTA ("Interest on Lawyers' Trust Accounts"), established by bar associations in each state. In this program, interest on money held by lawyers for their clients is given to groups providing legal services to the poor. This money adds up to a substantial amount, estimated at more than $200 million in 2001. Opponents of IOLTA argued that the program constitutes an unconstitutional taking of clients' property, but the Supreme Court rejected that argument by a 5–4 vote in 2003.[87]

There are other means to provide assistance to the poor in legal matters, including law-school programs and donations of time by individual attorneys. After his term as governor of Georgia, for instance, Roy Barnes worked for the Atlanta Legal Aid Society for six months for no salary.[88] But it appears that all these mechanisms together meet only a small portion of the legal needs of the poor. A 2005 study by the Legal Services Corporation found that because of funding limitations, LSC-funded programs turned away slightly greater numbers of eligible clients than they served. The study also found that most of the time low-income people obtained no legal assistance for legal problems they identified as very important.[89]

Advertising   Of course, people above the poverty line also face financial barriers to their use of lawyers. Just as programs exist to increase the access of the poor to lawyers' services, other mechanisms are aimed at enhancing access for working-class and middle-class people. To some extent they are designed to reduce fears about the costs of legal services; to some extent, they actually reduce these costs. These mechanisms have developed in the private sector, though government has played a key role in making them possible.

Advertising by lawyers is significant in itself and a foundation for other developments.[90] Traditionally, state rules prohibited most forms of advertising by lawyers. In 1977, however, the Supreme Court struck down state prohibitions of advertising by lawyers as a violation of free speech rights.[91]

Lawyers were slow to begin advertising, but gradually advertising became a common practice among lawyers whose clients are primarily individuals rather than institutions. The growth of advertising is visible in the telephone yellow pages, which feature large numbers of display ads by attorneys. In 2003, lawyers spent about $1 billion on yellow-page ads, the most of any business or profession.[92] Television commercials are less common, but some lawyers rely heavily on them to attract clients. It has become a standard practice for lawyers to use websites to attract business, sometimes advertising to alert potential clients to their sites. A Maryland firm co-sponsored a NASCAR racing team.[93] Lawyers' advertising can contain a variety of messages. Exhibit 3.6 provides a sampling of the messages in lawyers' yellow-page ads.

Lawyers sometimes solicit clients more directly. Some send mailings to people who have been involved in accidents or who have been arrested. After a child died because of apparent negligence by a day care center, an Alabama lawyer sent a wreath to the funeral home with a brochure and a note soliciting the parents' business.[94]

While most advertising is fairly restrained in content, some lawyers take a more flamboyant approach. A Las Vegas lawyer who represents plaintiffs in personal injury cases has run a television commercial with "a giant gorilla taking bananas from him to space aliens seeking legal help for a vehicle accident" and another with "a car-sized telephone dropping down on a hapless group of people."[95] Fears of such ads helped to spur efforts to regulate lawyers' advertising after it was legalized, and there has been a good deal of battling over what practices are allowable. Every state regulates the content of advertising by attorneys, and most have adopted a set of rules recommended by the American Bar Association. State regulations are fairly restrictive. For instance, the Florida Supreme Court in 2005 applied several of its state regulations to rule that a firm could not use the image of a pit bull in a commercial.[96] Some restrictions on advertising have been challenged on the ground that they are inconsistent with the Supreme Court's 1977 decision, and the successful challenges have broadened the range of advertising that lawyers can use.

EXHIBIT 3.6   Examples of Appeals by Lawyers in Yellow-Page Ads

---

Costs

People worry that lawyers are expensive. Personal injury lawyers who take cases on a contingency basis reassure potential clients that, in the words of a Kansas City ad, "nothing is paid by you unless and until the case is successfully resolved." Lawyers who charge regular fees to clients sometimes indicate the cost of a particular service, and a Seattle lawyer who does criminal defense says, "payment plans accepted." A Baltimore firm addresses another issue of cost: "free parking available."

Convenience

Ads frequently emphasize the ease of dealing with a lawyer or firm. A Kansas City firm offers "online traffic ticket help." A Chicago firm has "10 different offices to serve you near your home." Another Chicago firm has "staff on call 24 hours a day, 7 days a week," and a Miami lawyer "will personally come to your home or hospital."

Empathy

People who look for lawyers are often in difficult situations, and there is widespread distrust of lawyers. Some ads address one or both of these realities by seeking to show that a lawyer identifies with a potential client's situation. According to a Baltimore ad, "Insurance companies don't care about you . . . we do!" At a Philadelphia firm, "we only represent the interests of people, not large corporations." A Denver firm offers "professional, compassionate representation."

Credentials

Why hire one lawyer rather than another? Lawyers frequently point to indications of their competence—the length of time they have been in practice, the training they received, the honors they have won. One Philadelphia lawyer is a "former state senator, former assistant district attorney." A Chicago firm is "the LARGEST personal bankruptcy law firm in the country!" A Los Angeles lawyer "has degrees in both medicine & law." Taking a cue from product ads, a lawyer in Philadelphia announces: "As seen on TV!"

Past results

Some firms appeal to readers by describing what they have achieved for clients in the past—usually large verdicts in personal injury cases. A criminal lawyer's ad in Kansas City includes the headlines and the first few lines of real or mock newspaper stories about victories he won for defendants. Ads in Baltimore and Seattle include testimonials from clients.

Prospect of good outcomes

Both sides cannot win a case, and it probably would not be credible for a lawyer to guarantee a good outcome. (Such a guarantee might also get a lawyer in trouble with the state agency that regulates lawyers' conduct.) But ads nonetheless can be aimed at indicating that a good result is likely. According to a Kansas City ad, "there is no such thing as a hopeless tax problem." A Philadelphia ad says: "Accident? Injured? Make them pay!!" And lawyers frequently combine reassurance about costs with an implied guarantee. In the words of a Baltimore ad, "You don't pay a fee until we win!"

Source: Selected telephone books available in 2006.

Law firms that serve business clients seldom use mass advertising. But large firms have always sought to make contacts with potential clients, and increased competition for business clients gives these firms greater incentive to seek out clients. Many firms now use websites, brochures, and newsletters to advertise their services. Some advertise in specialized newspapers that are read by potential clients and lawyers who might refer business to them.

Those who favored the allowance of advertising by lawyers argued that advertising would lower lawyers' fees and make lawyers more accessible to individuals. The impact on fees is uncertain. But advertising does seem to have become an important means for people to find attorneys when they have a legal problem. Studies have found that many of the people who consult lawyers after they have been injured in accidents found those lawyers through advertising.[97]

Legal Services Plans   In the past few decades, a variety of programs have developed to provide lawyers' services to people for no fee or reduced fees, programs that go under the general heading of legal services plans.[98] The most popular form of these programs is "access plans," in which people are referred to lawyers who typically offer free brief consultations (often up to thirty minutes) and reduced rates for further work. Access plans are inexpensive to provide. As a result, some employers and groups such as labor unions and AARP (formerly the American Association of Retired Persons) offer these programs as a free benefit to their members. Altogether, a great many people—perhaps a majority of the population—are covered by these access plans. It appears that most people who are provided this benefit never make use of it. When access plans *are* used, it is most often for the kinds of matters that are common among working-class and middle-class people: marriage and divorce, real estate, landlord-tenant relations, and wills.

Another form of legal service plan, usually labeled "prepaid legal services," provides participants with more substantial legal services at no cost. Because the benefits are greater, often covering most of the legal services that an individual might need, prepaid legal services are more expensive to provide than access plans. As a result, they cover far fewer people than access plans. Some employers provide prepaid legal services as a benefit to their employees, and some people buy coverage for themselves.

Lawyers who participate in legal services plans typically are providing their services at a discount from standard fees. They are willing to do so because of the value of obtaining new business and contacts with new clients. The same incentives have led lawyers to develop other kinds of programs to appeal to individuals with relatively low fees and ready availability. In the 1970s and 1980s there was a burgeoning of "legal clinics" that sought to attract a high volume of work for middle-income clients, but these clinics declined because of economic difficulties. A current version of this approach is the three "Legal Grind" cafes in Southern California that provide a range of law-related services, including access to lawyers who sit in the cafe and offer fifteen-minute consultations for $25. The cafe receives the $25 and a portion of the fees that lawyers are paid if clients retain them for further legal work.[99]

The Contingent Fee   Somewhat different from all these other developments is a long-standing system under which a lawyer's fee in a case is contingent upon its outcome.[100] Under the contingent or contingency fee system, a lawyer represents a client who has a legal claim for money without requiring an advance payment (except, in some instances, for some of the lawyer's expenses). In a pure contingent fee system, if the client recovers money, either through a court decision or through a settlement with the other party, the attorney's fee will be a proportion of that sum. But if the client wins nothing, the attorney also receives nothing. The proportion that the attorney receives sometimes depends on how far the case goes before resolution; where the fee is fixed, one-third of the recovery is the most common proportion.

The contingent fee is used almost entirely in representation of individuals rather than institutions. It is employed most often in personal injury cases, where it is the predominant form of payment. One study found that contingent fees were used 97 percent of the time in this area.[101]

In deciding whether to take a case on a contingency basis, lawyers must consider the likelihood of winning a recovery and the prospective size of that recovery. In one study, lawyers accepted about half of the potential cases that were brought to them.[102] For those whose cases are accepted, the existence of the contingent fee is critical. If a sizable advance payment were required, many people could not hire a lawyer, and if a significant fee had to be paid regardless of the outcome, hiring a lawyer would strike many people as an unacceptable risk. Thus, for one important type of legal problem, the contingent fee overcomes much of the financial barrier to the use of legal services. Indeed, one purpose of legal advertising is to inform individuals of the contingent fee and thus to allay their fears about the financial risks of litigation.

The Overall Picture

The cost of legal services would seem to make it difficult for most people to take advantage of them; it would also seem to create a strong relationship between wealth and the ability to hire a lawyer. On the other hand, several mechanisms have been developed to overcome the usual financial barriers. In light of all this, what is the impact of costs on the use of lawyers?

Individuals who are not wealthy still face great constraints when they need to use lawyers for more than limited purposes. Some people under some circumstances can avail themselves of very good legal services—for example, the indigent criminal defendant in a city with an excellent public defender's office or the injured person who has a strong case involving a large potential recovery. By and large, however, the great majority of individuals are limited in the quantity and quality of services they can obtain. They must refrain from using lawyers at times when legal help would be useful. When they do employ an attorney, they may have to settle for less than the full level of the services they need. Nor can they afford to hire the most expensive attorneys.

Individuals sometimes have little choice but to hire attorneys, usually because they become defendants in serious criminal or civil cases. In these situations, even minimal use of lawyers' services may have a disastrous financial impact. And even people with relatively high incomes may have difficulty paying their legal expenses when they run into serious difficulties. However, corporate executives sometimes are reimbursed by their companies, and political leaders can raise money from supporters. By 2005, former House Speaker Tom DeLay had received several hundred thousand dollars for his legal defense fund to help defray the costs resulting from ethics investigations and criminal charges.[103]

If we leave aside the wealthy, the relationship between individuals' income and their ability to use a lawyer is complicated. People with higher incomes certainly are in a better position to pay for lawyers' services. Not surprisingly, one study of divorce lawyers found that lawyers did more on behalf of clients who had a greater ability to afford legal expenses.[104] The near-poor may now be in a weaker position than the poor, and the relative positions of low-income and middle-income people vary with such factors as the strength of a local Legal Services program and the availability of legal services plans. The contingent fee provides access to lawyers' services for individuals with attractive personal injury cases, regardless of their economic status. As a result, surveys of the public have not found a strong relationship between income and a person's use of lawyers to deal with legal problems.[105]

Compared with the great majority of people, large institutions such as corporations and the state and national governments can afford much higher levels of legal services. Large corporations are in an especially strong position, both because of their wealth and because legal fees are tax-deductible as a business expense—in effect, a very large government subsidy. Thus major corporations, like some governments, can pay large sums for legal services. Because they engage in a great many activities that require lawyers, large institutions do spend a great deal to employ lawyers, and corporations spend a great deal more for the help of outside attorneys.

The ready availability of attorneys provides a great advantage in utilizing the legal system. This advantage becomes most evident in a dispute between parties that differ in their access to attorneys. A working-class or middle-class individual may have great difficulty in combating a large business or the Internal Revenue Service. The largest corporations probably are in the strongest position. In a case with high stakes, even the federal government may be at a disadvantage against such a corporation, which can hire the most expert attorneys and assemble a much larger legal staff than the one available to the government.

This kind of advantage is also reflected in corporate influence on government policy. By employing attorneys as advocates in all three branches of government, large corporations can shape the development of the law. Where legal issues involve conflicts between corporations and sectors of society with less access to attorneys (as in consumer law), corporate interests generally have a greater capacity to achieve favorable rules of law.

There are many exceptions to this rule. Legal Services lawyers, interest groups, and public interest law firms have sometimes done quite well in securing judicial doctrines that favor relatively powerless segments of society, such as racial minority groups and consumers. On the whole, however, large institutions have the greatest ability to use lawyers to shape the law.

THE LAWYER-CLIENT RELATIONSHIP

Clients come to lawyers with legal problems or opportunities, seeking assistance in achieving their goals. In allowing lawyers to represent them, clients put themselves in a dependent position. A client who hires an attorney turns over to that attorney some control over the course of events. As a result, a lawyer's ability and willingness to serve a client have much to do with the client's success in dealing with the legal system. An incompetent lawyer or one who does not represent a client's interests faithfully may do considerable damage to those interests.

Competence

Differences among lawyers in their skills have an obvious but important impact: the more competent an attorney, the better off are the lawyer's clients. That impact is especially visible in the courtroom, where the litigant with the better attorney may gain a clear advantage over the other party. This reality is disturbing but unavoidable.

Less tolerable is work by lawyers that falls below a minimal level of competence. When people give responsibilities to their lawyers, they typically assume that those lawyers have at least a moderate degree of ability. If that assumption is incorrect, the client may suffer grievously. A poorly drafted contract, inaccurate tax advice, and ineffective courtroom advocacy can all have very serious consequences.

Because lawyers are licensed only after intensive training and a lengthy examination, we might assume that few of them are incompetent. But law school does not cover the full range of skills that lawyers need, and even with the growth of clinical programs law students often graduate with limited practical skills. The bar examination is necessarily only a partial test of the ability needed to practice successfully. Moreover, lawyers' competence may decline over time.

Indeed, many critics have pointed to what they see as widespread inadequacies in the work of lawyers. One of these critics was federal judge David Bazelon. Referring to the constitutional provision that guarantees the right to counsel, Bazelon said that many criminal defense lawyers were "walking violations of the Sixth Amendment."[106] And as Exhibit 3.7 illustrates, some judges have offered highly negative critiques of the work done by lawyers appearing before them.

Problems of competence are widely recognized, and efforts have been made to address them. The most important is the development of continuing education requirements. Forty-one states now require a certain amount of continuing education for lawyers to renew their licenses, typically ten to fifteen hours per year. Many states require specific components to that work, most often legal ethics.[107] Some states allow lawyers to choose from a wide range of programs, and providers of these programs try to make their classes attractive to lawyers. In the past few years Florida lawyers could take a course on "Protecting Your Retirement Lifestyle," New York lawyers could watch a play and hear a commentary on its ethical relevance to lawyers, and California lawyers could attend a program in Fiji that was conducted by the Association of Surfing Lawyers.[108] It is uncertain how much effect continuing education requirements have on lawyers' competence, though they undoubtedly enhance the skills of some attorneys.

The law is a broad field, and no lawyer can be competent in every area. There have been proposals for mandatory certification, under which lawyers could practice in some specific fields only if they met certain requirements. But lawyers prize their freedom to practice in whatever fields they wish, and no state has adopted such a plan. However, some states have set up voluntary programs to certify lawyers as specialists in certain fields. Many others have accepted certification by private organizations in those fields. Lawyers who have won

EXHIBIT 3.7   Some Judicial Complaints About the Quality of Lawyers' Work

---

From time to time, judges comment on the performance of the lawyers who appear in their courts. A few examples make it clear that their evaluations are not always positive.

1. In 2004 a federal magistrate judge in Philadelphia reduced the legal fees that a lawyer for the victorious party sought from his opponents. The judge explained that the lawyer's work was "careless, to the point of disrespectful." He added that "some of the Amended Complaint was nearly unintelligible." In response to his opponents' reference to typographical errors in his written work, the lawyer submitted an argument that contained additional typographical errors. "If these mistakes were purposeful," the judge noted, "they would be brilliant. However, based on the history of the case" and the lawyer's prior written work, "we know otherwise."

2. In 2001 a federal district judge in Texas expressed his unhappiness with the written work by the lawyers on both sides of a case before him. He could not resist indicating his opinion that "this case involves two extremely likable lawyers, who have together delivered some of the most amateurish pleadings ever to cross the hallowed causeway into Galveston, an effort which leads the Court to surmise but one plausible explanation. Both attorneys have obviously entered into a secret pact—complete with hats, handshakes and cryptic words—to draft their pleadings entirely in crayon on the back sides of gravy-stained paper place mats, in the hope that the Court would be so charmed by their child-like efforts that the utter dearth of legal authorities in their briefing would go unnoticed."

3. In 2004 another Texas district judge complained about the warring between the lawyers on the two sides of a case. When he "accepted the appointment from the President of the United States of the position now held," the judge said, "he was ready to face the daily practice of law in federal courts with presumably competent lawyers. No one warned" him "that in many instances his responsibilities would be the same as a person who supervised kindergarten." He concluded that "if the lawyers in this case do not change, immediately, their manner of practice and start conducting themselves as competent to practice in the federal court, the Court will contemplate and may enter an order requiring the parties to obtain new counsel."

Sources: In order, *Devore v. City of Philadelphia*, 2004 U.S. Dist. LEXIS 3635, 6–8 (E.D. Pa. 2004); *Bradshaw v. Unity Marine Corporation, Inc.*, 147 F. Supp. 2d 668, 670 (S.D. Texas 2001); and *Klein-Becker, LLC v. Stanley*, 2004 U.S. Dist. LEXIS 19107, 4, 6 (W.D. Texas 2004).

---

certification in a field can then advertise that fact. It is not clear to what extent potential clients are aware of certification and take it into account in selecting a lawyer.

Faithful Representation

Rules of professional conduct for lawyers require them to represent their clients faithfully, but the rules also require lawyers to do so within the limits of law and ethics.[109]

Lawyers frequently are criticized for acting on behalf of clients in ways that may be socially undesirable and ethically questionable. In the past few years, much of this criticism has focused on the lawyers who represented Enron and other large corporations in which high-level officials were later charged with serious misdeeds. In a 2006 decision a federal judge ruled that tobacco companies had conspired to prevent people from learning of the health consequences of smoking, and she denounced attorneys who represented the companies for their part in this effort.[110]

While inappropriate actions on behalf of a client represent a serious issue, more pervasive is the problem of failure to represent clients faithfully. Inevitably, lawyers' self-interest sometimes diverges from the interests of their clients. One example concerns fees. A lawyer who is paid on an hourly basis may have a financial incentive to devote more time to a case than a client needs. In contrast, a lawyer who is paid a flat fee has an incentive to resolve a matter by spending the minimum time necessary. The contingent fee system seems to meld the interests of lawyer and client, but it often creates a conflict of interest. The additional expenditure of time necessary to gain the maximum settlement for a plaintiff may not provide the lawyer with an adequate return to be financially worthwhile.

In situations that involve a conflict of interest, clients are at a disadvantage. Even though lawyers have a duty to elevate clients' interests over their own, in practice they may have a strong temptation to follow the course of action most favorable to their own interests. That temptation is increased by the difficulties that clients face in evaluating a lawyer's decisions. Lacking full information about the alternatives that a lawyer faced, a client may not recognize that the lawyer took a course of action that did not serve the client well. As a result, clients do not always receive the most faithful representation from their attorneys.

The failure of some attorneys to represent their clients faithfully is illustrated by class action lawsuits. In these lawsuits, one or more plaintiffs stand in for a larger class of people in similar situations. Class actions have proved to be a very useful means to attack practices that injure large numbers of people, especially when the damage to each individual is small. But the class action device also offers temptations to lawyers, who sometimes bring class action suits on behalf of large numbers of people and then reach settlements that give them large fees while providing very little to members of the class they formally represent except for the few "named plaintiffs." The other class members may receive coupons that are nearly worthless or, in some instances, nothing at all. In 2006 a federal grand jury indicted a law firm that specialized in class action cases, charging that it paid illegal kickbacks to three named plaintiffs in a series of lawsuits in order to secure their cooperation in participating as plaintiffs and accepting settlements that were highly favorable to the law firm. But even lawyers who adhere to the law often settle suits in ways that do not serve the great majority of class members who are their clients.[111] Occasionally, a court refuses to accept such settlements. In one instance, a federal district judge did accept it, but that decision was overturned by a court of appeals. In its opinion, the court of appeals summarized the problem of conflict of interest in class actions:

> Would it be too cynical to speculate that what may be going on here is that class counsel wanted a settlement that would give them a generous fee and Fleet [Mortgage Corporation, the defendant] wanted a settlement that would extinguish 1.4 million

claims against it at no cost to itself? The settlement that the district judge approved sold these 1.4 million claimants down the river.[112]

Some lawyers depart from their clients' interests in a more straightforward way: they behave dishonestly. Although many people think that lawyers are unusually prone to dishonesty, one legal scholar argued that "lawyers are about as honest as other people, given their opportunities. Unfortunately, they have many more opportunities than most people to be dishonest."[113] The two forms of dishonesty that seem most common among lawyers both reflect these opportunities.

One is the misuse of clients' funds. Attorneys entrusted with the proceeds of an estate or money to be placed in a trust sometimes "borrow" these funds for their own use, intending to pay back what they have taken. A few simply steal money—in some instances, a great deal of money.

The second form of dishonesty involves fees. Clients frequently are billed for more time than lawyers actually work for them, and lawyers sometimes inflate the expenses for which they charge clients or charge for questionable items. In the classic example, a Los Angeles law firm charged clients for the flowers it sent to their funerals.[114] One reason that fraudulent billing practices are widespread is the strong incentive that individual lawyers and law firms have to bill for as much time as possible; another is that these practices are very difficult for clients to detect. Even more serious, lawyers sometimes accept money for services they never perform. As a result, the unsuspecting client may forfeit legal rights. For example, an attorney's inaction can cause a client to miss the deadline for filing a lawsuit.

On rare occasions lawyers engage in more direct conflict with their clients. One Ohio attorney apparently hit a client in a criminal case during a court recess. A Texas lawyer was arrested for kidnapping a client at his wedding in an effort to get him to pay the forfeited bail bond she had put up for him and the legal fees she said he owed her.[115] These would not seem to be instances of good representation.

Variation in the Lawyer-Client Relationship

In general, lawyers are in a good position to dominate their relationships with clients. They possess information and expertise that their clients lack, and they are the ones who directly act in legal matters. As a result, people are usually not in a good position to oversee and control what their lawyers do.

Still, lawyer-client relationships vary a good deal. Much of this variation simply reflects how willing lawyers are to serve their clients' best interests regardless of their own self-interest. Some lawyers take advantage of clients who are dependent on them, but other lawyers go to great lengths to help such clients. One example is described in Exhibit 3.8.

The most systematic source of variation is by type of client: between organizations and individuals. As John Heinz and Edward Laumann argued, organizations such as corporations generally can exert considerably more control over their lawyers than can individuals.[116]

In the sector of the bar that serves individuals, lawyers typically represent clients on a one-time basis, and they have a great many clients. Thus no single client is very

EXHIBIT 3.8   A Law Firm Keeps Its Promise to a Client

In 1986, a Texas lawyer named Rex Houston represented Robbie Linton in a workers' compensation case, winning $34,000 for Linton in an administrative proceeding the next year. Houston then issued Linton a letter certifying that Linton's injury costs were covered by insurance, and he told Linton that if there were ever a problem, Houston's firm would help Linton.

In 1997 Linton returned to the firm when an insurance company refused to pay for two prescriptions costing $77.55. He recounted Houston's promise to James Holmes, another lawyer with the firm, and Holmes agreed to help. Nine years later, in 2006, Holmes won a verdict for the full $77.55 for Linton. The case cost the firm $25,000 in court costs and legal fees, for which it did not charge Linton. "They always treated me fair," Linton said. "So it didn't surprise me when they did what they did."

Source: John Council, "Texas Firm Pays Big for a Small Verdict," *National Law Journal*, March 20, 2006, 10.

important to a lawyer's professional position or income, and the lawyer need not worry a great deal about incurring a client's disfavor. For their part, few individual clients have an opportunity to scrutinize the performance of a lawyer over time or to develop independent expertise in the law. Further, lawyers who represent individuals have considerable capacity to shape their clients' perceptions of their situations. In the divorce field, for instance, lawyers can set clients' expectations about what they will get out of their case by referring to their own knowledge of the law and of judges.[117] A similar process occurs with lawyers who represent plaintiffs in personal injury cases.[118] Clients in these cases are far from powerless in their interactions with lawyers, but these individuals typically have limited control over their lawyers' choices. To a considerable degree, then, they are dependent on the willingness of those lawyers voluntarily to serve their interests well.

The situation in the sector of the bar that serves institutions is different. Here some lawyers are employed by a single client, a business corporation or a government. In the case of a corporation, this arrangement gives the client some control because corporate executives can evaluate a lawyer's work over time and because the lawyer depends on the corporation for employment. Full-time government lawyers are in a similar situation in some respects, though their "clients" often are in other agencies and thus may have little direct control over them.

Because of their independent status and their multiple clients, large law firms would seem to be in a much stronger position than lawyers who work for a single client. But large firms often provide continuing services to a set of corporate clients. These long-term relationships give clients a good chance to scrutinize and evaluate their lawyers' work, and they also require lawyers to satisfy their clients in order to keep their business. Moreover, corporations are powerful organizations that can affect the standing of a lawyer or firm.

The control that institutional clients gain over the lawyers and law firms that represent them should not be exaggerated. In his study of medium-sized litigation, Herbert Kritzer concluded that "there is little evidence of significant control of the lawyer by the client, regardless of whether the client is an individual or an organization (even if that organization is a large insurance company on which the lawyer is highly dependent)."[119] It is noteworthy that corporations, like individuals, are victims of outrageous and even dishonest billing practices.[120]

Yet the dependence of lawyers in the corporate sector on their major clients means that those clients gain significant influence over lawyers' choices. On the whole, then, institutions do achieve greater control over their attorneys than do individuals. Thus they gain one more advantage in their use of legal services. Not only do they get more and often better services, the services they get are more likely to be consistent with their interests.

Remedies

As noted already, education programs and certification of specialists have been used to improve the representation that lawyers provide to their clients. For people who feel they have been badly served by their lawyers, there are more specific remedies. If a lawyer's dishonesty has cost a client money, the client can apply to a state's client security fund for restitution. The effectiveness of these funds in reimbursing clients for losses varies across the states, and in many states they do not work very well.[121] Two other remedies are malpractice suits and complaints to disciplinary bodies. These mechanisms can provide redress to a disgruntled client, and their existence may deter lawyers from engaging in undesirable practices.

Malpractice Suits   Like other professionals, lawyers can be sued for malpractice on the ground that they failed to serve their clients adequately. Suits can also be brought by other people who claim that they have suffered losses because of a lawyer's representation of a client.

A substantial number of people make malpractice claims against lawyers. A quite incomplete study for the years 2000–2003 found more than seven thousand claims per year.[122] The bases for these claims range widely, involving both the quality of lawyers' performance and their alleged failure to take needed action in a case.

As is true of other types of cases, most malpractice claims are resolved without the filing of a lawsuit. In the 2000–2003 study, about 30 percent of claimants received a payment either through settlement of the case or a trial. Typically, the payment is fairly low; the mean was about $10,000 in that study. But in 2003, a jury awarded a hotel chain $21 million in a malpractice suit against the large law firm that had represented it.[123]

There is a widespread perception that the number of malpractice claims and lawsuits against lawyers has grown rapidly, but it is unclear whether this is actually true. If claims actually have become more common, the primary reason may be that clients are now more skeptical about the quality of legal work and more willing to seek redress when they feel that they have been badly served. It seems unlikely that the quality of lawyers' work has worsened. One lawyer who represents people bringing malpractice suits has a simple explanation for the relatively large number of lawsuits: "There are idiots out there practicing law."[124] But if that is true now, it was true in the past as well.

Discipline   Clients or others who feel that a lawyer has acted unethically can complain to the agencies in each state that are responsible for disciplinary action against attorneys. Discipline is ultimately the responsibility of state supreme courts, but typically most of the disciplinary process is delegated to bar association committees or to lawyers' disciplinary groups established by the supreme court. In this process, a lawyer's conduct is assessed against standards adopted by the state supreme court, standards that are usually similar to those in the American Bar Association's Code of Professional Responsibility.

Most disciplinary proceedings begin with a complaint to the appropriate agency. The agency may set a complaint aside without further action or investigate it. After an investigation, it may file formal charges against the attorney and hold a hearing. Based on what it finds, the agency can then recommend disciplinary action, which may range from a private reprimand to permanent disbarment from legal practice in that state. The state's supreme court must make the final decision to impose disciplinary action.

In 2004, the state disciplinary agencies across the country received 127,000 complaints, a striking number.[125] Of the complaints that these agencies acted on in 2004, nearly half were dismissed for lack of jurisdiction, generally meaning that the charges they made would not constitute a violation of the ethical standards even if they were true. Of the complaints that agencies went ahead to investigate, about half were dismissed as unfounded. Although only a small proportion of complaints result in some action against attorneys, sanctions are not rare. In 2004, 2300 lawyers received a private sanction and 3400 some kind of public sanction. About 1400 were suspended from practice. More than 900 were disbarred, either through action by the disciplinary body and supreme court or by consent of the attorney. But it should be noted that disbarred lawyers are often readmitted to practice after some interval.

The most common basis for disciplinary action is failure to perform competently on behalf of clients or neglect of clients.[126] Mishandling of funds is another common reason for sanctions. But many lawyers are sanctioned on the basis of matters such as criminal convictions that are unrelated to their dealings with clients. In 2000, for instance, the Committee on Professional Misconduct of the Arkansas Supreme Court recommended disbarment of President Clinton for giving misleading testimony about his relationship with Monica Lewinsky in the sexual harassment lawsuit against Clinton brought by Paula Jones. On the day after he left office in January 2001, Clinton reached an agreement with Robert Ray, Kenneth Starr's successor as independent counsel in the investigation of Clinton's conduct. As part of that agreement Clinton agreed to give up his Arkansas license to practice law for five years, an outcome that the Committee on Professional Misconduct found acceptable.[127]

The disciplinary system for lawyers has been criticized a good deal, primarily on the grounds that too few complaints are given serious consideration and that the discipline applied to miscreant lawyers is too lenient. There is considerable support for this criticism: complaints often seem to be dismissed too readily, and sanctions for serious misconduct are not always heavy. But some states have acted to strengthen their systems through measures such as increasing the resources with which disciplinary agencies can investigate and act on allegations of misconduct. And with all the weaknesses in the disciplinary process, lawyers probably do a better job of punishing wrongdoers than do most other professions.

CONCLUSIONS

This chapter offers only a first look at lawyers. Discussions of their roles in specific areas of the court system will provide a fuller picture of what lawyers do and how they fit into the judicial process. But even this first look should make clear the importance of lawyers in the legal system. More specifically, it indicates their importance in two respects.

First, access to lawyers makes a difference to people, increasing their ability to employ the law effectively. Those who can make use of lawyers' services have a better capacity to take advantage of legal rights than those without lawyers. In some situations, such as a trial with major stakes, the assistance of attorneys is critical.

Second, access to lawyers is not enough. Lawyers do not necessarily have a high level of competence, and they do not always serve their clients' interests faithfully. There is considerable variation in both lawyers' skills and their willingness to act on behalf of their clients.

A final lesson of the chapter is that access to lawyers and the quality of lawyers' services vary systematically. In particular, large organizations typically get more and better legal services than do individuals who are not wealthy. To a degree, this difference reflects the needs of corporations and governments. But its impact is to give them an advantage in using the legal system to their benefit. Of course, that advantage does not guarantee success in legal conflicts. The discussions of trial and appellate courts later in the book will probe more fully into patterns of success and failure in the courts.

FOR FURTHER READING

Baker, Nancy V. *General Ashcroft: Attorney at War*. Lawrence: University Press of Kansas, 2006.

Clayton, Cornell W., ed. *Government Lawyers: The Federal Legal Bureaucracy and Presidential Politics*. Lawrence: University Press of Kansas, 1995.

Heinz, John P., Robert L. Nelson, Rebecca L. Sandefur, and Edward O. Laumann. *Urban Lawyers: The New Social Structure of the Bar*. Chicago: University of Chicago Press, 2005.

Kritzer, Herbert M. *Risks, Reputations, and Rewards: Contingency Fee Legal Practice in the United States*. Stanford, Calif.: Stanford University Press, 2004.

Mather, Lynn, Craig A. McEwen, and Richard J. Maiman. *Divorce Lawyers at Work: Varieties of Professionalism in Practice*. New York: Oxford University Press, 2001.

Sarat, Austin, and William L. F. Felstiner. *Divorce Lawyers and Their Clients: Power and Meaning in the Legal Process*. New York: Oxford University Press, 1995.

Seron, Carroll. *The Business of Practicing Law: The Work Lives of Solo and Small-Firm Attorneys*. Philadelphia: Temple University Press, 1996.

Wice, Paul B. *Public Defenders and the American Justice System*. Westport, Conn.: Praeger, 2005.

Zitrin, Richard, and Carol M. Langford. *The Moral Compass of the American Lawyer: Truth, Justice, Power, and Greed*. New York: Ballantine Books, 1999.

Online Study Center Go to college.hmco.com/PIC/baum6e for ACE practice test questions and additional resources.

NOTES

1. American Bar Association, "National Lawyer Population by State" (http://www.abanet .org/marketresearch/2006_national%20_lawyer_population_survey.pdf).
2. This typology of lawyers' activities is based on Martin Mayer, *The Lawyers* (New York: Harper & Row, 1967), 29.
3. See Patrick Schmidt, *Lawyers and Regulation: The Politics of the Administrative Process* (New York: Cambridge University Press, 2005).
4. *California Business and Professions Code*, sec. 6125 (2006).
5. Suzanne Hoholik, "Lawyer's Objection Gets Nurse in Trouble," *Columbus Dispatch*, March 25, 2005, A1, A4; "Nurse Cleared of Allegations," *Columbus Dispatch*, August 20, 2005, 3C.
6. Lynn Mather, "Changing Patterns of Legal Representation in Divorce: From Lawyers to Pro Se," *Journal of Law and Society* 30 (March 2003): 142–144.
7. Administrative Office of the United States Courts, *Judicial Business of the United States Courts: Report of the Director (2004)* (Washington, D.C.: Administrative Office of the United States Courts, n.d.), 43, 88.
8. Siobhan Roth, "Can the Lawyers Fix the Damage?" *Legal Times*, October 27, 2003, 1.
9. Peter Lewis, "Crash Victim Beats the Odds in High Court," *Seattle Times*, July 16, 2004, A1. The case was *Mulcahy v. Farmers Insurance Company*, 95 P.3d 313 (Wash. 2004).
10. See Erica J. Hashimoto, "Defending the Right to Self-Representation: An Empirical Look at the *Pro Se* Criminal Defendant," *North Carolina Law Review* 85 (January 2007), 423–487; and Leandra Lederman, "Do Attorneys Do Their Clients Justice? An Empirical Study of Lawyers' Effects on Tax Court Litigation Outcomes," *Wake Forest Law Review* 41 (2006), 1235–1295.
11. American Bar Association, "Comprehensive Guide to Bar Admission Requirements," Chart III (www.abanet.org/legaled/baradmissions/bar.html).
12. "2005 Statistics," *The Bar Examiner* 75 (May 2006): 26.
13. "Skipping Law School," *New York Times*, September 21, 2005, A21.
14. American Bar Association, "Standards for Approval of Law Schools," Standard 304(e) (www.abanet.org/legaled/standards/standards.html).
15. Ibid., Standard 304(b).
16. "2005 Statistics," *The Bar Examiner*, 26.
17. State Bar of California, "Law Schools" (calbar.ca.gov/state/calbar/calbar_generic.jsp?cid= 10115&id=5128).
18. Ameet Sachdev, "Law Deans Linked to Accrediting Task," *Chicago Tribune*, February 15, 2004, sec. 5, 1–2; American Bar Association, "ABA-Approved Law Schools by Year" (www.abanet.org/legaled/approvedlawschools/year.html).
19. Leigh Jones, "Law School Deans Feel the Heat From Ranking," *National Law Journal*, April 5, 2006, 6. See Michael Sauder and Ryon Lancaster, "Do Rankings Matter? The Effects of *U.S. News & World Report* Rankings on the Admissions Process of Law Schools," *Law & Society Review* 40 (2006): 105–134.
20. Leigh Jones, "Salaries Rise, So Does Debt," *National Law Journal*, January 30, 2006, 1, 12; American Bar Association, "Average Amount Borrowed for Law School 2001–2004" (www.abanet.org/legaled/statistics/stats.html).
21. Jonathan D. Glater, "High-Tuition Debts and Low Pay Drain Public Interest Law," *New York Times*, September 12, 2003, A1, A25.
22. Tresa Baldas, "Paying the Way," *National Law Journal*, July 5, 2004, 1, 18.

23. Sheri Qualters, "Shorter Route to JDs Offered," *National Law Journal*, September 18, 2006, 4.

24. Information on the form of the bar examination is taken from American Bar Association, *Comprehensive Guide to Bar Admission Requirements*.

25. "2005 Statistics," *The Bar Examiner*, 23–24.

26. James Bandler and Nathan Koppel, "Raising the Bar: Even Top Lawyers Fail California Exam," *Wall Street Journal*, December 5, 2005, A1.

27. David Margolick, "At the Bar," *New York Times*, September 13, 1991, B9.

28. Matthew A. Ritter, "The Ethics of Moral Character Determination: An Indeterminate Ethical Reflection Upon Bar Admissions," *California Western Law Review* 39 (Fall 2002): 18–22.

29. *In the Matter of Hamm*, 123 P.3d 652 (Ariz. 2005).

30. *Kohlmayer v. National Railroad Passenger Corporation*, 124 F. Supp. 2d 877, 878 (D.N.J. 2000).

31. American Bar Association, "Enrollment and Degrees Awarded 1963–2005" (www.abanet .org/legaled/statistics.stats.html).

32. Cynthia Fuchs Epstein, *Women in Law* (New York: Basic Books, 1981), 4; Robert Benenson, *Editorial Research Reports: Lawyers in America* (Washington, D.C.: Congressional Quarterly, 1984), 535.

33. Epstein, *Women in Law*, 51.

34. American Bar Association, "First Year and Total J.D. Enrollment by Gender 1974–2005" and "Total Minority J.D. Enrollment, 1971–2005" (www.abanet.org/legaled/statistics/ stats.html).

35. Clara N. Carson, *The Lawyer Statistical Report: The U.S. Legal Profession in 2000* (Chicago: American Bar Foundation, 2004), 3.

36. See Nancy J. Reichman and Joyce S. Sterling, "Sticky Floors, Broken Steps, and Concrete Ceilings in Legal Careers," *Texas Journal of Women and the Law* 14 (Fall 2004): 27–76.

37. The proportions of lawyers in private practice, business, and government are from Carson, *Lawyer Statistical Report*, 6.

38. The proportions of lawyers in firms and in large firms are from Carson, *Lawyer Statistical Report*, 7–8, 15.

39. John P. Heinz, Robert L. Nelson, Rebecca L. Sandefur, and Edward O. Laumann, *Urban Lawyers: The New Social Structure of the Bar* (Chicago: University of Chicago Press, 2005), 163.

40. Tamara Loomis, "Survey Shows Post-Convergence Stability," *National Law Journal*, September 12, 2005, S3.

41. Lindsay Fortado, "Going Up Still," *National Law Journal*, December 12, 2005, S1–S7.

42. "The NLJ 250," *National Law Journal*, November 13, 2006, S39–S50.

43. National Association for Law Placement, "Salaries Up at Largest Firms for First Time Since 2000" (press release, August 1, 2006) (http://www.nalp.org/press/details.php?id=62); Leigh Jones, "Big-Firm Associate Pay Soars by $10K in 2006," *National Law Journal*, August 7, 2006, 10.

44. These associates had graduated from law school in 2000, so most were in their second year of practice. Ronit Dinovitzer et al., *After the JD: First Results of a National Study of Legal Careers* (Overland Park, Kansas, and Chicago: NALP Foundation and American Bar Foundation, 2004), 36.

45. Leigh Jones, "Mentoring Plans Failing Associates," *National Law Journal*, September 18, 2006, 1.

46. Lily Henning, "Deep Freeze," *Legal Times*, January 23, 2006, 1.

47. Marie Beaudette, "Diversity Still Elusive at Top Firms," *Legal Times*, November 3, 2003, 1, 27, 29; Alicia Upano, "Breaking Into the Boys Club," *Legal Times*, November 10, 2003, 17–18.

48. Brenda Sandburg, "Brobeck to End Turmoil by Going Out of Business," *National Law Journal*, February 3, 2003, A15; Reynolds Holding, Harriet Chiang, and Christian Berzthelsen, "How High-Flying Firm Fell," *San Francisco Chronicle*, February 3, 2003, A1, A10.

49. Anthony Lin, "Ten Firms Hit $2M Per Partner in Profits in '05," *National Law Journal*, May 8, 2006, 10.

50. "The 200 Largest Legal Departments," *Corporate Legal Times*, August 2005, 32–34.

51. Joan C. Williams, Cynthia Thomas Calvert, and Holly Cohen Cooper, "Better on Balance? The Corporate Counsel Work/Life Report," *William & Mary Journal of Women and the Law* 10 (Spring 2004): 389.

52. Robert L. Nelson and Laura Beth Nielsen, "Cops, Counsel, and Entrepreneurs: Constructing the Role of Inside Counsel in Large Corporations," *Law & Society Review* 34 (2000): 457–494.

53. Dinovitzer et al., *After the JD*, 36, 43, 44.

54. See Todd Lochner, "Strategic Behavior and Prosecutorial Agenda Setting in United States Attorneys' Offices," *Justice System Journal* 23 (2002): 271–294.

55. Nancy V. Baker, *General Ashcroft: Attorney at War* (Lawrence: University Press of Kansas, 2006).

56. Vanessa Blum, "Culture of Yes: Signing Off on a Strategy," *Legal Times*, June 14, 2004, 1, 12.

57. Marty Graham, "Elected City Attorney Shakes Up a City Hall," *National Law Journal*, February 28, 2005, 6.

58. Leonard Post, "Making Their Mark," *National Law Journal*, April 10, 2006, 1, 22; Tresa Baldas, "AGs Find Payoff in Big Drug Lawsuits," *National Law Journal*, June 12, 2006, 1, 26.

59. Heinz, Nelson, Sandefur, and Laumann, *Urban Lawyers*, 37.

60. Heinz, Nelson, Sandefur, and Laumann, *Urban Lawyers*, ch. 2; Donald D. Landon, *Country Lawyers: The Impact of Context on Professional Practice* (New York: Praeger, 1990), 129.

61. John P. Heinz and Edward O. Laumann, *Chicago Lawyers: The Social Structure of the Bar* (New York: Russell Sage Foundation, 1982), 319. This discussion of the "two hemispheres" is based primarily on that book and on Heinz, Nelson, Sandefur, and Laumann, *Urban Lawyers*.

62. Heinz, Nelson, Sandefur, and Laumann, *Urban Lawyers*, ch. 7.

63. John Heinz, quoted in Francis J. Flaherty, "The Myth—and Reality—of the Law," *National Law Journal*, August 6, 1984, 45. In this passage, Heinz was quoting a 1968 federal commission report on race relations in the United States.

64. Heinz, Nelson, Sandefur, and Laumann, *Urban Lawyers*, 42–43.

65. The membership figure is from the ABA website, at www.abanet.org/about/home.html.

66. The membership figure is from the ATLA website, at www.atla.org/about/index.aspx.

67. This title is borrowed from Michael J. Kelly, *Lives of Lawyers: Journeys in the Organizations of Practice* (Ann Arbor: University of Michigan Press, 1994).

68. Patrick J. Schiltz, "On Being a Happy, Healthy, and Ethical Member of an Unhappy, Unhealthy, and Unethical Profession," *Vanderbilt Law Review* 52 (1999): 872.

69. Heinz, Nelson, Sandefur, and Laumann, *Urban Lawyers*, 257.

70. Dinovitzer et al., *After the JD*, 47.

71. Heinz, Nelson, Sandefur, and Laumann, *Urban Lawyers*, 273.

72. *Gideon v. Wainwright*, 372 U.S. 335 (1963).

73. Robert L. Spangenberg, Marea L. Beeman, and James Downing, *State and County Expenditures for Indigent Defense Services in Fiscal Year 2002* (West Newton, Mass.: The Spangenberg Group, 2003), 35.

74. Caroline Wolf Harlow, *Defense Counsel in Criminal Cases* (Washington, D.C.: Bureau of Justice Statistics, U.S. Department of Justice, 2000), 1.

75. Each state's system is described in Spangenberg, Beeman, and Downing, *State and County Expenditures*.

76. Vivian Berger, "Time for a Real Raise," *National Law Journal*, September 13, 2004, 27.

77. *State v. Citizen*, 898 So. 2d 325 (La. 2005); *Lavallee v. Justices*, 812 N.E.2d 895 (Mass. 2004).

78. Commission on the Future of Indigent Defense Services, *Final Report to the Chief Judge of the State of New York*, June 18, 2006.

79. American Bar Association Standing Committee on Legal Aid and Indigent Defendants, Gideon's *Broken Promise: America's Continuing Quest for Equal Justice* (Chicago: American Bar Association, 2004), 16.

80. Steve Bogira, *Courtroom 302: A Year Behind the Scenes in an American Criminal Courthouse* (New York: Alfred A. Knopf, 2005), 138.

81. Allan K. Butcher and Michael K. Moore, *Muting Gideon's Trumpet: The Crisis in Indigent Criminal Defense in Texas* (Austin: State Bar of Texas, 2000).

82. Paul B. Wice, *Public Defenders and the American Justice System* (Westport, Conn.: Praeger, 2005), 19–20.

83. *Lassiter v. Department of Social Services*, 452 U.S. 18 (1981).

84. Legal Services Corporation, *Documenting the Justice Gap in America* (Washington, D.C.: Legal Services Corporation, 2005), 16.

85. *Legal Services Corporation v. Velazquez*, 531 U.S. 533 (2001).

86. Legal Services Corporation, *2003–2004 Annual Report* (Washington, D.C.: Legal Services Corporation, n.d.), 18–19.

87. *Brown v. Legal Foundation of Washington*, 538 U.S. 216 (2003). The estimate for 2001 is from p. 223 of the Court's opinion.

88. Rachel Tobin Ramos, "Georgia Governor Heading to the Legal Aid Society," *National Law Journal*, December 23–30, 2002, A8.

89. Legal Services Corporation, *Documenting the Justice Gap*.

90. This discussion is based in part on William Hornsby, "Clashes of Class and Cash: Battles from the 150 Years War to Govern Client Development," *Arizona State Law Journal* 37 (Summer 2005): 255–305, and Geoffrey C. Hazard, "Advertising and Intermediaries in Provision of Legal Services: Bates in Retrospect and Prospect," *Arizona State Law Journal* 37 (Summer 2005): 307–319.

91. *Bates v. State Bar*, 433 U.S. 350 (1977).

92. Kerry Randall and Andru J. Johnson, *The Lawyer's Guide to Effective Yellow Pages Advertising*, 2d. ed. (Chicago: American Bar Association, 2005), 8, 11.

93. Gail Diane Cox, "Revving for Clients," *National Law Journal*, May 10, 2004, 16.

94. David Margolick, *At the Bar: The Passions and Peccadilloes of American Lawyers* (New York: Simon & Schuster 1995), 170–171.

95. Lisa Kim Bach, "Lerner Takes State Bar to Court Over Advertising," *Las Vegas Review-Journal*, April 13, 2006, 1B.

96. *Florida Bar v. Pape*, 918 So.2d 240 (Fla. 2005).

97. Deborah R. Hensler et al., *Compensation for Accidental Injuries in the United States* (Santa Monica, Calif.: Rand Corporation, 1991), 134; Herbert M. Kritzer and Jayanth K. Krishnan, "Lawyers Seeking Clients, Clients Seeking Lawyers: Sources of Contingency Fee Cases and Their Implications for Case Handling," *Law & Policy* 21 (October 1999), 351.

98. This discussion is based in part on Michael Z. Green, "Ethical Incentives for Employers in Adopting Legal Service Plans to Handle Employment Disputes," *Brandeis Law Journal* 44 (Winter 2006): 402–404; and Judith L. Maute, "Pre-Paid and Group Legal Services: Thirty Years After the Storm," *Fordham Law Review* 70 (December 2001): 915–943.

99. Regan Morris, "Offering Legal Tips Over Cup of Latte," *New York Times*, August 5, 2004, C5; Legal Grind website, at www.legalgrind.com/.

100. This discussion of contingency fees is based largely on Herbert M. Kritzer, *Risks, Reputations, and Rewards: Contingency Fee Legal Practice in the United States* (Stanford, Calif.: Stanford University Press, 2004).

101. Herbert M. Kritzer, *The Justice Broker: Lawyers and Ordinary Litigation* (New York: Oxford University Press, 1990), 151.

102. Kritzer, *Risks, Reputations, and Rewards*, 72.

103. Glen Justice, "DeLay Shown Facing Growing Legal Bills," *New York Times*, June 16, 2005, A18.

104. Lynn Mather, Craig A. McEwen, and Richard J. Maiman, *Divorce Lawyers at Work: Varieties of Professionalism in Practice* (New York: Oxford University Press, 2001), 124, 142.

105. Barbara C. Curran, *The Legal Needs of the Public: The Final Report of a National Survey* (Chicago: American Bar Foundation, 1977), 152–157; "Project: An Assessment of Alternative Strategies for Increasing Access to Legal Services," *Yale Law Journal* 90 (1980),

140–141; Bruce Campbell and Susette Talarico, "Access to Legal Services: Examining Common Assumptions," *Judicature* 66 (February 1983), 313–318.

106. Laurence Meyer, "Conference to Weigh Lawyer Competency," *Washington Post*, May 21, 1979, C1.

107. Information on continuing education requirements is taken from the American Bar Association's website on continuing legal education, www.abanet.org/cle/.

108. Gail Diane Cox, "Back to School (or Not Really)," *National Law Journal*, September 9, 2002, A16; Gail Diane Cox, "Lawyers Take the Stage But Audience Gets Credit," *National Law Journal*, September 23, 2002, A18; website of the Association of Surfing Lawyers, www.surfinglawyers.com.

109. See American Bar Association, *Annotated Model Rules of Professional Conduct*, 5th ed. (Chicago: American Bar Association, 2003), 41, 315–321. On issues in lawyers' representation of clients, see Richard Zitrin and Carol M. Langford, *The Moral Compass of the American Lawyer: Truth, Justice, Power, and Greed* (New York: Ballantine Books, 1999).

110. Emma Schwartz, "Where There's Smoke, There's Ire," *Legal Times*, August 21, 2006, 1, 8.

111. Julie Creswell, "U.S. Indictment for Big Law Firm in Class Actions," *New York Times*, May 19, 2006, A1, C9; Julie Creswell and Jonathan D. Glater, "For Law Firm, Serial Plaintiff Had Midas Touch," *New York Times*, June 6, 2006, A1, C8; Michael C. Dorf, "The Indictment of the Milberg Weiss Law Firm and America's Love/Hate Relationship with Class Action Litigation," *Findlaw: Legal News and Commentary*, May 22, 2006 (http://writ.news.findlaw.com/dorf/20060522.html).

112. *Mirfasihi v. Fleet Mortgage Corporation*, 356 F.3d 781, 785 (7th Cir. 2004).

113. James D. Gordon III, *Law School: A Survivor's Guide* (New York: HarperCollins, 1994), 109.

114. Ralph Nader and Wesley J. Smith, *No Contest: Corporate Lawyers and the Perversion of Justice in America* (New York: Random House, 1996), 234.

115. Tim Doulin, "Mistrial Declared After Lawyer Hits Client," *Columbus Dispatch*, July 17, 2002, B1–B2; Cindy V. Culp, "Waco Attorney Arrested for Kidnapping Own Client," *Waco Tribune-Herald*, January 13, 2006.

116. Heinz and Laumann, *Chicago Lawyers*, 353–373.

117. Mather, McEwen, and Maiman, *Divorce Lawyers at Work*, 96–101.

118. Kritzer, *Risks, Reputations, and Rewards*, 118–124, 169–176.

119. Kritzer, *The Justice Broker*, 167.

120. See Lisa G. Lerman, "Blue-Chip Bilking: Regulation of Billing and Expense Fraud by Lawyers," *Georgetown Journal of Legal Ethics* 12 (Winter 1999), 205–365.

121. Elizabeth Amon, "Client Funds Improved, Still Flawed," *National Law Journal*, September 27, 2004, 1, 24.

122. The study is American Bar Association, *Profile of Legal Malpractice Claims 2000–2003* (Chicago: American Bar Association, 2005).

123. "Starwood Awarded $21 Million From Former Law Firm," *New York Times*, September 24, 2003, C4.

124. Richard Pérez-Peña, "When Lawyers Go After Their Peers: The Boom in Malpractice Cases," *New York Times*, August 5, 1994, B12.

125. Data on complaints and action by disciplinary bodies in 2004 are from American Bar Association, "Survey on Lawyer Disciplinary Systems" (https://www.abanet.org/cpr/discipline/sold/home.html). The totals are underestimates, because some states provided only partial data to the ABA.

126. Information on the bases for disciplinary action is taken from recent reports by state disciplinary agencies.

127. Eric Lichtblau, "Clinton Strikes Indictment Deal," *Los Angeles Times*, January 20, 2001, A1.

4

The Selection of Judges

J udges are at the center of the judicial process. In the cases that come to court, judges preside over proceedings and make decisions. Those decisions, significant in themselves, also influence the outcomes of disputes and situations that never get to court. This chapter deals with the process by which judges are selected, and the following chapter examines their characteristics and their behavior as judges.

Judicial selection is consequential. Its most direct effect derives from the fact that different people would behave in different ways as judges. For this reason, the process by which some people become judges rather than others helps determine what the courts do. Further, the selection process affects judges' choices. A judge who wants to stay in office may have to take into account the need to win a new term. Aside from its effects, the selection process merits consideration because it reveals some important realities about the courts, the larger political system, and the relationship between the two.

The selection of judges has been a subject of debate throughout U.S. history. That debate has focused chiefly on formal rules for judicial selection, reflecting a widespread belief that formal rules have great impact on the results of the selection process. Differences among the various formal systems used in the United States do have an impact, but one that is more limited than most people think. Perhaps their most important similarity is that each formal system provides considerable room for the influence of other political institutions, including political parties and the other branches of government. Indeed, judicial selection is the point at which courts are shaped most directly by their political environments.

GENERAL ISSUES IN JUDICIAL SELECTION

Debates about methods for selecting judges are largely debates about what people want from the courts and how to achieve it. In these debates, two questions have been dominant. The first is whether to give priority to judicial independence or to political accountability. Many people argue that judges should be selected in a way that maximizes their freedom from control so they can apply the law in the way they think appropriate. But others contend that judges are important policymakers, so they should be accountable to the people they serve—either directly or through the other branches of government.

The second question is how to obtain the most competent judges. The answer to this question is far from obvious, and the question is complicated by disagreement about the kind of competence that is desirable in a judge. Some people seek only legal competence, a mastery of the law and legal procedures. Others see a broader under-standing of politics and government policymaking as important for judges.

The United States differs from most other democratic nations in its emphasis on accountability and its relatively limited emphasis on legal competence. In continental Europe, for instance, prospective judges typically receive special training as judges and then enter a professional corps that resembles a civil service system. In the United States, in contrast, judges reach office through a highly unstructured process in which no spe-cialized training is required and people move into judgeships from other careers. And unlike most European countries, elected officials and the general public play the central roles in putting American judges on the bench and determining whether they stay there.

Within this general pattern, formal rules of selection vary considerably. The fed-eral and state governments use several distinct selection systems, systems that differ in both the goals they emphasize and the ways they are designed to achieve these goals.

The mix of judicial selection systems in the United States has a strong historical element.[1] Different systems have been popular in different periods, reflecting changes in people's views about goals and the best means to achieve them. Until the 1840s, the federal government and most states gave power over judicial selection to the other branches of government—the chief executive, the legislature, or both. This approach reflected a desire to minimize direct popular control over the judiciary. And the federal government and a majority of states gave judges lifetime terms in order to maximize their independence.

In the nineteenth century, a growing movement for popular control over govern-ment led to support for partisan election of judges who would hold terms of limited length. For several decades from the 1840s on, most new states and many existing states adopted this system.

By the late nineteenth century, political parties had come into some disfavor. Be-cause party leaders exercised so much power, many people came to see parties as bar-riers to popular control of government rather than as means to achieve it. As a result, nonpartisan elections gained support as a method for selection of public officials. The movement for nonpartisan elections had perhaps its greatest success in the judiciary: in the half century that began in the 1880s, most new states and several existing ones chose this system.

Early in the twentieth century, former president William Howard Taft and other prominent lawyers expressed dissatisfaction with all the existing methods of judicial selection, arguing that they provided for too little judicial independence and gave in-sufficient weight to legal competence. This feeling was reflected in the reform agenda of the American Judicature Society (AJS), founded in 1913, whose leaders sought a new method of judicial selection. The AJS helped devise a system in which a state governor would choose a new judge from a list of nominees provided by an indepen-dent commission, with the voters later having the chance to approve or disapprove the governor's choice.

Supporters of this new system had their first success when Missouri adopted it for some of its courts in 1940. For that reason it is often called the Missouri Plan, although its supporters prefer the term *merit selection.* Other states followed Missouri, at first slowly and then more rapidly, so that a large minority of states use the Missouri Plan for at least some of their courts. But efforts to establish the Missouri Plan have encountered resistance, largely because voters are reluctant to give up their power to choose between judicial candidates. In the past two decades few states have changed their formal systems for judicial selection, and people who disapprove of judicial elections now devote most of their attention to the functioning of elective systems rather than efforts to eliminate them.

Debates over formal systems of judicial selection have reached the federal level. In 1977, President Jimmy Carter incorporated Missouri Plan–style commissions into his procedures for selecting lower-court judges. Some senators have continued to employ commissions to help them recommend candidates for judgeships. But there has never been a sufficient consensus to change the constitutional procedures for selecting federal judges, and these procedures continue to reflect the views about judicial selection that predominated two centuries ago.

THE SELECTION OF FEDERAL JUDGES

The formal rules for selection of federal judges are fairly simple. All judges are nominated by the president and confirmed by the Senate. A simple majority of the senators voting is required for confirmation, but confirmation can be blocked by the Senate Judiciary Committee or by a filibuster that prevents a vote from being taken. (Under current rules, sixty votes are required to end a filibuster.) A filibuster was used to block a vote on the confirmation of Abe Fortas as chief justice of the Supreme Court in 1968, after which Fortas (already an associate justice) withdrew from consideration. After the Republicans gained a Senate majority in 2003, Democratic senators began to use the filibuster to prevent the confirmation of lower-court nominees.

When the Senate is in recess, the president can make a recess appointment, under which a nominee takes the bench immediately and can serve until the end of the next Senate session. There is disagreement about what constitutes a recess—whether the president can make recess appointments only after the end of the year-long congressional session, or whether even a few days out of session is sufficient. Between the mid-1960s and the early 2000s that issue was of little interest, because presidents made few recess appointments. But in 2004 President George W. Bush made two recess appointments to federal courts of appeals after Senate Democrats blocked confirmation of the two nominees. One of those appointments was made within the year-long session, and it was challenged on that basis. A federal court of appeals upheld the appointment, giving a broad interpretation to the recess appointment power, and the Supreme Court chose not to hear the case. By that time, however, President Bush had agreed not to make any further recess appointments in exchange for the unblocking of twenty-five lower-court nominees by Senate Democrats.[2]

With the exception of the specialized courts established under Article I of the Constitution, such as the Tax Court and the Court of Federal Claims, federal judges hold their positions for life. This means that vacancies on federal courts occur at irregular intervals: when a sitting judge resigns, retires, or dies—or, occasionally, when new judgeships are created. In turn, judges can influence which president gets to replace them through the timing of their retirements or resignations, and judges are more likely to leave the bench when a president of their own party wins office.[3]

The actual selection process is more complicated than the formal rules suggest. It also differs a good deal among the three major sets of federal courts.

The Supreme Court

Most people see the Supreme Court as unique among courts in its importance. This perception makes the selection of Supreme Court justices unique as well, both in the way that justices are chosen and in the mix of criteria used to choose them.

The Nomination Process   Every president must select hundreds of federal officials, but presidents make the great majority of these appointments in name only. A few appointments are deemed too important to delegate to subordinates, and foremost among these are positions on the Supreme Court. Thus, when a vacancy occurs on the Court, the president usually plays a very active role in filling it. One reflection of this role is the common practice of having a president meet personally with one or more potential nominees before making a final choice, a practice that George W. Bush has followed. But in identifying and choosing from candidates for nominations, presidents get considerable assistance from Justice Department officials and from members of their own staffs.

A variety of individuals and groups outside the executive branch seek to influence the president's choice. Interest groups that are close to the administration may participate privately in the nomination process, and other groups sometimes seek to exert pressure through the mass media. When President Bush had to replace William Rehnquist and Sandra Day O'Connor in 2005, groups with conservative positions on "social issues" such as abortion pushed both publicly and privately for the selection of nominees who had strong conservative records. Sitting members of the Court sometimes participate by identifying or endorsing candidates. Chief Justice Warren Burger played an important role in O'Connor's 1981 nomination by President Reagan and a crucial role in President Nixon's nomination of Burger's old friend Harry Blackmun in 1970.

A seat on the Supreme Court is a very attractive prize, and some prospective nominees make efforts to advance their candidacies. They may try to mobilize political support for themselves, and Martin Ginsburg worked to build support for his wife Ruth Bader Ginsburg prior to her nomination by Bill Clinton in 1993.[4] A sitting judge might cast votes and write opinions that are aimed in part at appealing to presidents and their advisers, and occasionally there are suspicions that a federal judge has done so in a particular case.

Criteria for Nominations   Not surprisingly, presidents use a variety of criteria in selecting Supreme Court nominees. The most important of these criteria fall into four categories.

The first includes what might be called the *qualifications* of prospective nominees: their competence and ethical standards. A nominee who falls short on either criterion may fail to gain Senate confirmation, and an unqualified candidate who does get confirmed but serves poorly on the Court may embarrass the appointing president. As a result, relatively few nominees are susceptible to attack on either ground. Indeed, most rate very high for their legal competence, and some have brought truly distinguished records to the Court.

The second category concerns the attitudes of the nominee toward issues with which the Court deals—that is, the nominee's *policy preferences*. Because Supreme Court decisions are so important, presidents seek appointees who share presidential views about policy. A liberal president, for example, wants to select justices who take liberal positions on most issues. As a result, administration officials usually scrutinize the views of potential nominees with considerable care. All but one nominee since 1975 have been lower-court judges, primarily because judges' records help in predicting their behavior on the Court.

A president is not guaranteed that a justice will actually behave as expected. To take one example, David Souter has been considerably less conservative than the first President Bush hoped. But such unexpected developments are the exception rather than the rule. More typical is the record of President Clinton's appointees. Both Ginsburg and Stephen Breyer have established themselves as moderate liberals, which seems to be what Clinton sought. And the early records of John Roberts and Samuel Alito suggest that they will be the strong conservatives George W. Bush wanted.

The third category of criteria might be labeled *reward*. Until the 1970s, nominations often went to personal and political associates of the president. That has become uncommon; Harriet Miers, President Bush's unsuccessful nominee in 2005, was the first close associate of a president to win a nomination since 1968. It remains true that the overwhelming majority of all nominees come from the president's party; one reason is the belief that such important prizes should be awarded to people within the party.

The final category is *pursuit of political support*. Some nominations are used to appeal to important interest groups or segments of the population. Most often a president tries to appeal to voters in a large demographic group by selecting a member of that group. For instance, President Bush's selection of Clarence Thomas in 1991 was intended to appeal to black voters—especially because Thomas would succeed the Court's only black justice, Thurgood Marshall.

Presidents differ in the weight they give to particular criteria, but for recent presidents—with the partial exception of Clinton—policy preferences have had the highest priority. The preeminence of policy preferences reflects the growing recognition that the Supreme Court plays a significant role in national policymaking and the increased salience of Supreme Court policies to people whose support is important to presidents. But other criteria continue to play a part in presidents' choices. The interplay of criteria is reflected in the successive nominations to replace Sandra Day O'Connor, described in Exhibit 4.1.

Senate Confirmation   The Senate's power to veto a presidential nomination gives it a critical role in the selection process. The Senate confirms the great majority of the nominees that it considers, twenty-six out of thirty since 1949, and few confirmation votes are close. Yet confirmation is never automatic, and in the current era the Senate consistently gives nominees close scrutiny. The most public form of this

EXHIBIT 4.1   Replacing Justice O'Connor

When Justice Sandra Day O'Connor announced her intention to retire in July 2005, George W. Bush gained his first opportunity to nominate a Supreme Court justice. Conservative interest groups pushed hard for a nominee whose record was one of strong conservatism, so that the replacement of O'Connor with a new justice would move the Court somewhat to the right. President Bush nominated John Roberts, a judge on the federal court of appeals for the District of Columbia. Conservative groups had already indicated that Roberts was acceptable to them, and Roberts's impressive record as a lawyer gave him strong credentials for the Court. Liberal interest groups were not happy with Roberts, and some Democratic senators were also unhappy, but as summer went on Roberts seemed to be headed toward confirmation.

Then, in early September, Chief Justice William Rehnquist died. President Bush quickly nominated Roberts to succeed Rehnquist. This meant that the president needed to find another nominee for Justice O'Connor's position. He chose Harriet Miers, the White House Counsel. Miers's nomination aroused strong opposition from an unexpected source, conservative interest groups. In part because Miers had not served as a judge, those groups were not confident that she was strongly conservative. They attacked her on that ground and on two other grounds: she lacked the expertise in constitutional law that a justice should have, and her nomination represented "cronyism" because she had long been a close associate of President Bush. Meanwhile, Democrats remained largely on the sidelines. Under the pressure, Miers withdrew from consideration.

Shortly afterwards, the president chose Samuel Alito for O'Connor's position. Alito, a judge on the federal court of appeals in Philadelphia, was similar to Roberts in most respects. His fifteen years of work on the court of appeals indicated that he was an able judge. Just as important, he was highly acceptable to the conservative groups that had mobilized against Miers. The record that pleased those groups was likely to arouse opposition from the other side of the ideological divide, but the Republican majority in the Senate seemed likely to guarantee Alito's confirmation— as indeed it did. Thus President Bush was able to strengthen his support among interest groups that were important to his political base and, it appeared, to advance his goal of shifting the Supreme Court's collective point of view in a conservative direction.

Sources: Newspaper articles.

scrutiny is the hearings held by the Judiciary Committee, in which nominees are questioned at length and other witnesses are heard.

The combination of close scrutiny and a high rate of success reflects some basic realities about the confirmation process. Aware of the Senate's active role, presidents look for nominees who are likely to win confirmation.[5] This was especially true of Bill Clinton, who chose not to nominate strong liberals partly in order to minimize opposition from Senate Republicans. For their part, senators generally begin with a presumption in favor of confirmation. Although that presumption usually holds up, it can be overcome under the right circumstances—or, from a nominee's perspective, the wrong ones. These circumstances relate to both the specific nominee and the situation in which a nomination is made.[6]

For the nominee, one unfavorable condition is strong and widespread opposition to the nominee's views on legal issues, especially if interest groups sharing that opposition mobilize against a nominee. On the whole, strongly liberal Democratic nominees and strongly conservative Republican nominees are more vulnerable than moderates. Another unfavorable condition is a credible challenge to the competence or ethical behavior of a nominee. Nixon nominee G. Harrold Carswell was defeated in 1970 after opponents mustered evidence of his limited legal skills. Reagan choice Douglas Ginsburg withdrew in 1987 before his formal nomination because disclosures about his use of marijuana made confirmation unlikely.

The most important aspect of the situation is the partisan makeup of the Senate. Nominees are much better off when the president's party controls the Senate. Presidents have a poor record of success in the last year of a term, primarily because senators from the other party want to keep a seat open in case their own party wins the next election. When the Supreme Court is closely divided between liberal and conservative justices and a new justice might shift the Court's collective position, contention over nominees tends to increase because the stakes are higher. And the current era is a relatively difficult one for nominees because of strong polarization between the parties and mobilization of interest groups that care a great deal about the Court's policies.

The confirmations of John Roberts in 2005 and Samuel Alito in 2006 reflected several circumstances. By choosing judges who seemed to be strong conservatives, President Bush ensured that there would be opposition from liberal senators and interest groups. But the 55–45 Republican majority in the Senate ensured that the nominees would be confirmed if no more than a few Republicans defected—so long as Democrats chose not to filibuster, which they did. Both Roberts and Alito demonstrated impressive legal skills in their records and their Senate testimony. No questions were raised about Roberts's ethical behavior; Alito's participation in a case involving a conflict of interest was questioned, but most senators concluded that this was a minor and inadvertent error. Roberts was confirmed by a 78–22 margin, with about half the Democrats voting against him. Alito won by only a 58–42 vote, with negative votes from all but four Democrats as well as one Republican. The closeness of the vote compared with that on Roberts reflected the clearer evidence of Alito's strong conservatism and the fact that he would replace Justice O'Connor, a "swing" vote on the Court. Roberts would succeed Chief Justice Rehnquist, himself a strong conservative, so his appointment would not have as much effect on the Court's ideological balance. The forty-two votes against Alito were an extraordinarily large number, but because of Republican unity his confirmation was never in much doubt.

The Lower Courts

Judges on the district courts and the courts of appeals differ from Supreme Court justices in that they serve only one region of the country—in the case of district judges, a single state or part of a state. Of course, there are far more lower-court judges than there are positions on the Supreme Court. For these reasons, the process and criteria for selection of lower-court judges once differed radically from those for the Supreme Court. But these differences have been reduced, primarily because presidents and senators now see lower-court judgeships as significant to their political and policy goals. In turn, these changing perceptions reflect heightened recognition that lower courts have an impact on national policy, increased polarization between the parties, and the development of interest groups that give a high priority to the selection of federal judges.[7]

The Nomination Process   Presidents delegate the nomination of lower-court judges to staff members in the White House and Justice Department. Each administration develops its own procedures for selecting nominees; the procedures used in George W. Bush's first term provide one example.[8]

The work of making judicial nominations was done primarily in the Office of Legal Policy within the Justice Department and the office of the White House Counsel. People in those two offices met frequently in the Judicial Selection Committee, a coordinating body chaired by White House Counsel Alberto Gonzales (who became attorney general in President Bush's second term). That committee would recommend to the president when a potential nominee to a judgeship should be given a detailed investigation by the Office of Legal Policy and the FBI. If investigation of a candidate suggested that a nomination was appropriate, once again a recommendation would be made for the president's approval.

Like Supreme Court nominations, the selection of lower-court nominees is made with the Senate in mind. Traditionally, the Senate's role was centered on senators from a nominee's state, because of senatorial courtesy. Under the practice of senatorial courtesy, when a presidential nomination to a federal position within a state requires Senate confirmation, the Senate as a whole gives deference to the wishes of the senators from that state—very strong deference to a home-state senator of the president's party. District judges represent a single state. The courts of appeals cover multiple states, so senatorial courtesy is not as strong at that level, but specific seats usually are treated as belonging to a particular state.

Thus administrations have an incentive to take home-state senators' views into account when they make nominations. At an extreme, a senator from the president's party might dictate a specific nominee. But the leverage of individual senators has weakened, in part because presidents and their administrations are less willing to yield control over nominations. In the Bush administration the White House Counsel's office consults with senators a good deal, but home-state senators have less power than they once held, and Democratic senators seldom play key roles in selecting nominees.

As in the selection of Supreme Court justices, interest groups try to influence the president's choices. The American Bar Association has been an important group, because most administrations since the 1950s allowed the ABA to screen candidates for judgeships before their nomination. Republicans have become unhappy with the ABA because of its perceived liberalism, and the George W. Bush administration has eliminated this role for the ABA. Other groups that concern themselves with the selection of federal judges play a part in the nomination process. In the Bush administration, conservative groups have worked to secure the nominations of strong conservatives.

In contrast with the Supreme Court, people who would like to become lower-court judges routinely campaign for those positions. One important kind of campaigning is amassing support from people and groups that are politically significant to the administration and home-state senators.

Criteria for Selection   The criteria that influence Supreme Court nominations apply to the lower courts as well, but their relative importance differs. Traditionally, reward was the primary criterion for nominations to the district courts and courts of appeals, while qualifications and policy preferences had less weight than they did for the Supreme Court. These differences followed from the belief that the lower courts were less significant than the Supreme Court, so who occupied those courts did not matter a great deal. Thus, lawyers who had personal or political ties with presidents, Justice Department officials, and senators held a great advantage in winning judgeships. The best way to become a federal judge, one Senate staff member joked, "is that you should have the foresight to be the law school roommate of a future United States senator; or, that failing, to pick a future senator for your first law partner."[9]

Over time, primarily since the 1960s, the criteria for nominations to the courts of appeals have become more like those for the Supreme Court. To a lesser degree, the same thing has happened to the district courts. The reason is simple: increasingly, presidents, senators, and interest groups recognize that the lower federal courts do make important policy choices. As a result, it has become less attractive to put political associates of dubious qualifications on the lower courts and more compelling to select nominees on the basis of their perceived attitudes toward issues of judicial policy.

The extent of the change should not be exaggerated. Connections with the people who help select nominees are still helpful (to take one example, George W. Bush's district court nominees included the son of Kentucky's Republican senator Jim Bunning), lawyers whose capabilities could be questioned still win some nominations, and some nominees' policy preferences seem distant from those of the administration that selects them. What stands out is variation—between the district courts and courts of appeals, from one nomination to the next, and among administrations.

Variation among administrations is highlighted by the differences between Bill Clinton and George W. Bush. For Clinton, putting liberals on the federal bench was less important than it had been to Lyndon Johnson and Jimmy Carter. The relative moderation of Clinton's appointees frustrated liberal groups that cared about judicial policy. But judicial policy was not a high priority for Clinton and his advisers, and they saw important advantages to the selection of moderates. The nomination of relatively moderate judges helped Clinton to maintain good relations with the Senate and assisted him in getting his nominees confirmed, especially when there was a Republican Senate majority. It also may have served the president in his effort to present a moderate image to the voters. Like Carter, Clinton selected record numbers of female and nonwhite judges. This record was motivated in part by the belief that enhanced diversity in the judiciary was desirable in itself, but it also reflected the desire to maintain support for the administration among groups that were important to it.[10]

George W. Bush has been very different from Clinton in his approach to lower-court nominations. Bush was unhappy with what he perceived as the undue liberalism of the federal courts. For many of his legal advisers and for some conservative interest groups, shifting the courts in a conservative direction was a high priority. As a result, policy preferences became the primary criterion for selection of court of appeals nominees, a criterion that also advanced Bush's goal of maintaining support from groups that were part of his political "base."

The approach taken by President Bush is symbolized by the high proportion of his court of appeals nominees who had been members of the Federalist Society, by far the most important conservative legal group—a little less than half between 2001 and 2005.[11] In part, this record reflected personal ties between these nominees and administration officials who themselves were Society members. More important, membership in the Society indicated a commitment to strongly conservative views that made prospective nominees more attractive to the Bush administration. Indeed, one study suggests, among nominees who won confirmation Federalist Society members have had more conservative records on the bench than other Bush appointees.

The Bush appointees as a group have been strongly conservative, reflecting the administration's priorities. A study of district court decisions found that judges selected by George W. Bush have reached a somewhat higher proportion of conservative decisions than those chosen by prior Republican presidents. In contrast, the Clinton appointees had a lower proportion of liberal decisions than those chosen by Lyndon Johnson and Jimmy Carter.[12]

Senate Confirmation   The confirmation process for lower-court judges has changed fundamentally since the late 1970s.[13] Traditionally, confirmation was closely tied to senatorial courtesy. If home-state senators from the president's party did not indicate their support for a nomination, the Judiciary Committee did not consider it. In this way, the committee enforced the requirement that the Justice Department reach agreement with those senators. Home-state senators from the other party had less power, but they still exercised a veto over nominees under some circumstances. If a candidate did have the support of the home-state senators, the committee and the Senate confirmed the nomination automatically rather than giving it collective scrutiny; this is the other side of senatorial courtesy.

In the past three decades, the negative side of senatorial courtesy has remained largely intact, in that home-state senators from the president's party can prevent confirmation. But the positive side has weakened substantially: the support of the home-state senators no longer guarantees confirmation. As a result, the average time from nomination to confirmation has lengthened considerably, and a higher proportion of nominees never win confirmation.

This change has accelerated since 1994. After winning a majority in that year's elections, Senate Republicans took an aggressive stance in scrutinizing President Clinton's nominees. Even though Clinton's nominees as a whole were relatively moderate, several were denied confirmation and others were confirmed with difficulty because they were perceived as overly liberal.

More broadly, Senate Republicans sought to limit the number of Clinton appointees on the bench. A Senate controlled by the opposition party usually is slow to confirm the president's nominees, but the pace was especially slow during the Clinton administration. Here too, the primary reason was ideological: with the lower courts predominantly conservative after the Reagan and Bush appointments, Republican senators were reluctant to see that situation changed. Clinton gave Senate Republicans a larger role in nominations in an effort to smooth the confirmation process, but doing so reduced his problems only marginally. Clinton was still able to change the partisan and ideological composition of the courts a good deal, but less than would be expected for a two-term president.

After George W. Bush was elected in 2000, Senate Democrats sought to return the favor. They were able to do so because of the mid-2001 decision of one Republican senator to become an independent and vote with the Democrats on organization of the Senate, thereby creating Democratic control of the Judiciary Committee. The committee blocked some nominees to the courts of appeals, primarily on the ground that they were unduly conservative. Republicans gained control of the Senate in 2002 and a larger majority in 2004, largely removing the Judiciary Committee as an obstacle. But Senate Democrats used procedural devices, especially the filibuster, to prevent confirmation of some court of appeals nominees. In response, Republicans threatened to eliminate the filibuster in judicial confirmations, an action that was labeled the "nuclear option" because it would represent a major change in Senate procedures and would trigger fierce battling between the parties. The bitterness between Senate Democrats and Republicans was reflected in suggestions by Judiciary Committee staff members "that the Department of Homeland Security screen senators for weapons and sharp objects before they enter the hearing room."[14] In 2004, a report by the Senate sergeant-at-arms concluded that two Republican staff members had gained unauthorized access to the files of staff for Democratic committee members to gather information on Democratic strategy.[15]

In 2005, fourteen moderate senators—seven from each party—reached an agreement under which Democrats in that group agreed to filibuster nominees only under "extraordinary" circumstances and the Republicans agreed to vote against changing the filibuster rule.[16] That agreement avoided a severe escalation of interparty conflict. But battles over confirmations continued, because the stakes involved in the selection of federal judges remained high.

Even during the Clinton and George W. Bush administrations, most court of appeals nominees and an even higher proportion of district court nominees have been confirmed. Some run into difficulty because of specific circumstances that produce opposition from home-state senators; others arouse opposition from interest groups for ideological reasons, and those groups in turn mobilize opposition by sympathetic senators. A sampling of Clinton and Bush nominees who faced strong opposition, shown in Exhibit 4.2, illustrates the changes that have occurred in the confirmation process.

EXHIBIT 4.2   Selected Episodes in Senate Consideration of Lower-Court Nominees by Bill Clinton and George W. Bush

William Fletcher. Despite twelve years of appointments by Ronald Reagan and George Bush, the Ninth Circuit Court of Appeals on the West Coast remained relatively liberal in the mid-1990s. For that reason Senate Republicans were especially reluctant to allow Bill Clinton to appoint judges to that court. In 1995, Clinton nominated Fletcher, a law professor, to the Ninth Circuit. Senator Orrin Hatch, chair of the Judiciary Committee, argued that under federal law Fletcher could not serve on the same court as his mother, sitting judge Betty Fletcher. That problem was overcome when Betty Fletcher agreed to become a senior judge. Some observers labeled this episode, "Throw Momma from the Bench." Still, the Judiciary Committee did not act on William Fletcher's nomination. Finally, in 1998, Clinton agreed to a deal with Washington Republican senator Slade Gorton in which Clinton would nominate Gorton's choice to another Ninth Circuit seat in exchange for Fletcher's confirmation. Hatch then acted to bring Fletcher's nomination to the floor over opposition from other Republican senators. Fletcher was confirmed by a 57–41 vote, with all the negative votes coming from Republicans.

Ronnie White. In 1999 Clinton nominated White, a justice on the Missouri Supreme Court, to a district court seat. Missouri Republican senator John Ashcroft led opposition to White, arguing that White had voted too frequently to overturn death sentences and calling him "pro-criminal." White came before the Senate for a confirmation vote, but he was defeated by a 54–45 margin, with all Democrats supporting him and all Republicans opposing him; he was the first nominee to a federal judgeship to lose a full Senate vote since 1986. White was black, and Democrats charged that his defeat reflected a Republican tendency to give greater scrutiny to nonwhite nominees. Whether or not this was the case, White's defeat apparently reflected the willingness of Republican colleagues to help Ashcroft create an issue for his reelection campaign in 2000. Ashcroft lost that contest, but shortly afterwards George W. Bush chose him to be attorney general.

Miguel Estrada. In 2001 President Bush announced his first eleven nominees to the federal courts of appeals. One of the eleven, Miguel Estrada, was nominated to serve on the federal court of appeals for the District of Columbia—a court often considered second in importance to the Supreme Court. Estrada had clerked for Supreme Court justice Anthony Kennedy and had served in the office that represents the federal government in the Supreme Court before going into private practice. Senate Democrats and liberal groups were suspicious of Estrada because he appeared to be strongly conservative, and some thought that if Estrada was confirmed he was likely to receive a Supreme Court nomination later in the Bush administration. Supporters of Estrada touted his status as an immigrant from Honduras; Hispanic groups divided on the nomination, which became fodder for the battle between the parties to win the support of Latino voters. With a bare Senate majority, Democrats blocked Estrada's nomination. He was renominated in 2003, after the Republicans gained a slight majority of their own, but Democrats prevented a vote on his confirmation with a filibuster. In September, Estrada asked that his nomination be withdrawn.

Priscilla Owen. A member of the Texas Supreme Court, Owen was another of Bush's original nominees to the federal courts of appeals. Owen was one of the more conservative members of a conservative court, and Senate liberals charged that she had taken extreme positions on economic issues and on abortion. They gleefully pointed to a 2000 opinion in which her colleague Alberto Gonzales—who became White House Counsel in 2001—said that if the court adopted the position that she and other dissenters took in an abortion case, it would be "an unconscionable act of judicial activism." Owen's nomination, like that of Estrada, was blocked in the 107th and 108th Congresses. But Owen did not withdraw. Bush renominated her in 2005. After the compromise between the parties that year the Democrats did not filibuster against her, and she was confirmed by a 55–43 vote that followed party lines almost perfectly.

Brett Kavanaugh.   In 2003 Bush nominated Kavanaugh to the federal court of appeals for D.C. Relatively young at thirty-eight, Kavanaugh served as associate counsel to the president. He drew opposition from Senate Democrats for his work in that position but even more for his service as a deputy to special prosecutor Kenneth Starr. In that position, Kavanaugh was a principal author of the report to Congress that provided the impetus for impeachment of President Clinton. Senator Charles Schumer said that Kavanaugh's nomination was "payment for political services rendered." Democrats blocked Kavanaugh's nomination, which was allowed to die in 2004. The president renominated Kavanaugh in 2005, but even with their reduced numbers Senate Democrats were able to prevent confirmation again. But after one more nomination the next year, Kavanaugh was finally confirmed: as with Owen, Democrats decided against using a filibuster to block a vote, and he won confirmation by a 57–36 vote.

Sources: Newspaper articles. The quotations are from Michael Grunwald, "Coming Up Short on an Appeals Circuit," *Washington Post*, October 6, 1998, A21 (Fletcher); Charles Babington and Joan Biskupic, "Senate Rejects Judicial Nominee," *Washington Post*, October 6, 1999, A12 (White); *In re Doe*, 19 S.W.3d 346, 366 (Texas 2000) (Owen); and Emma Schwartz, "The Next Generation," *Legal Times*, March 6, 2006, 12 (Kavanaugh).

THE SELECTION OF STATE JUDGES

The history discussed at the beginning of this chapter has left states with a variety of formal systems for selection of judges, systems that continue to change with decisions by state governments and voters. These systems work in practice to produce an even wider array of selection processes.

The Formal Rules

Any classification of the formal systems in the states oversimplifies the variation among them. But those systems can be placed in five categories:

1. *Gubernatorial appointment.* In this system, as the title indicates, the governor appoints judges. In nearly every state that uses gubernatorial appointment, the governor's choice must be confirmed. Usually, the confirming body is the state senate.
2. *Legislative election.* In this system, now used in only two states, the legislature elects judges.

3. *Partisan election.* Here voters choose between party nominees in a general election, with party labels indicated on the ballot. The nominees generally are selected through partisan primary elections.
4. *Nonpartisan election.* Under this system, voters choose between candidates in a general election, with no party labels indicated on the ballot. Usually, the top two candidates in a nonpartisan primary are placed on the general election ballot. In several states, however, there is no general election if one candidate receives a majority of votes in the primary.
5. *Missouri Plan.* In this complex system, a commission is established to nominate candidates for judgeships. Most often, the commission includes lawyers who have been selected by their colleagues and non-lawyers selected by the governor. In many states, a judge also serves. When a judgeship needs to be filled, the commission produces a short list (usually three names) of nominees, and the governor makes the appointment from this list. After the judge has served for a short time, and at periodic intervals thereafter, voters are asked whether or not to retain the judge; there is no opposing candidate.

Exhibit 4.3 shows the current distribution of these five systems among the states. As the exhibit shows, historical patterns in the popularity of different systems are reflected in their distribution across regions. Gubernatorial appointment and legislative election are found almost exclusively on the eastern seaboard, among the original thirteen states. Similarly, partisan election of judges is most common in the South and Midwest, whose states were formed when this system was most popular. Because they developed relatively late, nonpartisan election and the Missouri Plan have the weakest geographical patterns.

The exhibit also indicates the complexity of the states' formal rules. For one thing, many states use different selection systems for different courts. Indiana, for example, uses the Missouri Plan to choose appellate judges and partisan election to select nearly all its trial judges. The special systems that many states use for minor trial courts, not shown in the exhibit, complicate the picture even further.

Further, as the "M"s in the exhibit indicate, many of the systems used by the states do not fit neatly into a single category. And even the systems that fit a single category can vary considerably. This is especially true of the Missouri Plan, in which the details differ a good deal from state to state.

Another respect in which the states vary is in the length of judges' terms. Rhode Island gives its judges life terms, and judges in Massachusetts and New Hampshire hold office until the age of seventy. Elsewhere judges have fixed terms. In many states, these terms are longer for appellate judges than they are for trial judges. The most common term length is six years, but some states give trial judges four-year terms, and most New York judges serve fourteen-year terms. Most states have mandatory retirement ages or ages beyond which judges cannot seek new terms, usually seventy.

Vacancies can occur during judges' terms because of resignation, retirement, or death. In states that do not use partisan or nonpartisan elections, such vacancies are usually filled by the method that is ordinarily employed to select judges. But in most states with elective systems, the governor makes interim appointments. In some of these states, the selection is made from nominees of a Missouri Plan–style commis-

EXHIBIT 4.3   Formal Systems for the Selection of State Judges

Partisan Election	Nonpartisan Election	Gubernatorial Appointment	Legislative Election	Missouri Plan
Alabama	Arizona*	California* (M)	South	Alaska
Illinois (M1)	Arkansas	Delaware	Carolina	Arizona*
Indiana*	California*	Maine	Virginia	Colorado
Kansas*	Florida*	Maryland (M)		Connecticut
Missouri*	Georgia	Massachusetts		(M3,M4)
New York*	Idaho	New Hampshire		Florida* (M4)
Pennsylvania	Kentucky	New Jersey		Hawaii (M3,M4)
(M1)	Louisiana (M2)			Indiana*
Tennessee*	Michigan (M2)			Iowa
Texas	Minnesota			Kansas*
West Virginia	Mississippi			Missouri*
	Montana (M)			Nebraska
	Nevada			New Mexico (M)
	North Carolina			New York* (M4)
	North Dakota			Oklahoma*
	Ohio (M2)			Rhode Island
	Oklahoma*			(M3,M4)
	Oregon			South Dakota*
	South Dakota*			Tennessee*
	Washington			Utah (M3)
	Wisconsin			Vermont (M3,M4)
				Wyoming

Note: The states in this table are classified according to the system they use for the regular selection of judges rather than the system for filling vacancies in the middle of terms. The systems used only for minor trial courts or for a small number of major trial judgeships are not listed. An asterisk indicates that another system is also used in that state (in such cases, both systems are listed in the table).

An "M" indicates that the system used in a particular state is a significant modification of that described in the text. For modifications used in multiple states, "M" is followed by a number. "M1" designates states in which judges are initially selected through partisan elections and face retention elections when they seek additional terms. "M2" designates states in which elections are primarily nonpartisan but there are significant partisan elements. "M3" designates states in which judges are selected through the Missouri Plan but the governor's choice must be confirmed by the state legislature. "M4" designates Missouri Plan states in which there are no retention elections, either because judges are chosen for new terms through another method or (in Rhode Island) they hold office for life.

States that have established nominating commissions for appointments through executive order rather than through constitutional or statutory provisions are classified as gubernatorial appointment states. Delaware and Maryland have long-standing nominating commissions based on executive order.

Source: American Judicature Society, "Judicial Selection in the States" (www.ajs.org/js/).

sion. In most states with interim appointees, an appointee must face the voters fairly soon, even if the term has not expired.

Formal rules are important to the selection of judges, but they provide only the starting point in determining how judges are actually chosen. The discussions that follow consider the ways that the various formal systems work in practice.

The Operation of Elective Systems

Nearly two-thirds of the states choose some or all of their judges through partisan or nonpartisan elections. The difference between those two forms of election is consequential, and each form operates quite differently across the states that use it. Still, there are some general patterns in judicial elections.

Campaigns and Voters   By no means are all judicial elections contested. To take one example, Ohio features relatively high levels of competition for judgeships, but in 2004 only 41 percent of its judicial races were contested.[17] In the Los Angeles trial court, about one-hundred fifty judges' terms ended in 2006, but there were only eight contests for those seats.[18] Because we think of judgeships as prized positions, it may be surprising that judicial candidates often run unopposed. But judgeships are *not* always attractive. Many lawyers have incomes that far exceed judicial salaries, and trial-court judgeships lack the prestige to compensate for economic sacrifice. And where one candidate seems to have a great advantage, potential opponents may see no reason to run a futile campaign.

When elections are contested, they vary in several respects. Much of this variation can be captured by a continuum between "quiet" and "noisy" contests. Most judicial elections are fairly quiet. The candidates may campaign actively, but exciting issues are absent. Levels of campaign spending are low to moderate, and the news media give only limited coverage to the candidates.

In quiet contests, voters are unlikely to learn much about the candidates before they go to the polls. As a result, they must rely heavily on what the ballot itself tells them. In states that use partisan elections, one key piece of information on the ballot is the candidates' party affiliations. Most voters identify themselves as Democrats or Republicans, so they are likely to give weight to partisan considerations when they know little else about the candidates. This means that one candidate may have a great advantage because of the party balance in a state or district.

This effect is especially clear in the South. When the Democratic party was dominant in the region, Republican candidates had no chance to win judgeships in states that employed partisan elections. As dominance has shifted to the Republican party in much of the South, the situation has been reversed. In Texas, Republicans have won every election since 1996 for the two courts whose judges are elected statewide.[19] In such states the most heated battles may take place in the primary elections of the dominant party. This was true of Alabama in 2006, when there was a set of contests between factions of the Republican party for nominations to the supreme court. In one contest, an associate justice ran for chief justice against the incumbent in what observers labeled a "bare-knuckle fight" and "a political mud bog."[20] The incumbent won, with the result that the two combatants would be sitting together on the court for some time.

In New York State, nominations to the primary trial court are made by party nominating conventions that typically are controlled by local party leaders. In judicial districts where one party is dominant, these party leaders effectively determine who becomes a judge. The same is true in competitive districts when the parties "essentially divvy up the judgeships," as they do more often than not. In 2006 a federal district judge held that the New York system as it works in practice violates the rights of those who seek to challenge the party leaders' favored candidates, and until the legislature acted he ordered that the state use primary elections instead of party conventions to choose nominees.[21]

Whether or not a state uses a partisan ballot, of course, the ballot discloses the candidates' names. In most states that use nonpartisan judicial elections, the candidates' names are the *only* information the ballot provides about them. Thus, a recognizable name can be a major asset. Someone who is well known usually gains a distinct advantage, and someone with the good fortune to have the same name as a well-known officeholder can gain the same advantage. County auditor Frank Russo made himself a familiar figure in the county that includes Cleveland, and six other Russos now sit on the county's major trial court. (There might be a seventh, except that a candidate named Scott Miller who changed his middle name to "Russo" was not allowed to include the new middle name on the ballot in 2004. Deprived of that benefit, he lost by a wide margin.)[22] For that matter, some names can attract votes because they are pleasant sounding or because of their ethnic connotations. The impact of candidates' names is suggested by the unexpected defeat of a Los Angeles judge, described in Exhibit 4.4.

Even in relatively quiet contests, candidates for judgeships have some ability to get their messages to the voters during the campaign. This ability has increased in the states and localities where levels of spending by judicial candidates have grown. But in contests that lack exciting issues, the primary effect of campaigning is to enhance a candidate's name recognition. That is not a trivial effect: a candidate who is better known than a rival has a distinct advantage, especially in a nonpartisan election. Thus judicial candidates have good reason to raise and spend as much money as they can.

In noisy contests, candidates spend substantial amounts of money. Interest groups may run independent campaigns in support of the candidates they favor. And the campaigns often raise issues relating to judicial policy—the decisions an incumbent has reached or the kinds of positions that a candidate would take if elected to a judgeship. Only a small proportion of contests fit in this category. But contests of this type are becoming more common, especially at the supreme court level.[23] This trend has roots in two related developments.

First, interest groups are increasingly aware of the importance of state court decisions to their fortunes. In particular, rules established by state supreme courts for cases involving personal injuries have considerable effect on labor unions, consumers, manufacturers, medical professionals, insurance companies, and the lawyers who represent plaintiffs or defendants in injury cases. One focus of conflict in recent years is the statutes that a number of legislatures have adopted to strengthen the interests of defendants in injury cases. These statutes routinely are challenged in court suits, and decisions whether to uphold the statutes or strike them down can have enormous

EXHIBIT 4.4   A Judge's Name Contributes to Her Defeat

In June 2006, Los Angeles Superior Court judge Dzintra Janavs lost by a 7 percent margin to challenger Lynn Diane Olson in a nonpartisan election. The defeat was a surprise, in that Janavs was considered a diligent and effective judge. Some lawyers thought she was abusive toward people she dealt with in the courtroom, but that criticism was not widely publicized. Olson, successful in business, had not practiced law actively since 1992.

One reason for Olson's victory was that she spent about $100,000 on her campaign, outspending Janavs by about a 2–1 margin. Most of the money was used to buy her a place on "slate mailers" that are sent to voters to guide them in their decisions. And in a heavily Democratic county, Olson undoubtedly benefited by emphasizing that she was a Democrat and Janavs a Republican.

But election observers widely perceived that Janavs was hurt by having a Latvian name that sounded unfamiliar, one that contrasted with Olson's more common name. Olson could have run against dozens of judges; some people speculated that she chose Janavs as her opponent because of the name, although Olson denied that this was the case. In any event, it seems likely that Janavs would have survived the challenge had it not been for her name.

Janavs did not have to contemplate her defeat for long. Three days after the election, Governor Arnold Schwarzenegger announced that he would appoint Janavs to a vacant seat on the same court. The governor said that the "unfortunate result" of the election "should not rob California of a fine jurist." He also noted that "I can relate to the problem of having a name that is hard to pronounce."

Sources: Articles in the *Los Angeles Times*. The quotations are from Jessica Garrison, "Gov. Is the Judge: Janavs Back to the Bench," *Los Angeles Times*, June 10, 2006, B1.

economic impact. Thus groups are willing to spend large sums to win election for candidates whom they perceive as favorable to their positions. This willingness helps to account for the general increase in the levels of spending in judicial elections.

Second, aspiring judges, parties, and other interested groups have found that effective campaigns can be waged against judicial candidates on the basis of policy issues. By no means do all campaigns in noisy contests revolve around policy issues. Candidates may focus on raising doubts about their opponents' qualifications, especially where an incumbent judge has been charged with corruption, incompetence, or intemperate behavior. But increasingly, questions of judicial policy play a central role in judicial campaigns.

Two kinds of issues predominate. One is personal injury law, in which candidates and groups on either side can claim to represent the public interest: enabling consumers and workers to get adequate compensation for injuries, or fighting against baseless lawsuits that extract large sums of money from businesses and ultimately from consumers. Even more effective as an issue is criminal law, since the great majority of voters believe that the courts are too lenient toward criminal defendants. A candidate who is seen as "soft on crime" may be quite vulnerable. For this reason, even groups that care only about personal injury law may emphasize criminal justice issues in their appeals to voters.

A Supreme Court decision in 2002 eliminated long-standing rules in most states that severely limited the discussion of policy issues by judicial candidates.[24] Most judicial candidates still refrain from directly taking positions on such issues, but this practice is becoming more common. For instance, one candidate for the Arkansas Supreme Court in 2006 stated his opposition to the court's school funding decision in the preceding year.[25] Some interest groups are asking candidates to indicate their positions on certain issues. In any event, parties and interest groups often stand in for the candidates in discussing policy issues. Indeed, some judicial contests have two largely separate components: campaigns by the candidates, which focus on matters such as experience and qualifications, and campaigns by groups, which focus on matters of judicial policy.

In recent years, several states have had well-funded and highly visible contests for the state supreme court. Among them are Alabama, Michigan, Mississippi, and Ohio. Republican and conservative candidates have won most of those contests. One reason is that these candidates usually have more money spent on their behalf than their opponents do. Perhaps more important, they are often able to connect effectively with voters' conservatism on the issues they raise. That success and the conduct of noisy judicial elections are illustrated by two supreme court contests in 2004, discussed in Exhibit 4.5.

The Situation of Incumbents   Despite the growth of large-scale campaigns for judgeships, it remains true that the great majority of sitting judges win re-election. In this respect, judges are like other public officials who run for new terms. However, judges are more likely than most other officials to run unopposed, and this is especially true below the supreme court level.

Judges' success in winning new terms largely reflects the advantages held by incumbents in any office. Voters usually know them better than their opponents; they usually come from the majority party in their state or district; and they generally can raise more campaign funds than any challenger. However, the lack of visibility of most judges and most judicial contests puts judges in a somewhat different position from incumbents such as governors and members of Congress. On the one hand, the small scale of most judicial campaigns makes it more difficult for challengers to persuade voters to vote against a sitting judge. On the other hand, judges generally are not in a good position to build name recognition and political support. Thus, under unfavorable conditions they may be vulnerable to defeat.

Indeed, supreme court justices lose at a higher rate than members of Congress and at about the same rate as governors.[26] However, the overall rate of defeat masks an enormous difference between types of elections. In 1990–2000, counting uncontested races, justices lost 5 percent of the time in nonpartisan elections and 31 percent of the time in partisan elections. For the most part, this difference reflects the vulnerability of judges when their party is in the minority or there is an unfavorable party tide in a particular election.

Judges can also lose when opponents convince enough voters that an incumbent has been ineffective or has taken unpopular positions. The large-scale campaigns that have become more common in recent years typically center on charges against an

EXHIBIT 4.5 Two 2004 Contests for State Supreme Courts

Illinois: Karmeier vs. Maag

Justices of the Illinois Supreme Court are chosen by district in partisan elections. In 2004 there was an open seat in a district in southern Illinois, a seat that both parties had a reasonable chance to win. The candidates, both state appellate judges, were Republican Lloyd Karmeier and Democrat Gordon Maag. Business groups were especially interested in the seat because plaintiffs in this judicial district had won large verdicts in tort cases, one for $10 billion against a tobacco company. The supreme court fills vacancies on the lower courts, and the "local" justice typically makes the choices of new judges. Business groups contributed heavily to Karmeier, and lawyers who represent tort plaintiffs made large contributions to Maag. Setting a national record, the two candidates raised $9.4 million—an extraordinary total for an election in which fewer than six hundred thousand votes were cast—and independent groups spent additional money in the contest.

"While the candidates behaved politely in person," according to one report, "they fought a no-holds-barred battle on television." The candidates and groups supporting them spent the bulk of their money on television, airing 7,500 commercials during the campaign. Many of the commercials attacked the opposing candidate for past decisions, positions on issues, or ties with interest groups. One commercial on behalf of Maag attacked Karmeier for contributions he had received "from big corporations and Washington DC lobbyists," including the tobacco and asbestos industries. One flyer from a group supporting Karmeier charged that "Gordon Maag's decisions caused businesses and jobs to flee southern Illinois," but it devoted most of its space to six decisions in which it charged that he was unduly favorable to criminal defendants. A pro-Maag commercial attacked Karmeier for a decision of his own in a criminal case. Ultimately, Karmeier won with 55 percent of the vote. It appears that he and his supporters were able to define the issues in the election in a way that worked in his favor.

West Virginia: McGraw vs. Rowe and Benjamin

The Illinois contest was tame compared with one in West Virginia, which also uses partisan elections for its supreme court. In 2004 the court was perceived as having a 3–2 majority that generally favored plaintiffs in personal injury cases. The U.S. Chamber of Commerce targeted Democrat Warren McGraw, one of the three pro-plaintiff justices. As its first step, the Chamber spent $850,000 on behalf of McGraw's opponent in the Democratic primary election. McGraw won, but with only 57 percent of the vote.

In the general election, McGraw's opponent was Brent Benjamin, a lawyer who initially was little known. His campaign sought to build name recognition and a favorable image for him. At the same time, the Benjamin campaign and an independent group called "For the Sake of the Kids" aired television commercials that attacked McGraw for his vote in a case involving a child molester. For its part, the Chamber of Commerce criticized McGraw for a decision in a drunk driving case. As one scholar said, "the criminal issues were put in as a surrogate for what the battle was really about." McGraw counterattacked with his own large-scale campaign, supported by labor unions and lawyers who represent personal injury plaintiffs. Ultimately, the candidates in the primary and general elections and independent groups spent about $2 million on television commercials, most of them attack ads, that aired 5,000 times.

About two-thirds of the ads were against McGraw. His opponents outspent him by a considerable margin, primarily because of an estimated $3.5 million spent on behalf of

Benjamin by the head of a coal company. The Benjamin campaign and its allies seemed effective in shaping voters' perception of McGraw. Despite his enormous advantage in name familiarity at the beginning of the year, an advantage strengthened by his brother's position as state attorney general, McGraw received only 47 percent of the vote and lost his position.

Sources: Newspaper articles; Deborah Goldberg et al., *The New Politics of Judicial Elections 2004* (Washington, D.C.: Justice at Stake, n.d.); Seth Stern, "West Virginia Supreme Court Election Shows Effectiveness of Interest Groups," *Judicature* 89 (July–August 2005), 38–40; data on campaign spending at www.followthemoney.org. The quotations, in order, are from Paul Hampel, "Karmeier Wins Illinois Supreme Court Race," *St. Louis Post-Dispatch*, November 2, 2004; Goldberg et al., *New Politics of Judicial Elections*, 18; "In Southern Illinois, the 'Wheels of Justice' Have Ground to a Screeching Halt . . .", flyer from the Coalition for Jobs, Growth, and Prosperity; and Stern, "West Virginia Supreme Court Election," 39.

incumbent, as illustrated by the West Virginia contest described in Exhibit 4.5. The charges can relate to either the quality of a judge's performance in office or the substance of the judge's decisions. The most common subject is a judge's decisions in criminal cases, often votes to overturn death sentences. In one extreme case, a newspaper advertisement charged that an incumbent municipal judge in California had never sentenced a defendant to prison. The ad did not mention the fact that municipal judges had no power to sentence defendants to prison.[27] Issue-based challenges to incumbents fail more often than they succeed. In 2004, for instance, a supreme court justice in Washington State won by a 3–2 margin after she was attacked for a decision in criminal justice, and a Georgia justice won by a similar margin despite a campaign that depicted her as liberal, activist, and a supporter of same-sex marriage.[28] But the campaigns against the two justices did not run television commercials, and more massive campaigns against incumbents enjoy a higher rate of success. Sitting judges have more reason to feel vulnerable than they did in the past.

Interim Appointment   In all but two states that elect judges, the governor fills vacancies between elections. These interim appointments are important because vacancies occur with some frequency and because appointees generally are successful in winning subsequent elections, though less successful than incumbents who had won previous elections. (In Arkansas, appointees are prohibited from running for election to keep their positions.) As a result, many of the judges in states with elective systems gained their positions initially through appointments. Between 1964 and 2004, about half of all new supreme court justices in those states were appointed rather than elected, and the proportion for lower courts seems to be about the same.[29] For this reason, elective systems should be considered both elective *and* appointive.

The success of appointees in winning election is understandable: an appointed judge shares some of the advantages of long-time incumbents, and most appointees are too new to create enemies or to arouse concerted opposition. In some states, appointed judges from the minority party in their district or the state as a whole can be vulnerable to defeat, but even in those states most newcomers hold their positions. In other states, they seldom lose.

The proportion of judges who gain office through appointment varies considerably from state to state. In Minnesota, appointment is dominant. Under state law, an appointed judge must run for election in the next general election more than one year after the appointment. It has been common practice for judges to leave office in the last year before their term ends, allowing the governor to appoint a new judge and canceling what would have been an election if the judge had stayed on until the end of the term. When the appointee does face an election, there typically is no opposition. The state supreme court has had to decide several cases involving challenges to the use of resignations to avoid judicial elections under various circumstances.[30]

The Operation of Appointive Systems

Of the three nonelective systems of judicial selection, legislative election is so rare today that it requires no further discussion. But gubernatorial appointment and the Missouri Plan are of considerable importance, the former because it is commonly used to fill vacancies in states that elect judges and the latter because of its widespread and increasing use.

Gubernatorial Appointment   Six states on the East Coast give their governors the general power to select judges, and California governors appoint the state's appellate judges. Since governors make so many interim appointments in states that elect judges, at any given time a high proportion of all judges in the United States reached the bench through a governor's appointment. The seven states in which governors have general selection power all require that the governor's choice be confirmed by another body, most often the state senate. In the great majority of elective states, interim appointments do not require confirmation.

Governors with regular or interim appointment powers often set up commissions to screen prospective judges, thus importing a key element of the Missouri Plan. In some states this arrangement has lasted for more than thirty years, but governors can always modify or eliminate it. Massachusetts has had a nominating commission since 1975, but in 2006 Governor Mitt Romney reduced the commission's role to determining that prospective judges meet a set of minimum qualifications.[31]

In making their selections, governors can consult with a wide array of individuals and groups. The views of people who are politically important to the governor tend to get serious consideration. Legislators may also influence the governor's choices, particularly in states in which the senate must confirm nominees. In New Jersey, under a variant of senatorial courtesy in Congress, any senator from the county in which a nominee resides holds an informal veto power over the nominee's confirmation, and in making a choice the governor needs to take the home-county senators' views into account. Texas requires senate confirmation of interim appointments, and the senator in whose district a nominee resides can veto the nominee. In 2005 the governor's legal counsel won a supreme court nomination after moving from the district of a senator who questioned a nomination to that of a more compliant senator. (The nominee said that he had moved for other reasons.)[32]

The criteria that governors apply in making judicial appointments fall into the same general categories as those employed by presidents. Reward plays a powerful role, and governors' associates and political allies win a good many appointments. In 2005, for instance, Kentucky governor Ernie Fletcher appointed his general counsel to the state supreme court, and Arizona governor Janet Napolitano chose a supreme court justice whom she had known for two decades and who had worked with her in legal positions and in her gubernatorial campaign.[33]

As with the lower federal courts, growing awareness that state courts play a significant role in public policymaking has increased the weight that governors give to the policy preferences of potential judges. This is especially true of state supreme courts, which have made highly visible decisions on issues ranging from school funding to same-sex marriage in recent years. In part because of ideological considerations in appointments, in part because governors usually choose judges from their own party, Democratic appointees tend to have liberal views on judicial issues and Republican appointees conservative views.

Where the governor's choices have to be confirmed by another body, few nominees fail to win confirmation—in part because governors avoid making nominations that might displease the confirming body. But nominees sometimes run into difficulties, and scrutiny by state senates and other confirming bodies seems to be increasing. In 2004 the Hawaii Senate rejected a trial-court nominee whom the state bar association had rated as unqualified.[34] The Connecticut Senate also defeated a trial-court nominee that year. The defeat resulted in part from the weakness of Governor John Rowland, who resigned three months later under the threat of impeachment because of corruption charges.[35]

In states with gubernatorial appointment of judges, as in legislative election states, the general practice is to grant an additional term to a judge who wishes to continue in office. As a result, appointments to judgeships generally constitute lifetime appointments in practice. But a few judges do fail to win reappointment. In 1997, for instance, New York governor George Pataki chose not to reappoint an appellate judge whom he saw as unduly liberal in criminal cases.[36]

The Missouri Plan   Twenty states now use some form of the Missouri Plan as the formal selection system for at least some of their courts.[37] Several states that elect judges have established truncated Missouri Plan systems (involving commission nomination and gubernatorial appointment) to fill vacancies between elections, some governors have voluntarily established commissions to select nominees for regular or interim appointments, and two states (Illinois and Pennsylvania) use retention elections when judges who were initially chosen through partisan elections seek new terms.

The composition of the nominating commissions varies considerably among states. Typically, there are equal or nearly equal numbers of lawyers and non-lawyers, and in about half the states a judge also serves on the commission. Non-lawyer commissioners are generally chosen by the governor, sometimes in conjunction with legislators. Lawyer members are usually chosen by the state's lawyers in some fashion, but the governor or legislature may participate in the selection of those members, and in some states lawyers play no part in determining which attorneys serve on the commissions.

When a judicial vacancy arises, the commission's task is to solicit applications from prospective judges and then choose nominees for the governor to consider. Most often, state rules ask a commission to submit three nominees without ranking them. The goal behind adoption of the Missouri Plan is that the commission bases its choices solely on the qualifications of potential judges. But judgments about qualifications can be affected by other considerations. Commissioners may favor people whom they know personally and candidates who share their partisan affiliations or their policy views.

The governor is in a strong position to influence the choice of nominees. Commissioners who were selected by the governor may view themselves as the governor's representatives, and it is not difficult to ensure that the list of nominees includes at least one candidate whom the governor favors. Further, although governors are generally bound to select a judge from the commission's list, a governor may simply refuse to make an appointment. When a vacancy appeared on the New York Court of Appeals, the state's highest court, there was a widespread perception that the appointment would go to one candidate who was close to Governor George Pataki or another candidate who had a geographical advantage, so many potential candidates held back from applying. The head of the bar association in New York City "begged people to apply in a newsletter article headlined with the lottery slogan, 'Hey, you never know.'" Ironically, the commission did not nominate the candidate close to the governor, and Pataki did not choose the candidate with a geographical advantage—though the well-credentialed candidate whom he did choose had made substantial contributions to Pataki and to the state Republican party.[38]

In Florida, Governor Jeb Bush (1999–2007) sought to change the orientation of the state's appellate courts, which he perceived as too liberal and Democratic. In 2001, the Republican legislature changed the state's rules so that Bush could choose all members of the nominating commissions. (The state bar association could nominate candidates for the lawyers' positions on the commission, but the governor was free to reject all nominees.) As a result, the Missouri Plan in Florida became close to a system of gubernatorial appointment. When a commission produced a set of nominees for the state supreme court in 2002, its chair said that he thought Governor Bush would like the nominees. "I know the governor and have a pretty good feel for what he looks for."[39] One result is that partisan and ideological considerations became more prominent in the selection of judges.[40]

In some states with the Missouri Plan, the other branches of government determine whether a sitting judge wins a new term. But in most states, the voters have this choice through retention elections in which they vote "yes" or "no" on judges. Except in Illinois (60 percent) and New Mexico (57 percent), a judge needs to win a simple majority to remain in office. Most judges are in an excellent position to do so; in a retention election, all the ordinary advantages of incumbency are strengthened by the absence of an opposing candidate. The results are highly favorable to judges: the overwhelming majority of judges win, and generally by large margins. In ten states with retention elections, only fifty-two judges failed to win voter approval between 1964 and 1998, about 1 percent of those facing the voters.[41] Twenty-eight of the fifty-two were in Illinois, with its requirement of a 60 percent majority for retention.

Because of their limited information, voters tend to cast the same votes for every judge on the ballot. As a result, the proportions of the vote that judges receive typically depend less on their individual qualities than on overall levels of political trust and support for the judiciary. In the past decade, however, growing activity by interest groups that are unhappy with court policies has led to more frequent targeting of individual judges for defeat.[42] These judges are typically charged with taking overly liberal positions in cases, especially on criminal justice issues.

Most of the targeted judges win their retention elections, albeit with smaller majorities than they otherwise would have achieved. In 2004, for instance, the successful judges included an Iowa judge who was attacked for approving the dissolution of a civil union that two women had obtained in Vermont, a Kansas judge who was charged with lenient sentencing, and a Missouri judge who was opposed as too liberal.[43] But some other judges have been defeated, including several supreme court justices who were depicted as unwilling to uphold death sentences. And judges occasionally lose for idiosyncratic reasons. This was true of a part-time Colorado trial judge whose narrow defeat in 2004 resulted from several considerations that led some voters to oppose her; as one reporter concluded, she seemed to be largely "a victim of small-town politics."[44] And in 2005, as described in Exhibit 4.6, a supreme court justice in Pennsylvania lost primarily because he was the most convenient target of voter anger. Still, the overwhelming majority of judges win retention elections, and few face significant opposition.

EXHIBIT 4.6   A Pennsylvania Judge Loses a Retention Election

Pennsylvania initially selects its judges through partisan elections, but sitting judges face retention elections. As in other states, judges typically win retention elections by large margins. But in 2005, two justices on the state supreme court ran into difficult circumstances. In July, state legislators enacted substantial pay raises for themselves and for other state officials. This action led to widespread anger among individuals and interest groups.

But legislative elections would not come until 2006, so opponents of the pay raise targeted two supreme court justices who faced retention elections, Russell Nigro and Sandra Schultz Newman. Those justices had nothing to do with the pay raise. But they were among its beneficiaries, the court's chief justice had proposed the raise, and opponents charged that the court's past decisions had made possible the secretive procedure that legislators used to enact the raise. It may be that broader unhappiness with the courts also played a part in the opposition.

The opposition had considerable impact on the voters: Newman won with only 54 percent of the vote, and Nigro won 49 percent and lost his position. Both justices were disadvantaged by patterns of voter turnout across the state. Newman's higher proportion of the vote probably resulted in part from her being a Republican rather than a Democrat. Nigro's defeat can be characterized as a classic case of being in the wrong place at the wrong time.

Sources: Newspaper articles.

The Impact of Formal Selection Systems

A great deal of effort has been expended on debates over alternative systems for the selection of state judges. Has that effort been justified? In other words, how much do the various formal selection systems actually differ in practice? This question can be considered at three levels: the actual processes by which judges are selected, the characteristics of the people who are chosen as judges, and the behavior of judges and courts.

Effects on Selection Processes   On paper, the five major systems for selecting judges look very different. In practice, these systems do operate differently. Judges are more likely to be removed from office in states with partisan elections than in states that use other systems. Partisan election also gives political parties the best opportunity to influence the selection process. Of course, governors have the greatest control over the selection of judges in states that give them the sole power to nominate judges.

But the differences are not as great as the formal rules might suggest, in at least three respects. First, the governor typically has a great deal of impact across all the major systems. In states with judicial elections, governors select a high proportion of judges by filling vacancies. Because the governor's appointees usually win subsequent elections, interim appointment gives the governor considerable power to staff the judiciary. In Missouri Plan states, the governor makes the final choice from a commission's list. As we have seen, the governor often has considerable influence over the list itself.

Second, in each system judges are likely to remain in their positions as long as they want. Governors nearly always reappoint incumbents. Few judges lose retention elections, and the rate of re-election is high for nonpartisan elections. States with partisan elections are a partial exception, but even in these states lower-court judges generally do well when they run for re-election.

Finally, all judicial selection systems are political in the sense that considerations other than the merits of prospective judges come into play. We would expect this to be true of most systems, but even the Missouri Plan leaves room for a good deal of politics. Members of nominating commissions have partisan and ideological biases, and governors select commissioners and choose from nominees on political bases. And the relatively few judges who lose retention elections are generally not removed because of a perceived lack of competence; more often, they have aroused opposition on other grounds such as the content of their decisions.

A state's political conditions and traditions can have greater impact on the process of judicial selection than does the formal system it uses. For this reason, the same system can work quite differently in two different states. By the same token, changing formal rules for judicial selection might have only limited impact in some states. Thus, in states with partisan traditions and strong party organizations, such as New York, partisan considerations would play an important part under any formal system. In states with a nonpartisan ethos or weak party organizations, the same system would be less partisan. This produces an irony: in states in which judicial selection is heavily permeated by partisanship, so that the Missouri Plan seems most attractive to reformers, the plan is least likely to minimize partisanship.

Effects on Characteristics of Judges   For those who debate methods of selecting judges, one central concern is the kinds of people who are selected. Supporters of the Missouri Plan, for instance, argue that it will strengthen the qualifications of judges, as reflected in characteristics such as educational attainments and legal experience.

There are two reasons to be skeptical about such arguments. The first is the similarities among formal selection systems in the ways they actually work. The second is the fact that any system draws judges from the pool of eligible and interested lawyers, a pool that is affected only in limited ways by the formal rules for selection. Even so, the formal systems still might make a difference.

Over the years, several studies have probed whether the background characteristics of state judges are affected by formal selection systems. The greatest attention has been given to the racial and gender composition of state supreme courts.[45] The findings of these studies are mixed, but on the whole they have not found that the traits of judges vary greatly by selection system. However, formal systems might produce stronger effects on traits that have not yet been studied. For instance, the Missouri Plan may produce fewer judges who are actively involved in political party organizations. When better means to gauge the competence of judges are developed, we might find that some systems produce abler judges than others—and if such differences exist, they would provide a strong basis for choosing among selection systems. But it seems unlikely that the various systems produce judges who differ dramatically in any significant respects.

Effects on the Behavior of Judges   Ultimately, the most consequential effects of formal selection systems—to the extent that there *are* effects—are on judges' choices as decision makers. Advocates of a particular system often argue that it produces better justice, but not everyone agrees on what better justice actually means. Leaving aside this question, we might expect selection systems to influence court policies for either of two reasons: the systems put different kinds of judges on the bench, or they subject judges to different kinds of influences once they reach the bench.

As just discussed, there is some reason to discount the first possibility. The second possibility, however, is an intriguing one. For example, judges who are subject to party nominations may take party interests into account in their decisions more than do judges who run in nonpartisan elections. Judges who are appointed by the chief executive might support the positions of the executive branch more often than those who are elected.

Perhaps the most likely type of effect is also the most important: the impact of elective systems on judges' responses to public opinion. Judges who require the approval of voters to keep their positions may avoid taking positions that challengers could use against them in a campaign. The most dangerous positions in this sense are decisions that can be depicted as unduly favorable to criminal defendants, such as lenient sentencing by trial judges and votes to overturn death sentences by state supreme court justices. Challengers sometimes point to such decisions in their campaigns, and this kind of attack on incumbent judges has become more common in recent years. Thus it seems reasonable to posit that elected judges will take pains to avoid being depicted as "soft on crime." On the other hand, even appointed judges might seek to avoid that label. Missouri Plan judges do not face opponents in retention elections, but they too have been confronted with campaigns that attack them for their positions on criminal justice issues.

The evidence we have suggests that some judges in states with partisan or nonpartisan elections do act on their fears of electoral opposition. Supreme court justices in those states seem more reluctant to overturn death sentences, especially under conditions that make them more vulnerable to defeat.[46] Elected trial judges in Pennsylvania become more stringent sentencers as elections approach. The same effect occurs for judges in Kansas, but only in counties that use partisan elections rather than retention elections.[47] Of course, judicial elections and other selection mechanisms work differently in different states, so this and other effects of these mechanisms might depend on the political context. In any event, what we know about the possible effects of formal selection systems remains quite incomplete.

CONCLUSIONS

In the federal and state court systems, a variety of formal systems are used to select judges. The most important lessons of this chapter concern those formal systems.

First, formal systems seem to make less of a difference than the heated debates over competing systems would suggest. The choice of one system rather than another does have an impact. Some differences among selection systems may become more apparent in the future as we gain a better capacity to measure those effects. But similarities across systems are more striking than their differences, especially in the ways that the selection process works in practice.

Second, from a broader perspective the similarities among the selection systems used in the United States are even more striking. Some other nations use civil service–like systems to choose judges for most of their courts. In contrast, each of the systems in the United States gives a central role to other political institutions in the selection of judges, thereby emphasizing accountability rather than judicial independence.

Third, there is considerable variation in judicial selection that is not the product of formal rules. All federal judges are chosen under the same rules, but the actual process of choosing Supreme Court justices is very different from the process for district judges. In the same way, each of the formal systems used in the states operates quite differently across the states. These differences reflect such matters as the strength of political parties and attitudes toward courts and judges.

The selection of judges is significant because it can affect what judges do. The next chapter considers the impact of judicial selection and other factors that shape judges' behavior.

FOR FURTHER READING

Abraham, Henry J. *Justices, Presidents, and Senators: A History of the U.S. Supreme Court Appointments from Washington to Clinton*, rev. ed. Lanham, Md.: Rowman & Littlefield, 1999.

Bell, Lauren Cohen. *Warring Factions: Interest Groups, Money, and the New Politics of Senate Confirmation.* Columbus: Ohio State University Press, 2002.

Comiskey, Michael. *Seeking Justices: The Judging of Supreme Court Nominees.* Lawrence: University Press of Kansas, 2004.

Dubois, Philip L. *From Ballot to Bench: Judicial Elections and the Quest for Accountability.* Austin: University of Texas Press, 1980.

Goldman, Sheldon. *Picking Federal Judges: Lower Court Selection From Roosevelt Through Reagan.* New Haven, Conn.: Yale University Press, 1997.

Scherer, Nancy. *Scoring Points: Politicians, Activists, and the Lower Federal Court Appointment Process.* Stanford: Stanford University Press, 2005.

Sheldon, Charles H., and Linda S. Maule. *Choosing Justice: The Recruitment of State and Federal Judges.* Pullman: Washington State University Press, 1997.

Streb, Matthew, ed. *Running for Judge: The Rising Political, Financial, and Legal Stakes of Judicial Elections.* New York: New York University Press, 2007.

Yalof, David Alistair. *Pursuit of Justices: Presidential Politics and the Selection of Supreme Court Justices.* Chicago: University of Chicago Press, 1999.

Online Study Center Go to college.hmco.com/PIC/baum6e for ACE practice test questions and additional resources.

NOTES

1. F. Andrew Hanssen, "Learning About Judicial Independence: Institutional Change in the State Courts," *Journal of Legal Studies* 33 (June 2004), 431–473.

2. Neil A. Lewis, "Deal Ends Impasse Over Judicial Nominees," *New York Times*, May 19, 2004, A17. The court of appeals decision was *Evans v. Stephens*, 387 F.3d 1220 (11th Cir. 2004).

3. See David C. Nixon and J. David Haskin, "Judicial Retirement Strategies: The Judge's Role in Influencing Party Control of the Appellate Courts," *American Politics Quarterly* 28 (October 2000), 458–489.

4. Eleanor Randolph, "Husband Triggered Letters Supporting Ginsburg for Court," *Washington Post*, June 17, 1993, A25.

5. See Bryon J. Moraski and Charles R. Shipan, "The Politics of Supreme Court Nominations: A Theory of Institutional Constraints and Choices," *American Journal of Political Science* 43 (October 1999), 1069–1095.

6. On the factors that shape Senate confirmation decisions, see Lee Epstein, René Lindstädt, Jeffrey A. Segal, and Chad Westerland, "The Changing Dynamics of Senate Voting on Supreme Court Nominees," *Journal of Politics* 68 (May 2006), 296–307.

7. Nancy Scherer, *Scoring Points: Politicians, Activists, and the Lower Federal Court Appointment Process* (Stanford: Stanford University Press, 2005).

8. Sheldon Goldman, Elliot Slotnick, Gerard Gryski, Gary Zuk, and Sara Schiavoni, "W. Bush Remaking the Judiciary: Like Father Like Son?" *Judicature* 86 (May–June 2003), 284–293; Sheldon Goldman, Elliot Slotnick, Gerard Gryski, and Sara Schiavoni, "W. Bush's Judiciary: The First Term Record," *Judicature* 88 (May–June 2005), 245–256.

9. Joseph C. Goulden, *The Benchwarmers: The Private World of the Powerful Federal Judges* (New York: Weybright and Talley, 1974), 23.

10. See Sheldon Goldman and Matthew D. Saronson, "Clinton's Nontraditional Judges: Creating a More Representative Bench," *Judicature* 78 (September–October 1994), 68–73.

11. Information in this paragraph is taken from Nancy Scherer and Banks Miller, "The Federalist Society's Influence on the Federal Judiciary" (paper presented at meeting of the Midwest Political Science Association, April 2006, Chicago).

12. Robert A. Carp, Ronald Stidham, and Kenneth L. Manning, "The Voting Behavior of George W. Bush's Judges: How Sharp a Turn to the Right?" in *Principles and Practice of American Politics: Classic and Contemporary Readings*, 3d ed., ed. Samuel Kernell and Steven S. Smith (Washington, D.C.: CQ Press, 2007), 429–447.

13. See Sarah A. Binder and Forrest Maltzman, "Congress and the Politics of Judicial Appointments," in *Congress Reconsidered*, 8th ed., ed. Lawrence C. Dodd and Bruce I. Oppenheimer (Washington, D.C.: CQ Press, 2005), 297–317; and Lauren Cohen Bell, *Warring Factions: Interest Groups, Money, and the New Politics of Senate Confirmation* (Columbus: Ohio State University Press, 2002).

14. Neil A. Lewis, "Where the Gloves Are Nearly Always Off," *New York Times*, October 28, 2003, A19.

15. Neil A. Lewis, "Report Finds Republican Aides Spied on Democrats," *New York Times*, March 5, 2004, A14.

16. Carl Hulse, "Bipartisan Group in Senate Averts Judge Showdown," *New York Times*, May 24, 2005, A1, A16.

17. The data are from J. Kenneth Blackwell, *Ohio Election Statistics for 2003–2004* (Columbus: Office of the Secretary of State, n.d.).

18. The data are from the website for the Los Angeles Registrar-Recorder/County Clerk, www.lavote.net.

19. The data are from the website for the Texas Secretary of State, http://elections.sos.state.tx.us/elchist.exe. See Kyle Cheek and Anthony Champagne, *Judicial Politics in Texas: Partisanship, Money, and Politics in State Courts* (New York: Peter Lang, 2005).

20. Drew Jubera, "There's Nothing Civil About Ala. Judicial Race," *Atlanta Journal-Constitution*, June 5, 2006, 1A.

21. *Lopez Torres v. New York State Board of Elections*, 411 F. Supp. 2d 212 (E.D.N.Y. 2006). The quotation in this paragraph is from p. 231 of the decision.

22. James F. McCarty, "Ballot Benchmark: Russos Prevail," *Cleveland Plain Dealer*, June 4, 2004, A1.

23. Deborah Goldberg et al., *The New Politics of Judicial Elections 2004* (Washington, D.C.: Justice at Stake, n.d.); Research and Policy Committee, Committee for Economic Development, *Justice for Hire* (New York: Committee for Economic Development, 2002).

24. *Republican Party v. White*, 536 U.S. 765 (2002).

25. Jake Bleed, "2 High Court Candidates Declaring Stands on Issues," *Arkansas Democrat-Gazette*, April 25, 2006.

26. Melinda Gann Hall, "State Supreme Courts in American Democracy: Probing the Myths of Judicial Reform," *American Political Science Review* 95 (June 2001), 315–330; Chris W. Bonneau, "Electoral Verdicts: Incumbent Defeats in State Supreme Court Elections," *American Politics Research* 33 (November 2005), 818–841. The figures for 1990–2000 are from p. 824 of the Bonneau article.

27. Gail Diane Cox, "Jerry's Judges," *National Law Journal*, May 25, 1992, 31.

28. See Tracy Johnson, "Judge Seeks to Oust a Justice Over Felony Murder Law," *Seattle Post-Intelligencer*, September 6, 2004; and Bill Rankin, "Divisive Fight Ends in Victory for Sears," *Atlanta Journal-Constitution*, July 21, 2004, 1D.

29. Lisa M. Holmes and Jolly A. Emrey, "Court Diversification: Staffing the State Courts of Last Resort Through Interim Appointments," *Justice System Journal* 27 (2006), 6. See John Bigeaut, "Bench Battle," *ABA Journal*, August 2000, 43.

30. See *Zettler v. Ventura*, 649 N.W.2d 846 (Minn. 2002).

31. Governor Mitt Romney, Executive Order 470, February 3, 2006; Michael Levenson, "Romney Curtails Panel Advising on New Judges," *Boston Globe*, April 9, 2006, B1.

32. Gardner Selby, "Perry Picks Former Bush Helpmate for High Court," *Austin American-Statesman*, August 25, 2005, A1.

33. Tom Loftus, "Fletcher Picks Judge," *Louisville Courier-Journal*, June 11, 2005; Chip Scutari, "Democrat Joins High Court," *Arizona Republic*, June 15, 2005.

34. Lynda Arakawa, "Senate Rejects Hong," *Honolulu Advertiser*, March 13, 2004.

35. Ken Dixon, "Senate Denies Megacci Judgeship," *Connecticut Post*, March 26, 2004.

36. Jan Hoffman, "A Prominent Judge Retires, Objecting to the Governor's Litmus Test," *New York Times*, December 14, 1997, sec. 1, p. 49.

37. Information on nominating commissions is taken from *Judicial Merit Selection: Current Status* (Chicago: American Judicature Society, 2003). On the operation of the Missouri Plan overall, see Malia Reddick, "Merit Selection: A Review of the Social Scientific Literature," *Dickinson Law Review* 106 (2002), 729–745.

38. James C. McKinley Jr., "Pataki Puts Nonjudge on Court of Appeals," *New York Times*, November 5, 2003, B5. The quotation is from Yancey Roy, "Court of Appeals Spot Fails to Get Applicants," *Albany Times Union*, October 11, 2003, B2.

39. Peter Wallsten, "Florida Supreme Court Panel Grills Bush Ally," *Miami Herald*, June 6, 2002. See Julie Kay, "Not Taken on Faith," *Miami Daily Business Review*, January 13, 2004.

40. Rebecca Mae Salokar, D. Jason Berggren, and Kathryn A. DePalo, "The New Politics of Judicial Selection in Florida: Merit Selection Redefined," *Justice System Journal* 27 (2006), 123–142.

41. Larry Aspin, "Trends in Judicial Retention Elections, 1964–1998," *Judicature* 83 (September–October 1999), 79–81.

42. Susan M. Olson, "Voter Mobilization in Judicial Retention Elections: Performance Evaluations and Organized Opposition," *Justice System Journal* 22 (2001), 263–285.

43. "Group Forms to Unseat Judge in Gay Divorce," *Des Moines Register*, August 14, 2004; Eric Weslander, "Embattled District Judge Stays on Bench," *Lawrence Journal-World*, November 3, 2004; William H. Lhotka, "High Court Judge Faces Ouster Effort," *St. Louis Post-Dispatch*, October 27, 2004, D1.

44. Mike McPhee, "One of 84 Jurists Removed," *Denver Post*, November 4, 2004, B3.

45. Among these studies are Henry R. Glick and Craig F. Emmert, "Selection Systems and Judicial Characteristics: The Recruitment of State Supreme Court Judges," *Judicature* 70 (December–January 1987), 228–235; Barbara Luck Graham, "Do Judicial Selection Systems Matter? A Study of Black Representation on State Courts," *American Politics Quarterly* 18 (July 1990), 316–336; Mark S. Hurwitz and Drew Noble Lanier, "Women and Minorities on State and Federal Appellate Benches, 1985 and 1999," *Judicature* 85 (September–October 2001), 84–92; and Margaret S. Williams, "Women Judges: Accession at the State Court Level" (paper presented at the Annual Meeting of the Midwest Political Science Association, Chicago, April 2003).

46. See Paul R. Brace and Melinda Gann Hall, "The Interplay of Preferences, Case Facts, Context, and Rules in the Politics of Judicial Choice," *Journal of Politics* 59 (November 1997), 1206–1231.

47. Gregory A. Huber and Sanford C. Gordon, "Accountability and Coercion: Is Justice Blind When It Runs for Office?" *American Journal of Political Science* 48 (April 2004), 247–263; Sanford C. Gordon and Gregory A. Huber, "Incumbent Incentives and the Informational Role of Challengers" (paper presented at the Annual Meeting of the Midwest Political Science Association, Chicago, April 2005). See Richard R.W. Brooks and Steven Raphael, "Life Terms or Death Sentences: The Uneasy Relationship Between Judicial Elections and Capital Punishment," *Journal of Criminal Law and Criminology* 92 (2002), 609–639, and Jason J. Czarnezki, "Voting and Electoral Politics in the Wisconsin Supreme Court," *Marquette Law Review* 87 (2003), 323–356.

5

Judges

Because judges are at the center of the judicial process, who they are and what they do make a great deal of difference for the outcomes of that process. The chapters that follow will examine judges' work in specific settings; this chapter discusses judges at a more general level. The first section looks at the characteristics of the people who become judges, characteristics that affect what they do. The second section surveys the work and work lives of judges. The last section assesses the quality of judges' performance and considers means to improve their performance.

WHO JUDGES ARE

There are few formal restrictions on who can become a judge. The U.S. Constitution establishes no requirements at all for federal judges. In contrast, the states do have some restrictions.[1] The great majority of states require that judges be licensed as lawyers, though some states exempt their lowest courts from this requirement. Many specify a minimum number of years that a judge has been a lawyer or, in some states, actually has practiced law; the longest time required is ten years. Other requirements found in some states are a period of residency in the state and U.S. citizenship. Some states establish a minimum age for judges, but the ages are low enough to have little practical effect. Most states have a maximum age. Such a maximum *does* have a practical effect, bringing an end to many judicial careers.

Whether or not there is a formal requirement, in practice judges on all but the lowest courts are attorneys. Thus, for someone who would like to be a judge, achievement of that status is the first hurdle. The last hurdle is winning election or appointment to a judgeship. Those two hurdles provide a perspective from which to view the characteristics of people who become judges. I will examine three sets of characteristics: social backgrounds, career experiences, and political activity.

In these discussions I frequently refer to characteristics of federal judges and of judges on the state supreme courts. The information on characteristics of federal judges is based on judges who were appointed to the district courts and courts of appeals between 1993 and 2004; much of that information is summarized in Exhibit 5.1. The information on characteristics of state supreme court justices is based on justices who were serving in 2006.[2] Because the available data on state judges are incomplete in some respects, they are not shown in an exhibit.

EXHIBIT 5.1   Selected Background Characteristics of Federal Court Appointees, 1993–2004

Characteristic	District Courts (%)	Courts of Appeals (%)
Social background		
White	77.6	75.8
Male	74.2	71.6
White male	57.7	54.7
Private undergraduate school[a]	54.5	58.9
Ivy League	11.2	20.0
Career		
Experience as a judge	53.7	60.0
Judge at time of appointment	49.0	50.5
Experience as prosecutor	42.3	36.8
Private practice at time of appointment	37.8	29.5
Firm of 100 or more lawyers[b]	21.2	32.1
Firm of 25–99 lawyers[b]	26.3	21.4
Firm of 5–24 lawyers[b]	32.4	39.3
Firm of 1–4 lawyers[b]	20.1	7.1
Economic status at time of appointment		
Net worth under $200,000	10.8	5.3
$200,000–500,000	20.9	16.8
$500,000–1,000,000	24.9	26.3
Over $1,000,000	43.3	51.6
Political activity		
Past party activism	49.7	58.9
Member of president's party[c]	93.2	93.3

[a] Includes Ivy League.
[b] The percentages are of those engaged in private practice.
[c] Excludes judges who did not indicate a party affiliation.

Source: Sheldon Goldman, Elliot Slotnick, Gerard Gryski, and Sara Schiavoni, "W. Bush's Judiciary: The First Term Record," *Judicature* 88 (May–June 2005), 269, 274.

Social Background

Whatever people accomplish in their own lives, they begin with certain characteristics they cannot control. One is their parents' social and economic status. Others are race and gender. In each of these respects, judges, like other public officials, are far from a random sample of the population.

Social and Economic Status   Most judges come from families of higher than average status. This pattern reflects the advantages that relative wealth and high social status confer. A high family income helps a person to become a lawyer, most directly by making it easier to pay the costs of a college education and law school. Inherited social status affords some people an advantage in entering the most prestigious schools and law firms and in advancing their careers in politics and government.

High family status is most common among judges on the highest courts. The Supreme Court in particular has been populated mostly by people from high-status backgrounds, and to a lesser extent the same is true of lower federal courts. One indicator of family status for federal judges is the schools they attended. It is noteworthy that more than half of the federal court appointees since 1993 attended private undergraduate colleges and that 20 percent of the court of appeals appointees went to Ivy League schools, which account for a very small proportion of all college graduates.[3] State supreme court justices are not quite as elite a group in this respect: although slightly over half of the 2006 justices went to private undergraduate schools, only 7 percent attended Ivy League schools.

Lower-court judges appear to be a more heterogeneous group, and in some localities there is a good deal of upward mobility into the state trial courts. It is not unusual for people from relatively poor families to make their way through law school (perhaps attending classes at night while working during the day) and then become candidates for judgeships through legal work or political activity. And fewer judges at the lower court levels come from highly advantaged backgrounds.

Race and Gender For most of American history, the judiciary consisted almost entirely of white men. As late as 1977, about 96 percent of the judges on major state trial courts were white, and about 98 percent were male. More than 99 percent of the state supreme court justices in 1980–1981 were white and 97 percent male.[4] The Supreme Court was entirely white until 1967, entirely male until 1981.

The numerical dominance of white men in the judiciary resulted from several social realities. Poverty and discrimination limited the numbers of nonwhite citizens who could obtain college and legal educations. Largely because of admissions policies, women had a difficult time getting to law school. Women and members of racial minority groups who did manage to become lawyers found that many career and political opportunities were closed to them. After finishing near the top of her class at Stanford Law School in 1952, future Supreme Court Justice Sandra Day O'Connor discovered that no California law firm would offer her anything more than a secretarial position.

The proportion of judgeships held by women and members of racial minority groups has grown enormously since the 1980s.[5] In 2005, by one count, 23 percent of all judges were women.[6] And women are a little better represented in higher courts, with 26 percent of the appointments to federal courts since 1993 and 29 percent representation on state supreme courts in 2006. A few state supreme courts have had female majorities, and in 2005 a Texas court of appeals with seven members became all female. Similarly, the numbers of judges from racial minority groups have grown substantially, especially in the federal courts. These increases reflect the changing composition of the legal profession, reduced discrimination in the profession, the enhanced political power of groups representing racial minorities and women, and changing attitudes of people who select judges. In particular, some chief executives such as President Bill Clinton and Kentucky governor Paul Patton have increased the diversity of the judiciary with their appointments. Patton, who served from 1995 to 2003, used his interim appointments to increase the proportion of female judges in Kentucky from 10 percent to 27 percent.[7]

White men continue to hold judgeships well beyond their proportion in the general population. But the numbers of female and minority-group judges are certain to increase further with the representation of these groups in the legal profession. The growth in diversity in this respect is likely to increase the diversity of experience that judges bring to the bench.

Career Experience

Except at the very lowest levels of the judiciary, nearly all of today's judges were educated in law school. But a wide variety of career paths can lead from law school to a judgeship. Because there are many ways of making useful contacts and establishing a reputation for competence, the variation in career paths is understandable. But certain kinds of career experiences are especially common because they provide major advantages.

Private Practice   Like other attorneys, the great majority of judges engaged at some point in the private practice of law. A high proportion of judges on state trial courts come directly from private practice. This path is less common in higher courts, because lawyers often move from practice to a first judgeship and then to a higher court. Even so, about one in five state supreme court justices serving in 2006 came directly from private practice, and more than one-third of the federal district judges chosen since 1993 were in practice when they were appointed.

The judges on higher courts who practiced law generally came from practices that brought them high incomes and prestige. One imperfect but meaningful indicator of income and prestige is firm size. In the legal profession as a whole, half of all lawyers in private practice have solo practices, and only about one in seven are in firms with one hundred or more lawyers.[8] In contrast, among the lawyers in private practice who came to the federal courts between 1993 and 2004, only 7 percent were solo practitioners and 23 percent were in firms of one hundred or more.

We have more direct information on the financial status of federal judges. Among the appointees from 1993 through 2004, more than two-thirds had a net worth of at least $500,000, and nearly half were millionaires. In part, this level of wealth reflects judges' family backgrounds; in part, it reflects the financial rewards of high-status legal practice.

Lower-court judges are less likely to come from elite segments of the bar. State trial courts contain a broader cross section of private practitioners than do the federal courts of appeals. One reason for this difference is that highly successful lawyers are much less likely to seek positions in lower courts, which carry only limited power and prestige. Another reason is that participants in judicial selection tend to demand higher levels of achievement for higher courts.

The Other Branches of Government   A great many attorneys practice law for the government at some point in their careers, and this is true of lawyers who become judges. Some spent the first few years after law school working for the government and then moved into private practice. Others came to the bench directly from government service.

A lawyer who works for the government has an advantage in coming to the attention of people who choose judges. Thus lawyers in the Justice Department are in a good position to be recognized and rewarded with a judgeship. To take one example, in 2003 Jay Bybee moved from a position as assistant attorney general in George W. Bush's administration to a judgeship on a federal court of appeals. At the state level, a prominent government lawyer such as an attorney general has the sort of visibility that helps in winning an election or appointment to the courts. Government lawyers also have a good chance to develop the courtroom experience that is often deemed essential for a judge.

Criminal prosecution is the most common form of prior government service for judges. From 1993 through 2004, about 40 percent of the lawyers appointed to federal courts had been prosecutors; in 2006, about one-quarter of the state supreme court justices across the country had that experience. These figures reflect both the large numbers of lawyers who serve as prosecutors at some point in their careers and the credibility of prosecutors as candidates for judgeships. This credibility stems partly from a prosecutor's advantage in projecting a "law and order" image that most voters favor, and the growing importance of criminal justice as an issue in judicial elections has probably enhanced prosecutors' advantage.

Some people become judges after holding high positions in government that do not involve legal work as such. These positions can be a brief way station or a person's primary career. Because state legislators are in a good position to extract appointments from governors and to win judicial elections, the state courts include a liberal sprinkling of former legislators. (Not surprisingly, judges are especially likely to have legislative experience in the two states where the legislature chooses judges. In South Carolina, four of the five supreme court justices in 2006 were former legislators.) It is less common for a chief executive to become a judge. The only president to do so was William Howard Taft, who was defeated for re-election in 1912 and became chief justice of the U.S. Supreme Court in 1921, after a strenuous campaign for the position. Over the years, however, a number of former governors have become state supreme court justices.

The Judicial Career Ladder   Judges in many countries serve within a kind of civil service system, attaining their first judgeships early in their legal careers and progressing upward through the ranks. The system in the United States is fundamentally different. Here most judges reach the bench at middle age or later, and service on one court is not required to obtain a seat on the court above it.

Still, in both the federal and the state court systems, it is common for judges to ascend upward. One reason is the widespread feeling that service on a lower court helps to qualify a person for a higher judgeship. Besides, a prospective appointee's abilities and policy preferences can be gauged more easily from a judicial record than from most other career experiences. And where judges are elected, prior service on a lower court can give a candidate name recognition.

This promotional pattern is especially strong in the state courts. About two-thirds of the state supreme court justices in 2006 had been serving on a lower state court when they won a supreme court seat. But promotion is frequent in the federal courts as well, as state judges and federal magistrate judges win appointments to the district courts and district judges move up to the courts of appeals. And the last eight people appointed to the Supreme Court came directly from the federal courts of appeals. It has become more common for justices to come from lower courts, but it is not clear whether there is a movement toward more of a career ladder in the judiciary as a whole.

Political Activity

Most judges were active in politics prior to their selection. As Exhibit 5.1 shows, more than half of the federal judges appointed between 1993 and 2004 had records of activism in a political party. Undoubtedly many others were involved in politics in some way. In all likelihood, the proportion of state judges who had been active in politics is even higher.

The frequency of political activity is quite understandable. In a judicial election, a candidate who has already been involved in politics has an easier time building an organization and often has the advantage of name recognition among voters. Even more important, political activity helps in winning the support of the public officials and political leaders who play key parts in every selection system.

These people tend to favor political activists for two reasons. First, one goal in the selection of judges is to reward political supporters. Second, since most of the people who help to select judges are political activists themselves, many of their acquaintances are also activists. Even if the selectors cared only about the qualifications of potential judges, they would have the greatest confidence in people they already knew.

For the same reasons, a considerable proportion of all judges have personal ties with the officials who help to select them. This is often true of federal judges with senators and state judges with governors. In a statement that is widely quoted, a judge and novelist put the matter succinctly: "a judge is a member of the Bar who once knew a Governor."[9] People who want to become judges often participate in politics solely as a means to develop these personal ties and the other advantages of political activism.

The kinds of political activity that lead to judgeships differ considerably. Some judges, especially on higher courts, worked in leadership roles of political campaigns or party organizations. At the other end of the spectrum, many state trial judges were party activists at what is sometimes called the clubhouse level of politics. Attorneys may work for years in unglamorous local party jobs and contribute money to party coffers in order to obtain a judicial appointment or a party nomination to a lower court. This traditionally has been true in Chicago, to take one prominent example. And in Chicago, as in other places, links to powerful political figures have often led to the bench. When Mayor Richard J. Daley (father of the current mayor, Richard M. Daley) controlled the Democratic organization, he secured a party endorsement for a lawyer named Joseph Gordon. According to one account,

> Gordon, a bright and highly regarded former law professor, would have been an outstanding member of any judiciary, but that had little to do with why Daley selected him. When Daley's youngest son, William, was having trouble with his grades at John Marshall Law School, Gordon tutored him privately. For this, Daley was grateful. He expressed his gratitude by making Gordon a judge.[10]

Of course, political activity in itself hardly guarantees a person's selection as a judge: there are far more lawyers active in politics than there are judgeships. To a considerable extent, the translation of activism into a judgeship is a matter of good fortune—of alliance with someone who ends up in a position to help select judges. After all, most rising state politicians do not become governors, just as most law school roommates do not become senators. But if political activity is not sufficient for selection, it is often necessary.

The Impact of Judges' Characteristics

There is a good deal of variation in the lives that people experience before they become judges. That diversity of experience is reflected in the two examples of state supreme court justices in Exhibit 5.2. Yet judges are not a random sample of the legal profession in their backgrounds, and they are even less representative of the general population. This reality has some symbolic importance, affecting the ways that people in different segments of society think and feel about the courts. It also has practical importance. People with different experiences may develop different sets of attitudes toward political and social issues;[11] in turn, judges' attitudes influence the decisions that they reach on the bench.

Background characteristics that are widely shared among judges might be reflected in their behavior. The legal training received by all judges above the lowest levels of the courts undoubtedly influences their thinking about the issues that come before them. The past involvement of most judges in partisan politics may incline them to view some cases in terms of their effects on political parties and factions.

Especially interesting is the possible impact of judges' social backgrounds. As we have seen, judges are distinctly higher in family status than the general population. Whites and men also predominate in comparison with their share of the population. What difference do these characteristics make for the behavior of the judiciary?

What to expect is uncertain. Surveys of the general population show that opinions on policy issues differ between people of higher and lower economic status and between women and men. The differences between African Americans and whites are even greater.[12] Some of these differences can be characterized as ideological, with whites, men, and people of higher status more conservative than those in other groups. There is also reason to expect that judges will have greater empathy for people who share their own characteristics.

On the other hand, those people who achieve judgeships tend to share certain experiences and perspectives no matter what their origins were. The person from a humble economic background who becomes a successful attorney and then a judge may develop values similar to judges who grew up in more advantaged circumstances. And those who select judges, whether voters or political leaders, may look for people with particular outlooks no matter what their origins were.

Studies of judges' race and gender have differed in their findings about the impact of these characteristics on decisions.[13] Across the full range of issues that judges address, there do not appear to be dramatic differences in the behavior of men and women or of people from different racial groups. At the federal level, the absence of dramatic differences reflects the choices of presidents. George W. Bush's preference for conservatives applies to the people he appoints from *all* groups. If a reputation for being tough on crime is important to winning judicial elections, as it is in Texas today, both women and men on the bench are likely to be conservative on criminal justice issues.[14]

EXHIBIT 5.2   Two Unusual Paths to the State Supreme Courts

Alan Page

Page was born in 1945 and grew up in Canton, Ohio. He went to college at Notre Dame, where he starred as a football player and received his B.A. in political science in 1967. He went on to play eleven years in the National Football League with the Minnesota Vikings and three with the Chicago Bears, ultimately winning selection to the pro football hall of fame. While with the Vikings, he held leadership positions with the NFL Players' Association.

As a child, Page thought about becoming a lawyer. In 1975 he entered the University of Minnesota law school as a full-time student while playing for the Vikings. He graduated in 1978. He began to work at a law firm in Minneapolis during the years he was still playing football. He stayed at the firm for three years after his football career ended and then worked at the state attorney general's office for eight years.

Page was interested in running for the state supreme court, but a Minnesota tradition of avoiding electoral contests for judgeships worked against him. He challenged an incumbent justice in 1990, but the incumbent then resigned, and under the state's rules the governor's appointee to fill the vacancy could not be challenged that year. Two years later Page tried to challenge another incumbent, but the governor tried to extend the incumbent's term by two years to prevent the challenge. Page went to court, and after a favorable ruling he was allowed to run against the incumbent and won. He joined the Minnesota Supreme Court in 1993 and has served on the court since then. A visitor reported that his office at the court is filled with memorabilia related to issues of racial equality rather than football.

Joyce Kennard

Kennard was born in 1941 in Java (now part of Indonesia), then occupied by the Japanese. "I'm of Indonesian, Dutch, and Chinese descent." Her father died when she was one year old. She and her mother lived in Indonesia under difficult circumstances during and after World War II. When she was fourteen, they moved to Holland so she could get an adequate education. After some resistance resulting from her limited preparation, she was allowed to enter school. But six months later, a tumor on her leg resulted in its amputation above the knee, and she had to drop out of school. She studied typing and shorthand, and at the age of sixteen she became a secretary.

Because of her Dutch citizenship and her situation in Indonesia, Kennard fell under a special immigration rule that allowed her to move to the United States in 1961. On arriving in California, she took a secretarial job. Six years later, after her mother died, a small inheritance enabled her to begin junior college at the age of twenty-seven. She completed her undergraduate work at the University of Southern California three years later, and she then received degrees in law and public administration from USC.

After graduation, Kennard worked for the state attorney general's office for four years and then for seven years as a staff attorney with a state court of appeal. In 1986 she was appointed to the Municipal Court in Los Angeles County. Each of the following three years she received appointments to a higher court—the Superior Court, the Court of Appeal, and finally the state supreme court. She has served on the supreme court since 1989. Like Justice Page, she has received several honorary degrees and an array of other honors.

Sources: official biographies on court websites; biographical sources; Steve Rushin, "Thanks, Your Honor," *Sports Illustrated*, July 31, 2000, 132–137; Michael Abramowicz, "Page Puts on Big Rush in Minnesota Court Bid," *Washington* Post, October 24, 1992, G1, G4; Elizabeth Vrato, *The Counselors: Conversations with 18 Courageous Women Who Have Changed the World* (Philadelphia: Running Press, 2002), 157–161. The quotation is from p. 157 of the Vrato book.

But race and gender may affect some aspects of judges' work on the bench. For instance, a study of Pennsylvania found that black judges were somewhat more likely to sentence defendants to prison than their white counterparts. One explanation for this finding was suggested by a black judge in Pennsylvania:

> Really, as far as toughness, the black judges I know are as tough or tougher than white judges. They know in a personal way how crime affects the lives of people and will feel in a personal way the need to do something about it.[15]

The differential experiences of men and women and of different racial groups can affect their perspectives in ways that are too specific to measure across whole categories of cases. In a dispute over child custody, for instance, a female judge may see the consequences of spousal and child abuse as crucial, while her male colleagues may regard evidence of abuse as irrelevant.[16]

There is little systematic evidence about the impact of social class. But it seems likely that the higher-status backgrounds of most judges subtly influence their work by affecting the perspectives that they bring to cases. One example, considered in Chapter 6, is the traditional lenient sentencing of white-collar criminals. As judges themselves have noted, they tend to identify with defendants whose backgrounds and social circumstances are similar to their own. As I discuss in Chapter 7, business creditors who sue individual debtors are quite successful. This success results in part from judges' tendency to regard the creditor as the more respectable and responsible party. In turn, this perception is related to the family backgrounds and careers of most judges, which make it easier for them to identify with the owner of a business than with a low-income debtor.

The impact of race, gender, and class on the courts should not be overstated. To a great extent, judges with divergent backgrounds behave in similar ways. But judges' backgrounds do affect their behavior. For that reason, the predominance of white men from higher-status backgrounds on the bench has had practical effects as well as symbolic importance.

Overview   In Chapter 4, I argued that differences among judicial selection systems in the United States are less significant than their similarities. In this section, I have made a similar point about judicial backgrounds: although judges differ a good deal, most share some important characteristics.

The two points are related. The traits shared by most judges result in part from the systems by which they are selected. If the United States followed the example of most other nations and chose judges through a civil service system, judges' ties to political parties would be much weaker. Under such a system, judges would still be disproportionately male, white, and upper status in background, but almost surely this tendency would be weaker than it actually is.

To a degree, then, the systems used to select judges link the courts with the patterns of economic and political power in the United States. These systems favor those whose backgrounds and personal attainments give them relatively high status. They also favor people who are connected with the holders of political power. This is one important way in which the courts are shaped by the larger society in which they operate.

JUDGES ON THE BENCH

Though judges have much in common, their work as judges and how they do that work differ a good deal. This variation makes it difficult to generalize about the work of judges on the bench. In this section I will examine both general patterns in judging and some of the important differences.

Judges' Work

Judges' work varies in several respects. One distinction is between the majority of judges who serve full-time and those—primarily at the lowest levels of the state systems—who combine judging with other pursuits. Perhaps the most fundamental difference is between trial and appellate judges, though members of some major trial courts also hear appeals from decisions of minor trial courts. Some judges are generalists who hear a wide range of cases, while others focus on single fields such as taxes and domestic relations. State and federal judges operate within different systems and hear different kinds of cases, and individual courts and judges develop their own ways of operating. However, the work of all judges can be described in terms of three broad categories.[17]

The first category, *adjudication*, involves formal decision making. This activity comes most readily to mind when we think about judges, and it is at the heart of what judges do. It also consumes the largest share of most judges' work time.

Adjudication varies in form along several lines. Perhaps most important, it looks somewhat different in trial and appellate courts. Trial court decisions are nearly always made by single judges. In contrast, appellate decisions are group products; even if judges do most of their work on decisions apart from their colleagues, they ultimately reach a collective decision. The timing of decisions also differs. Trial judges frequently make and announce their decisions in open court, but appellate decisions are generally made outside the courtroom and announced later.

The most familiar decisions are those that directly resolve the merits of cases—whether a defendant is guilty or innocent, whether a lower-court decision is affirmed or reversed. But judges also make preliminary decisions on matters such as the admission of evidence and dismissal of criminal charges, and these preliminary decisions often determine the outcomes of cases.

In trial courts, different kinds of cases have their own typical forms of adjudication. Trials in criminal and civil cases with high stakes are usually lengthy and formal, while cases with lower stakes may be processed in speedy and routine fashion. Appellate courts also distinguish between cases that require close judicial consideration and those that can be resolved in more summary fashion.

In *negotiation*, the second category, judges seek to resolve cases without formal adjudication by encouraging the parties to reach settlements. The great majority of cases are terminated prior to trial through settlements, and a smaller proportion of appeals are settled between the parties. Settlements often occur without the judge's participation, but judges may play active roles in bringing them about.

Trial judges are more likely to involve themselves actively in negotiation of civil settlements, largely because opinion is divided on the legitimacy of judges' participation in plea bargaining. Appellate judges are less involved in efforts to settle cases. Judges' role in negotiating settlements in all types of cases has grown over time because of the pressures created by growing caseloads.

The final category, *administration*, was discussed in Chapter 2. As the size of courts and the number of cases they handle have grown, so has the volume of administrative work needed for a court to function adequately. The staffs that support judges have grown in size, taking on some of the burden of administration, but supervision of the staff is itself a significant task.

Among the judges on a court, the chief judge has the primary responsibility for administration. Court management may consume the largest share of the chief judge's time. But no judge can escape administrative work altogether. This is especially true of trial courts, where individual judges and their staffs largely run their own courtrooms.

The Difficulties and Rewards of Being a Judge

Like any other job, the position of judges has both positive and negative features. The negatives are substantial, and they are a good place to start.

Many Skills Required, Little Preparation   My catalogue of judges' activities suggests that a good judge must possess a diverse range of skills. This is especially true at the trial level. Effective performance by a trial judge requires a good knowledge of legal rules and court procedures, the capacity to run trials, a talent for negotiation, skill in managing court operations, and an ability to make instantaneous rulings. Appellate judging is not as demanding: court proceedings are more orderly, judges sit with colleagues rather than alone, and they typically make rulings after careful deliberation. Even so, the job is not easy.

The task of learning the job is made more difficult by the lack of prior training for judges. In nations with a career judiciary, aspiring judges study how to carry out the work they will face. In the United States, no such formal preparation exists. As a result, the extent of judges' preparation depends on their pre-judicial careers. Serving as a law clerk in an appellate court provides background for someone who later becomes an appellate judge. Lawyers who appear regularly in a trial court, as prosecutors do, gain a sense of court procedure that they can bring with them to the bench. But new judges who lack that kind of experience may know little about how to handle their jobs. And judges will find it difficult to handle cases in legal areas that are new to them. "When I did my first divorce," one trial judge reported, "I made notes of all the questions and the attorneys each rested, and then I was supposed to say something. I had no idea what I was supposed to say. I ran into the back room of my office and I quickly looked through a notebook. . . . I went back in the courtroom with the notebook. I read through and made the findings that both attorneys, luckily, agreed had to be made, and I read the order out of the outline in the notebook. Then I called the attorneys up to the bench, and I whispered to them, 'Are these people divorced yet?' "[18]

Inevitably, novices on the bench turn for help to those who have more experience—other judges and members of the court staff as well as the lawyers who appear before them. And increasingly, judges are given formal assistance in learning their jobs. The federal judiciary and nearly all the states now provide some kind of training for their judges, and many judges make use of educational programs such as the National Judicial College in Reno. As one Louisiana judge reports, however, such programs do not fully solve the problems that judges face in preparing for their jobs.

> Shortly after taking the bench, while I was attending the Institute of Judicial Administration at New York University, I hailed a taxicab one night. The taxi driver . . . asked me what I was doing in New York. When I said that I had just recently become a judge and was in town for a judicial education program, he observed that he would have felt a whole lot better if I had received my judicial education *before* becoming a judge.[19]

Stresses of the Job   Several characteristics of the judge's job create stress. Most fundamentally, judges have to make a large number of decisions with potentially serious consequences under less than ideal conditions. In a full trial, a judge often must hand down a series of procedural rulings with little time to consider them and with the prospect that an appellate court will find a ruling in error, perhaps overturning the trial verdict as a result. Both trial and appellate judges frequently must choose between two competing sides when it is not clear where the facts and the law point. And many decisions—criminal sentences and custody of children, for instance—can have enormous effects on people's lives.

Another source of stress is court caseloads, which are heavier in some courts than judges can manage easily. That situation has become increasingly common as the volume of cases grows faster than the number of judgeships. Both trial and appellate judges find themselves scrambling to dispose of cases in order to prevent unacceptable backlogs. One commentator has said that American judges "are coming to resemble harried bureaucrats."[20] Aside from the stresses involved, one result is that judges are doing less of the work that they find most satisfying.

Just as caseloads have grown, so has scrutiny of judges' work from outside the court system. Increasingly, the mass media and interest groups observe judges at work and issue criticisms when they disagree with decisions. Judges receive the greatest scrutiny in criminal justice, where observers—including officials in the other branches of government—often castigate judges whom they see as unduly lenient. In 2006 a Vermont judge was denounced for his sentence of a sex offender by people who included the governor (who asked him to resign), state legislators (who suggested he be impeached), and a national television news commentator (who said he might be "the worst judge in the USA"). Under the pressure, the judge re-sentenced the offender to a much longer term.[21] After a newspaper columnist charged that he had acted improperly in a case, the chief justice of the Illinois Supreme Court took a different course: he sued the newspaper for libel, asking compensation for the income he might lose if his damaged reputation cost him additional terms on the court, a federal court appointment, or a position in a private law firm. In 2006 a jury awarded him $7 million in damages.[22]

As in the Vermont episode, judges are sometimes threatened with loss of their positions when they make unpopular decisions. In the past decade congressional Republicans have discussed possible impeachment of several judges on that ground. Some state judges have been subject to similar efforts. The Nevada Supreme Court made a ruling in 2003 that created an exception to the requirement of a two-thirds legislative majority to raise taxes. The ruling aroused strong opposition, including the beginning of an effort to remove one justice from office through a public vote called a recall. A year later, that justice decided not to run for re-election because her health problems ruled out a vigorous campaign.[23] As this example illustrates, it has become increasingly common for judges to face electoral opposition based on their decisions, and some are defeated. Inevitably, that prospect concerns some judges.

Judges have reason to fear even worse consequences. Harassment and threats of violence against judges are common, and occasionally actual violence occurs. In 2005 a criminal defendant killed an Atlanta judge along with a court reporter and a deputy sheriff at a courthouse. A federal district judge in Chicago was threatened with violence because of a decision she reached in 2000, and a man was sentenced to prison for soliciting her murder. In 2005 the same judge's husband and mother were killed by a disgruntled litigant in an unrelated case.[24] Inevitably, these dangers weigh on judges' minds. When monitored home security systems were offered to federal judges in 2006, two-thirds of the judges asked for them.[25] In the same year, the New York Advisory Committee on Judicial Ethics responded to a judge's query by saying that it did not violate any ethical rules to "carry a pistol while you are on the bench," though it advised judges to keep any firearms concealed.[26]

Finances   Compared with the average American, most judges are paid well, and many are paid very well. At the beginning of 2006, the median salary for judges on major state trial courts across the states was $116,000; the median for state supreme court justices was $128,000. Federal district judges received $165,000, and Supreme Court justices were paid $203,000.[27]

But people's satisfaction with their income depends largely on comparison with people they consider their peers and on what they think they could earn in another pursuit. By these criteria, most judges do not feel well paid. It is true that for many lawyers a judgeship would bring a substantial increase in salary. But judicial salaries are considerably lower than those of lawyers in private practice who enjoy financial success. As a result, judges may feel that they have sacrificed a good deal financially.

Federal judges have been especially vocal in expressing dissatisfaction with their salaries. Chief Justice William Rehnquist frequently exhorted Congress to raise judicial salaries, and new Chief Justice John Roberts followed Rehnquist's example in his first year-end report on the federal courts.[28] One reason is that federal judges are more likely to compare themselves with highly paid lawyers; another is that, in contrast with the states, the salaries of federal judges have not kept up well with inflation. Whether or not judges are justified in feeling underpaid, the feeling creates dissatisfaction.

The Attractions of Judgeships   Judging is hardly unique in having its negative aspects, and the negatives of many other occupations are considerably greater. A member of the British comedy troupe Beyond the Fringe, taking the perspective of a coal miner, concluded that judges were considerably better off than miners. "You're not troubled by falling coal, for one thing."[29]

Negatives aside, judging has powerful attractions, attractions indicated by the high level of interest in the position. Governors and presidents usually find many aspirants eager to fill a judicial vacancy, and lawyers are often willing to undergo difficult campaigns to win judgeships through elections. It is true that some judges give up their positions voluntarily, either because they are unhappy with conditions on the bench or because they seek higher incomes in the private sector. Exhibit 5.3 describes one case of a judge who left a high level of the judiciary for another pursuit. Still, the great majority of federal judges stay on the job at least until retirement age. In the state courts, many judges work very hard to win re-election. And many judges clearly enjoy their jobs a great deal.

One attraction of the position is the degree of freedom that judges enjoy. Certainly they face constraints, both from audiences outside the courts and from the lawyers and judges with whom they work. Heavy caseloads create constraints of their own. On the whole, however, it is judges' freedom that stands out. This freedom is reflected in

EXHIBIT 5.3   Judge Luttig Resigns from the Federal Court of Appeals for the Fourth Circuit

J. Michael Luttig enjoyed great success in the legal profession from the start. After receiving his law degree from the University of Virginia in 1981, he worked for a year as an attorney in the Office of the President in the Reagan administration and then clerked for Judge Antonin Scalia and Chief Justice Warren Burger. After four years in private practice, he joined the administration of President George H.W. Bush. In 1991 Bush appointed him to the federal court of appeals for the Fourth Circuit. He became a prominent judge, and he was considered a leading candidate for the Supreme Court in a Republican administration. He apparently was given serious consideration for the Court positions that President George W. Bush filled in 2005.

Then, in May 2006, Luttig resigned from the court of appeals to take a position as general counsel of the Boeing aircraft company. That decision surprised and shocked observers of the federal courts. Why did Luttig give up his judgeship? Some people speculated that he was unhappy about being passed over for the Supreme Court. Others said he was upset as a result of an action by the Bush administration in a case involving the treatment of suspected terrorists. (After Luttig's opinion ruling in favor of the administration in the case, the government in effect abandoned the position it had taken before his court. In a second opinion after the government's shift, Luttig strongly criticized the government.) Luttig's letter of resignation did not mention those matters. Instead, he referred to the attractions of his new position and alluded to the economic benefits of moving to Boeing at a time when his children were getting close to college age.

There is no way to know what considerations actually influenced Luttig's decision. In any case, he is a clear exception to the rule. He was fifty-one years old when he resigned, and only a small proportion of federal judges leave the bench at so early an age. The willingness of most judges to remain in the judiciary rather than leave for other positions reflects the attractions of being a federal judge.

Sources: biographical sources; Jess Bravin and J. Lynn Lunsford, "Breakdown of Trust Led Judge Luttig to Clash with Bush," *Wall Street Journal*, May 11, 2006, A1; other newspaper articles; *Padilla v. Hanft*, 432 F.3d 582 (4th Cir. 2005); Judge Luttig's letter of resignation to President Bush, May 10, 2006 (http://www.ca4.uscourts.gov/pdf/ltpres.pdf).

work styles. Judges typically set their own work schedules, and they have considerable leeway in allocating their time among the various parts of their job. Another reflection of judges' freedom is differences in the positions they take on the same legal issues. To a considerable degree, judges can apply the law as they see fit.

A further attraction is the status of the job. In the courtroom, judges are generally accorded great deference by court personnel, lawyers, and other participants. Outside of court, many people—including lawyers—give automatic respect to a person who holds the title of judge. Some judges achieve high levels of public regard as individuals for actions they take on the bench, and some gain a degree of fame that outlives them.

Along with a judge's status comes a considerable measure of power. Judges routinely make decisions that affect people's lives in important ways. Some decisions have broader impact on people throughout a state or the nation. If the responsibility for important decisions sometimes creates stress, it also allows judges to make a difference, to do what they see as good. And because judgeships *are* powerful positions, they attract lawyers who enjoy the exercise of power for its own sake. Judges sometimes speak of the burdens of the powers they hold, such as criminal sentencing, but they frequently employ these powers with enthusiasm.

THE QUALITY OF JUDICIAL PERFORMANCE

Because judges have so much impact, the quality of their performance is important. But it is very difficult to assess the performance of American judges as a group. For one thing, observers cannot agree on the criteria for assessment and how to apply those criteria. Polls of lawyers often produce substantial disagreement about the performance of a particular judge. For another, there are so many judges serving across the country that even active trial lawyers can have only a partial sense of the overall level of performance.

We should begin with reasonable expectations. With luck, the process of selecting judges favors people who would perform their jobs at a relatively high level. But the selection process is highly imperfect, and those who become judges are likely to vary considerably in their strengths and weaknesses. And judges cannot be expected to differ fundamentally from other people. Abraham Lincoln often quoted from a letter by Thomas Jefferson on this point: "Our judges are as honest as other men, and not more so. They have, with others, the same passions for party, for power, and the privilege of their corps."[30]

Keeping in mind both the need for realistic expectations and the difficulty of evaluating judges, it is still useful to consider what we know about their performance.

Several Areas of Performance

Judges can be assessed according to several criteria. Perhaps the most important are competence, commitment to the job, "judicial temperament," and impartiality.

Competence and Commitment   The most basic element of a judge's performance is an ability to handle the job effectively. Of all the qualities of judges, however, competence is perhaps the most difficult to define and measure.

Except at the lowest levels, all judges have received legal training. In that sense, they all have basic preparation for their jobs. But legal education does not guarantee competence as a judge any more than it guarantees competence as an attorney. For this reason, even very good judges often had to go through a period in which they performed poorly while they learned the task of judging.

Once they have had the chance to learn, judges differ widely in their competence. A great many are highly regarded, but others are considered unable to carry out their jobs effectively. In a 2005 survey by the Dallas Bar Association in 2005, according to one report, "a staggering 67 percent of attorneys responded 'no' when asked if [one judge] correctly applied the law. As one lawyer put it, 'How can someone be a judge if they don't know the law?'"[31] Federal judges are widely thought to have a higher level of skills, on average, than their state counterparts. But as Exhibit 5.4 shows, even within the federal courts there is considerable variation in perceived competence.

Judges' relative freedom from direct supervision gives them considerable leeway in determining how much and how hard they will work. Some judges respond by working long hours, even driving themselves to exhaustion. Judges who are not inclined to work so hard may give their job something less than a full commitment. Some judges routinely take Fridays off or work only half days. In one extreme case described by the California Commission on Judicial Performance, a Los Angeles trial judge was absent from his job for long stretches of time, among them a total of ten months in one year.

EXHIBIT 5.4   Lawyers' Assessments of Some Federal Judges

The *Almanac of the Federal Judiciary* is a compilation of information on federal judges, including lawyers' anonymous evaluations of judges' legal abilities. On the whole, those evaluations are quite positive. Even allowing for a tendency to be charitable, this pattern suggests that the overall level of ability of federal judges is high. But by no means are the evaluations uniformly positive, as a perusal of the comments on district judges indicates.

Some judges receive high praise from all the lawyers who assess them. "She is great. She is just superb." "His legal ability is outstanding. He is an intellectual heavyweight." "She is a super judge. She is fabulous—she really is." But others are viewed less favorably, drawing mixed or negative comments from many (or most) of the lawyers who evaluate them. "His ability is at the bottom of the scale." "He still hasn't learned the simple things." "She's a terrible judge."

One noteworthy aspect of the evaluations is the wide divergence in assessments of some individual judges by different lawyers. One attorney referred to a judge as "an able judge. He is bright." According to another lawyer, "His ability is poor. He's a crummy judge." And a judge was viewed by one lawyer as having "a very strong legal ability," while another concluded that "I don't think he has any business being on the bench." That divergence is a reminder of the difficulties and biases involved in evaluating the quality of judging.

Source: Almanac of the Federal Judiciary, 2006-1 edition, volume 1 (New York: Aspen Publishers, 2006).

The judge claimed that he was ill for much of that time, including periods when he was taking or teaching courses. He resigned after the commission ordered that he be removed from office.[32]

The appropriate commitment seems lacking when a judge does not deal seriously with cases. Although the coin-tossing judge would seem to be matter of legend, from time to time judges actually do flip coins to reach decisions.[33] And other means to avoid responsibility, such as polling of the courtroom audience, have occurred as well.

Judicial Temperament   What lawyers call "judicial temperament" is one of those qualities that is difficult to define but easier to recognize. Judges have enormous power over the lawyers and litigants who come before them, and they receive a great deal of deference. Especially in trial courts, they often find themselves in stressful situations. Judges with a judicial temperament maintain their composure and refrain from misusing their power by bullying the people who come before them or acting arbitrarily.

Many, perhaps most, judges meet this standard. They handle job pressures with calm and good humor, and they treat the people in their courtrooms with respect. It appears, however, that a substantial number of judges fall short of this standard. The worst cases are indeed bad:

1. In a West Virginia case, a criminal defendant mumbled curses after his bail request was denied. The judge left the bench, took off his robes, and ultimately bit the defendant's nose. The judge agreed to resign from his position.[34]
2. A small-town Missouri mayor initiated a decision not to provide health insurance payments for elected officials. The town's municipal judge then ordered that all fines for the next two weeks would be $1 plus $21 in court costs, regardless of the offense. The judge later talked about killing the mayor and displayed a bumper sticker supporting an effort to impeach the mayor. The state supreme court suspended the judge for the remainder of his term.[35]
3. Filling in for a colleague one day, a Pittsburgh judge became increasingly unhappy with the way that traffic citations were handled in the courtroom. According to the state judicial conduct board, he ultimately said, "Well, then, let's just find everybody not guilty!" When he announced this judgment to the people awaiting hearings for their cases, many of them were confused about what to do—in part because they were unsure that he was actually their judge. The judge then became angry at the defendants, threatening that "if you don't leave, I'm going to find everyone guilty!"[36]
4. In several cases a California judge threatened defendants that he would increase their sentences because of what they said at their hearings, and in some of those cases he did so. The judge told one defendant that he would be jailed for twenty days for failing to meet a condition of probation. When the defendant offered an explanation for his failure, the judge increased the sentence to thirty days and said, "If you care to keep talking about the same issue, I'll give you 60 days." The defendant spoke twice, and the judge set a sentence of seventy-five days.[37]

Impartiality   One quality that everyone would want from a judge is impartiality between the litigants. No judge can be perfectly impartial, because all people have political and social attitudes that incline them in favor of some types of parties or legal claims. To take one example, liberals and conservatives on the Supreme Court come to criminal cases with different points of view. But a judge should be sufficiently open-minded to give a fair hearing to both sides. Thus it can be troubling when a judge's views about a particular class of cases are so strong that the judge's decision in such cases seems preordained.

Even the appearance of bias is undesirable, so judges are expected to recuse themselves (not participate) in cases when their open-mindedness might be questioned. A defendant in a Texas murder case sought the recusal of a judge from her appeal; her lawyers alleged that the judge had told a law clerk that if any clerk wrote a draft opinion that recommended reversing a criminal conviction, "I'll fire them."[38] Judges generally decide for themselves whether it is appropriate to recuse themselves from a case; in this case, the judge's court as a whole denied a motion to require recusal.

One form of bias arises from attitudes toward specific groups in the population. Historically, some judges have demonstrated considerable prejudice against women and members of racial minority groups. Such bias has become less common as social attitudes have changed and the bench has become more diverse. But blatant discrimination has hardly disappeared, as both systematic studies and anecdotal evidence indicate,[39] and there are still some judges who openly make ethnic and racial slurs.[40]

Judges may exhibit bias that is based on their political affiliations and interests. In one form of political bias, some judges are inclined to favor the interests of their political party in relevant cases. For instance, it has been found that judges are more likely to uphold legislative redistricting plans if those plans favor the interests of their own party.[41] In an era in which spending in election campaigns for judgeships has grown considerably, judges might be swayed in favor of litigants and lawyers who have contributed to their campaigns. Judges seldom if ever recuse themselves from cases involving contributors, even when litigants ask that they do so. For instance, in 2006 a member of the West Virginia Supreme Court chose to participate in an appeal of a $50 million jury award against a company even though the company's head had contributed at least $3 million to a campaign committee supporting the justice in 2004.[42] (That contest was described in Exhibit 4.5.) In a 2003 case a Michigan Supreme Court justice declined to recuse herself from a case in which a contributor to her campaign had filed a brief, but she acknowledged the problems that arise from high-cost judicial campaigns: "The judiciary cannot afford to be perceived by the public as 'bought and paid for.'"[43]

Judges who seek to keep their positions or to obtain promotions might be biased by those career interests. As discussed in Chapter 4, elected judges may avoid making unpopular decisions in order to avoid alienating voters. It can be argued that taking the electorate into account is quite appropriate, but if judges' concern about re-election has so great an impact that they come to cases with a closed mind, that impact is troubling.

Judges may have financial conflicts of interest in some situations. The most common situation is one in which a decision could affect the value of a judge's stocks or other financial holdings. For Supreme Court justices, this is the most common reason for recusals from cases. In a variant of this situation, judges have received financial benefits from people with an interest in their decisions. According to a newspaper story about the Las Vegas courts, one judge participated in cases in which litigants were involved in his real estate investments, another judge participated in cases in which a litigant was associated with a foundation that had provided a college scholarship for the judge's son, and a third judge ruled in cases involving a litigant who provided a discount for a wedding reception for the judge's daughter.[44] Exhibit 5.5 describes a more complicated situation in which federal judges receive benefits from groups that care about their decisions. The most extreme situation is bribery, the direct selling of decisions. It is impossible to ascertain the frequency with which judges accept bribes, but two conclusions seem safe: this kind of corruption touches only a small minority of judges, but it does occur. In 2003, for instance, a West Virginia judge was convicted

EXHIBIT 5.5   The Controversy over Education Programs for Federal Judges

Several organizations sponsor educational programs for federal judges, and some of these organizations have positions on issues that come before the courts. For several years the Community Rights Counsel (CRC), a liberal group, has criticized judges' participation in some of these programs on two grounds. First, the CRC argues that the groups involved present a conservative point of view in an effort to sway judges' thinking. Second, the programs sponsored by these groups usually take place in attractive places, so the CRC contends that the sponsoring groups provide a benefit to the judges who participate and thereby gain an inappropriate advantage. One of the CRC's reports cited three conservative groups that were active in providing seminars for federal judges. The report gave particular attention to one of these groups, the Foundation for Research on Economics and the Environment (FREE), which the CRC has described as "wining, dining and vacationing judges, while instructing them how and why to roll back environmental laws."

Some commentators and members of Congress have joined in the criticism of judges' participation in these programs, but the organizations that provide the programs defend the judges and themselves. Two leaders of FREE argued in a commentary that their programs are balanced rather than ideologically skewed, and they cited positive evaluations from independent observers. "The CRC fantasizes that our programs are lavish corporate-sponsored getaways at posh resorts intended to brainwash intellectually pliant federal judges. They are none of that: neither lavish nor sponsored by special interests nor intended to influence anyone."

In response to the controversy and pressure from some members of Congress, in 2004 a committee of the federal judiciary revised its guidelines relating to judicial education programs. But some people argued that the new guidelines weakened rather than strengthened limits on participation and reporting requirements for judges. Some members of Congress proposed legislation to establish tighter controls. The legislation has not yet been enacted, and it will probably not become law. But in 2006 the federal Judicial Conference responded to the congressional criticism with new rules that allow judges to attend education programs only if the sponsors disclose their sources of funding and that require judges to disclose their attendance at these programs within thirty days.

Sources: News articles, group websites. The quotations are from CRC News Release, "Despite Years of Growing Outrage, Corporate Junkets for Judges Increase by 60%," April 28, 2006 (http://www.communityrights.org/Newsroom/crcNewsReleases/jud04-28-06.asp); and John A. Baden and Pete Geddes, "Free to Learn," *Legal Times*, March 20, 2006, 76.

and sentenced to prison for demanding and receiving bribes from criminal defendants or their friends.[45] Rare though bribery may be, the existence of even a very small proportion of corrupt judges is troubling.

Enhancing the Quality of Judging

In discussing the performance of judges, I have given special attention to the judges whose work is deficient. It is worth emphasizing that those judges are far from representative. Still, given judges' power, the inadequacies that do exist represent a real problem. The extent of these inadequacies might be reduced and the overall quality of judging enhanced in three ways: selecting better judges, removing inadequate judges, and improving the performance of sitting judges.

Selecting Better Judges   Perhaps the best way to improve the quality of judging is simply to put the most qualified people on the bench. For many lawyers and judges, the primary means to achieve that goal is adoption of the Missouri Plan. Advocates of the Missouri Plan see its nominating commissions as a device to identify the most promising candidates. They have won enough support that a majority of states now use some version of the Missouri Plan by law or in practice for at least some of their courts.

As suggested in Chapter 4, it is uncertain whether the Missouri Plan actually affects the quality of judges. It seems unlikely that adoption of the Missouri Plan would have any dramatic impact on that quality. Criteria other than qualifications affect the selection of judges under the Missouri Plan, and it is not clear that judges' performance can be predicted very well from their records prior to their selection. It is also noteworthy that the background characteristics of Missouri Plan judges, including those related to their qualifications, are similar to the characteristics of judges selected under other systems.

Another approach is to raise judicial salaries so that good judges will have a greater incentive to remain on the bench and good prospective judges will be more interested in serving. Better compensation might improve the quality of the judiciary by broadening the pool of candidates. On the other hand, judgeships would be more attractive to less competent people as well as to the most competent. In any case, it has proved very difficult to secure legislative approval for substantial increases in judicial salaries. If inadequate compensation does weaken the quality of the judiciary, that problem is likely to continue.

Removing Inadequate Judges   If it is impossible to ensure that only good judges will be put on the bench, an obvious remedy is to remove judges whose performance proves to be inadequate. Several removal methods exist.

Where judges do not hold life terms, the simplest method is to deny them reappointment or reelection when their terms end. This is a highly imperfect method, chiefly because sitting judges tend to win new terms no matter what their level of performance. And the judges who do lose their seats are not necessarily those whose work is most deficient. Rather, unpopular decisions, unfavorable partisan tides, and other factors unrelated to the quality of judging are responsible for most failures to win a new term. Still, a judge's bad performance occasionally leads to electoral defeat or non-reappointment.

In the federal courts and nearly all the states, judges are subject to impeachment. The procedure generally used is that judges can be removed if impeached (in effect, charged with an offense) by the lower house of the legislature and convicted by the upper house. For the most part, legislators seriously consider impeachment only where corruption or other criminal offenses are alleged, so this mechanism has little application to problems such as tyrannical behavior. Because the impeachment procedure is so extreme and so unwieldy, it is not always employed even when there are serious allegations of criminal conduct.

In recent years, it has become more common to threaten judges with impeachment when they make unpopular decisions. Such threats seldom lead to formal proceedings. But in a complex situation in 2000, Chief Justice David Brock of the New Hampshire Supreme Court was impeached by the lower house of the state legislature. The impeachment was based on allegations of misconduct. But it apparently was motivated in part by other sources of unhappiness with the state supreme court, especially its decisions striking down the state's system for funding of public education. The state senate acquitted Brock of the four charges against him by large margins.[46] That outcome underlined the widely shared perception that removal of judges through impeachment should be reserved for extreme cases of misconduct.

Faced with the limitations of other methods, since 1960 every state has adopted a new structure with which to investigate and act on complaints against judges. The agencies that carry out these functions have various names. One common name, judicial conduct commission, can be used to refer to all of them.[47] People can make complaints against judges to the commission (which usually includes judges, lawyers, and lay members) on such grounds as misconduct in office and failure to perform judicial duties.

Typically, the judicial conduct commission screens complaints, investigates those that have possible merit, and recommends disciplinary action to the state supreme court. Such action can take several forms, ranging from private admonition to removal or retirement. In assessing judges' behavior and considering sanctions, most commissions are guided by their state's version of the Code of Judicial Conduct, developed by the American Bar Association.

Commissions receive large numbers of complaints, several thousand across the country each year. Michigan's Judicial Tenure Commission compiles data on complaints, and in 2005 more than 90 percent came from parties to cases and parties' friends or families. The majority of complaints asked the commission to review the merits of a case, and these complaints were dismissed because they were outside the commission's powers. Altogether, the commission found misconduct in only about 5 percent of the cases it considered. In nearly all those cases, it communicated its finding privately to the judge.[48]

This does not mean that commissions never issue significant sanctions to judges. In the twenty-five years from 1980 through 2004, they removed 325 judges from office. In 2004, eighteen judges were removed, another ten resigned as a result of disciplinary proceedings, and eleven were suspended from office.[49] One of the eighteen removals was part of a widely publicized controversy, described in Exhibit 5.6. Despite these numbers, some commissions are regarded as unable or unwilling to respond adequately to judicial misconduct.

EXHIBIT 5.6   The "Ten Commandments" Judge Is Removed from Office

Roy Moore became an Alabama trial judge in 1992. He put up a copy of the Ten Commandments in his courtroom, an action that became the subject of litigation. An Alabama court ruled against Moore, but the controversy won Moore fame as the "Ten Commandments" judge as well as wide support in and outside the state. Drawing on his popularity, in 2000 Moore was elected chief justice of the Alabama Supreme Court.

After taking office, Chief Justice Moore installed a large monument of the Ten Commandments in the rotunda of the building in which the Supreme Court held its sessions. His action was challenged in a lawsuit. In 2002 a federal district judge ruled against Moore and, after Moore refused to remove the monument, issued an injunction ordering that the monument be removed. The court of appeals for the Eleventh Circuit upheld the district judge's decision, and the Supreme Court did not hear the case. Moore refused to obey the district court's injunction, arguing that the district court decision was invalid, but his eight colleagues ordered removal of the monument.

The state Judicial Inquiry Commission then brought a complaint against the chief justice in which it charged that he had violated several provisions of the state's Canons of Judicial Ethics by refusing to obey the district court injunction. The complaint was heard by the Alabama Court of the Judiciary, a court with the sole function of hearing such complaints. In 2003 the court ruled that Moore had violated the Canons and ordered that he be removed from office. Moore appealed to the state supreme court. All of the justices recused themselves, so seven temporary members were put on the court under the state's rules. In 2004 the supreme court ruled unanimously against Moore, and he lost his position.

This decision and the continuing controversy made Moore even more of a hero to those who shared his views, but others opposed what they saw as his defiance of the law. In 2006 Moore ran in the Republican primary for governor against the incumbent, and he was defeated by a large margin.

Sources: newspaper articles; *Moore v. Judicial Inquiry Commission*, 891 So. 2d 848 (Ala. 2004).

The federal courts do not have an equivalent system. As described in Chapter 2, the judicial councils of the circuits have the power to act as judicial conduct commissions for federal judges. Congress did not allow the councils to remove judges from office, chiefly because of doubts that such action would be constitutionally acceptable. However, several judges have quietly retired after complaints about them were made to circuit councils.

Improving Sitting Judges   Inevitably, the methods used to select judges and to remove inadequate judges are imperfect. For the most part, we have to live with the judges we have: a set of people whose performance varies considerably. This reality has become increasingly clear to people who care about the quality of the judiciary, so more attention is now given to improving the quality of judges' work.

One form of these efforts is organized educational programs, mentioned earlier in the chapter. Orientation programs for new judges have become standard practice. There has also been growth in continuing education for sitting judges, including several national programs. Only a few states require training for all their judges, but a large minority impose such requirements on nonlawyer judges and those who serve on specialized courts. These programs undoubtedly improve the skills of most judges who participate in them, but their overall impact is difficult to assess.

Some effort has also been made to provide help for sitting judges who are identified as having problems. Indeed, one function of the state conduct commissions is to warn judges of deficiencies that need correction. Some states have established programs to help judges who suffer from alcoholism and psychological problems. In 2005 the chief justice of the Massachusetts Supreme Court initiated a "judicial enhancement" program to improve the work of judges in the state whose work appeared to be deficient on the basis of evaluations by lawyers and other people in the courts. But many judges expressed resentment of the program, and it was unclear how effective it would be.[50]

Attempts to improve the performance of sitting judges, like efforts to select good judges and remove bad ones, have significant limitations. Inevitably, some of the judges whose performance is most deficient will be least willing to try to improve their work. Even judges who want to do better may be limited in their capacity to improve. Thus we will continue to have some judges who perform poorly, just as we have others who meet the highest standards.

CONCLUSIONS

This chapter has discussed a wide range of issues involving judges and their work. These discussions suggest some conclusions about similarities and differences among judges in the United States.

The similarities are important. Judges all do the same general kind of work, and most are subject to the same kinds of stresses in their jobs. Most judges share certain background characteristics, including relatively high socioeconomic status and involvement in politics.

But the differences are even more striking. Judges' values and the ways they approach their jobs vary a great deal. Perhaps most important, there is wide variation in the quality of their performance. Thus it does make a difference which people sit on the bench, and the energy devoted to the selection of judges is justified.

Thus far I have described judges' work and performance only in broad terms. The examinations of trial and appellate courts in the remaining chapters look more closely at judges as decision makers and at the forces that shape their behavior.

FOR FURTHER READING

Barrow, Deborah J., Gary Zuk, and Gerard S. Gryski. *The Federal Judiciary and Institutional Change.* Ann Arbor: University of Michigan Press, 1996.

Burbank, Stephen B., and Barry Friedman, eds. *Judicial Independence at the Crossroads: An Interdisciplinary Approach.* Thousand Oaks, Calif.: Sage Publications, 2002.

Volcansek, Mary L. *Judicial Impeachment: None Called for Justice.* Urbana: University of Illinois Press, 1993.

Washington, Linn. *Black Judges on Justice: Perspectives From the Bench.* New York: The New Press, 1994.

Online Study Center Go to college.hmco.com/PIC/baum6e for ACE practice test questions and additional resources.

NOTES

1. *The Book of the States, 2005 Edition* (Lexington, Ky.: Council of State Governments, 2005), 313.
2. Data on the characteristics of state supreme court justices were obtained primarily from the websites of the state courts, with two additional sources: *Judicial Yellow Book*, vol. 11, #2 (New York: Leadership Directories, Inc., 2006); and *The American Bench: Judges of the Nation*, 16th ed. (Sacramento: Forster-Long, 2006). Members of the Court of Criminal Appeals in Oklahoma and Texas, the highest court for criminal cases, are not included.
3. All figures on federal judges appointed in 1993–2004 were taken from Sheldon Goldman, Elliot Slotnick, Gerard Gryski, and Sara Schiavoni, "W. Bush's Judiciary: The First Term Record," *Judicature* 88 (May–June 2005), 269, 274, the same source used in Exhibit 5.1. These figures exclude Supreme Court justices (too small in number to affect the percentages) and magistrate and bankruptcy judges.
4. John Paul Ryan, Allan Ashman, Bruce D. Sales, and Sandra Shane-DuBow, *American Trial Judges: Their Work Styles and Performance* (New York: Free Press, 1980), 128; Henry R. Glick and Craig F. Emmert, "Stability and Change: Characteristics of State Supreme Court Justices," *Judicature* 70 (August–September 1986), 108.
5. See Mark S. Hurwitz and Drew Noble Lanier, "Women and Minorities on State and Federal Appellate Benches, 1985 and 1999," *Judicature* 85 (September–October 2001), 84–92; and Elaine Martin and Barry Pyle, "Gender and Racial Diversification of State Supreme Courts," *Women & Politics* 24 (2002), No. 2, pp. 35–52.
6. *The American Bench.* (This publication does not have page numbers.)
7. John Cheves, "Patton Legacy: Women as Judges," *Lexington Herald-Leader*, December 5, 2003.
8. Clara N. Carson, *The Lawyer Statistical Report: The U.S. Legal Profession in 2000* (Chicago: American Bar Foundation, 2004), 7–8.
9. Curtis Bok, *Backbone of the Herring* (New York: Alfred A. Knopf, 1941), 3.
10. James Tuohy and Rob Warden, *Greylord: Justice, Chicago Style* (New York: G. P. Putnam's Sons, 1989), 47.
11. See, for instance, C. Neal Tate and Roger Handberg, "Time Binding and Theory Building in Personal Attribute Models of Supreme Court Voting Behavior, 1916–88," *American Journal of Political Science* 35 (May 1991), 460–480; and James J. Brudney, Sara Schiavoni, and Deborah J. Merritt, "Judicial Hostility Toward Labor Unions? Applying the Social Background Model to a Celebrated Concern," *Ohio State Law Journal* 60 (1999), 1675–1771.
12. See Carroll J. Glynn, Susan Herbst, Garrett J. O'Keefe, and Robert Y. Shapiro, *Public Opinion* (Boulder, Colo.: Westview Press, 1999), 226–238.
13. See, for instance, Donald R. Songer and Kelly A. Crews-Meyer, "Does Judge Gender Matter? Decision Making in State Supreme Courts," *Social Science Quarterly* 81 (September 2000), 750–762; Jennifer A. Segal, "Representative Decision Making on the Federal Bench: Clinton's District Court Appointees," *Political Research Quarterly* 53 (March

2000), 137–150; and Barbara Palmer, "Women in the American Judiciary: Their Influence and Impact," *Women & Politics* 23 (2001), 91–101.

14. See Jeffrey Toobin, "Women in Black," *The New Yorker,* October 20, 2000, 48–55.
15. Darrell Steffensmeier and Chester L. Britt, "Judges' Race and Judicial Decision Making: Do Black Judges Sentence Differently?" *Social Science Quarterly* 82 (December 2001), 749–764. The quotation is from p. 762.
16. *Patricia Ann S. v. James Daniel S.,* 435 S.E.2d 6 (W. Va. 1993). See also *Office of Disciplinary Counsel v. Mestemaker,* 676 N.E.2d 870 (Ohio 1997).
17. This list of categories is adapted from a list in Ryan et al., 6–7; some of the material in this subsection was drawn from that source.
18. Karen Abbott, "Judges, Too, Get 1st-Day Jitters," *Rocky Mountain News* (Denver), August 5, 2002.
19. Marc T. Amy, "Judiciary School: A Proposal for a Pre-Judicial LL.M. Degree," *Judicature* 87 (July–August 2003), 30.
20. Mary Ann Glendon, *A Nation Under Lawyers: How the Crisis in the Legal Profession Is Transforming American Society* (New York: Farrar, Straus and Giroux, 1994), 149.
21. The quotation is from Christopher Graff, "Judge Edward Cashman Is Best Known for His Pro-Law Stands," Associated Press State & Local Wire, January 11, 2006.
22. (38.1). Eric Herman, "Justice's Libel Suit Figures His Losses," *Chicago Sun-Times,* July 10, 2006, 12; Dan Rozek and Abdon M. Pallasch, "Top Judge Gets 7 mil.," *Chicago Sun-Times,* November 15, 2006, 7.
23. Brendan Riley, "Nevada High Court Justice Won't Seek Second Term," Associated Press State & Local Wire, April 15, 2004.
24. Jodi Wilgoren, "Haunted by Threats, U.S. Judge Finds New Horror," *New York Times,* March 2, 2005, A1, A16; Jodi Wilgoren, "Electrician Says in Suicide Note That He Killed Judge's Family," *New York Times,* March 11, 2005, A1, A15.
25. Lynne Marek, "Most Federal Judges Are Opting for Home Security Measures," *National Law Journal,* July 17, 2006.
26. New York State Advisory Committee on Judicial Ethics, Opinion 06-51, May 18, 2006 (http://www.nycourts.gov/acoje/opinions/06-51.htm).
27. *Survey of Judicial Salaries* 30 (January 1, 2006), 15.
28. John G. Roberts, Jr., "2005 Year-End Report on the Federal Judiciary," 4–6 (http://www.supremecourtus.gov/publicinfo/year-end/2005year-endreport.pdf).
29. Quoted in posting at the web log slaw.ca, February 23, 2006 (http://www.slaw.ca/2006/02/20/i-never-had-the-latin/).
30. Quoted in Charles M. Haar, *Suburbs Under Siege: Race, Space, and Audacious Judges* (Princeton, N.J.: Princeton University Press, 1996), 156.
31. Nate Blakeslee, "The Worst Judges in Texas," *Texas Observer,* February 10, 2006.
32. California Commission on Judicial Performance, Inquiry No. 157 (2001) (http://cjp.ca.gov/CNCensure/Murphy%20Censure%20Bar%205-10-01.pdf).
33. "Kids' Christmas Was Up in the Air," *National Law Journal,* February 11, 2002, A22.
34. Gail Diane Cox, "Stupid Judge Tricks," *National Law Journal,* May 4, 1998, A25.
35. *In re Hill,* 8 S.W.3d 578 (Mo. 2000).
36. Jim McKinnon, "2 District Judges Charged with Misconduct," *Pittsburgh Post-Gazette,* February 17, 2005; Pennsylvania Court of Judicial Discipline, *In re Ernest L. Marraccini,* 2 JD 05, Notice of February 16, 2005.
37. Bob Egelko, "Judge Again to be Investigated Over Courtroom Behavior," *San Francisco Chronicle,* April 29, 2006, B2.
38. George Flynn, "Running Over the Defense?" *Houston Press,* October 7, 2004.
39. See, for instance, Ohio Commission on Racial Fairness, *Reviewing the Fairness of Ohio's Legal System* (Columbus: Ohio Supreme Court, 1999); "The Effects of Gender in the Federal Courts: The Final Report of the Ninth Circuit Gender Bias Task Force," *Southern California Law Review* 67 (May 1994), 745–1106; and Sheila Weller, "America's Most Sexist Judges," *Redbook,* February 1994, 83–87.

40. Lynne Duke, "Panel Faults Remarks by U.S. Judge," *Washington Post*, October 22, 1993, A14; "Mass. Judge Quits Prior to Hearing on Conduct," *Boston Globe*, May 29, 1993, Metro section, 1.
41. Randall D. Lloyd, "Separating Partisanship from Party in Judicial Research: Reapportionment in the U.S. District Courts," *American Political Science Review* 89 (June 1995), 413–420; Mark Jonathan McKenzie, "The Politics of Judicial Decision-Making and Redistricting: Do Federal Judges Revert to Partisanship When It Comes to Representation?" (paper presented at the annual meeting of the American Political Science Association, September 2–4, 2004, Chicago).
42. Peter Geier, "Recusal Fight Highlights Judicial Election Concerns," *National Law Journal*, April 24, 2006, 6.
43. *Gilbert v. DaimlerChrysler Corporation*, 669 N.W.2d 265, 267 (Mich. 2003).
44. Michael J. Goodman and William C. Rempel, "Special Treatment Keeps Them Under the Radar," *Los Angeles Times*, June 10, 2006, A1.
45. Toby Coleman, "Ex-Magistrate Sentenced to Seven Years for Bribery," *Charleston (West Virginia) Daily Mail*, July 22, 2003, 8A.
46. Jeffrey Toobin, "The Judge Hunter," *The New Yorker*, June 12, 2000, 49–54; Ralph Ranalli, "N.H. Senate Acquits State's Chief Justice," *Boston Globe*, October 11, 2000, A1.
47. See Cynthia Gray, *How Judicial Conduct Commissions Work* (Chicago: American Judicature Society, 1999).
48. Michigan Judicial Tenure Commission, "2005 Statistics & Budget" (http://jtc.courts.mi .gov/).
49. Cynthia Gray, "18 Judges Removed in 2004," *Judicial Conduct Reporter* 26 (Winter 2005), 1.
50. Jonathan Saltzman, "Judges Fume Over Remedial Program," *Boston Globe*, June 6, 2005, A1.

6

Trial Courts: Criminal Cases

T he courts hear and decide a wide array of cases. But the attention that people give to the courts goes primarily to one area of their work, criminal law. In part, this interest stems from the deep concern about crime that so many people feel. In part, it reflects the drama of crime and punishment, a quality demonstrated by the seemingly endless coverage of real and fictional criminal cases on television.[1]

In a way, the focus on criminal cases slights other issues that courts address. But what the courts do in criminal law has great importance. A high proportion of all cases are criminal. The outcomes of those cases affect millions of lives directly, and indirectly they shape public policy and American life.

This chapter examines the work of trial courts in criminal cases (what I will call, for convenience, the work of criminal courts). I discuss the ways that criminal courts deal with cases, emphasizing the conditions and motivations that shape their practices. One concern of the chapter is the impact of efforts to reform these practices, an impact that is often surprising and disappointing.

Criminal courts vary a good deal. The chapter describes general patterns in their operation and differences among them. The proportion of criminal cases that go to federal court has grown considerably in the past century, but it remains true that the great majority of criminal cases are filed in state courts. For that reason, this chapter gives primary attention to the state level.

After a general look at criminal courts, the chapter explores four key processes: bringing cases to court, plea bargaining, trials, and sentencing.

AN OVERVIEW OF CRIMINAL COURTS

To provide an overview of criminal courts, this section surveys three subjects—types of criminal cases, participants in criminal proceedings, and procedures for the handling of cases.

Types of Criminal Cases

In general, criminal cases are those in which government charges people with offenses for which they may be punished if found guilty. However, the line between criminal and civil cases is not entirely clear-cut. And the two sides of the law overlap, in that a single incident such as an automobile accident can lead to either type of case or both.

By enacting statutes, Congress and the state legislatures determine what acts are defined as criminal offenses. For this reason, the coverage of the criminal law should be viewed as a product of political decisions. This political character is hardly visible for offenses such as murder and robbery, which always have been treated as criminal by consensus. But such a consensus does not exist for some other acts such as gambling, for which the laws vary a great deal across states and over time. One of the most heated national debates today is about the circumstances under which abortion should be treated as a criminal offense. And legislatures debate other issues such as how crimes by corporations and their leaders should be defined.

The number of criminal offenses tends to grow over time. Between 1960 and 2000, the Illinois Criminal Code reportedly grew from 35 pages to nearly 800 pages.[2] The primary reason for this growth is that legislators often react to news of social problems by enacting new criminal laws. For instance, the increasing use of computers has led to a range of new criminal laws.

Statutes label criminal offenses as felonies or misdemeanors. Felonies are the most serious offenses, those punishable with the most severe sanctions. Some states define felonies as offenses for which a defendant may be sentenced to death or to imprisonment in a state prison (as opposed to a local jail). Other states and the federal government define felonies as offenses for which at least one year's imprisonment is possible. Violent offenses are almost always treated as felonies, while relatively minor crimes such as petty theft and gambling are usually misdemeanors. But the line between the two categories is arbitrary and varies from state to state.

Felonies constitute only a minority of criminal cases, but their seriousness gives them an importance beyond their numbers. For that reason, and because we know the most about them, this chapter gives primary attention to felonies. Typically, felony cases are tried in the major trial courts of a state system, so the chapter focuses chiefly on those courts.

Misdemeanor cases typically go to minor trial courts in the states, and most federal misdemeanors are handled by magistrate judges rather than district judges. Nearly all traffic and parking offenses are classified as misdemeanors, sometimes in a separate category. These cases greatly outnumber all others in the criminal courts. But because most are relatively minor in seriousness and possible sanctions, I give little attention to them.

Crimes allegedly committed by younger people can be either felonies or misdemeanors. But they also constitute a special category, which may be called juvenile offenses.[3] Every state has established juvenile courts, sometimes as divisions of other courts. Below a designated age, usually eighteen, defendants generally go to juvenile courts. In addition to "regular" crimes, juvenile courts handle offenses that apply only to juveniles such as truancy and running away from home.

When juvenile courts were created, the goal was to emphasize treatment rather than punishment; indeed, juvenile cases were no longer defined as criminal. The idea of treatment has lost support over time, largely because of a perceived growth in serious offenses by juveniles. One reflection of this change in thinking is a growing willingness to try juvenile defendants as adults. In the 1990s, nearly all states enacted legislation to facilitate the transfer of certain juvenile cases to adult court.

Participants in Criminal Courts

Of all the people who take part in the work of criminal courts, the most important are those who hold three positions: judges, prosecutors, and defense attorneys. Together, these three sets of participants have the greatest impact on the processing of cases and on their outcomes. Typically, the judges and lawyers who handle criminal cases do so on a regular basis. As a result, they get to know each other well. To use two terms suggested by students of criminal courts, lawyers and judges are at the center of the "courtroom work group" and the "courthouse community."[4]

The closeness of relationships within this community differs from court to court, based in part on the stability of the work group and its size (smaller groups tend to have closer relationships). Because of their familiarity with each other and the benefits of cooperation, the core members of the working group often get along very well. (In an extreme instance, in 2006 a federal magistrate judge donated a kidney to an assistant U.S. Attorney.[5]) But their relationships are not always harmonious.

This is especially true of prosecutors and defense attorneys. They are adversaries who represent competing sides, and the competition is especially direct in cases that go to trial. Their reputations and careers depend heavily on their success in those cases. For all these reasons, serious personal conflicts can develop. In an extreme instance, an Alaska judge found that the decision of Anchorage prosecutors to bring felony charges against a public defender after a traffic accident was "spiteful and malicious," based on bad feelings between prosecutors and defense attorneys.[6]

Lawyers on both sides can also get into conflicts with judges, despite the obvious benefits for lawyers of maintaining judges' good will. Unhappy with a district attorney's strong criticisms of their decisions, the Board of Judges in Philadelphia voted to make a formal complaint of ethical misconduct against her.[7] A federal prosecutor in Chicago charged that a federal district judge was "hostile" and "bizarre," and the judge asked the Justice Department to investigate the prosecutor's conduct.[8]

No matter what the state of their relationships is, in any court judges, prosecutors, and defense attorneys are all so central to criminal cases that the actions each takes and the interactions among them are crucial to what happens in court.

Judges   Most trial judges hear criminal cases at least part of the time. Some state judges sit on courts that hear only criminal cases, and some judges on other courts are assigned permanently or for long periods to criminal cases.

Judges, of course, play a central role in criminal cases. Simply by presiding in court, they influence the proceedings before them. But they also make several kinds of decisions about cases. At pretrial stages, judges set bail and determine whether there is sufficient evidence to maintain a case against the defendant. When defendants plead guilty, judges determine whether to accept the plea. In a nonjury trial, the judge decides whether to convict or acquit. If a defendant pleads guilty or is convicted after a trial, a judge usually makes the sentencing decision.

This list of responsibilities exaggerates the judge's importance somewhat. Even where a judge holds the ultimate power of decision, the actual exercise of that power is influenced by other people in the courts, especially prosecutors and defense attorneys. In interactions among the three work group members, judges have the advantage of their power to make binding decisions. But this power does not necessarily give judges control over what happens to cases. Sentencing decisions, for instance, are often constrained by plea bargaining agreements between the prosecutor and defense attorney. Even so, judges hold great influence over the processing of cases and their outcomes.

Prosecutors   In minor cases, police officers sometimes act as prosecutors. With that exception, in criminal cases the government is represented by attorneys. Some prosecutors work in offices that deal only with criminal cases, but it is common for those offices to handle other government legal work as well.[9]

Prosecutors' offices generally follow the same geographical lines as courts. In the federal court system, for instance, each judicial district has an office of the United States Attorney as well as a district court. Where a state court serves a county, there is usually a county prosecutor's office. But in Alaska, Connecticut, and Delaware, the state attorney general is responsible for prosecution throughout the state.

The structure of a prosecutor's office varies with its workload. In state systems, many rural counties have only a single part-time prosecutor. In contrast, most metropolitan counties have large offices with scores of full-time assistants to the chief prosecutor. The largest offices include several hundred assistants. In larger offices, individual assistants often specialize in specific kinds of cases. And in such offices, power over the handling of cases may be highly decentralized.

The official who heads a prosecutor's office in a state system may have any of several titles—most often district attorney, county attorney, or prosecuting attorney. U.S. Attorneys are appointed by the president and confirmed by the Senate. In the states, nearly all chief prosecutors are elected, most for four-year terms. Like other incumbent officeholders, prosecutors generally win re-election, but occasionally they lose their positions because of dissatisfaction with their performance.

Some assistant prosecutors make a career of prosecution, but others take this position shortly after graduation from law school and move on to private practice after a few years. Because of this initial inexperience and fairly rapid turnover, at any given time a significant proportion of prosecutors are still in the process of learning their jobs. But the large numbers of cases they handle reduce the time required to develop expertise.

Like judges, prosecutors make important decisions at several stages in the processing of criminal cases. Initially, they decide which cases will go to court and on what charges. Prosecutors present the government's case throughout the pretrial and trial stages, and they also reach plea bargains with defendants. Finally, if defendants are convicted, the prosecutor's recommendation usually influences the judge's sentencing decision, and that recommendation is often the primary influence on the sentence.

Thus prosecutors have a good deal of power over the outcomes of potential and actual criminal cases. It is probably true that in most courts the prosecutor is even more important than the judge. The growing use of rules that restrict judges' discretion over sentencing further strengthened prosecutors. "Over the past 15 to 20 years," a commentator wrote in 2000, "there has been a tremendous shift in power . . . from judges to prosecutors."[10]

Defense Attorneys   In the most minor cases, such as those involving routine traffic offenses, a defendant is unlikely to have an attorney. But defense attorneys are

EXHIBIT 6.1   A Defense Lawyer Finds a Crucial Piece of Evidence

In 2003, Los Angeles police arrested Juan Catalan for murder, and he was jailed prior to trial. Catalan asked to take a lie-detector test, but the police refused. He said that he had been at Dodger Stadium watching a baseball game with his six-year-old daughter when the murder took place, but the police did not accept his alibi.

Catalan's attorney Todd Melnik tried to find direct evidence for that alibi. He obtained videotapes of the game from the Dodgers and the television network that broadcast the game, but he could not locate a clear picture of Catalan. However, he discovered that on the night of the murder, the HBO series "Curb Your Enthusiasm" had shot scenes at the stadium, and the show's star and co-executive producer Larry David allowed Melnik to watch all the footage that had been shot at the stadium. Melnik found two pictures of Catalan at the stadium for which he could pinpoint the time. He also found cell-phone records which showed that Catalan had taken calls in or near the stadium at the time when the murder was committed.

When presented with this evidence at Catalan's preliminary hearing, the judge dismissed the case and released Catalan from jail after more than five months. Larry David said, "I tell people that I've now done one decent thing in my life, albeit inadvertently."

Source: Jeffrey Toobin, "Face in the Crowd," *The New Yorker*, June 7, 2004, 34–36.

generally present in more serious cases. Defense attorneys have less power than judges and prosecutors. But they automatically exert an impact as the representatives of defendants in plea bargaining and in court.

Defense attorneys can be put into three categories: public defenders, private attorneys paid by their clients, and private attorneys who are assigned and paid by courts to represent indigent defendants. Public defenders share several characteristics with prosecutors. They generally work out of local offices, which are part of statewide systems in some states. Some public defenders are full-time, others part-time. Like assistant prosecutors, many public defenders move on to private practice after a few years.

Some private attorneys handle criminal cases only occasionally, while others spend much or even most of their time in the criminal field. A small proportion of the lawyers who do substantial work in criminal defense are both prosperous and well regarded, but the income and standing of defense attorneys as a group are relatively low. In a survey of Chicago lawyers, criminal defense ranked thirty-first in prestige among forty-two categories. (Prosecution ranked nineteenth.)[11] And victories are not plentiful: the overwhelming majority of defendants are convicted or plead guilty. One Washington, D.C., lawyer reported that "if you win three times in a year, people hear about you."[12] Exhibit 6.1 describes one pretrial victory that garnered publicity for a defense lawyer.

Other Court Personnel   Other people in the courts also influence the handling of cases. Courtroom clerks schedule and arrange cases, and their decisions can affect the disposition of cases by giving one side a tactical advantage. Parajudges such as magistrates sometimes act in place of judges, usually in minor cases and in the preliminary stages of other cases.

Probation officers supervise convicted defendants who have been given probation rather than a prison sentence. Within the court, they produce presentence reports that judges use in sentencing decisions.

Defendants   Defendants occupy the most ambiguous position of all the participants in criminal cases. Although defendants must approve their lawyers' decisions, they stand outside the core work group of the court. As a result, they may have only limited impact on the course of events in their cases. Depending on the extent of their prior experience with the criminal courts, they may have considerable expertise in the workings of the courts, or they may be heavily dependent on their lawyer's expertise.

Beyond responding to their lawyers' advice, defendants affect the course of cases through their testimony, if they appear as witnesses, and through their behavior in court proceedings. Their impact is most obvious when they make bad choices. A Pennsylvania defendant charged with drunk driving appeared at his trial in a highly drunken state.[13] A Missouri defendant charged with theft stole the gavel of her trial judge.[14]

Defendants are far from a random sample of the population. Most have low incomes: at least in felony cases in large counties, the great majority have lawyers from programs to serve indigent defendants.[15] Most have limited educations as well. Defendants are disproportionately male and members of racial minority groups.[16]

The Prosecutor's Clients   In the abstract, the prosecutor's clients are the government and the citizenry as a whole. But prosecutors have two more direct clients: law enforcement agencies and the people who bring complaints of crimes. Since police departments and other agencies make the arrests that allow criminal prosecutions, prosecutors' activities depend on the kinds of arrests police make. Prosecutors also depend on the quality of the evidence police gather, which has considerable effect on the strength of cases in court. Law enforcement officers often are important witnesses in court as well. And they serve as a significant audience for the criminal courts, an audience that exerts direct and indirect pressure against leniency toward defendants.

People who make criminal complaints are generally the victims of the crimes involved. Prosecutors depend on their cooperation to make effective cases against defendants, yet victims traditionally have been excluded from decisions about the handling and disposition of their cases. In recent years, however, the federal government and most states have changed their laws to give victims more extensive rights to participate in cases. Most states now allow a victim to make a statement, usually in writing, at a sentencing hearing. Several require consultation with the victim in the plea bargaining process. A 2004 statute gives a broad set of rights to crime victims in federal cases.

Witnesses and Jurors   In general, law enforcement officers and complainants are the most important witnesses in trials. Of course, other people also serve as witnesses. They are not given a high priority in the concerns of courtroom professionals, who often fail to inform them about what they need to do. They may appear in court only to find cases postponed, and repeated postponements can discourage them from reappearing—which is often the goal of the defense attorney who seeks postponements.

Two sets of jurors, members of *grand juries* and *petit*, or *trial, juries*, take part in criminal cases. Both are selected from the general population. Trial jurors (and in most states, grand jurors) are chosen through methods intended to produce a fairly representative cross section of the public; typically, they are drawn from lists of people who are registered to vote or who hold driver's licenses. The reluctance of many people to undertake jury service has sometimes made it difficult to assemble jury pools. In places such as Miami and Los Angeles, only a small minority of the people called for jury service respond and appear for duty.[17] A Michigan juror actually failed to return for the second day of a trial, and a Cincinnati juror left for vacation in the middle of deliberations. The judges in their cases sentenced both to short terms in jail.[18]

Grand juries exist in the federal system and in most states to determine whether there is sufficient evidence to indict a defendant and thus bring the defendant to trial. Unlike trial juries, they sit continuously for a substantial period of time and hear large numbers of cases. They have little independent power, because they are guided through cases by the prosecutor and nearly always follow the prosecutor's recommendations. In 2003 a Cleveland grand jury issued a report that cited pressures from prosecutors to indict defendants. Because prosecutors indicated that cases rejected by this grand jury could be brought to a different grand jury, the report said the jurors got the impression that their role "was strictly a token one."[19] Typically, defendants do not testify before grand juries because doing so might weaken their cases at trial. But in New York City in recent years, some defense attorneys have allowed their clients to testify before the grand jury, occasionally winning a decision not to indict.[20] Grand jury proceedings are supposed to be confidential. As Exhibit 6.2 illustrates, the issue of confidentiality has led to several controversies in recent years.

Trial juries have more impact on the outcomes of cases. In the cases that actually go to jury trials, the jury decides whether to convict the defendant and, in some states, determines the sentence for a defendant it finds guilty. Only a small proportion of criminal cases culminate in jury trials, but the handling of other cases is affected by predictions of jurors' potential behavior. For instance, if a jury would be unlikely to convict a particular defendant, the prosecutor might be inclined to drop the case or offer a relatively favorable plea bargain.

Criminal Courts and Their Environments   The judges and attorneys who handle criminal cases have considerable freedom to act on the basis of their own goals and interests. One reflection of that freedom is their continued use of plea bargaining despite its unpopularity. But by no means are criminal courts entirely free from external influences.

These influences generally favor severity toward criminal defendants. In a 2002 national survey, respondents were asked: "In general, do you think the courts in this area deal too harshly or not harshly enough with criminals?" Altogether, 9 percent

EXHIBIT 6.2   Three Grand Juries and the Rule of Secrecy

Grand juries meet in private, and under the law their proceedings are supposed to remain secret. This requirement of secrecy and breaches of that requirement have come into play in two well-publicized cases.

Between 2004 and 2006 two reporters for the *San Francisco Chronicle* published a series of articles and then a book about the alleged use of steroids by Barry Bonds of the San Francisco Giants and other athletes. The reporters drew on an array of sources, including the testimony of Bonds and other people before a federal grand jury in 2003. The story garnered enormous publicity, largely because of Bonds's celebrity.

In 2006 another federal grand jury investigated the leaks of testimony from the earlier grand jury. The two reporters received subpoenas to testify about the sources of their information. Prosecutors argued that other evidence had not led to those sources and that they needed the reporters' testimony to determine who had violated the law. The reporters and their attorneys argued that reporters have legal protections against disclosure of their sources that should allow them to refuse to testify. In 2006 a federal district judge held the reporters and the *Chronicle* in contempt and ordered that the reporters be jailed if they did not reveal their source and their appeal failed. But in 2007 their source came forward, so there was no longer any need for their testimony.

In 1989 a federal grand jury was convened to investigate suspected environmental crimes at the Rocky Flats Nuclear Weapons Plant in Colorado. The grand jury served for three years, until federal prosecutors reached a plea bargain with the operator of Rocky Flats, Rockwell International Corporation.

Shortly before the final plea agreement was reached, the grand jury—acting on its own—submitted to the district court a report of its findings along with proposed indictments of people working for Rockwell and the federal Department of Energy. The U.S. Attorney rejected the proposed indictments. The grand jurors were unhappy with what they saw as lenient treatment of wrongdoers, and they wanted to make their report public, but a district judge allowed release of only a limited version. Under federal rules of criminal procedure, the grand jurors themselves were prohibited from disclosing what they had learned. Some of the jurors battled in the courts and elsewhere to win the right to disclose that information. In 2006 they won a favorable ruling on a procedural issue in a federal court of appeals, but fourteen years after their work ended they were still a long way from winning the right to tell what they had learned.

Sources: Newspaper articles; *In re: Special Grand Jury 89-2*, 450 F.3d 1159 (10th Cir. 2006).

thought that the courts were too harsh, 67 percent not harsh enough. That 67–9 margin was actually narrower than it had been—in 1994, it was 85–3—perhaps because the trend toward increasingly severe sentences became clear to some people.[21]

As discussed in Chapter 5, criticism of judges for perceived leniency creates pressures that affect some judges' choices. Judges may feel more specific pressures in their handling of one type of criminal offense or even their treatment of a specific defendant. Occasionally, those pressures favor leniency rather than rigor. For instance, community attitudes may foster judicial sympathy for a popular defendant.

A Summary of Court Procedures

Criminal courts operate under laws and rules that establish a series of formal procedures for the handling of cases. These procedures serve as a framework for court action, but that action is also shaped by informal procedures and routines. Thus both the formal procedures and the ways they operate in practice are important.

Formal Procedures   Formal criminal court procedures differ a good deal among states and individual courts, and even within a court different cases are often subject to different procedures. But it is possible to provide a broad description of the stages through which cases usually go.[22] Exhibit 6.3 summarizes a typical set of procedures for felony cases.

Felony cases usually begin with an arrest by the police. This arrest can be based on an individual's formal complaint, on a warrant (an authorization to arrest that is issued by a judge to the police), or on police observation of a possible crime. After the arrest, a complaint against the defendant is filed with the court.

The suspect then makes an initial appearance in court. At the initial appearance, the suspect is informed of the criminal charges and of the applicable procedural rights. Counsel is generally appointed for an indigent defendant at this stage. If required, bail is set. This appearance is sometimes called an arraignment, a label that creates confusion because another procedure with that label comes later in the process.

At the preliminary hearing or preliminary examination, the prosecution must show probable cause to believe that the defendant committed the crime indicated by the charge. To do so, the prosecutor presents evidence that the defense may then contest. If the judge finds probable cause, the defendant is held for further proceedings.

In federal court and in the states that use the grand jury, the prosecutor then presents evidence to that body. On the basis of this evidence, the grand jury decides whether to indict the defendant and on what charges. In states that do not use grand juries, the prosecutor simply files what is called an information, attesting that there is sufficient evidence to try the defendant.

EXHIBIT 6.3   Typical Major Stages of Formal Action in Felony Cases

1. Arrest and booking
2. Filing of a complaint
3. Initial appearance by the defendant in court
4. Preliminary hearing or examination
5. Grand jury indictment or filing of information by the prosecutor
6. Arraignment of the defendant
7. Procedures to prepare the case for trial: discovery, motions, conference
8. Trial
9. Verdict
10. Sentencing (if the defendant has been found guilty)

In states where the early stages of felony cases are handled in a minor trial court, the case now moves into a major court. The next stage is arraignment, at which the defendant is formally presented with the charge or charges. The defendant enters a plea to the charge.

After the arraignment, several procedures are used to prepare the case for trial. Discovery allows the defendant to examine the prosecution's evidence. If the defendant does so, the prosecutor may examine evidence held by the defense. In the federal courts and in some states, either side or the judge may initiate a pretrial conference to clarify the issues. The prosecution and defense can also make pretrial motions. For example, the defense may move to suppress evidence on the ground that the police obtained it illegally.

The last three stages of court action are the most familiar. At the trial, both sides present evidence and arguments on the issue of the defendant's guilt. When the trial has ended, the judge or jury reaches a verdict, convicting or acquitting the defendant or, in some instances, convicting on some charges and acquitting on others. After the verdict, if the defendant is found guilty, the judge or jury (usually the judge) chooses a sentence.

During a trial, the judge may intervene by granting a defense motion for acquittal on the ground that the evidence is insufficient to sustain a conviction. After the trial, on such a motion, the judge may override a conviction by the jury. (A judge cannot override a jury acquittal.) After a conviction, the judge may grant a defense motion for a new trial on the ground that the original trial was seriously flawed.

The formal procedures for misdemeanors are simpler than those for felonies. Grand juries are not used, and other pretrial stages such as the preliminary hearing are often omitted. For relatively minor misdemeanors, states may dispense with the right to a jury trial.

The premise that juvenile offenders should be treated rather than punished led to some important differences between juvenile and adult courts. In general, juvenile courts were intended to be governed less fully by formal rules and procedures. Juvenile courts remain less formal than adult courts today. But this difference has been narrowed, in part because of a 1967 Supreme Court decision that gave juvenile defendants most of the procedural rights granted to adults under the Constitution.[23]

Court Procedures in Practice   As noted earlier, this description of formal procedures gives only a partial picture of how cases are actually processed. Several aspects of case processing in practice merit emphasis.

First, cases go through a winnowing process, in which most drop out at some point between arrest and trial. This winnowing occurs in several ways. Early on, some cases are eliminated through a prosecutor's decision not to file charges, a decision that can occur at any of several stages in the set of procedures I have described. After charges are filed, a case may be dismissed by the judge, often at the instigation of a prosecutor. Alternatively, cases may be diverted to some kind of treatment or rehabilitation program, or adjudication of a case can be deferred (meaning that the case will be dismissed at a later time if the defendant meets certain conditions). Finally, defendants may plead guilty, so that no trial is necessary. These cases do not actually drop out, since sentencing still occurs, but a guilty plea has the effect of telescoping the proceedings and terminating cases early.

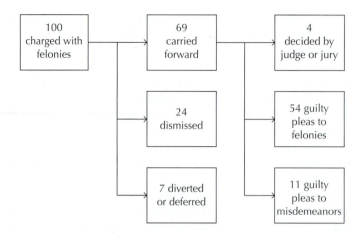

FIGURE 6.1   Outcomes of Cases for Defendants with Felony Charges at Arrest in the 75 Largest U.S. Counties, 2002, per 100 Defendants

Source: Thomas H. Cohen and Brian A. Reaves, *Felony Defendants in Large Urban Counties, 2002* (Washington, D.C.: U.S. Department of Justice, 2006), 24.

Starting with cases in which prosecutors actually have brought charges, Figure 6.1 shows the other forms of winnowing in felony cases in the state courts of large cities. As the figure shows, only a small proportion of cases with felony charges actually result in trials. The same is true in federal court. The proportion of misdemeanor cases going to trial is even lower. Trials were always the exception to the rule, but they have become even less common in the past three decades. A study of thirteen states found that 9 percent of all felony cases went to trial in 1976; by 2002, that proportion had fallen to 3 percent.[24]

A second important aspect of court procedure in practice is the frequent bypassing or abbreviation of the prescribed procedures. Even defendants who plead not guilty may waive some preliminary procedures, such as the pretrial hearing and the grand jury's consideration of indictment. Just as important, formal procedures may be undertaken with far more speed and less care than the rules would suggest. The most extreme abbreviation occurs in busy misdemeanor courts, which often carry out their business so rapidly that the formal stages are virtually unrecognizable.

A third important procedural matter is the length of time between an arrest and the final disposition of a case. Criminal courts have both legal and practical reasons to keep this time short. The Constitution guarantees the right to a speedy trial, and Congress and many state legislatures have backed this right by setting limits on the time for disposition of cases. Delay also penalizes defendants who are jailed prior to trial. At the same time, delay often makes convictions more difficult as witnesses become unavailable or their memories fade.

Judges and prosecutors generally succeed in completing cases within a reasonable time. In the seventy-five largest counties in 2002, the median length of time to dispose of cases with felony charges was 98 days, and 87 percent were completed within a year.[25] But that accomplishment comes at a cost: because of the pressure to dispose of cases in a reasonable time, some defendants are not charged, others have their cases dismissed or diverted, and plea bargains are made and accepted. Thus this pressure has a pervasive effect on criminal courts.

BRINGING CASES TO COURT

The large volume of criminal cases in many courts obscures a very important reality: only a small fraction of the cases that might be brought to court actually get there and last beyond the earliest stages of court action. The reasons for this phenomenon lie chiefly in the domains of the police and of prosecutors.

The Police: Making Arrests

Relatively few crimes result in arrests. A three-state study estimated probabilities of arrest that ranged from about one in four for aggravated assaults to about one in a thousand for drug deals.[26]

Most criminal offenses do not result in arrests simply because there is no opportunity to make them: the police cannot detect a crime or cannot apprehend a likely suspect. Unless a crime is committed in the presence of a police officer, law enforcement agencies must rely on others to inform them of it. But even when crimes involve great injury, victims often do not make complaints to the police. A national survey in 2004 found that only about 40 percent of all victims reported crimes to the police, with reporting rates generally highest for the most serious crimes.[27] For crimes that have no direct victims, such as drug sales and highway speeding, the rate of reports to police is very low. Thus only through active surveillance can the police detect these kinds of offenses.

Even when the police are aware of an offense, they cannot always apprehend a suspect. When an officer observes a crime directly or when a complainant singles out a suspect who is easily located, the task is easy. But in other cases, it is often much more difficult to identify a suspect. And even when a suspect is known, police officers may lack the time to locate the suspect and make an arrest. For the most serious criminal offenses in 2004, the proportion of offenses known to the police that were "cleared" through an arrest was only 20 percent; the clearance rate was 46 percent for violent crimes, 16 percent for property crimes.[28]

When police officers identify a likely suspect, they generally make an arrest. Indeed, they often have reasons to do so even when a conviction is far from certain. For example, an arrest may seem an appropriate way to deal with an immediate problem, such as a fight, or it may allay public concern about a well-publicized crime. And police departments and individual officers are judged in part by the volume of arrests they make and the proportion of crimes they clear through arrests.

Yet there are also reasons not to make every possible arrest. Police resources are often stretched thin, so officers may choose not to arrest suspects in cases that appear to be trivial. Resources aside, an officer may conclude that an arrest in a particular situation is not the best action to take. The ability to make these judgments gives the police considerable discretion. In turn, discretion creates power. Arrest in itself constitutes a kind of punishment, and it can lead to additional punishments in the criminal justice system. By the same token, a decision not to arrest ordinarily leaves a person free from possible punishment.

The Prosecutor: Charging Decisions

When a case comes to the attention of prosecutors, usually through an arrest, they must decide whether to carry the case forward or drop it. There are several points at which a prosecutor can make such a decision. In what is probably the most common pattern, prosecutors do most of their screening when they decide whether to file charges against someone who has been arrested. But in some places the police file felony charges themselves, and prosecutors then decide whether to maintain those cases in court or to dismiss them. For convenience, I refer to the prosecutor's screening of cases as the charging decision, though the screening may actually come at a later point.

The prosecutor has more choices than simply charging the suspect or dropping the case. If a suspect is to be charged, the prosecutor must also decide what charges to bring. The prosecutor may also take action other than criminal prosecution. For instance, in some cases it may seem preferable to institute a civil case against a suspect. The proportion of cases in which prosecutors make and carry forward charges varies from place to place, but in most courts prosecutors screen out a high proportion of the cases that are brought to them.

Choices about whether to carry cases forward, like arrest decisions, are made in the context of limited resources. Few if any prosecutors' offices have sufficient personnel and other resources to take every case that comes to them. Many are heavily overburdened. The effect of resource limitations is to tighten the standards for charging suspects. Cases that might not appear trivial in the abstract may be treated as trivial in light of competing demands in the prosecutor's office.

Criteria for Charging Decisions   The charging decisions of prosecutors are based on many criteria, which can be classified in various ways.[29] A few criteria are especially important.

The first is the *likelihood of conviction*, a criterion that rests primarily on the quality of the prosecutor's evidence. To take a case to trial and then lose it constitutes a waste of time and effort. And because prosecution puts heavy burdens on a defendant, a decision to prosecute someone who will probably be acquitted often seems unfair. Further, defeats in court hurt prosecutors by lowering the winning percentage of both individual prosecutors and their offices. Defeats also weaken the prosecutor's position in plea bargaining with defense attorneys.

Studies consistently show that weak evidence is the most common reason for dropping cases.[30] These studies also show that conviction may be doubtful for any of several reasons. Sometimes it is simply uncertain that the defendant committed a crime, but problems may arise even when a prosecutor is confident that the defendant is guilty. A great many dismissals, for instance, result from the withdrawal of a complaint because of the complainant's relationship with the defendant or fear of the defendant. The unwillingness of other witnesses to testify, sometimes because of intimidation, may also weaken the case against a defendant. And since prosecutors are more concerned with the likelihood of a conviction than with factual guilt, a case is unlikely to go forward without a cooperative complainant and needed witnesses.

This criterion helps to create an unofficial presumption of guilt in the minds of most people in the criminal courts. Knowing that prosecutors generally reject weak cases, judges and even defense attorneys often assume that if the prosecutor has chosen to carry a case forward, the defendant is probably guilty and is likely to be convicted if the case goes to trial. This presumption affects the ways that cases are perceived and handled at later stages, especially in plea bargaining.

The second criterion can be called *policy priorities*. Prosecutors make judgments about the kinds of cases that they see as most important, and those judgments are reflected in decisions whether to bring charges against particular defendants and what charges to bring. Some prosecutors' offices give high priority to drug cases, some to white-collar crime.

At the federal level, U.S. Attorneys across the country differ in their priorities, differences reflected in the charging decisions that their offices make. But they operate under general policies established by the Attorney General and other officials in Washington. For instance, the level of presidents' concern with illegal drugs is reflected in the volume of federal drug prosecutions.[31] In the Bush administration, the Justice Department has given a much higher priority than its predecessors to prosecutions for production and distribution of adult pornography.[32] Disagreements over priorities and other issues are common within prosecutors' offices and between U.S. Attorneys and Justice Department officials in Washington, as illustrated by the episode described in Exhibit 6.4.

Another set of criteria, relating to the situations in individual cases, can be labeled *pragmatic*. There may seem to be little point in charging a suspect who already faces serious charges in another case or another place. The facts of a case (which might suggest that the suspect is not very blameworthy) or the characteristics of a suspect (such as the absence of prior offenses) sometimes suggest that prosecution would be inappropriate. If a case is important to law enforcement officials or the general public, a prosecutor may conclude that the case should be carried forward even though other considerations would argue against bringing charges. The availability of what seem to be appropriate alternatives, such as arranging restitution to the victim or psychiatric treatment for the suspect, may lead prosecutors not to bring charges. When a prosecutor concludes that a felony charge is not justified, one option is to bring a misdemeanor charge that subjects the suspect to more limited sanctions. Where misdemeanors are prosecuted by another office, choosing that option also reduces the prosecutor's workload.

Charging Decisions and the Power of Prosecutors   Just as discretion in arrest decisions gives power to the police, so too does a similar discretion in charging decisions give power to prosecutors. Of course, this power affects the fates of individual suspects. More broadly, by establishing and applying criteria for charging suspects, prosecutors in effect rewrite the criminal law.

At the broadest level, prosecutors reshape the law with their treatment of various crimes. They elevate the importance of certain offenses by prosecuting those offenses

EXHIBIT 6.4   A U.S. Attorney Makes Waves

In September 2001, Thomas DiBiagio became U.S. Attorney for Maryland. Responding to the recent terrorist attacks, officials in the Department of Justice said that federal prosecutors should give terrorism the highest priority. But DiBiagio indicated that he had different priorities, among them corruption by public officials.

During his tenure DiBiagio took other actions that underlined his independence from his superiors in the Justice Department. He did not appear at some meetings in the Department. At one meeting, while Attorney General John Ashcroft was speaking, DiBiagio said that he had "work to do" and left. Meanwhile, DiBiagio's plans and priorities for his office alienated some of his prosecutors.

In July 2004, the *Baltimore Sun* reported messages from DiBiagio to his staff in which he said that he wanted three "front-page" indictments for white-collar crime or public corruption by November and expressed his frustration that "this Office has not convicted an elected official of corruption since 1988." A deputy attorney general announced that any proposed indictments in public corruption cases would have to be submitted to him for review. In November, Justice Department officials interviewed prosecutors in the Maryland office in a special review of DiBiagio's performance, and it was reported that several prosecutors said he should be removed. A month later DiBiagio announced that he was leaving his position. While he cited personal reasons for that decision, it seems likely that his superiors' long-standing unhappiness with him had something to do with that choice. Those superiors may have seized on the controversies in 2004 as a way to solve what they had seen as a problem in Maryland.

Sources: Stories in the *Baltimore Sun* and other newspapers. The quotations are from, in order, Doug Donovan and Laura Sullivan, "Prosecutor Could Face Political, Credibility Issues After Remarks in E-Mail," *Baltimore Sun*, July 16, 2004; and Doug Donovan, "Critics See Confidential Comments as Proof of U.S. Attorney's Political Motives," *Baltimore Sun*, July 15, 2004.

---

aggressively. On the other hand, they can effectively write certain offenses out of the law by choosing not to undertake prosecutions. U.S. Attorneys and state district attorneys sometimes establish official or unofficial policies that they will not prosecute certain minor offenses.

Prosecutors' power is underlined by a special kind of charging decision, whether to seek the death penalty in murder cases. In the Bush administration, Attorney General John Ashcroft (2001–2005) sought to increase the use of capital punishment, and he frequently overrode decisions of U.S. Attorneys not to ask for the death penalty in particular cases.[33] In Maryland, the prosecutor in Baltimore County (which includes suburbs around Baltimore but not the city itself) decided that it was most equitable to seek the death penalty in every case where the facts seemed to fit the legal criteria for that penalty. In contrast, prosecutors in the city of Baltimore and elsewhere were more reluctant to ask for the death penalty. As a result, in 2002 two-thirds of the state's death row inmates were from Baltimore County. The governor declared a one-year moratorium on executions, in part because of what he called "a lottery of jurisdiction."[34]

PLEA BARGAINING

Every criminal defendant must choose whether to plead guilty or not guilty. Typically, at least in serious cases, the defendant initially pleads not guilty. The choice then is whether to change the plea to guilty at some point before trial. (Occasionally, a defendant pleads *nolo contendere*, or no contest. This plea, like a guilty plea, waives the right to trial, but it does not constitute an admission of guilt.)

In most courts, the great majority of felony cases carried forward by the prosecutor are resolved through guilty pleas. This means that convictions generally result from guilty pleas rather than trials. In both the federal courts and state courts in large cities, around 95 percent of all convictions result from guilty pleas rather than trials.[35] Trials are rare in many, perhaps most, misdemeanor courts and even in some felony courts. In one county, according to a former public defender, trials in either felony or misdemeanor cases were "rare and precious events, like Christmas, or one's wedding day, or going off to war."[36]

A defendant may plead guilty for a variety of reasons. In minor cases, for instance, the likely penalty may be so light that it would not be worth the expense and trouble of going to trial. But the most common reason is that the defendant expects to receive a more favorable sentence by pleading guilty rather than being convicted at trial.

This expectation may be based on an explicit agreement in which the defendant is promised benefits related to the sentence in exchange for a guilty plea. Even if there is no explicit agreement, the defendant still may perceive that a guilty plea will produce a more advantageous sentence. This calculation, sometimes called an implicit bargain, is especially common in misdemeanor cases.

We can define plea bargaining to include only explicit bargains or to encompass implicit bargains as well. The question of definition is more than a technical matter, as it affects judgments about whether it is possible to eliminate plea bargaining. I think the broader definition is more appropriate, because a defendant who pleads guilty in the belief that a more favorable sentence will result is in effect making a bargain. When prosecutors and judges give signals that guilty pleas indeed are rewarded, as they often do, it is not just the defendant who perceives that a bargain is occurring.

The practice of plea bargaining affects every aspect of the adjudication of felony cases. The handling of cases in their early stages is influenced by the expectation of bargaining, and the existence of a bargain constrains judges in their sentencing decisions. And the knowledge that a case was *not* settled by a bargain can influence its outcome. Judges, for instance, often impose heavier sentences on defendants who refused to plead guilty and were convicted at trial.

Forms of Plea Bargaining

The implicit bargain represents one form of plea bargaining.[37] Explicit plea bargains take a variety of forms, which can be placed in three categories. The first is the *charge bargain*, in which the prosecutor reduces the defendant's potential sentence liability by reducing the package of charges. This reduction may be horizontal, with the number of multiple charges for an offense such as burglary reduced in exchange for a guilty plea

EXHIBIT 6.5   Creative Plea Bargains in Iowa

In 2004 the *Des Moines Register* reported that in two Iowa counties, defendants in cases involving traffic violations were frequently allowed to plead guilty to having defective "cowl lamps," a piece of automobile equipment that had largely disappeared after the 1930s. In two cases, it turned out, defendants charged with non-traffic offenses—theft and public intoxication—had their charges reduced to cowl lamp violations.

In response to this disclosure, the state supreme court issued a statement asking that "questionable" plea bargains in traffic cases be investigated. In 2005 the court suspended the licenses of two prosecutors, citing a rule of legal ethics that prohibits the filing of criminal charges for which there was no probable cause and other rules that prohibit false statements. The supreme court also found that the two prosecutors had committed a second type of violation: prosecuting defendants whom they also represented in criminal cases.

The *Register* reported another common practice: in some Iowa counties, defendants in serious traffic cases had their charges reduced or the cases dismissed in agreements under which they made monetary contributions to police agencies. The supreme court asked that the statute used to justify this practice be repealed.

Sources: Clark Kauffman and Tom Beaumont, "Court Questions Driver Deals," *Des Moines Register,* February 25, 2004; *Iowa Supreme Court Attorney Disciplinary Board v. Howe*, 706 N.W.2d 360 (Iowa 2005); *Iowa Supreme Court Attorney Disciplinary Board v. Zenor*, 707 N.W.2d 176 (Iowa 2005).

---

to the remaining charges. Or the reduction may be vertical, with the highest charges dropped in exchange for a guilty plea to lesser ones. The latter may be charges already in existence or new ones brought in as substitutes.[38] Reduction of felony charges to a misdemeanor is especially common. Police officers and prosecutors sometimes set the stage for charge bargains by "overcharging" defendants initially—bringing some charges that they have little intention of carrying forward.

Because the defendant's sentence liability is reduced in order to make a guilty plea attractive, the charges to which a defendant pleads guilty may bear little relationship to the original charges or even to the actual offense. Indeed, according to one commentator, "it is no oversimplification to say that courthouse personnel first decide what a defendant's punishment shall be and then hunt around to find a charge that is consistent with their decision."[39] Exhibit 6.5 describes one version of that practice in Iowa.

The second category is the *prosecutor's sentence bargain.* Here the prosecutor gives the defendant some assurance about the sentence that a judge will hand down. Most often, the prosecutor agrees to recommend a particular sentence, with the expectation that the judge will follow that recommendation. The judge is not obliged to do so, and judges sometimes reject bargains where they deem the terms to be inadequate. Some sentence bargains involve less direct concessions by the prosecutor, such as an agreement to make no sentence recommendation or to allow the defendant to go before a lenient judge. In one case a defendant agreed to plead guilty in exchange for a guarantee that he would not be moved from county jail to a state prison facility for a week. He knew from past encounters with the criminal justice system that he could watch television in jail but not in the prison, and he wanted to see an important football game.[40]

The final category is the *judge's sentence bargain.* A judge indicates the likely sentence that would follow a guilty plea, and the defendant pleads guilty on the assumption that this sentence will actually be imposed. This is almost surely the least common form of bargaining in felony cases, and its legitimacy is not fully accepted. For instance, in one case the Massachusetts Supreme Court sought "to remind judges that they are not to participate as active negotiators in plea bargaining discussions."[41] Even so, judicial sentence bargaining flourishes in some places. For instance, one Maryland judge took regular trips to the county jail to resolve cases with guilty pleas.[42]

Multiple forms of bargains sometimes are combined in a particular case. For instance, a prosecutor may reduce the charges against a defendant and offer to recommend a particular sentence in exchange for a guilty plea. Each courthouse community develops its own practices, with different kinds of bargains dominant in different places.

The Bargaining Process

The process of plea bargaining varies as much as its form. Much of that variation stems from the different forms themselves, which determine whether the defendant and defense attorney negotiate primarily with the prosecutor or with the judge—or, in the case of implicit bargaining, reach a decision to plead guilty without any negotiation. Defense attorneys usually bargain on behalf of their clients. In cases involving minor misdemeanors, however, defendants often represent themselves and negotiate or choose to plead guilty on their own. Plea bargaining most often occurs shortly before the trial is scheduled to begin, but it can come earlier or even later. One Virginia murder defendant agreed to a sentence of forty years even while, as it turned out, the jury was in the process of acquitting him.[43]

In each court, routines develop for the initiation and transaction of bargains. In some places, prosecutors "hold court" prior to court sessions in order to negotiate with attorneys who have cases scheduled for trial that day. Some courts use pretrial conferences as a forum for bargaining. But bargaining is not necessarily restricted to a single point in the proceedings; the two sides may negotiate at several points along the way to trial until they reach a mutually acceptable result.[44]

To a considerable extent, there is also a routine to the *terms* of plea bargains. Members of the courtroom work group become accustomed to the most common forms of particular offenses, such as burglary and assault. For these "normal crimes," as one scholar has called them,[45] standard terms of bargains—"going rates"—are likely to develop. These standard terms can then be adjusted for special circumstances in cases.

Both the going rates and the terms of bargains in specific cases reflect multiple factors. One of them is the participants' sense of justice and fairness, as applied to a specific offense and defendant. Perhaps more fundamental is the bargaining power of the participants. Bargaining power rests largely on estimates of what would happen if a case went to trial—the likelihood of conviction and the likely sentence if a defendant is found guilty. But other considerations come into play as well. Among them are the severity of the caseload pressures in the prosecutor's office, the financial incentives of defense attorneys, the negotiation skills of the two sides, and the length of time that a defendant has spent in jail awaiting trial.[46] Federal prosecutors tend to be in strong bargaining positions. Their cases typically are strong, stringent federal sentencing rules provide them with leverage, and they have better resources than many state prosecutors. As a result, when they engage in bargaining, they are in a good position to get the terms they prefer.

Explaining the Prevalence of Plea Bargaining

Not only is plea bargaining prevalent today, it has a long history that extends back to the nineteenth century.[47] Thus it must serve important goals for people in the criminal courts. Observers of the courts disagree on the relative importance of different motivations for plea bargaining, but two broad motivations clearly are dominant: reducing the time required to dispose of cases and achieving outcomes that seem desirable.

Saving Time and Other Resources   One basic motivation for plea bargaining is the desire of lawyers and judges to save time. Time is required to reach bargains and ratify them in court, but trials ordinarily require even more time—especially jury trials in serious cases. This difference is fundamental to plea bargaining. Indeed, historical research suggests that bargaining became popular partly because trials became more time consuming. Growing caseloads were also a factor. For example, the large flow of cases involving liquor offenses during Prohibition in the 1920s helped to increase the reliance of federal courts on guilty pleas.[48]

Judges and full-time prosecutors and public defenders gain obvious advantages from reducing the time required to dispose of cases. Plea bargaining allows them to work shorter days, handle more cases in the same workday, or achieve some combination of the two.

Private defense attorneys and part-time prosecutors gain financially from speedy disposal of cases. The less time that part-time prosecutors devote to their public duties, the more they can devote to their private practices. For private defense attorneys, quick turnover of cases is the most profitable mode of practice. Ordinarily, the attorney's fee—whether paid by the client or by the court—will not increase enough to pay for the extra time required to try a case rather than avoid trial through a guilty plea.

Where there are heavy caseload pressures on judges, prosecutors, and public defenders, the incentive to dispose of cases quickly is especially strong. Indeed, in many cities it would be impossible to hold full-scale trials in more than a small proportion of cases. As a result, plea bargaining, or some equivalent, is necessary to avoid complete chaos. In Manhattan, one judge said, "We go to plea bargaining out of necessity, not out of desire. It is inescapable."[49] But an interest in speed is not confined to courts with burdensome caseloads. As one scholar put it, "regardless of caseload, there will always be *too many cases* for many of the participants in the system, since most of them have a strong interest in being some place other than in court."[50]

Not only do trials require more time than guilty pleas, they require more effort. Attorneys and judges work much harder in trying cases than they do in resolving cases through bargains. Understandably, many lawyers and judges prefer the easier route to the more difficult one, whether their workloads are light or heavy. This is one reason why plea bargaining exists even in courts where caseload pressures are relatively light.

Achieving Desirable Results   For its participants, plea bargaining serves purposes that go beyond speed. Most important, plea bargains are a means for both the prosecution and the defense to secure acceptable results in cases and eliminate the possibility of highly undesirable outcomes.

In a plea bargain, the prosecutor gains a guaranteed conviction. Any case that goes to court carries at least a small risk of an acquittal, and some carry a substantial risk. By eliminating this risk, a plea bargain helps to build high winning percentages for the individual prosecutor and the prosecutor's office. By reaching bargains and helping to set their terms, prosecutors can also bring about what they see as the appropriate level of sanctions for defendants. In many cases, prosecutors gain the testimony of one defendant against another defendant who is more important to them.

On the other side, the defense attorney and the defendant get what they perceive as advantages in sentencing. Virtually all participants in the criminal courts assume that, all else being equal, a defendant who pleads guilty will receive a lighter sentence than one who has been convicted at trial. Pointing out that large numbers of jury trials would overwhelm the resources of the criminal courts in Chicago, one observer described how judges deal with that problem: "The simple solution: make the defendant pay for a trial. Not with money, of course, but with a stiffer sentence if he rolls the dice and loses. The trial tax is as much a part of the courthouse as its limestone columns."[51] Some judges readily acknowledge this policy. As one Chicago judge remarked of a defendant who might go to trial, "He takes some of my time— I take some of his."[52]

Perhaps because they are uncomfortable with the idea of a trial tax, some judges adopt another rationale for giving lighter sentences to defendants who plead guilty: those defendants have taken responsibility for their offenses rather than hoping for a lucky acquittal. The defendant who has good reason to go to trial may not be punished, but others can expect to pay for their trials. As one Pennsylvania judge put it, "I don't mind worthwhile trials, where there's actually some question about what happened—then I get to feel like a real judge. But some people are just jerking around the system. You can't have that. It's not really a penalty for the trial, it's more that they've abused the system. . . ."[53]

It is difficult to measure the advantage that defendants gain from pleading guilty, because the cases resolved with guilty pleas are not fully comparable with those that go to trial. But it does appear that defendants who plead guilty are rewarded at sentencing—at least in comparison with defendants who are convicted in jury (rather than bench) trials—and this advantage may be quite substantial.[54] In any event, a plea bargain generally eliminates the risk that a judge will hand down an unusually heavy sentence. One reason for the decline in the proportion of cases that go to trial is that the tough sentencing laws enacted in the past three decades increase the risk of going to trial.[55] When a bargain ensures that a defendant will not go to prison, this assurance is especially attractive. And since defense attorneys believe that the great majority of defendants would have little chance of victory at trial, pleading guilty in exchange for a sentencing benefit typically appears to be an excellent bargain.

Because defense attorneys have multiple reasons to resolve cases through plea bargains, there is a risk that they will induce clients to accept bargains that are not in their best interests. Attorneys tend to emphasize the advantages of guilty pleas; one public defender tells "my clients they can have a trial, but they have to understand they are gambling with their lives, and the state has two dice and they have one."[56] Defense attorneys may put considerable pressure on clients to plead guilty, in part because they assume that defendants *are* guilty. An innocent defendant, such as the Ohio man who was mistakenly linked with warrants for someone with a similar name, may encounter an attorney who simply tells him to plead guilty.[57] Yet defendants often are quite willing, even eager, to plead guilty. Like their attorneys, most defendants think they will be convicted if they go to trial, so the more lenient sentence to be gained from a guilty plea usually looks attractive to them.

The Impact of the Work Group   As already noted, the people who make up the core of the courtroom work group—attorneys and judges—tend to develop close working relationships through their constant interaction and interdependence. Indeed, as one lawyer observed of public defenders and prosecutors, "It's like prison guards and prisoners: They're all locked in together."[58] Plea bargaining is facilitated by these relationships, which foster the development of regular bargaining procedures and tacit understandings about feasible terms under particular circumstances.[59]

The interdependence of work group members also strengthens the pressures for plea bargaining. Lawyers and judges who refused to engage in plea bargaining would encounter so much resistance that they could not do their jobs effectively. Further, the general acceptance of plea bargaining as normal and appropriate shapes the thinking of members of the work group who initially question its use.

A lawyer or judge who routinely participates in plea bargaining can still balk at its use in specific cases, but the pressure to make and accept bargains reduces the frequency of that behavior. In a 2004 case a California federal judge said that a bargain between the prosecutor and defense was unduly lenient: "I don't feel that I can go along with the plea agreement." But two months later she accepted the bargain, saying that she had changed her mind. "It does seem," she said, "that the sentence that's proposed by the parties is one that is in line with the evidence that was presented against this defendant."[60] Another case in which a judge questioned a plea bargain had a different ending. In 2002 a federal judge in Buffalo was presented with a plea agreement in a high-profile case that he rejected on the ground "that the public good would not be served" by its acceptance. The judge did not back down, but the case was moved to another federal district, and eight months later a judge in that district accepted the bargain.[61]

Exceptions to the Dominance of Plea Bargaining

Prevalent as plea bargaining is, its dominance is not total. In some courts, a high proportion of cases go to trial; in all courts, some cases go to trial. These phenomena require explanation in light of the strong incentives that exist to avoid trials.

Trials in High-Bargaining Systems Even in courts that rely very heavily on plea bargaining, some felony cases are resolved through trials. Probably the most common reason is a bargaining failure. Where bargains are negotiated between the prosecutor and the defense attorney, as they usually are in felony cases, the two may assess a case so differently that they cannot reach agreement. For instance, they may disagree on the likelihood of conviction or on the weight to be given to any special circumstances. And both sides want to avoid yielding too much to reach a bargain in one case in order to maintain a strong bargaining position in future cases. Sometimes bargaining fails because the defendant refuses to accept the bargain reached by the prosecutor and the defense attorney. Some defendants are innocent, or see themselves as innocent, and balk at admitting guilt; others think the proposed bargain is a bad one.

Some kinds of cases simply do not lend themselves to bargains. Most often these are cases that are viewed as very serious, in terms of the offense and the defendant's prior record. In such cases, even a bargain probably would lead to a lengthy prison term. For this reason the defense may see an advantage in going to trial, even if the chances of acquittal seem slim. For their part, prosecutors in such cases may see no point in offering any concessions to a defendant when a conviction appears to be assured. These considerations help to explain the relative frequency of trials in cases involving serious charges of white-collar crimes. Another factor in these cases is the wealth that defendants such as corporate executives can devote to their defense, allowing them to go to trial despite the heavy monetary costs of doing so.[62]

Some cases go to trial because one or both sides have political goals that are best served by a trial. In trials of defendants with notorious reputations, for instance, the prosecutor may choose not to bargain because a trial will help satisfy public demands for retribution and provide the prosecutor with favorable publicity. And some defendants refuse to bargain because they find trials attractive as forums in which to proclaim their political beliefs and perhaps to gain additional support. Yet, as the example in Exhibit 6.6 indicates, even cases that are highly political in their content often end in plea bargains.

Beyond the characteristics of particular cases, many judges and attorneys get satisfaction from participating in at least occasional trials. It is in trials that they can make best use of their legal skills, and many enjoy the trial setting. A prosecutor or defense attorney who is successful in trials gains a stronger bargaining position in the future. But this is not true of everyone. Some defense lawyers look for opportunities to try cases; others do all they can to avoid them.

High-Trial Systems and the Use of Bench Trials Trials are relatively common in some courts. These have included, in some periods, the felony courts of Los Angeles, Baltimore, Pittsburgh, and Philadelphia. During one period, only 30 to 40 percent of the cases carried forward by Philadelphia prosecutors were resolved by guilty pleas.[63] In each of these cities, however, there were relatively few jury trials; rather, trials were generally conducted before a judge alone.

In general, trials before judges—bench trials—consume much less time than jury trials. For this reason, their frequent use creates less strain on the resources of courts and their participants than would large numbers of jury trials. In at least some courts, bench trials are highly abbreviated. In Chicago, which has high proportions of guilty

EXHIBIT 6.6   The "American Taliban" Reaches a Plea Bargain

In December 2001 it was announced that the United States had imprisoned John Walker Lindh, a twenty-year-old U.S. citizen, in Afghanistan. According to the U.S. government, Lindh had been fighting with the Taliban forces with which the U.S. fought there. Early in 2002, Lindh was charged with ten criminal counts that included conspiracy to kill U.S. citizens abroad, providing support to terrorist organizations, and engaging in prohibited transactions with the Taliban regime. If convicted, he could be sentenced to life in prison.

The administration seemed eager to try Lindh, and his primary defense lawyer was explicit about his own eagerness: "Don't miss this trial. Be there." In February, the trial date was set for August.

Then, in July, Lindh pled guilty to two charges in exchange for the dropping of the other charges and a recommendation of a twenty-year sentence. The judge accepted that recommendation, and the case ended.

The timing of the plea bargain was significant. The judge had not yet ruled on whether incriminating statements that Lindh had made while in U.S. custody could be introduced at his trial. It appeared that the judge would allow the admission of those statements, but that outcome was not guaranteed, and a ruling against the government would weaken its case considerably. Further, a trial might show that Lindh had been treated badly in custody and that he had been a less serious threat than the government originally said after his capture. For Lindh, the bargain required him to serve a long sentence but one well short of the life sentence that was a serious possibility if he was convicted at trial.

Thus, both sides decided that they would be better off avoiding the gamble of a trial. As one headline put it, it was an "ordinary outcome for an extremely odd court case."

Sources: Newspaper stories. The quotations are from, respectively, Katherine Q. Seelye, "American Charged as a Terrorist Makes First Appearance in Court," *New York Times*, January 25, 2002, A1; and Reynolds Holding, "Ordinary Outcome for an Extremely Odd Court Case," *San Francisco Chronicle*, July 16, 2002, A1.

pleas, judges use what is called a stipulated bench trial in other cases. As one reporter observed, these "stip benches"

> are Cliff's Notes versions of real trials. They're usually conducted when the state won't reduce a charge that the judge thinks should be reduced. The two sides go through the motions of a trial as rapidly as possible, substituting for actual testimony the capsule stipulations of what they believe witnesses would say. . . . The judge informs the defendant of the result ahead of time. "Verdict and sentence first—trial afterward," the Queen of Hearts might say.[64]

In Chicago, as in some cities that rely more heavily on bench trials, such a trial is sometimes called a "slow plea of guilty."[65] On the other hand, a scholar who studied bench trials in Philadelphia concluded that they generally were "real" trials in which the defense made a significant effort to secure acquittal.[66] But most bench trials in Philadelphia were brief, not much more time consuming than cases with guilty pleas.

And in Philadelphia, as in some other cities, judges usually gave defendants who were convicted at jury trials much heavier sentences than they gave those who pled guilty or chose bench trials.[67] Observers might disagree about just how "real" bench trials were in Philadelphia, but it seems clear that the Philadelphia court could operate with a relatively limited reliance on guilty pleas only by using speedy bench trials and largely avoiding jury trials.

Attacks on Plea Bargaining

Some participants and observers of criminal courts defend the regular use of plea bargaining. For some of its defenders, plea bargaining is simply a necessity: the system could not function without plea bargains as a means to avoid full-scale trials. Others take a more positive view, depicting bargains as a rational and desirable way to resolve criminal cases. According to one scholar, "Plea bargaining is our predominant method of concluding criminal cases because it is fair and just; happily, it also increases court efficiency."[68]

But defenders of plea bargaining are in the minority, and some of the opponents express their opposition in strong terms. "There is no glory in plea bargaining," writes one law professor. "In place of a noble clash for truth, plea bargaining gives us a skulking truce."[69] The many critics of widespread bargaining rest their criticisms on different premises. Some oppose it on principle as a departure from the formal model of criminal procedure. As they see it, trials are the fairest means to resolve criminal cases and the best way to reach an appropriate result.

A related argument is that plea bargaining victimizes defendants. In the view of some observers, lawyers and judges put heavy pressure on defendants to give up their fundamental rights and accept bargains. Innocent people are sometimes pressured to plead guilty. But whether they are innocent or guilty, defendants who might be acquitted at trial give up that chance in favor of a bargain that may not be advantageous. In 2004 a California appellate court ruled that a defendant should be allowed to withdraw his guilty plea on the ground that the trial judge had unduly pressured the defendant to give up his right to trial: "when the trial court abandons its judicial role and thrusts itself to the center of the negotiation process and makes repeated comments that suggest a less-than-neutral attitude about the case or the defendant, then great pressure exists for the defendant to accede to the court's wishes."[70] But it is rare for defendants to appeal in such cases; far more often, they accede to such pressure from judges, prosecutors, or their own attorneys.

The most common criticism, however, is that plea bargaining allows criminals to escape full punishment. In this view, prosecutors and judges weaken the criminal law by reducing sentences in exchange for guilty pleas. The law loses some of its deterrent effect because the cost of committing a crime is reduced, and the victim and the community are deprived of adequate retribution for criminal acts.

Primarily because of concern about excessive leniency, efforts have been made in several places to limit the use of plea bargaining. In the 1990s, the district attorney in one borough of New York City prohibited charge bargaining after indictment; the district attorney in another borough said he would stop bargaining with people who were charged with certain gun offenses; and the governing body of the New Jersey courts prohibited judges from accepting plea bargains after the pretrial conference under most circumstances.[71] Dick Thornburgh, attorney general under President Reagan and the first President Bush, issued guidelines to U.S. Attorneys to limit their participation in plea bargaining. Clinton attorney general Janet Reno largely eliminated those limits, but Attorney General John Ashcroft re-established several restrictions on plea bargaining in 2003.[72] In some places, efforts have been made to eliminate plea bargaining altogether. The most noteworthy effort occurred in Alaska, where both the state attorney general (who supervises all prosecutors) and the state supreme court prohibited plea bargaining in the late 1970s.[73]

Our evidence on the effectiveness of these measures is incomplete. But the evidence that does exist depicts a complex reality. It appears that some kinds of prohibitions, if seriously enforced, can substantially reduce the incidence of explicit bargaining. But it is clear that plea bargaining has strong survival powers, because of a combination of two powerful factors: the great incentives that people have to bargain and the means that exist to circumvent prohibitions.

The most extensive evidence exists on the restrictions on plea bargaining adopted by voters in California and on the effort to eliminate it altogether in Alaska. In 1982, California voters approved a ballot proposition that prohibited plea bargaining for any defendant charged with a serious felony "unless there is insufficient evidence to prove the people's case, or testimony of a material witness cannot be obtained, or a reduction or a dismissal would not result in a substantial change in sentence."[74] The provision was presented to voters as a prohibition of plea bargaining.

But the exceptions listed in the provision seemed to provide considerable room to continue plea bargaining. An even bigger exception was more difficult to discern: the provision did not affect plea bargaining prior to indictment or information. Indeed, plea bargaining continued at high rates, and the proportion of felony defendants pleading guilty actually increased from 78 percent in 1982 to 90 percent in 1991.[75] Because of all their incentives to bargain, participants in California criminal cases simply adapted to the new rules rather than reduce their reliance on plea bargaining.

The abolition effort in Alaska achieved partial success.[76] The attorney general's 1975 prohibition of plea bargaining reduced the incidence of explicit bargaining drastically. But high proportions of defendants continued to plead guilty, chiefly because they believed they would receive more severe sentences if they lost at trial. In this sense, explicit plea bargaining was largely replaced by implicit bargaining. Some charge bargaining continued despite the ban, and it became much more common over time. The main reasons for this increase apparently were a reduced commitment to the ban in the attorney general's office and state revenue problems that made the avoidance of trials more attractive. When the attorney general's prohibition on bargaining was rescinded in 1994, one commentator explained that this change was "designed to bring the Department's written policies into line with the actual practices of the last ten years."[77]

Thus it appears that plea bargaining is very difficult to eliminate, especially if we define it to include implicit bargaining. The proportion of cases resolved by bargains *can* be reduced, at least under some circumstances, and some courts operate with relatively low rates of guilty pleas. But at least in courts with heavy caseloads, such low rates seem to require the standard use of short bench trials, which achieve some of the same goals as plea bargaining for lawyers and judges. This fact underlines the lesson that people who participate in criminal courts shape court practices on the basis of their own incentives, and efforts to change these practices must take this reality into account.

CRIMINAL TRIALS

Of all the activities in criminal courts, trials receive by far the most attention. In one sense, this attention is undeserved: only a small proportion of cases are actually tried. Yet trials are an important part of what happens in criminal courts. First of all, many cases do go to trial, and those involving the most serious charges are more likely than others to be tried. Further, trials set standards for other court processes, in that decisions by prosecutors on whether to bring charges and the terms of plea bargains are heavily influenced by estimates of what would happen at trial.

Trials merit attention for another reason as well. Much of the criticism of plea bargaining reflects a belief that trials are a better means to resolve the issue of guilt. But comparison of trials and bargains is often based on an idealized version of the criminal trial. Instead, it needs to be based on trials as they actually operate. For that reason, the central concern of this section is the effectiveness of trials as means to determine guilt and innocence.

The Trial Process

Under the Constitution and Supreme Court decisions, a criminal defendant has the right to a jury trial in cases in which imprisonment of more than six months is possible. Federal courts use twelve-member juries in criminal cases. The great majority of states also require twelve-member juries in felony cases, but about three-quarters allow smaller juries in misdemeanor cases. Most defendants who go to trial in felony cases opt for juries, though the proportion of bench trials varies a good deal from place to place. Bench trials are more common in less serious cases.

In jury trials, the first important step is the selection of jurors. Selection from the jury pool centers on the voir dire, in which either the lawyers or the judge questions prospective jurors about matters deemed relevant to the trial. A lawyer may ask that the judge dismiss a juror for cause if possible bias or incompetence has been established. Each side also has a certain number of peremptory challenges, which are used to dismiss a juror without showing cause. In federal court, the government has six peremptory challenges and the defendant ten in felony cases; each side is allowed three peremptory challenges in misdemeanor cases.

At the start of a jury trial, each attorney may make an opening statement. The prosecutor then presents evidence, primarily through testimony by witnesses; the defense attorney may cross-examine these witnesses. After the prosecution has presented its case, the defense offers its own case in the same manner. Throughout this process, the attorneys may make motions and object to questions or the introduction of other evidence, and the judge rules on these motions. The trial ends with closing arguments by attorneys for each side.

After the closing arguments, the judge instructs the jury on the legal rules that are relevant to the decision. The jury then retires to discuss the case and reach a verdict. In all states except Louisiana and Oregon, a unanimous vote is required in felony cases. Finally, the jury's verdict is announced. If the jury cannot reach a decision, it will be dismissed and a mistrial declared. The prosecutor can then initiate a retrial.

Bench trials are generally simpler, briefer, and less formal than jury trials, primarily because procedures used to select jurors and to aid them in reaching a decision are absent. This difference is highlighted by the extreme example, the speedy bench trials of routine traffic offenses in misdemeanor courts. But with or without a jury, long trials are the exception to the rule. Even in federal court, where trials are relatively formal and lengthy, two-thirds of the trials in 2005 lasted three days or less.[78]

The Effectiveness of Trial Decision Making

How effectively do trials operate to produce correct judgments about guilt or innocence? The concept of a correct judgment requires some discussion. In every case, there is a factual reality and a set of applicable legal rules. Occasionally, the law and the facts combine in such a way that they leave the correct verdict uncertain. But in the great majority of cases, a decision maker who was all-seeing, learned, and objective would invariably reach the correct verdict. The issue here is the extent to which real judges and juries, functioning in real trials, can reach correct verdicts.

Decision Making in Trials   Judges and juries decide cases on the basis of the information they are given. In practice, this information is often both incomplete and inaccurate.

Incomplete information is a widespread problem. Sometimes, what would be valuable evidence does not exist. For instance, there might be no witnesses to a burglary. Evidence that does exist, such as a weapon, may be undiscovered. Witnesses sometimes do not come forward. And even available evidence does not always get to court. Witnesses may fail to appear, and the prosecution or defense may lack the resources to conduct tests on physical evidence.

The evidence introduced in court is not necessarily accurate. This problem is especially clear for witnesses, the primary sources of information in most cases. People's recollection of what they observe is highly imperfect. A witness's identification of a suspect is often the most persuasive evidence for the prosecution, but eyewitness identifications are mistaken a high proportion of the time. Even confessions may be false, sometimes as a result of police coercion.

Physical evidence would seem immune from these problems, but that is not necessarily the case.[79] Despite a widespread belief to the contrary, reading fingerprints is an inexact science. In 2004 an Oregon lawyer was arrested and jailed as a suspect in terrorist bombings in Spain on the basis of the FBI's match of his fingerprint with one found on a piece of evidence, but two weeks later it was determined that the match was an error.[80] In a few instances, repeated errors or false reporting by individuals who work at crime laboratories have infected large numbers of cases.[81]

Thus a judge or juror may be handicapped by inadequate information. Processing that information to reach a verdict adds further difficulties.[82] First of all, jurors and judges are, in effect, the witnesses of trials, and their recollections too may be both incomplete and inaccurate.

The judge or jury must also analyze the evidence to choose the most credible version of the facts. This process is fairly easy in some trials, because there is only one credible version. But in trials where differing interpretations of the facts are possible, the choice may be exceedingly difficult. For instance, assessing the truthfulness of witnesses is often one critical part of the task. Such assessments are highly prone to error. Summarizing the relevant research, one scholar said that "decisions about whether a statement is the truth or a lie are made about as well as if one were tossing a coin."[83] For all these reasons, a judge or jury is likely to do a highly imperfect job of ascertaining the relevant facts. Jerome Frank, a legal scholar and judge, summarized this imperfection bluntly: "Facts are guesses."[84]

The final step for a judge or juror is to apply legal rules to the facts—rules that frequently are ambiguous and difficult to apply. Perhaps most important, it is necessary to determine whether the defendant is guilty beyond a reasonable doubt, but the meaning of "reasonable doubt" is murky. A Rhode Island Supreme Court justice has argued that jurors often have an inaccurate sense of what the term means, largely because judges fail to give them clear instructions.[85] Judges' instructions on this and other legal questions are important to jury decisions, but these instructions are typically couched in complex language that is difficult to understand. Exhibit 6.7 discusses California's effort to overcome that problem.

A decision-making task of high difficulty and ambiguity, such as the task faced by judges and juries in close cases, provides fertile ground for irrelevant information to influence judgments. "In a trial-advocacy lecture," one prosecutor reported, "we were warned never to ask jurors after a trial how they had reached their verdict. Their answers would be too disturbingly unrelated to the facts."[86]

The Impact of the Adversary System   The problems that have just been identified need to be put in the context of the adversary system, in which two sides contest a case at trial, because this system is designed to minimize such problems. Ideally, the trial operates as a kind of marketplace of ideas: if each side presents the strongest possible case, the truth will emerge from the confrontation of those cases.

Unquestionably, the adversary system in practice goes some distance toward meeting this ideal. For instance, the desire of prosecutors and defense attorneys to win cases gives them an incentive to ferret out relevant evidence. But the clash between the two sides cannot eliminate the inherent difficulty of reaching a correct verdict, and one or both sides may be incapable of presenting anything resembling the strongest possible case.

Moreover, the adversary system has negative as well as positive effects. The desire to make a strong case can cause an attorney to obscure the facts rather than illuminate them or to increase prejudice rather than reduce it. Each side, after all, is not fighting for the truth to emerge; it is fighting to win.

This problem is illustrated by jury selection, in which lawyers work hard to obtain jurors who are inclined to support their side. Lawyers have always used hunches and stereotypes to try to eliminate jurors who might be unsympathetic to their side and seat those who seem favorable. Today some lawyers employ jury consultants and use "scientific" methods to choose jurors.

EXHIBIT 6.7   Simplifying Jury Instructions in California

In 2005, the California Judicial Council approved new jury instructions that had been developed over eight years. The effort was aimed at replacing confusing legal language with language that was easier for jurors to understand. The state judge who chaired the task force that wrote the new instructions said that the committee sought "that exquisite balance between explaining the law accurately and explaining the law in ways that everyone can understand."

One example of the change concerned false testimony. The old and new instructions read as follows:

> (Old) A Witness who is willfully false in one material aspect of his or her testimony is to be distrusted in others. You may reject the whole testimony of a witness who willfully has testified falsely as to a material point, unless, from all the evidence, you believe the probability of truth favors his or her testimony in other particulars.

> (New) If you decide that a witness deliberately lied about something important, you should consider not believing anything that witness says. Or, if you think the witness lied about some things, but told the truth about others, you may simply accept the part that you think is true and ignore the rest.

Such changes in jury instructions undoubtedly make it easier for juries to apply legal rules to the facts of a case. But this can still be a difficult task for both jurors and judges. And most states have not yet simplified their instructions for criminal cases, so jurors in those states must still wrestle with instructions that can be incomprehensible.

Sources: Pamela A. MacLean, "Calif. Puts It in Plain English," *National Law Journal*, August 22, 2005, 4. The quotation is from Bob Egelko, "Criminal Juries to Hear Less Legalese," *San Francisco Chronicle*, August 27, 2005, B7. The old and new instructions on false testimony are from Judicial Council of California, "Before and After: Comparison of Jury Instructions," August 11, 2005, at http://www.courtinfo.ca.gov/presscenter/documents/before_after.pdf.

The adversary system also affects the testimony of witnesses. A witness is called by one side or the other, and most witnesses—especially defendants who testify on their own behalf—feel a stake in the outcome. Not surprisingly, attorneys prepare witnesses to testify in the manner that will be most favorable to their side, and many witnesses would do so even without such preparation. Sometimes, witnesses simply lie. Indeed, some judges see perjury as commonplace. According to a federal district judge in Atlanta, "I think people would be shocked if it were truly known how many witnesses lied under oath in a court of law every day."[87]

Cross-examination is a mechanism to expose false or misleading testimony, and it can serve well to clarify the facts of a case. But lawyers aim to weaken the effect of damaging testimony no matter how accurate it is. In a 2004 cartoon, a court official swears in a grinning lawyer before he is to cross-examine a witness: "Do you swear to misinterpret the testimony, misstate the facts, and cast aspersions on the character of the witness, regardless of the truth?"[88]

Both sides engage in questionable trial tactics, but more attention has been given to the tactics of prosecutors. Despite a Supreme Court decision to the contrary, for instance, prosecutors frequently fail to give defense attorneys evidence that favors the defendant, even evidence that indicates the defendant's innocence.[89] In one case, the federal government prosecuted Edwin Wilson, a former CIA officer, for exporting explosives to Libya. Wilson offered the defense that he was still doing work for the CIA. The prosecution introduced an affidavit from a CIA official that Wilson had had only one minor contact with the CIA after his regular employment ended. But government officials knew that there had been more than eighty such contacts. As a federal district judge described the situation,

> The government discussed among dozens of its officials and lawyers whether to correct the testimony. No correction was made. . . . Confronted with its own internal memoranda, the government now says that, well, it might have misstated the truth, but that it was Wilson's fault, it did not really matter, and it did not know what it was doing. Because the government knowingly used false evidence against him and suppressed favorable evidence, his conviction will be vacated.[90]

Exhibit 6.8 describes an episode in which misconduct by a law enforcement officer and a prosecutor resulted in serious consequences for a set of innocent defendants.

The adversary system is especially problematic when one side has an advantage over the other in the ability to make its case effectively. That advantage can arise from differences in the quality of the attorneys or in the ability to prepare the case for trial. To some extent, both differences reflect economics. The rare defendant with access to large sums of money, such as wealthy athletes, entertainers, and corporate executives, can afford preparations and advocacy that greatly outdistance the prosecution. While Martha Stewart was awaiting trial in federal court for offenses resulting from her sale of a stock, she engaged in what was estimated to be a "million-dollar campaign" to gain a more favorable image with the public and thus with prospective jurors.[91] More often, the prosecution holds the advantage. Of course, the side with more skilled attorneys and greater resources for trial preparation does not always win, but it gains advantages that can prove decisive.

Judges and Juries as Decision Makers   Thus far I have not distinguished between judges and juries as trial decision makers. Many people make a sharp distinction between the two, arguing that juries alone do a bad job of deciding cases. Jury verdicts in well-publicized cases often outrage observers who favored a different result, and their outrage sometimes extends to criticism of jurors' competence in general. In offering that criticism, they enter a long historical debate over the relative merits of judges and juries.

One key issue in this debate is the competence of juries as decision makers. Critics argue that jurors' lack of experience and expertise puts them at a great disadvantage in assessing the facts of a case and applying the law under the difficult circumstances of a trial. One experienced observer of the criminal justice system reported, "I am coming closer and closer to the conclusion . . . that jurors simply cannot be expected to do what they are required to do."[92]

Yet the difficulties involved in reaching the right decision are not restricted to juries. The same observer also underlined the limitations of judges: "Experience on

EXHIBIT 6.8   The Drug Prosecutions in Tulia, Texas

Tulia is a small county seat in northwestern Texas. In 1999, forty-six residents of Tulia were arrested on drug charges. Forty-three were black, more than 10 percent of the African American population in the city. (Accounts of this episode differ in their counts of arrestees and some other details.) The arrests resulted from an undercover investigation by Tom Coleman, part of a regional task force. Coleman had gathered and kept no physical evidence. But in the seven cases that were tried, his testimony against the defendants resulted in their convictions, and they received prison terms of twenty years or more. Most other defendants pled guilty; some were sentenced to prison and others given probation. Coleman was widely praised, and the Texas attorney general named Coleman "Officer of the Year."

Gradually, doubts about the arrests and prosecutions arose. The *Texas Observer*, a weekly magazine, published an article questioning the cases in Tulia, and the NAACP raised its own questions. Two defense attorneys became involved in the remaining prosecutions and secured dismissals of some cases. In 2003 a state judge held a special hearing on the cases, and the testimony raised serious questions about Coleman's behavior in these cases and about his past. The judge found that Coleman had committed "blatant perjury" and recommended that all the convictions be overturned. Prosecutors agreed. Later that year, Texas governor Rick Perry issued pardons to thirty-five defendants. In 2004 a lawsuit by the people who had been arrested in Tulia against several cities and counties resulted in a $5 million settlement.

The statute of limitations protected Coleman from prosecution for perjury in the Tulia trials, but in 2005 he was convicted of lying about his arrest record at the 2003 hearing. He was sentenced to ten years' probation. The same year, the state bar investigated Terry McEachern, the district attorney in Tulia, on charges that he failed to disclose information about Coleman's criminal history and failed to take any action when he knew that Coleman was testifying falsely. The bar found that McEachern had violated ethical rules and put him on probation as a lawyer for two years.

Sources: Newspaper articles; Nate Blakeslee, *Tulia: Race, Cocaine, and Corruption in a Small Texas Town* (New York: Public Affairs Press, 2005). The quotation is from Adam Liptak, "$5 Million Settlement Ends Case of Tainted Texas Sting," *New York Times*, March 11, 2004, A14.

the bench may teach judicial temperament—even a little law—but I have yet to be persuaded that it sharpens the skills of detecting honest error and conscious falsehood in the renditions of strangers."[93] Research in social psychology suggests that a multimember body has real strengths in reaching decisions in comparison with a single person. And some people argue that jurors have an advantage based on what one judge called "their diversity of experiences. . . . Judges are drawn from a particularly well behaved group of people of limited experience. Fortunately, jurors are more diverse in their experiences than we are."[94] There is reason to conclude that judges are more capable decision makers than juries, but the difference should not be exaggerated.

At least in felony cases, defense lawyers generally choose jury trials rather than bench trials. This tendency is based on the belief that juries are more likely to acquit. One lawyer declared that "it would be legal malpractice for me to waive jury in a criminal case."[95] A study of jury trials in four cities probed this belief by asking both judges and jurors about their perceptions of cases.[96] The study found that judge and jury agreed on guilt or innocence in a particular case about three-quarters of the time. In cases where they did disagree, three-quarters of the time the jury acquitted when the judge would have convicted. This result is consistent with defense lawyers' preference for juries.

Some evidence suggests that jurors' relative leniency reflects their tendency to modify the law to fit their own sense of equity. For instance, they resist convicting defendants under unpopular laws and take the victim's conduct into account in judging the defendant. But the difference between judges and juries might result chiefly from a tendency for jurors to demand a higher level of proof for conviction.[97]

Assessing Criminal Trials   Clearly, trials are a highly imperfect means to reach the correct verdict as I have defined it. In recent years, we have learned more about the frequency with which innocent defendants are convicted because of failures in the operation of the criminal justice system.[98] In all likelihood, the number of guilty defendants who are acquitted is far higher. Acquittals of some guilty defendants may be an unavoidable result of the procedural safeguards built into the system, but many other acquittals result from the same imperfections that lead to convictions of innocent people.

In assessing the impact of these imperfections, we should make a distinction between clear cases and close cases. In many trials, the facts and the law are such that one result is virtually guaranteed, and all the imperfections of trials are unlikely to have any effect. In many other cases, however, there is enough uncertainty that the process can have an effect and the wrong verdict may be reached.

The realities of trials should be taken into account in assessing other methods for resolving cases, especially plea bargaining. The weaknesses of plea bargaining must be balanced against the weaknesses of trials, and certainly neither should be idealized. It is a mistake to criticize plea bargaining in comparison with an ideal trial process that always produces the correct verdict. But it is also a mistake to prefer plea bargaining on the ground that it avoids the imperfections of the criminal trial. Since some of the same weaknesses affect both, and since trials set standards by which plea bargains are negotiated, the two processes differ less in result than they do in form.

SENTENCING DECISIONS

Most cases that prosecutors carry forward result in convictions through guilty verdicts or guilty pleas. For defendants who are convicted, sentencing is the court decision that largely determines their fate. From the perspective of society as a whole, sentencing decisions establish the actual pattern of sanctions in the criminal justice system.

Formal sentencing power lies primarily with trial judges. Only six southern and border states provide for sentencing by juries. (Other states do so for decisions whether to impose the death penalty.) Even in those six states, juries generally set sentences only in the small minority of cases involving jury trials, and judges have some power to revise jury recommendations for sentences. The federal government and an increasing number of states allow some appeals of judges' sentences, but in most states sentences still cannot be appealed if they are consistent with the applicable statutes.

Sentencing Systems

Congress and the state legislatures each select their own statutory systems for sentencing. The most important difference among these systems is in the amount of discretion that is lodged with two decision makers, the sentencing judge and the parole board that sets release dates for prisoners.

For most of the twentieth century, American sentencing systems generally granted broad discretion to judges. They could impose a variety of sanctions, including prison or jail, fines, probation, community service, and restitution. If judges did impose a prison sentence, they were given a wide range of sentence lengths from which to choose for any specific offense.

In the past few decades, every state and the federal government have amended their sentencing systems in an effort to reduce discretion. One widespread approach, taken by the federal government and more than one-third of the states, is to adopt sentencing guidelines for judges.[99] These guideline systems vary considerably in their form. The most important element of variation is how binding the guidelines are on judges. Some states created guidelines that were strictly voluntary for judges, while other states and the federal government adopted "presumptive" guidelines that were binding to one degree or another. However, Supreme Court decisions in 2004 and 2005 struck down the systems with binding guidelines in Washington State and the federal courts on constitutional grounds.[100] The long-term effects of those decisions are not yet clear, but at least in the short run they have made all the guidelines systems voluntary.

Another approach, which has been used everywhere, is to set mandatory minimum sentences for certain specific offenses. For instance, Michigan requires an additional two-year prison term for possessing a gun while committing a felony, and New York requires prison sentences for narcotics offenses. A popular variant of mandatory minimum sentences, adopted by the federal government and half the states in the 1990s, is the "three-strikes" laws that typically require long sentences after the third conviction for a serious felony.

A different type of change has the effect of increasing judges' control over sentences.[101] Fourteen states have eliminated parole, so that prisoners cannot be released early through the action of a parole board. Most states have adopted "truth-in-sentencing" laws that require prisoners to serve at least some stipulated proportion of their original sentence. This development has been encouraged by a 1994 federal law providing monetary grants for states that require at least 85 percent of each sentence to be served.

The Sentencing Process

There is considerable variation in the process by which judges hand down sentences, especially in its timing. Sometimes, most often in misdemeanor cases, the sentence is announced immediately after a defendant is found guilty or the judge accepts a guilty plea. But in felony cases, sentencing generally follows a sentencing hearing that is held some time after the trial or plea acceptance.

Before a sentencing hearing, the judge typically receives a presentence report that has been compiled by a probation officer. This report contains background information on the defendant, including such matters as prior criminal record and family situation. The report usually recommends whether to impose a prison sentence or probation, and sometimes makes a more specific sentence recommendation.

At the hearing itself, the judge usually hears from both the prosecutor and the defense attorney. Defendants are generally allowed to speak and sometimes do so. One Virginia defendant told the jurors who would sentence him that if he were imprisoned, he would teach "hardened criminals" how to commit credit card fraud. "And," he pointed out, "we're trying to prevent crime in America."[102] In some states, the victim of the defendant's crime also may speak. After these presentations, the judge usually imposes the sentence immediately. The judge may offer a brief oral justification of the sentence, but anything more extensive or more formal is unusual.

Sentencing Choices: A First Look

Most of the time, judges have considerable discretion in choosing sentences. How do they go about making these choices?

To begin with, a judge's real options in any specific case are often considerably narrower than the applicable statute suggests. First of all, judges develop views about the sentences that are appropriate under common circumstances; thus, they may consider only a limited range of possible sentences. Of course, judges' conceptions of appropriate sentences are affected by their interactions with other members of the work group.

The judge's response to a specific case is also influenced by other court participants. Probation officers have some impact with their reports and recommendations. Indeed, the federal sentencing system gives considerable importance to the framing of facts in presentence reports by probation officers. Prosecutors are even more important; their recommendations often carry great weight with judges, especially when they have reached a sentence bargain with the defense attorney. In such cases, although there is no compulsion to accept the prosecutor's recommendation, a judge who supports plea bargaining almost invariably does so.

People outside the work group also seek to influence the sentence in some cases. In cases that have aroused public concern, judges sometimes feel pressure to impose heavy sentences. More generally, elected judges are aware that a pattern of stringent sentences may protect them from possible defeat. On the other hand, politicians and other celebrities who face sentencing may try to mobilize support for leniency. After famed lobbyist Jack Abramoff pled guilty to fraud and conspiracy charges in 2006, the sentencing judge received 262 letters on his behalf. The letters offered a variety of reasons to give Abramoff a relatively light sentence, one noting that "people make mistakes."[103]

Significant as all these influences are, judges still have considerable control over sentences. The recommendations of other participants and the terms of sentence bargains constrain judges less than it might appear, because both are tailored in part to fit a judge's preferences. Judges, after all, are free to reject recommendations and bargains that they find unacceptable. Besides, there are many cases in which no sentence bargain has been reached. In such cases, judges often have wide ranges from which to choose in practice as well as in law. And only in a small minority of cases are external pressures so strong that they are too strong to resist.

Thus judges must make choices, and the task of choosing among alternative sentences is difficult. Sentences can be used to serve any of several goals, including *retribution* (giving offenders their "just deserts"), *general deterrence* (discouraging other people from committing crimes), *rehabilitation* (changing the attitudes and capabilities of offenders so they will not commit more crimes), and *incapacitation* (confining offenders so they cannot commit crimes outside of prison). A judge may support several of these goals but find that they point in different directions. More fundamentally, it is often unclear what kind of sentence best serves these goals.

These problems would make sentencing difficult in any case, but judges often have to make choices under conditions that are far from ideal. Time pressures may limit the care with which judges can consider a sentence, and they often lack the information that they should have. Practical problems frequently make some possible sentences less attractive. Many prisons are overcrowded, and prison conditions may be so bad that judges are reluctant to impose prison sentences in marginal cases. Probation services may be inadequate to provide real supervision of offenders. Fines are notoriously difficult to collect; in one Ohio county, over a dozen-year period only 3 percent of the fines and court costs imposed on defendants had been paid.[104] As a result, judges may feel that they are only choosing among a set of bad alternatives.

If judges are unhappy with their alternatives, many observers of the courts have been unhappy with judges' sentencing decisions. Some of this feeling relates to the general severity or leniency of sentencing. This issue is difficult to assess, because people differ considerably in their views about how severe sentences should be. Two other issues, both fundamental to sentencing, are more amenable to evaluation: the criteria on which sentences are based and the consistency with which they are meted out.

Criteria for Sentences

Judges can base their sentencing decisions on many criteria, either consciously or unconsciously. These criteria include attributes of both the criminal offense and the defendant. Some of these attributes, such as the seriousness of the offense and the defendant's criminal record, are generally regarded as legitimate bases for decisions. Others, such as the race and economic status of the defendant, are almost universally regarded as illegitimate. Still others, such as the defendant's employment status and family situation, are subjects of disagreement.

One critical issue in sentencing is the relative importance of legitimate and illegitimate criteria. Although the evidence on this issue is incomplete and ambiguous, we have considerable information about the impact of some criteria.

Seriousness of the Offense and the Defendant's Prior Record   Most people would agree that sentences should be based primarily on the seriousness of the offense and the defendant's prior criminal record. The research on sentencing indicates that

EXHIBIT 6.9   Sentences Imposed by State Courts for Felony Offenses, 2002

Offense	Percentage Sentenced to Prison or Jail (%)	Mean Maximum Sentence for Defendants Sentenced to Prison or Jail (months)
Murder	95	217
Robbery	86	79
Sexual assault	82	78
Aggravated assault	71	37
Burglary	72	36
Drug Trafficking	68	38
Larceny	67	22

Note: Death sentences are treated as sentences to prison. "Murder" includes nonnegligent man-slaughter; "larceny" includes auto theft. Figures in the table are estimates based on a sample of 300 counties.

Source: Matthew R. Durose and Patrick A. Langan, *Felony Sentences in State Courts, 2002* (Washington, D.C.: U.S. Department of Justice, Bureau of Justice Statistics, 2004), 2–3.

most of the variation in the severity of sentences can in fact be explained by these factors, especially by the seriousness of the offense.[105] Exhibit 6.9 illustrates the significance of the offense in determining whether defendants go to prison and the length of their prison sentences, though there might be disagreement about whether all the offenses are in the appropriate order.

The importance of these two criteria is not surprising. Sentencing statutes virtually guarantee a relationship between the seriousness of offenses and the severity of sentences by setting different ranges for different offenses. The effects of these statutory ranges are reinforced by the consensus among judges and other members of the courtroom work group that more serious offenses call for stronger sanctions. Some legislatures have established rules under which sentences are increased on the basis of defendants' prior records. Even where they have not, agreement in the courtroom on the relevance of this factor ensures that it will be important.

The significance of this finding should not be overstated, for there is a good deal of variation in the severity of sentences that cannot be explained by offense seriousness and prior record. If illegitimate criteria have an impact on sentences, even an impact much weaker than that of legitimate criteria, then a serious problem exists.

Race and Economic Status   Of the illegitimate criteria that may influence sentences, the defendant's race and economic status are the most troubling. It is a matter of concern if these characteristics affect any stage of the criminal justice process, but some commentators conclude that they exert a substantial impact on the process as a whole. According to one legal scholar, we have established two systems of criminal justice: one for the privileged, and another for the less privileged. Some of the distinctions are based on race, others on class, but in no true sense can it be said that all are equal before the criminal law.[106]

For this reason, an examination of sentencing reaches only one aspect of possible discrimination in the criminal justice system.

Most of the research on this issue aims at isolating the impact of race on sentencing by controlling for other factors that may influence sentences. The research has not produced a clear consensus: some studies find that race has a substantial impact on sentencing decisions, while others do not. At least in part, this disagreement reflects differences in actual sentencing practices. Discrimination appears to exist in some places, for some types of crimes, and for some judges, but not universally.[107] Two studies found evidence that racial disparities are strongest in the sentencing of young men.[108]

Discrimination may be related to the race of the victim as well as that of the defendant. This issue has been studied most intensively for capital punishment. In several states, it appears that people who have been convicted of murdering whites are more likely to receive the death penalty than those convicted of murdering blacks, even if other factors relevant to the sentence are taken into account.[109] One study found that the race of the victim also affects sentences for vehicular homicide. Holding other factors constant, a driver who killed a white person received a sentence about twice as long as a driver who killed a black person.[110]

On the economic status of defendants, there is reason to think that people with higher status tend to receive more lenient sentences than do people with lower status who are convicted of the same offenses. One reason is that higher-status people have more resources with which to make the case for leniency. Another is that they are more likely to enlist the sympathies of judges and other participants in sentencing. In a federal case in California, the judge overruled prosecutors' recommendation of a prison sentence for a businessman with a doctoral degree who had pled guilty to sending illegal threats to his wife after a separation. The judge cited the defendant's "resources, intellectual resources, an educational background, that is highly unusual." The implication was that a similar defendant without those advantages would have been sent to prison.[111] Economic status seems to have a decisive impact on the use of the death penalty. One defender of capital punishment acknowledged, "I don't know of any affluent people who have been sentenced to death," and a lawyer with long experience in capital cases concluded that "the death penalty is for poor people."[112]

The most important issue concerning economic status and sentencing decisions is the treatment of *white-collar crime.* The concept of white-collar crime is difficult to define, but it generally refers to offenses "committed by nonphysical means and by concealment and guile" for economic gain.[113] This definition encompasses offenses such as embezzlement, mail fraud, income tax fraud, price fixing, and forgery. Among the range of white-collar crimes, of particular interest are those committed by employees in order to benefit their companies—or by corporations themselves, which can be charged with crimes.

Defendants and potential defendants in white-collar cases appear to enjoy advantages at all stages of the criminal justice process. One advantage is the difficulty that often exists in detecting white-collar crimes and in building cases when the crimes involve complex financial dealings. Another is the ability of corporations to shape the criminal laws that apply to them and their executives. When the U.S. Sentencing Commission rewrote its guidelines for crimes by organizations in 2004, lawyers representing companies participated in the revision process.[114] As a commentator pointed out some years earlier, in similar situations groups such as "drug smugglers" and "bank robbers" were not in a position to shape sentencing policy.[115] Other advantages are similar to those enjoyed by high-status people who are charged with "ordinary" crimes: the quality and quantity of legal services they can employ and the sympathies of people in the criminal justice system who can identify with white-collar defendants. Judges may even feel that some white-collar offenses such as antitrust violations are not really crimes.

There has been a widespread perception that people who are convicted of white-collar crimes tend to benefit from undue leniency at the sentencing stage. It is difficult to determine the accuracy of this perception. On the whole, individuals convicted of white-collar crimes receive lighter sentences than those convicted of other crimes, even crimes that seem comparable. But this difference might result chiefly from factors other than judicial favoritism. For example, white-collar crime by definition involves no violence, and its perpetrators usually have no prior record and appear to be good candidates for rehabilitation. Judges and others generally consider leniency to be appropriate when these conditions exist. On the other hand, white-collar offenses are especially likely to involve the kind of rational calculations that would be most susceptible to deterrence by heavy sentences.

In recent years there have been signs that white-collar crimes by corporations and their executives are being treated more seriously. The trigger was a series of scandals involving major companies, most prominently the collapse of Enron in 2001. Outrage at the apparent misdeeds of high company executives led to demands for a tougher drive against corporate crime. This outrage was reflected in 2002 federal legislation that created some new white-collar crimes and increased the penalties for some existing crimes. High-level executives in several companies have been indicted and tried. Among them are a large number of Enron employees, and in 2006 the two top officials of Enron were convicted of securities fraud, conspiracy, and other charges. And federal agencies have taken some steps to reverse the historical pattern of weak enforcement of criminal laws against practices that endanger workers' safety.[116]

The extent and permanence of this change are uncertain. There are still complaints that people convicted of white-collar sentences tend to receive lenient sentences. For instance, some people were unhappy at the one-year prison sentence given to former Connecticut governor John Rowland after he pled guilty to a federal charge based on his taking $107,000 in gifts from companies with an interest in state policy and failing to pay taxes on them.[117] In 2006 a Justice Department official pointed out that the department's Corporate Fraud Task Force had secured criminal convictions of ninety-two presidents of corporations and eighty-two chief executive officers. Yet the big increases early in the decade in the numbers of corporate fraud cases initiated by the Justice Department and of defendants charged in those cases were reversed in 2004 and 2005.[118] The next several years will provide a better sense of trends in the enforcement of laws against white-collar crime.

Consistency in Sentencing

The issue of consistency in sentencing is about whether cases with the same characteristics end with the same sentences. Inconsistencies can arise at three levels. First, patterns of sentencing may differ among courts. Second, judges in the same court may adopt different sentencing practices. Finally, an individual judge may operate with no firm standards, dispensing different sentences in similar cases.

The severity of sentencing varies considerably from place to place, based partly on differences in state laws and partly on the characteristics of particular courts and localities. Such variation might be considered appropriate. But it is difficult to justify variation within a single court, either among judges or in a single judge's decisions. Within any single court, variation in sentencing is limited by the development of going rates for particular crimes. Still, it appears that a good deal of inconsistency does exist.

Inconsistency among judges seems inevitable, because judges approach sentencing with different premises and different values. Lawyers who handle criminal cases are well aware of differences among judges in their general severity and in their responses to particular crimes or types of defendants. When defendants in a New York federal court had an opportunity to choose the judge who would sentence them after a guilty plea, so many preferred one judge "that they almost needed a reservation."[119]

One sign of variation among judges is the unusual sentences and conditions for probation that individual judges sometimes impose. To a degree, these choices reflect judges' frustration with the standard range of possible sentences, but for some judges they may also be a means to garner attention. Some examples are shown in Exhibit 6.10.

EXHIBIT 6.10   Examples of Unusual Sentences and Conditions of Probation Imposed by Judges

Offense	Sanction
Playing a car sound system too loud	Spending three hours in the woods; (another judge) watching a recording of the opera *Carmen*.
Theft	Donating Green Bay Packers tickets to charity.
Stealing mail	Standing outside a post office wearing a sign with the message, "I stole mail. This is my punishment."
Conspiracy to use stolen credit cards	Not watching television for ten months (penalty ruled out by an appellate court).

Sources (in order): "Loud Stereo Leads to Silent Treatment For Man's Sentence," *Columbus Dispatch*, September 20, 2001, D3; Amie Parnes, "Opera-Fan Judge Makes Guilty Face the Music," *Boston Globe*, April 22, 2004, A3; "Across the USA," *USA Today*, April 26, 2005, 9A; *United States v. Gementera*, 379 F.3d 596 (9th Cir. 2004); *United States v. Bello*, 310 F.3d 56 (2d Cir. 2002).

Even a single judge can hand down inconsistent sentences. Judges are asked to apply abstract and often conflicting goals to complex situations, and most judges feel that they should try to tailor justice to the individual. Under those conditions, almost anyone would find it difficult to achieve uniformity. Judges' explanations of their sentencing decisions sometimes make this difficulty clear. A federal judge in New York State sentenced one defendant to prison for a shorter term than defendants usually would receive for the same pair of offenses. Part of the judge's explanation to the defendant was that "I just had a gut feeling about you."[120] Although the judge may have made the appropriate judgment in that case, acting on such feelings leads to idiosyncrasies that can conflict with the goal of equal justice.

Sentencing Reform Through New Systems

The available evidence supports a mixed evaluation of judges' sentencing practices. On the positive side, most judges seem to use their discretion well in some respects, giving the greatest weight to factors that most people regard as legitimate. On the negative side, illegitimate factors sometimes affect sentences, and inconsistency seems to be widespread.

In the late twentieth century, Congress and state legislatures made major changes in sentencing systems. One spur was growing concern with inconsistency and the use of illegitimate criteria in sentencing. At the same time, criminologists and others became increasingly skeptical about the ability of the criminal justice system to rehabilitate offenders. This skepticism led to greater emphasis on retribution and general deterrence, goals that point toward more uniform sentencing for particular crimes. Meanwhile, conservatives argued that judges introduced too much leniency into the criminal law through their sentencing decisions.

These criticisms differed in their implications, but each led to an interest in reducing the sentencing discretion of judges. As noted earlier, the result has been a widespread alteration of sentencing systems to channel or limit judicial discretion. The major changes have been the adoption of mandatory minimum sentences for particular offenses, "three-strikes" laws that allow or mandate long sentences for certain repeat offenders, and guidelines for sentencing across all offenses.

Like other institutional changes in the courts, the effects of these alterations are not obvious. For one thing, judges may resist efforts to limit their discretion because they prefer the freedom to make their own choices. And judges and lawyers may want to maintain sentencing practices that produce what they see as good results. Further, major changes in sentencing systems can have unexpected effects on sentencing outcomes and on the functioning of the courts. Although the impact of sentencing reforms is uncertain and disputed, we do have some sense of their effects.

Where new sentencing rules are optional rather than mandatory, they seem to have only limited effects. Studies have found this to be true of the suggested sentencing guidelines that several states adopted.[121] This result is understandable, because judges and lawyers are unlikely to make major changes in their practices when they are left free to continue those practices.

Systems that actually limit judges' discretion have greater potential to affect sentencing practices. In states with presumptive sentencing guidelines, judges were required to justify departures from the mandated range of possible sentences, and departures could be appealed and reversed. Studies suggest that high proportions of sentences were within the mandated range. As a result, variation in sentences for specific offenses declined. But the decline often was smaller than might be expected, in part because guidelines usually left judges with considerable leeway. The evidence on reduction in unjustified sentencing disparities among defendants is ambiguous.[122]

Mandatory minimum sentences for specific offenses introduce a degree of compulsion, especially where judges are not allowed to make exceptions. As a result, they have a substantial impact on sentencing practices. But sometimes judges simply impose a sentence that is more lenient than the minimum required by the law. Such noncompliance was found to be common for drunk-driving laws in Indiana and New Mexico.[123] For their part, prosecutors can refuse to charge a defendant with an offense for which there is a mandatory sentence.

Similarly, three-strikes laws have had only limited impact in most states.[124] Some of these laws are written narrowly, and judges and prosecutors have used their discretion to limit the laws' use. One study found that after three-strikes laws were enacted, it became more common for prosecutors to reduce felony charges to misdemeanors in situations in which a felony conviction would make a defendant subject to a three-strikes sentence.[125] Although this practice occurs in California as well, that state's three-strikes law diverges from the pattern in other states: it has had considerable impact. The California three-strikes law doubles the sentence for a felony conviction if the defendant had a prior conviction for a violent or other serious felony. On a third conviction, the law mandates a long sentence, most often twenty-five years to life. Although use of the law varies among California counties, on the whole it is heavily employed, and prison populations have grown substantially.

Congress made two major changes in the federal sentencing system in the 1980s, and together they have had a greater impact than the changes in most state systems. One change was the establishment of the first mandatory minimum sentence requirements for federal crimes, which ultimately were applied to more than sixty offenses. Although most of these provisions have never been used, four (three involving drug offenses) have been employed a good deal.

The second change was adoption of a sentencing guidelines system. In 1984, Congress created the U.S. Sentencing Commission to write rules for federal sentencing that would narrow judges' discretion. A detailed and complex set of presumptive guidelines became effective in 1987, and a number of amendments were added later. The Sentencing Commission created a grid based on 43 offense level categories and six criminal history categories, and for each cell in the grid a district judge was given a range of possible imprisonment lengths (such as 57 to 71 months). The judge was required to impose a sentence within that range unless the judge found a relevant aggravating or mitigating circumstance that the guidelines did not adequately take into account or the prosecution stated that the defendant had provided substantial assistance in another case. If the sentence was above or below the range in a cell, the defendant or prosecutor could appeal to a court of appeals.

The effects of these two changes were complex, but some general patterns can be identified. First, the guidelines and mandatory minimums effectively reduced judges' discretion over sentencing, causing them to give tougher sentences than they had in the past. Before the guidelines went into effect, only about half the people convicted of federal offenses were sentenced to prison; by the 1990s, more than 80 percent received prison sentences.[126] Mandatory minimum sentences contributed to a trend in which long sentences, including life in prison without the possibility of parole, became more common.

Second, most of the power lost by federal judges shifted to prosecutors. Since charges against defendants translated more directly into sentences than in the past, prosecutors' original charges and charge bargains gained much greater impact. Under the commission rules, prosecutors could have additional impact on sentences through their reporting of case-related facts to judges, especially facts concerning the assistance that defendants provided with other cases.

Finally, the adoption of tighter rules for sentencing did not fully eliminate inconsistency or arbitrariness. Although judges' decisions became more consistent in relation to the cases presented to them, some inconsistency remained. Additional inconsistency arose from prosecutors' decisions about which cases to present and in what form. As a result, some racial discrimination continued to exist,[127] and average sentences for the same offense varied from one district to another.[128]

Furthermore, federal statutes and sentencing rules themselves incorporated arbitrary features. For instance, drug "kingpins" sometimes came out better off than small-time violators because they had more information with which to assist prosecutors and the sentencing rules gave weight to this consideration. Under the sentencing guidelines, sentences for counterfeiting differed considerably depending on whether the defendant had altered bills or made them from scratch.[129]

In federal cases tried before judges, the rate of acquittals increased a great deal between the mid-1980s and the late 1990s, even while the acquittal rate for juries declined somewhat. One possible explanation is that district judges were consciously or unconsciously acquitting defendants where they thought that the sentences indicated by the guidelines were unduly harsh.[130] If so, the divergence between judges' values and those reflected in the guidelines led to a quite unintended result.

Changing the New Systems

While many people were happy with the adoption of these new sentencing systems, others were not. However, the criticisms were of different types. On one side were those who thought that mandatory minimum sentences and presumptive sentencing guidelines unduly limited judges' discretion and resulted in sentences that were inappropriately high. Federal district judges frequently protested what they saw as the undesirable effects of the federal sentencing guidelines in general or in specific cases. In 2004, for instance, a Utah district judge who had taken strongly conservative positions on criminal justice issues as a law professor nonetheless expressed his unhappiness with a mandatory minimum that required him to sentence a defendant to fifty-five years in prison. That sentence, he wrote, "appears to be unjust, cruel, and irrational," and he recommended that President Bush reduce the sentence through his commutation power.[131] In California, there was widespread discontent with the impact of the three-strikes law. And some state policymakers who supported tough sentencing laws on principle were concerned with the financial costs of growing prison populations. As a result, a majority of state legislatures have repealed some of their requirements for mandatory minimum sentences.

On the other side, some people were unhappy because they perceived that judges were watering down the effects of the new sentencing laws with undue leniency. In particular, conservatives in Congress complained about the frequency of sentences below the federal guidelines range: judges were far more likely to go below that range than above it. The picture was ambiguous. In 2003, for instance, 69 percent of the federal sentences were within the guidelines range, 30 percent below the range, and only 1 percent above it. But of the sentences below the range, the great majority resulted from the prosecution's initiative, based on substantial assistance by the defendant in other cases or on other considerations. Even when such cases were eliminated, downward departures were still much more common than upward departures, but judges initiated downward departures in only 8 percent of all cases.[132]

In any event, members of Congress directed considerable criticism at district judges for their sentencing practices and sought to change those practices. In 2003 Congress enacted legislation that required the Sentencing Commission to write new rules limiting downward departures and gave courts of appeals greater discretion to overturn sentences that departed from the guidelines. The legislation also set requirements for reporting of sentences that were intended to put pressure on judges to avoid downward departures.

Then the Supreme Court intervened. The federal sentencing guidelines and presumptive guidelines in the states required sentencing judges to take into account facts that had not been admitted by the defendant or proved at trial but that made the defendant deserve a heavier sentence. In *Blakely v. Washington* (2004), a case involving the Washington State guidelines, the Court held that this use of facts violated the constitutional right to a jury trial. The implications of the decision for sentencing guideline systems were not fully clear, and the Court provided clarification the next year in *United States v. Booker* (2005). In that case the Court said that what it had ruled in *Blakely* applied to the federal guidelines as well. It also held that because this feature was so central to the guidelines system, mandatory guidelines were unconstitutional, and the federal guidelines (and, by implication, similar state guidelines) must be made voluntary for judges. Some commentators thought that this solution to the constitutional problem was inappropriate, even illogical; the Court's choice reflected disagreements among the justices about both the constitutional issue and the solution.[133]

The Court invited Congress to rewrite the federal sentencing rules in light of its decision, but neither Congress nor the state legislatures acted quickly. In this situation, judges had to adapt to the new system of voluntary guidelines. At least at the federal level, sentencing practices did not change radically. Judges generally continued to use the guideline ranges as the bases for their choices, and rulings by the Sentencing Commission and the courts of appeals strongly favored adherence to the guidelines.[134] However, at least in the short run, the rates of upward and downward departures from the guidelines that were not initiated by prosecutors increased considerably.[135] States with sentencing guidelines have responded in various ways to the Supreme Court's decisions, some making their presumptive guidelines voluntary, others modifying their systems, and some interpreting the Court's rulings as irrelevant to their systems.[136] The long-term effects of those rulings will depend in part on further Supreme Court rulings but chiefly on action (or lack of action) by Congress and the state legislatures.

CONCLUSIONS

One theme of this chapter is that the criminal courts do not function nearly as well as we would like. Widespread perceptions of problems in the system have led to a long series of campaigns to improve the handling of criminal cases. Perhaps the most important lessons of the chapter concern those efforts at reform.

To begin with, reforms do not always produce the intended results. Plea bargaining survives attempts to eliminate it. New sentencing systems may create new problems without eradicating old ones. And changes in one part of the system often affect other parts in unexpected—and sometimes undesired—ways. Thus, for instance, reduction in the sentencing power of judges adds to the power of prosecutors.

Second, failures of reform often reflect unavoidable realities. In particular, plea bargaining survives because it serves important needs for participants in the courts. No matter how elaborate the efforts to abolish it, bargaining always returns. Reforms, then, have the best chance to succeed when they reflect a thorough understanding of the criminal courts. Such understanding allows people to take into account the possible effects of a change in the system.

Even so, the imperfections of the criminal courts cannot be solved fully. It is impossible to bring to court all the people who are probably guilty of serious crimes. There will always be a gulf between the goals of sentencing and the actual effects of sentencing decisions. The lesson is not that we should be satisfied with the current workings of the criminal courts or that we should abandon efforts to improve them. Rather, we need to be realistic about how much can be expected from those efforts.

FOR FURTHER READING

Bogira, Steve. *Courtroom 302: A Year Behind the Scenes in an American Criminal Courthouse.* New York: Knopf, 2005.

Calavita, Kitty, Henry N. Pontell, and Robert H. Tillman. *Big Money Crime: Fraud and Politics in the Savings and Loan Crisis.* Berkeley: University of California Press, 1997.

Cole, David. *No Equal Justice: Race and Class in the American Criminal Justice System.* New York: New Press, 1999.

Delsohn, Gary. *The Prosecutors: A Year in the Life of a District Attorney's Office.* New York: Dutton, 2003.

Fisher, George. *Plea Bargaining's Triumph: A History of Plea Bargaining in America.* Stanford: Stanford University Press, 2003.

Jonakait, Randolph N. *The American Jury System.* New Haven: Yale University Press, 2003.

Kennedy, Randall. *Race, Crime, and the Law.* New York: Pantheon, 1997.

Stith, Kate, and Jose A. Cabranes. *Fear of Judging: Sentencing Guidelines in the Federal Courts.* Chicago: University of Chicago Press, 1998.

Uviller, H. Richard. *The Tilted Playing Field: Is Criminal Justice Unfair?* New Haven, Conn.: Yale University Press, 1999.

Vogel, Mary E. *Coercion to Compromise: Plea Bargaining, the Courts, and the Making of Political Authority.* New York: Oxford University Press, 2007.

Online Study Center Go to college.hmco.com/PIC/baum6e for ACE practice test questions and additional resources.

NOTES

1. See Elayne Rapping, *Law and Justice as Seen on TV* (New York: New York University Press, 2003).
2. Janan Hanna, "Criminal Code's Clutter Awaits Cleanup Panel," *Chicago Tribune*, May 28, 2000, sec. 4, pp. 1, 3.
3. This discussion is based in part on Howard N. Snyder and Melissa Sickmund, *Juvenile Offenders and Victims: 2006 National Report* (Washington, D.C.: U.S. Department of Justice, 2006).
4. On "work groups," see James Eisenstein and Herbert Jacob, *Felony Justice: An Organizational Analysis of Criminal Courts* (Boston: Little, Brown, 1977), ch. 2. On "courthouse communities," see Peter F. Nardulli, James Eisenstein, and Roy B. Flemming, *The Tenor of Justice: Criminal Courts and the Guilty Plea Process* (Urbana: University of Illinois Press, 1988), ch. 5.
5. "Judge Donates the Gift of Life," *Kentucky Post*, June 23, 2006.
6. Peter Page, "Alaska's Top Prosecutor Out After Clash with Judges," *National Law Journal*, April 22, 2002, A5. The quotation from the judge's decision is from Sheila Toomey, "Judge Calls Tetlow Case Outrageous," *Anchorage Daily News*, April 2, 2002, B1.
7. Jill Porter, "DA Scorn Riles Judges," *Philadelphia Daily News*, January 7, 2003.
8. Steve Warmbir and Natasha Korecki, "Legal Battle Pits U.S. Attorney vs. Judge," *Chicago Sun-Times*, January 22, 2005, 3.
9. This discussion is based in part on Steven W. Perry, *Prosecutors in State Courts, 2005* (Washington, D.C.: U.S. Department of Justice, 2006). On the operation of a prosecutor's office, see Gary Delsohn, *The Prosecutors: A Year in the Life of a District Attorney's Office* (New York: Dutton, 2003).
10. Bob Herbert, "The Truth About Justice," *New York Times*, September 18, 2000, A31.
11. John P. Heinz, Robert L. Nelson, Rebecca L. Sandefur, and Edward O. Laumann, *Urban Lawyers: The New Social Structure of the Bar* (Chicago: University of Chicago Press, 2005), 84.
12. David Segal, "Verdict: The Defense Can't Rest Too Often," *Washington Post*, July 3, 1999, A14.
13. "Man Shows Up to Fight DUI Charge with Booze Breath," *San Francisco Chronicle*, August 5, 2004.
14. "Woman Accused of Stealing Gavel from Judge," *Detroit Free Press*, January 7, 2005.
15. Caroline Wolf Harlow, *Defense Counsel in Criminal Cases* (Washington, D.C.: Bureau of Justice Statistics, U.S. Department of Justice, 2000), 1.
16. Thomas H. Cohen and Brian A. Reaves, *Felony Defendants in Large Urban Counties, 2002* (Washington, D.C.: Bureau of Justice Statistics, U.S. Department of Justice, 2006), 4–7.

17. Marty Graham, "L.A. Jurors Ignore Jury Duty, as Well as Threats," *National Law Journal*, October 11, 2004, 6; Dan Christensen, "Fla. Supreme Court: Everyone Into the Pool," *Miami Daily Business Review*, January 3, 2005.
18. "Juror Gets Week in Jail for Leaving for Vacation," *Los Angeles Times*, February 26, 2002; "Skip Jury Duty, Go Directly to Jail," *National Law Journal*, October 24, 2006, 16.
19. Scott Hiassen and Karl Turner, "Grand Jury Members Say They Felt Pressured to OK Indictments," *Cleveland Plain Dealer*, January 16, 2003, A1.
20. William Glaberson, "New Trend Before Grand Juries: Meet the Accused," *New York Times*, June 20, 2004, A1.
21. *Sourcebook of Criminal Justice Statistics 2003* (Bureau of Justice Statistics, U.S. Department of Justice), 140–141 (www.albany.edu/sourcebook/index.html).
22. This discussion is based in part on Wayne R. LaFave, Jerold H. Israel, and Nancy J. King, *Criminal Procedure*, 4th ed. (St. Paul: Thomson/West, 2004), 6–23.
23. *In re Gault*, 387 U.S. 1 (1967).
24. Brian J. Ostrom, Shauna M. Strickland, and Paul L. Hannaford-Agor, "Examining Trial Trends in State Courts: 1976–2002," *Journal of Empirical Legal Studies* 1 (November 2004), 765.
25. Cohen and Reaves, *Felony Defendants, 2002*, 23.
26. Joan Petersilia, *Racial Disparities in the Criminal Justice System* (Santa Monica, Calif.: Rand Corporation, 1983), 45.
27. *Criminal Victimization in the United States, 2004: Statistical Tables* (Washington, D.C.: Bureau of Justice Statistics, U.S. Department of Justice, 2006), Table 91 (http://www.ojp.usdoj.gov/bjs/pub/pdf/cvus04.pdf).
28. Federal Bureau of Investigation, *Crime in the United States 2004* (Washington, D.C.: U.S. Department of Justice, n.d.), Table 25 (http://www.fbi.gov/ucr/cius_04/).
29. See Michael Edmond O'Neill, "Understanding Federal Prosecutorial Declinations: An Empirical Analysis of Predictive Factors," *American Criminal Law Review* 41 (2004), 1458–1463.
30. Richard S. Frase, "The Decision to File Federal Criminal Charges: A Quantitative Study of Prosecutorial Discretion," *University of Chicago Law Review* 47 (1980), 263–265; Celesta A. Albonetti, "Prosecutorial Discretion: The Effects of Uncertainty," *Law & Society Review* 21 (1987), 291–313; O'Neill, "Understanding Federal Prosecutorial Declinations."
31. Andrew B. Whitford and Jeff Yates, "Policy Signals and Executive Governance: Presidential Rhetoric in the War on Drugs," *Journal of Politics* 65 (November 2003), 995–1012.
32. Vanessa Blum, "DOJ's New Porn Police," *Legal Times*, March 8, 2004, 1, 14.
33. See Benjamin Weiser and William Glaberson, "Ashcroft Pushes Executions in More Cases in New York," *New York Times*, February 6, 2003, A1, C13.
34. Lori Montgomery, "Md. Questioning Local Extremes on Death Penalty," *Washington Post*, May 12, 2002, C1. See Lori Montgomery, "Eliminating Questions of Life or Death," *Washington Post*, May 20, 2002, B1.
35. Administrative Office of the United States Courts, *Judicial Business of the United States Courts: Report of the Director (2005)* (Washington, D.C.: Administrative Office of the U.S. Courts, n.d.), 245; Cohen and Reaves, *Felony Defendants, 2002*, 24.
36. David Lynch, "The Impropriety of Plea Agreements: A Tale of Two Counties," *Law and Social Inquiry* 19 (Winter 1994), 127.
37. This discussion of forms of plea bargaining is based in part on John F. Padgett, "The Emergent Organization of Plea Bargaining," *American Journal of Sociology* 90 (January 1985), 753–800.
38. Alfred Blumstein, Jacqueline Cohen, Susan E. Martin, and Michael H. Tonry, eds., *Research on Sentencing: The Search for Reform,* 2 vols. (Washington, D.C.: National Academy Press, 1983), I, 43.
39. Donald R. Cressey, "Doing Justice," *The Center Magazine* 10 (January/February 1977), 23.
40. "Forger Strikes Deal to See Game From Jail," *Columbus Dispatch*, November 19, 2003, A1.
41. *Commonwealth v. Gordon*, 574 N.E.2d 974, 976 n.3 (Mass. 1991).

42. Emily Bazelon, "Doling Out Justice on the 'Rocket Docket,'" *Washington Post*, August 24, 1998, D1, D5.

43. Don Nunes, "Acquitted Defendant Faces Years in Prison," *Washington Post*, August 20, 1982, A1, A10.

44. Debra S. Emmelman, "Trial by Plea Bargain: Case Settlement as a Product of Recursive Decisionmaking," *Law & Society Review* 30 (1996), 335–360.

45. David Sudnow, "Normal Crimes: Sociological Features of the Penal Code in a Public Defender's Office," *Social Problems* 12 (Winter 1965), 255–276.

46. Stephanos Bibas, "Plea Bargaining Outside the Shadow of Trial," *Harvard Law Review* 117 (June 2004), 2464–2547.

47. The history of plea bargaining and reasons for its dominance are discussed in Mary E. Vogel, *Coercion to Compromise: Plea Bargaining, the Courts, and the Making of Political Authority* (New York: Oxford University Press, 2007); George Fisher, *Plea Bargaining's Triumph: A History of Plea Bargaining in America* (Stanford: Stanford University Press, 2003); and Bruce P. Smith, "Plea Bargaining and the Eclipse of the Jury," *Annual Review of Law and Social Science* 1 (2005), 131–149.

48. John F. Padgett, "Plea Bargaining and Prohibition in the Federal Courts, 1908–1934," *Law & Society Review* 24 (1990), 413–450.

49. Harold J. Rothwax, *Guilty: The Collapse of Criminal Justice* (New York: Random House, 1996), 145.

50. Malcolm M. Feeley, *The Process Is the Punishment: Handling Cases in a Lower Court* (New York: Russell Sage Foundation, 1979), 272 (emphasis in original).

51. Steve Bogira, *Courtroom 302: A Year Behind the Scenes in an American Criminal Courthouse* (New York: Knopf, 2005), 38.

52. Albert W. Alschuler, "The Trial Judge's Role in Plea Bargaining, Part I," *Columbia Law Review* 76 (November 1976), 1089.

53. Jeffery T. Ulmer and John H. Kramer, "Court Communities Under Sentencing Guidelines: Dilemmas of Formal Rationality and Sentencing Disparity," *Criminology* 34 (1996), 396.

54. Candace McCoy, "Bargaining in the Shadow of the Hammer: The Trial Penalty in the USA," in *The Jury Trial in Criminal Justice*, ed. Douglas D. Koski (Durham, N.C.: Carolina Academic Press, 2003), 23–29.

55. Paul B. Wice, *Public Defenders and the American Justice System* (Westport, Conn.: Praeger, 2005), 111.

56. Martin Berg, "Playing the Chaos Game," *California Lawyer* 12 (August 1992), 37.

57. Bruce Cadwallader, "Man Finally Convinces Court It Had Wrong Guy," *Columbus Dispatch*, July 16, 2003, C1, C2.

58. Jonathan Barzilay, "The D.A.'s Right Arms," *New York Times Magazine*, November 27, 1983, 121.

59. Rebecca Hollander-Blumoff, "Getting to 'Guilty': Plea Bargaining as Negotiation," *Harvard Negotiation Law Review* 2 (Spring 1997), 135–147.

60. Henry K. Lee, "Judge Balks at Lack of Jail for Son of Sex Smuggler," *San Francisco Chronicle*, March 30, 2004, B5; Henry K. Lee, "Landlord's Son Fined in Illegal Worker Case," *San Francisco Chronicle*, June 8, 2004, B5.

61. Dan Herbeck, "Judge Kills Deal for Kopp's Friends," *Buffalo News*, August 22, 2002, A1; Andy Newman, "Couple Plead Guilty to Aiding Man Who Killed Abortion Provider," *New York Times*, April 16, 2003, D8. The quotation is from the Herbeck article.

62. Brooke A. Masters and Carrie Johnson, "Corporate Scandals Yield Few Plea Deals," *Washington Post*, January 11, 2004, A1.

63. See Stephen J. Schulhofer, "Is Plea Bargaining Inevitable?" *Harvard Law Review* 97 (March 1984), 1037–1107. The figure for Philadelphia is on p. 1096.

64. Bogira, *Courtroom 302*, 150.

65. Lynn Mather, *Plea Bargaining or Trial?: The Process of Criminal-Case Disposition* (Lexington, Mass.: Lexington Books, 1979), 55–56.

66. Schulhofer, "Is Plea Bargaining Inevitable?"

67. Thomas M. Uhlman and Darlene N. Walker, " 'He Takes Some of My Time; I Take Some

of His': An Analysis of Judicial Sentencing Patterns in Jury Cases," *Law & Society Review* 14 (Winter 1980), 323–341.

68. Candace McCoy, *Politics and Plea Bargaining: Victims' Rights in California* (Philadelphia: University of Pennsylvania Press, 1993), xiv. See also Douglas D. Guirorizzi, "Should We Really 'Ban' Plea Bargaining? The Core Concerns of Plea Bargaining Critics," *Emory Law Journal* 47 (Spring 1998), 753–783.

69. Fisher, *Plea Bargaining's Triumph*, 1.

70. *People v. Weaver*, 118 Cal. App. 4th 131, 150 (Cal. 4th App. Dist. 2004).

71. Roland Acevedo, "Is a Ban on Plea Bargaining an Ethical Abuse of Discretion? A Bronx County, New York Case Study," *Fordham Law Review* 64 (December 1995), 987–1013; Joyce Shelby, "Tough Talk From DA on Gun Law," *New York Daily News*, June 14, 1999, 1; Andrew Blum, " 'No Plea' Policies Sprout Across U.S.," *National Law Journal*, September 9, 1996, A1, A20.

72. Deborah J. Daniels, "Sentencing Guidelines and Prosecutorial Discretion: The Justice Department's 'Clarification' of the Thornburgh Memo," *Federal Sentencing Reporter* 6 (May–June 1994), 302–305; Eric Lichtblau, "Ashcroft Limiting Prosecutors' Use of Plea Bargains," *New York Times*, September 23, 2003, A1, A25; John Ashcroft, "Memo Regarding Policy on Charging of Criminal Defendants," September 22, 2003 (http://www.usdoj.gov/opa/pr/2003/September/03_ag_516.htm).

73. Michael L. Rubinstein, Stevens H. Clarke, and Teresa J. White, *Alaska Bans Plea Bargaining* (Washington, D.C.: U.S. Department of Justice, 1980); Teri Carns, "Plea Bargaining Policy Rescinded by Cole," *Alaska Bar Rag*, March–April 1994, 9, 20.

74. McCoy, *Politics and Plea Bargaining*.

75. Philip Hager, "Fewer Felony Trials in State Despite a Rise in Caseload," *Los Angeles Times*, September 27, 1992, A1.

76. Rubinstein, Clarke, and White, *Alaska Bans Plea Bargaining*; Teresa White Carns and John A. Kruse, "Alaska's Ban on Plea Bargaining Reevaluated," *Judicature* 75 (April–May 1992), 310–317.

77. Carns, "Plea Bargaining Policy Rescinded by Cole," 9.

78. Administrative Office of the United States Courts, *Judicial Business of the United States Courts (2005)*, 412.

79. David Feige, "Printing Problems," Slate Magazine (http://slate.com/), May 27, 2004. See Flynn McRoberts, Steve Mills, and Maurice Possley, "Forensics Under the Microscope," *Chicago Tribune*, October 17, 2004, sec. 1, 1, 15–17.

80. Susan Schmidt and Blaine Harden, "Lawyer Is Cleared of Ties to Bombings," *Washington Post*, May 25, 2004, A2.

81. Lois Romano, "Police Chemist's Missteps Cause Okla. Scandal," *Washington Post*, November 26, 2001, A1; Francis X. Clines, "Work by Expert Witness Is Now on Trial," *New York Times*, September 5, 2001, A12; Adam Liptak and Ralph Blumenthal, "New Doubt Cast on Crime Testing in Houston Cases," *New York Times*, August 5, 2004, A1, A18.

82. See Randolph N. Jonakait, *The American Jury System* (New Haven: Yale University Press, 2003).

83. Michael J. Saks, "Enhancing and Restraining Accuracy in Adjudication," *Law and Contemporary Problems* 51 (Autumn 1988), 263.

84. Jerome Frank, *Courts on Trial: Myth and Reality in American Justice* (Princeton, N.J.: Princeton University Press, 1949), ch. 3.

85. Stephen J. Fortunato Jr., "No Uncertain Terms," *Legal Affairs*, January–February 2004, 16–18.

86. David Heilbroner, *Rough Justice: Days and Nights of a Young DA* (New York: Pantheon Books, 1990), 95.

87. Mark Curriden, "The Lies Have It," *American Bar Association Journal*, May 1995, 69.

88. Wiley (Miller), "Non Sequitur," *Columbus Dispatch*, February 5, 2004, A6.

89. Bennett L. Gershman, "Reflections on Brady v. Maryland," *South Texas Law Review* 47 (Summer 2006), 685–728.

90. *United States v. Wilson*, 289 F. Supp. 2d 801, 802 (S.D. Texas 2003).

91. Constance L. Hays and Leslie Eaton, "Martha Stewart, Near Trial, Arranges Her Image," *New York Times*, January 20, 2004, A1, C2.
92. H. Richard Uviller, *Virtual Justice: The Flawed Prosecution of Crime in America* (New Haven, Conn.: Yale University Press, 1996), 310.
93. Ibid., 242.
94. *Grotemeyer v. Hickman*, 393 F.3d 871, 879–880 (9th Cir. 2004).
95. Andrew E. Leipold, "Why Are Federal Judges So Acquittal Prone?" *Washington University Law Quarterly* 83 (2005), 162.
96. Theodore Eisenberg et al., "Judge-Jury Agreement in Criminal Cases: A Partial Replication of Kalven and Zeisel's *The American Jury*," *Journal of Empirical Legal Studies* 2 (March 2005), 171–206.
97. James P. Levine, *Juries and Politics* (Pacific Grove, Calif.: Brooks/Cole, 1992), chs. 4–8; Eisenberg et al., "Judge-Jury Agreement in Criminal Cases."
98. Scott Christianson, *Innocent: Inside Wrongful Conviction Cases* (New York: New York University Press, 2004); Samuel R. Gross, Kristen Jacoby, Daniel J. Matheson, Nicholas Montgomery, and Sujata Patil, "Exonerations in the United States 1989 Through 2003," *Journal of Criminal Law & Criminology* 95 (2005), 523–560; "Wrongful Convictions of the Innocent" (special issue), *Judicature* 86 (September–October 2002), 64–121.
99. Richard S. Frase, "State Sentencing Guidelines: Diversity, Consensus, and Unresolved Policy Issues," *Columbia Law Review* 105 (May 2005), 1190–1208.
100. *Blakely v. Washington*, 542 U.S. 296 (2004); *United States v. Booker*, 543 U.S. 220 (2005).
101. Paula M. Ditton and Doris James Wilson, *Truth in Sentencing in State Prisons* (Washington, D.C.: U.S. Department of Justice, Bureau of Justice Statistics, 1999).
102. Chuck Shepherd, "News of the Weird," *The Funny Times*, June 1997, 21.
103. Amy Argetsinger and Roxanne Roberts, "The Reliable Source," *Washington Post*, April 2, 2006, D3.
104. Bruce Cadwallader, "Since '92, Criminals Have Paid 3% of Fines," *Columbus Dispatch*, December 27, 2005, A1, A4.
105. See Blumstein et al., *Research on Sentencing*, I, 83–87; and Jo Dixon, "The Organizational Context of Criminal Sentencing," *American Journal of Sociology* 100 (March 1995), 1157–1198.
106. David Cole, *No Equal Justice: Race and Class in the American Criminal Justice System* (New York: New Press, 1999), 9. See also Randall Kennedy, *Race, Crime, and the Law* (New York: Pantheon, 1997).
107. Martha A. Myers and Susette M. Talarico, "The Social Contexts of Racial Discrimination in Sentencing," *Social Problems* 33 (February 1986), 236–251; Stephen Klein, Joan Petersilia, and Susan Turner, "Race and Imprisonment Decisions in California," *Science* 247 (February 16, 1990), 812–816.
108. Darrell Steffensmeier, Jeffery Ulmer, and John Kramer, "The Interaction of Race, Gender, and Age in Criminal Sentencing: The Punishment Cost of Being Young, Black, and Male," *Criminology* 36 (1998), 763–797; Cassia Spohn and David Holleran, "The Imprisonment Penalty Paid by Young, Unemployed Black and Hispanic Male Offenders," *Criminology* 38 (2000), 281–306.
109. David C. Baldus, George Woodworth, and Charles A. Pulaski, Jr., *Equal Justice and the Death Penalty: A Legal and Empirical Analysis* (Boston: Northeastern University Press, 1990); Samuel R. Gross and Robert Mauro, *Death and Discrimination: Racial Disparities in Capital Sentencing* (Boston: Northeastern University Press, 1989).
110. Richard Morin, "Justice Isn't Blind," *Washington Post*, September 3, 2000, B5.
111. Reynolds Holding, "Privilege Tips Scales of Justice," *San Francisco Chronicle*, February 4, 2001, Sunday section, 2.
112. Bob Egelko, "Rich Never Face Death Sentence," *San Francisco Examiner*, August 15, 1994, A2.
113. Herbert Edelhertz, *The Nature, Impact, and Prosecution of White Collar Crime* (Washington, D.C.: U.S. Department of Justice, 1970), 3.
114. Marcia Coyle, "Walking a Careful Line with Penalties," *National Law Journal*, May 10, 2004, 1, 17.

115. Fred Strasser, "Corporate Sentences Draw Fire," *National Law Journal*, March 12, 1990, 3, 9.

116. David Barstow, "U.S. Rarely Seeks Charges for Deaths in Workplace," *New York Times*, December 22, 2003, A1, A20, A21; David Barstow and Lowell Bergman, "With Little Fanfare, a New Effort to Prosecute Employers That Flout Safety Laws," *New York Times*, May 2, 2005, A17.

117. Alison Leigh Cowan, "Former Governor's Sentence Brings Gasps, and Questions About Leniency," *New York Times*, March 19, 2005, B4.

118. Jason McLure, "White-Collar Prosecutions Dropping," *Legal Times*, July 17, 2006, 1, 12.

119. David Margolick, "At the Bar," *New York Times*, December 18, 1987, B6.

120. *United States v. Jones*, 460 F.3d 191, 194 (2d Cir. 2006).

121. Jacqueline Cohen and Michael H. Tonry, "Sentencing Reforms and Their Impact," in Blumstein et al., *Research on Sentencing*, II, 417.

122. Bureau of Justice Assistance, *National Assessment of Structured Sentencing* (Washington, D.C.: U.S. Department of Justice, 1996), 82–98. See Lisa Stolzenberg and Stewart J. D'Alessio, "Sentencing and Unwarranted Disparity: An Empirical Assessment of the Long-Term Impact of Sentencing Guidelines in Minnesota," *Criminology* 32 (May 1994), 301–310; and Shawn D. Bushway and Anne Morrison Piehl, "Judging Judicial Discretion: Legal Factors and Racial Discrimination in Sentencing," *Law & Society Review* 35 (2001), 733–764."

123. H. Laurence Ross and James P. Foley, "Judicial Disobedience of the Mandate to Imprison Drunk Drivers," *Law & Society Review* 21 (1987), 315–323.

124. On three-strikes laws, see David Schichor and Dale K. Sechrest, eds., *Three Strikes and You're Out: Vengeance as Public Policy* (Thousand Oaks, Calif.: Sage Publications, 1996); and John Clark, James Austin, and D. Alan Henry, " 'Three Strikes and You're Out': Are Repeat Offender Laws Having Their Anticipated Effects?" *Judicature* 81 (January–February 1998), 144–149.

125. David Bjerk, "Making the Crime Fit the Penalty: The Role of Prosecutorial Discretion Under Mandatory Minimum Sentencing," *Journal of Law and Economics* 48 (October 2005), 591–625.

126. Kate Stith and Jose A. Cabranes, *Fear of Judging: Sentencing Guidelines in the Federal Courts* (Chicago: University of Chicago Press, 1998), 5.

127. United States Sentencing Commission, *Mandatory Minimum Penalties in the Federal Criminal Justice System* (Washington, D.C.: U.S. Government Printing Office, 1991), 76–82; United States General Accounting Office, *Sentencing Guidelines: Central Questions Remain Unanswered* (Washington, D.C.: Government Printing Office, 1992), 111–142. For a different finding, see Joe Gorton and John L. Boies, "Sentencing Guidelines and Racial Disparity Across Time: Pennsylvania Prison Sentences in 1977, 1983, 1992, and 1993," *Social Science Quarterly* 80 (March 1999), 37–54.

128. See Stephanos Bibas, "Regulating Local Variations in Federal Sentencing," *Stanford Law Review* 58 (October 2005), 137–154.

129. See *United States v. Inclema*, 363 F.3d 1177 (11th Cir. 2004).

130. Leipold, "Why Are Federal Judges so Acquittal Prone?" 200–218.

131. *United States v. Angelos*, 345 F. Supp. 2d 1227, 1263 (D. Utah 2004).

132. United States Sentencing Commission, *2003 Annual Report*, 37 (http://www.ussc.gov/ANNRPT/2003/ar03toc.htm). The 2003 legislation discussed in the next paragraph became effective late in the 2003 fiscal year, so it may have affected these patterns somewhat. Unfortunately, full information on the sources of downward departures was not available until 2003.

133. See Michael W. McConnell, "The *Booker* Mess," *Denver University Law Review* 83 (2006), 665–684.

134. Nancy Gertner, "What Yogi Berra Teaches About Post-*Booker* Sentencing," *Yale Law Journal Pocket Part* 115 (2006), 137–141; Douglas A. Berman, "Reasoning Through Reasonableness," *Yale Law Journal Pocket Part* 115 (2006), 142–145.

135. United States Sentencing Commission, *Final Report on the Impact of* United States v. Booker *on Federal Sentencing* (March 2006), 57.

136. Steven L. Chanenson and Daniel F. Wilhelm, "Evolution and Denial: State Sentencing After *Blakely* and *Booker*," *Federal Sentencing Reporter* 18 (October 2005), 1–6.

7

Trial Courts: Civil Cases

U nlike criminal cases, civil cases seldom garner newspaper headlines or coverage on television news programs before the first commercial. Yet the civil side of the courts' work affects more people in more ways. The outcomes of civil cases determine the compensation that people receive for their injuries, the custody of children after divorce, the division of assets after death, and other matters that affect people's lives. Cumulatively, these outcomes shape national policy on issues ranging from health care to the family.

One characteristic of civil cases is the diversity of their subject matter, and this quality makes it difficult to generalize about them. For that reason, much of this chapter focuses on individual types of cases rather than civil cases as a whole. Taken together, the categories of cases considered in the chapter provide a sense of what trial courts do and how they operate in civil cases.

In discussing civil courts—shorthand for trial courts in civil cases—I give some emphasis to two issues. The first issue concerns litigation, the use of civil courts, and its alternatives. Matters that might be taken to court can be handled in a variety of other ways, and only a small minority of potential civil cases actually go to court. Whether or not potential cases become actual cases is consequential, because their outcomes may depend on whether they are resolved in court or elsewhere. Yet the possibility of litigation affects even those matters that never get to court: when people negotiate to resolve disputes, they often do so "in the shadow of the law."[1] For this reason, an examination of civil courts must take into account actions and decisions that occur outside the courts.

The second issue concerns the benefits and burdens that civil courts allocate. Court decisions affect a great many individuals and institutions. For this reason, it makes a good deal of difference who wins and loses cases in court and who is favored by the legal rules that courts establish. Litigation aimed at winning cases and gaining favorable rules often involves contention between parties of vastly unequal economic resources—for example, injured individuals and insurance companies or debtors and finance companies. We might expect advantaged litigants to do much better than the weaker parties with whom they contend. The extent to which this result actually occurs is an important concern of the chapter.

Both these issues relate to a central reality of the civil courts: they are a focus of political contention. Because civil cases have such high stakes, every group in American society wants a favorable position in court. Any formal or informal group—whether manufacturers or labor unions or consumers—would like to have the maximum access to the courts when its members would gain an advantage by using them. By the same token, every group would like to limit access to the courts for groups that might sue its members. Put differently, everyone wants the chance to be a *plaintiff*, the party that brings a lawsuit; nobody wants to be a *defendant*, the party against whom a suit is brought. In cases that do reach court, of course, every group wants the best possible chance of winning. The rules that determine who can get into court and that govern cases in court are set primarily by legislation and appellate court decisions. Interest groups do not leave the creation of rules to chance. Indeed, they expend massive resources to influence those rules. In this way, political processes in the legislative and judicial branches powerfully shape the work of civil courts.

AN OVERVIEW OF CIVIL COURTS

As with criminal cases, it is useful to begin with a general look at trial courts and their work. This section examines the purposes behind civil cases, the most common types of civil cases, and the participants and procedures in civil courts.

The Purposes of Civil Courts

People go to civil courts to seek what are called *remedies*—things they are asking the courts to give them.[2] The most common remedy is *damages* to compensate for a loss. The loss may be something concrete, such as the cost of a car repair after an accident, or more abstract, such as harm to a reputation resulting from a libelous publication. Along with compensatory damages, a plaintiff can be awarded *punitive damages*, intended to punish a defendant for wrongdoing. Closely related to damages is *restitution*, the return of something belonging to a person such as land or corporate bonds.

Another kind of remedy is *coercion*, in which a party asks the court to require that another party either take a particular action or refrain from an action. The major form of this remedy is an injunction, in which a court orders action such as the halting of a labor strike. The final type of remedy is a *declaration* of legal rights or status, such as the termination of marriage through divorce or a ruling that a statute is unconstitutional.

Government gives the courts the power to provide these remedies as a means to serve two broad goals, each tied to a general function of the courts discussed in Chapter 1.[3] The first is dispute resolution: the law offers remedies to people who have grievances in order to encourage the peaceful and orderly settlement of conflicts. The second is behavior modification: the law imposes costs on certain kinds of behavior with the intent of discouraging that behavior.

These broad goals enjoy general acceptance, but more specific issues elicit heated disagreement. This is especially true of behavior modification. There is considerable conflict over how the law should be written to discourage or prevent undesirable behavior such as drunken driving, the making of unsafe products, and medical malpractice. Should airlines, airports, and building owners be held responsible for some of the damages that result when terrorists fly planes into buildings? Should casinos be held liable if they encourage gambling by people who are compulsive gamblers?[4] Not surprisingly, there is seldom consensus about such issues.

As noted earlier, questions about when legal remedies should be available are resolved primarily by legislatures and appellate courts. In some areas of law, called "common law" fields, appellate courts were primarily responsible for establishing the basic legal rules, but legislatures have superseded some of those rules with statutes. In personal injury law, one common law field, the law today is a complicated mix of legislation and court decisions. In other legal areas, legislatures have established the basic rules by statute, and courts interpret these rules, filling in details that statutes leave uncertain. On many issues the law varies a great deal from state to state. For instance, in some states, landlords have a legal duty to provide reasonable protection against crime to their tenants, but in other states they do not. Of course, the legal rules that exist in any state at a given time reflect the political processes that shape every aspect of the civil courts.

Major Types of Civil Cases

Among the wide range of cases handled by civil courts, some occur much more frequently than others. The preponderance of cases fall into four categories.[5]

Most *contract* cases arise when one party to a contract claims that the other party has violated its terms. Such cases can involve the whole array of agreements that exist in our society. But most are brought by businesses against individuals on the basis of contracts for the sale or rental of goods, for the purchase of services, or for the lending of money. In these cases, the business alleges that it has not received the money owed to it and seeks restitution in the form of direct payment or through some other means, such as the foreclosure of a mortgage on property. I refer to this kind of contract case as *debt collection*.

Personal injury, property damage, and wrongful death cases can all be put under the heading of *personal injury* cases. In turn, personal injury cases constitute the largest part of the field called tort law. In these cases, the party who has suffered a loss seeks damages to compensate for that loss. Personal injury cases typically result from accidents, which can be triggered by everything from use of a household product to receiving medical care. However, a majority of personal injury cases arise from a single source, accidents involving motor vehicles.

Most *domestic relations* cases concern matters related to marriage. Courts provide the administrative service of granting marriage licenses and performing marriages. Even if we leave this service aside, the work of trial courts in domestic relations is still sizable. The preponderance of this work concerns divorce: awarding divorces, determining child custody, and allocating economic resources between the former wife and husband.

Finally, most *estate* or *probate* cases concern the assets of people who have died. In these cases, courts supervise the administration of wills and handle the estates of people who did not write wills. Also in this category are guardianships for juveniles and for adults who are declared mentally incompetent to handle their own affairs.

These four types of cases all come under the heading of private law. Only a small (but growing) minority of civil cases can be considered public law, which involves the government acting as government rather than in a role such as creditor. Because public law cases are more prominent at the appellate level, they are discussed primarily in Chapters 8 and 9.

Public law cases are likely to go to federal court, but the great majority of all civil cases are handled in state courts. For that reason this chapter, like the preceding one, gives most of its attention to the state level. However, the processes involved in civil litigation are similar at the state and federal levels, and I generally do not distinguish between the two sets of courts.

Participants in Civil Courts

As in criminal courts, the most important participants in civil courts are lawyers and judges. In both settings, they are the core of the courtroom work group. Another similarity is that the relationships among lawyers and judges are closer when a set of lawyers comes before a particular judge more frequently.

Judges   The great majority of judges spend at least part of their time hearing civil cases. Many judges sit on courts that hear only civil cases. Some specialize more narrowly, serving permanently on courts or divisions that handle only a specific type of case such as probate, domestic relations, or bankruptcy.

In most respects, the powers and responsibilities of judges in civil cases are similar to those in criminal cases. One difference is that a higher proportion of civil cases are heard by judges. In federal district courts in 2005, one-third of all criminal trials were before juries, compared with one-ninth of all civil trials.[6] And there are large categories of cases—bankruptcy in federal court, domestic relations and estates in state court—that seldom or never involve jury trials. This difference, of course, increases the judge's role as a decision maker. Another difference is that judges participate in negotiations between civil parties more often than they do in plea bargaining. But unlike criminal litigants who must await the judge's sentencing decision, civil parties who settle out of court ordinarily determine the specific terms of the settlement themselves.

Attorneys   As in criminal cases, attorneys appear in most civil cases that have substantial stakes. They are less common in cases with smaller stakes. Indeed, some small claims courts prohibit them altogether. And the numbers of people who represent themselves have been growing. In many areas of law, the lawyers who participate in cases are primarily specialists in those areas. But in nontechnical areas that have large numbers of cases, such as estates, much of the work is done by lawyers who are not specialists. This is especially true outside of big cities.

Some areas of law on the civil side resemble criminal law in the sense that lawyers specialize by the "side" they represent. For example, in areas that pit the government against private parties, such as taxes and economic regulation, the government is usually represented by its own full-time employees, while attorneys in private practice serve individuals and private organizations. In areas that typically involve conflicts between businesses and individuals, such as debt collection and personal injury cases, the attorneys who represent businesses generally are a separate group from those who represent individuals. In some other areas, however, most lawyers work on both sides. For instance, most divorce lawyers represent both husbands and wives.

Parties   Civil cases pit plaintiffs against defendants. Cases often have multiple plaintiffs, multiple defendants, or both. Under some conditions a case may be brought as a class action, in which one or more people sue on behalf of a larger set of people who share the same situation. One prominent example is the smokers and former smokers who have sued tobacco companies for damage to their health.

The parties to civil cases may be classified in several ways. Marc Galanter and other scholars have suggested the importance of three related distinctions.[7] The first is between individuals and organizations, primarily businesses and governments. The second is between what Galanter called "one-shotters," or "those claimants who have only occasional recourse to the courts," and "repeat players" such as insurance companies, finance companies, and some government agencies "who are engaged in many similar litigations over time."[8] Finally, Galanter distinguished between litigants by their economic status, dividing them into "haves" and "have-nots." These distinctions are linked, since organizations tend to be repeat players that have substantial economic resources, while individuals tend to be one-shotters who possess fewer resources.

Galanter argued that haves generally "come out ahead" in litigation.[9] To the extent this is true, the success of haves reflects several advantages that flow from economic resources and repeat-player status. The most obvious is that they can afford more and better legal services. In cases that pit haves and have-nots, the likely disparity in legal resources favors the haves. Further, those with more resources have a greater capacity to go to court in the first place. One effect is that haves can use litigation or the threat of litigation as leverage against those who have only a limited capacity to defend themselves in court. Repeat players can also seek to deter lawsuits against them with aggressive defenses that make such suits costly. Critics have charged that Allstate Insurance used this tactic in order to discourage lawyers from representing people who sought small amounts of damages from drivers insured by Allstate.[10]

As that example suggests, repeat players who have plentiful economic resources have both the incentive and the capacity to gain a favorable position in the future. Large businesses and governments go to appellate courts and to legislatures in order to win legal rules that will strengthen their positions in litigation or potential litigation that arises later on. Repeat players can also structure transactions in ways that put them in a favorable position in the event of a dispute, often by controlling the terms of their contracts with weaker parties. Exhibit 7.1 discusses some examples of this practice.

It may seem self-evident from their various advantages that on the whole, the haves do come out ahead in court. But our evidence on what actually happens in court cases is limited.[11] Further, that evidence is subject to different interpretations.

Within these limitations, the hypothesis that the haves come out ahead can be probed in types of civil cases that pit different types of parties against each other. In most debt collection cases, merchants and financial institutions sue low-income individuals. In most personal injury cases, individuals sue defendants who are represented by insurance companies. To what extent do litigants such as creditors and insurance companies—organizations, repeat players, and haves—succeed in court? The last section of this chapter examines the evidence on this question.

EXHIBIT 7.1   Contracts of Adhesion

In transactions between businesses and employees or consumers, it is common for a business to require that an employee or consumer sign a standard contract with terms favorable to the business. Someone who wants a job or a product or a service has no choice but to accept those terms. These are sometimes called "contracts of adhesion." Should a dispute arise between the business and the other party, the contract is likely to put the business in a strong position. Of all the contracts of adhesion, probably the most numerous are the agreements that consumers must accept to obtain credit cards. But such contracts can be found in a variety of other places as well.

Some contracts are quite elaborate, running more than ten thousand words. Those people who were members of the Hertz "#1 Club Gold" were made subject to a lengthy new agreement with Hertz at the beginning of 2006. That contract made several changes that favored Hertz—changes that, to the company's credit, it summarized rather than simply burying in the contract. Under one provision, as the summary explained, people who rented Hertz cars were now responsible for "loss or damage" resulting from "acts of nature or God beyond your control."

The contract that Carnival Cruise Lines presented to its passengers as of 2006 was not nearly as lengthy, but it had a wide range of provisions that favored the company. Carnival exempted itself from responsibility for such matters as passengers' safety in ports and actions of many of the service personnel on board its ships. The contract also capped Carnival's liability for loss of its passengers' property at $100 per room unless passengers paid an additional fee to the company. Under the contract Carnival could change its ship's course, port calls, and arrival and departure times "with or without notice, for any reason whatsoever." For their part, passengers were subject to a variety of restrictions. Among other things, they could bring on board only "a small quantity of non-alcoholic beverages at the beginning of the cruise during embarkation day only. Excessive quantities, as determined by Carnival, will be confiscated and discarded without compensation." One virtue of this contract was that its language was less technical and thus more understandable than that of many other contracts that consumers receive.

Participants in television reality shows may also be required to sign contracts that can work to their disadvantage. One example is the contract that boxers who participated in NBC's boxing "reality" show "The Contender" had to sign. Among other things, according to a newspaper report, contestants were required to allow the program to use information about them that might be "personal, private, surprising, defamatory, disparaging, embarrassing or unfavorable" and to let its producers "make certain misrepresentations to me and others" about some matters. Under another provision, a contestant might have to pay as much as $500,000 for disclosing information about the series even after all episodes had been shown on television.

The terms in contracts of adhesion are not always enforceable in practice, sometimes because they conflict with legal protections for employees and consumers. But these contracts often set up rules for potential lawsuits that favor the interests of the businesses that impose them—requiring, for example, that such lawsuits be brought in the "home" district of the business. In any event, those who accept these contracts seldom knew when terms of the contracts might be challenged successfully. Ordinarily, then, these contracts serve their purposes well.

(Continued on next page)

EXHIBIT 7.1 *(continued)*

Sources: David Lazarus, "Hertz Puts You in the Hot Seat," *San Francisco Chronicle*, January 13, 2006, C1; "Terms and Conditions Update and Notice of Amendment" (Hertz website, http://www .hertz.com/goldtermsupdate/); "Ticket Contract" (Carnival Cruise Lines website, http://www .carnival.com/CMS/Static_Templates/ticket_contract.aspx); David Foster Wallace, *A Supposedly Fun Thing I'll Never Do Again* (Boston: Little, Brown, 1997), 318 n. 89; Richard Sandomir, "For Fame and Fortune, Boxing Hopefuls Seal Their Lips and Sign Their Lives Away," *New York Times*, November 1, 2004, D1, D2. The quotations are from the Hertz and Carnival contracts and from the *New York Times* article.

Other Participants   Of the other participants in criminal courts, some—such as witnesses and court clerks—play similar roles in the civil courts. Law enforcement officers are far less important, although they often serve as witnesses in auto accident cases. Grand jurors and probation officers, of course, are absent altogether.

When a civil case is tried before a jury, the jury's position is somewhat different from that of the criminal jury. In suits for damages, civil court juries determine the amount to be paid if they find the defendant liable. Thus they exercise the equivalent of the judge's sentencing power in criminal cases. But the trial judge has more power in civil cases to override a jury's verdict or to take a decision away from a jury.

A Summary of Court Procedures

Both formal and actual procedures for civil cases vary a good deal. The basic and most common set of procedures is the one ordinarily used in suits for damages and restitution. I focus on those procedures, discussing other sets of procedures more briefly.[12]

The Basic System   In a typical set of procedures for civil cases, as shown in Exhibit 7.2, court action begins with the filing by the plaintiff of a *complaint* making

EXHIBIT 7.2   Typical Stages of Processing of Civil Suits for Damages or Restitution

1. Filing of a complaint by the plaintiff
2. Serving of process on the defendant
3. Filing of an answer to the complaint by the defendant
4. Discovery of evidence: depositions, interrogatories, and discovery of materials
5. Pretrial conference and order
6. Trial
7. Verdict on liability and (where liability is found) the remedy
8. Post-trial motions: for a judgment notwithstanding the verdict, to set aside the verdict
9. Compliance with or enforcement of the judgment

legal allegations against the defendant. (For the sake of simplicity, I assume that the case has only a single plaintiff and a single defendant.) The next step is notification of the defendant, called *serving process.* The defendant may then file an *answer* to the complaint. This answer offers defenses to the complaint, and it may also make counterclaims against the plaintiff—in effect, making the plaintiff a defendant as well. The complaint and the answer are called the *pleadings.*

A series of pretrial procedures follows the pleadings. In *discovery,* the parties gather evidence from each other, primarily in three forms. The first is *depositions,* in which the lawyer for one side questions the other party and the witnesses for the other side. The second is *interrogatories,* in which one party presents questions to the other party for more extensive written responses. The third is the *discovery of documents and other materials* held by the other party. The judge does not supervise discovery directly but settles any disputes that may arise at this stage.

These proceedings were created to eliminate the surprise element at trial, but they have come to play an important—sometimes crucial—role in civil cases. As one commentator has said, "The real action, the stuff that wins or loses a case, is far more likely to happen in a conference room than a courtroom."[13] It was President Clinton's testimony during discovery about his relationship with Monica Lewinsky that raised the question of whether he had committed perjury and ultimately led to his impeachment. Depositions and other discovery proceedings often become a battle between parties that seek to obtain as much information as possible and opponents that try to provide as little as they can. Lawyers use their questions of witnesses for the other side at depositions to weaken their testimony, and they sometimes try to intimidate witnesses with their questioning. Pretrial proceedings also provide an opportunity for lawyers to press for any advantage, no matter how small. That behavior is reflected in the case described in Exhibit 7.3.

After discovery is completed, the judge may schedule a *pretrial conference* with the parties. In some courts, the conference is mandatory. During the conference, the judge seeks to clarify the issues in the case and ready it for trial. Afterwards, the judge makes up a pretrial order listing the evidence that the parties will present.

Like criminal cases, civil cases can drop out along the way to trial. The plaintiff can drop the case voluntarily, perhaps because a favorable outcome seems unlikely or because filing the lawsuit was a symbolic action to express anger or dissatisfaction. In cases that plaintiffs do not drop, the parties usually reach a settlement out of court. Settlements in some types of cases require the judge's approval, while others are simply reached between the parties. Where approval is required, judges provide it in the great majority of cases. As in criminal cases, the high rate of settlements reflects the desire to limit costs as well as the desire to avoid an undesirable outcome.

Sometimes the judge reaches a decision in the case before it comes to trial. The judge may dismiss the case because of the plaintiff's failure to pursue it adequately. Similarly, the judge may issue a *default judgment* against the defendant for failure to file an answer or to meet other procedural requirements. Either party may also ask for a *judgment on* the basis of *the pleadings,* which the judge can grant if the other party has failed to make sufficient allegations to support a case. And the judge can grant a *summary judgment* to one party on the ground that the law compels a decision in favor of that party.

EXHIBIT 7.3   A Federal Judge Settles a Dispute over Discovery

In a Florida federal case involving a dispute over insurance, the lawyers on the two sides could not agree on where to hold the deposition of a witness, and one filed a motion to have district judge Gregory Presnell designate the location. Judge Presnell denied the motion, calling it "the latest in a series of Gordian knots that the parties have been unable to untangle without enlisting the assistance of the federal courts." But wanting to end the battle over location of the deposition, the judge ordered that the two lawyers "convene at a neutral site agreeable to both parties" at a designated time and place—adding that if they could not agree even on that, they would meet on the front steps of the federal courthouse.

Judge Presnell then described what the lawyers were to do: "Each lawyer shall be entitled to be accompanied by one paralegal who shall act as an attendant and witness. At that time and location, counsel shall engage in one (1) game of 'rock, paper, scissors.' The winner of this engagement shall be entitled to select the location for the 30(b)(6) deposition to be held somewhere in Hillsborough County during the period July 11–12, 2006." Recognizing that he could take nothing for granted, he added: "If either party disputes the outcome of this engagement, an appeal may be filed and a hearing will be held at 8:30 A.M. on Friday, July 7, 2006."

With the game pending, a reporter consulted the co-commissioner of the USA Rock Paper Scissors League, the governing body of the sport. He predicted that "both lawyers will open with paper. Lawyers open with paper 67 percent of the time, because they deal with so much paper." This official volunteered to officiate at the match, an offer that was unlikely to be accepted. As yet, there is no report of the outcome.

Sources: Avista Management, Inc. v. Wausau Underwriters Insurance Company, 2006 U.S. Dist. LEXIS 38526 (M.D. Fla. 2006); Adam Liptak, "Lawyers Won't End Squabble, So Judge Turns to Child's Play," *New York Times*, June 9, 2006, A20. The last quotation is from the Liptak article, the others from the decision.

In civil cases, as in criminal cases, the great majority of cases do drop out prior to trial. In 2005, for instance, only 1.4 percent of the civil cases terminated in federal district courts had gone to trial.[14] And even more than on the criminal side of the law, the rate of trials has declined. In 1936, at least 18 percent of all federal civil cases went to trial, and in the years that followed this proportion dropped bit by bit to its current low level.[15] Less dramatic declines have occurred in the states.[16] Noting these trends, some commentators have referred to "the vanishing trial."[17] The reasons for this decline are uncertain.[18] One factor may be increasing backlogs of cases in many courts, which make it less attractive to wait for trials. Another may be stronger efforts by judges to resolve cases at pretrial stages. One judge referred to a "settlement culture" in the federal courts.[19]

The trials that do occur resemble criminal trials. As a trial proceeds, the plaintiff seeks to prove the defendant's liability and the appropriateness of the desired remedy. In response, the defendant may contest either or both issues. On the remedy, the question usually is the amount of money to be paid in damages if liability is found. The standard of proof for liability generally is a preponderance of the evidence, a standard that is easier to meet than the proof beyond a reasonable doubt required of criminal prosecutors.

During a jury trial, the judge may grant a *directed verdict* in favor of one party at the close of the other party's case, on the ground that the evidence allows only one outcome. If there is no directed verdict, the judge or jury decides the contested issues after the trial. Where damages or restitution are to be provided, the amount is determined.

After a jury decision, the losing party can ask the judge for what is called a *judgment notwithstanding the verdict*, on the ground that there was insufficient basis for the jury's decision. A party can also ask the judge to set aside the verdict and order a new trial on the basis of problems in either the trial or the verdict.

If the court's judgment requires one party to provide a remedy to the other, that party may comply readily with the judgment. If voluntary compliance does not occur, the winning party can seek enforcement of the judgment by the sheriff or another official through a variety of methods, including garnishment (a process in which an employer withholds part of the losing party's wages and turns it over to the winning party) and the forced sale of the loser's property to pay the judgment.

Cases typically take considerable time to go through these stages. For the federal civil cases that were resolved by jury trials in 2005, the median time from filing to trial was slightly more than two years. In the state courts in Chicago in 2003, the median time was slightly more than three years.[20] Some cases take much longer. A case in Washington, D.C. that originated in 1981 as a dispute over $14,500 took a series of twists, and it was far from completion in 2004.[21]

Other Sets of Procedures   In civil cases with small stakes, as in similar criminal cases, formal procedures can be relatively simple. This is especially true of small claims courts, which are usually special divisions of trial courts designated to hear cases in which plaintiffs seek relatively small amounts of money or (in some states) remedies such as evictions. A significant proportion of all civil cases are heard under small claims procedures. Small claims courts were created to handle cases at relatively little expense to the parties and with less delay than in other civil courts. In line with these goals, small claims courts operate under special procedural rules. Pretrial procedures are shortened and simplified, and trials are held before judges with considerable informality. Even when lawyers are allowed in small claims courts, parties often proceed without them.

Cases in which the plaintiff seeks a coercive remedy are handled under a different set of procedures, which can be illustrated with injunctions. Prior to trial the plaintiff may ask for a *temporary restraining order*, sometimes without giving notice to the defendant. Later the plaintiff may seek a *preliminary injunction*, which the defendant can contest. Both are intended to prevent the defendant from taking irreversible action, such as demolishing a building. The trial itself, in which the plaintiff seeks a permanent injunction, is held before a judge alone. In many cases, the trial is relatively short because much of the relevant evidence was presented in the pretrial hearings. If an injunction is awarded, it can be enforced with a motion to hold a non-complying party in contempt of court. If a judge holds that party in contempt, the judge can impose a fine or prison sentence.

Cases involving divorces and the estates of deceased people have their own procedures as well. In both categories, most cases are uncontested: for example, nobody disputes a will, or a husband and wife both want a divorce and agree on the terms of the settlement. Such cases must go to court for approval of the uncontested action or agreement, but the hearings are generally routine and abbreviated. When divorce and estate cases are contested, they go through adversarial proceedings before a judge.

DECIDING WHETHER TO LITIGATE

One widespread image of Americans is that we are a litigious people who "will sue each other at the slightest provocation."[22] In this image, people in the United States—or at least a great many people—look eagerly for opportunities to file lawsuits. In particular, trivial or nonexistent injuries turn into claims for large amounts of money. Indeed, one legal scholar has argued that "we are the most litigious people in the world."[23] There is also a widespread belief that the United States has experienced a massive growth in litigation in recent years as people flock to the courts in unprecedented numbers.

Combining the two themes, a representative of the U.S. Chamber of Commerce said in 2005 that "in the last decade, we've had a litigation explosion in this country that is unmatched in the industrial world."[24] The courts themselves are thought to encourage this explosion by awarding damages in highly questionable circumstances. The result, according to some people, has been considerable damage to the American economy and American society: among other things, billions of dollars each year are drained from productive use to pay legal costs, companies stop making some useful products to avoid potentially disastrous lawsuits, and everyone suffers.

This section considers the accuracy of these images: to what extent are Americans litigious, and how much of a litigation explosion is actually occurring? But before those questions can be addressed directly, we need to take a broader look at decisions whether to engage in litigation.

As individuals or members of organizations, people often decide whether to take cases to court—that is, to litigate. These decisions emerge from situations in which a person develops a grievance or recognizes an opportunity that might be addressed through litigation. In such situations, people may do nothing at all, choosing to live with the grievance or to forgo the opportunity, or they may choose to take some action other than litigation. But they might decide to go to court, either as a first action or after trying one or more alternatives. Going to court itself involves two steps: filing a lawsuit and taking a case to trial. Although both steps are important, the second is the more decisive, for it means that the parties are putting their dispute before a court rather than settling it in another forum.

Some Types of Litigation

A good way to begin is by looking at litigation in specific areas of law. Since each area has its own patterns, I examine three somewhat different areas: discrimination, personal injuries, and disputes between businesses.

Discrimination Cases brought under the laws that prohibit discrimination are not among the most common types of litigation. But when commentators speak of today's Americans as litigious, they sometimes use discrimination claims to illustrate their arguments.[25]

Indeed, the number of discrimination cases brought to federal courts grew tremendously from the 1960s to the late 1990s, though that number has declined somewhat since then. Most discrimination cases concern employment, and the number of those cases filed in federal court tripled between 1990 and 1997.[26] However, this growth was not primarily a result of increased litigiousness. Rather, its main source was the enactment of federal statutes that provided new or expanded rights to challenge discrimination in court.

The facts of some discrimination cases suggest that the plaintiff was eager to litigate. Yet the most striking attribute of litigation over discrimination is how few people go to court. Surveys indicate that among those people who think they have been the victims of discrimination, a relative few—perhaps as few as one in one hundred—file lawsuits.[27]

There are several reasons for this infrequent use of litigation. For one thing, many people do not know what action they can take if they are denied an apartment or a job and feel that the denial was discriminatory. As a result, they may simply live with their grievance. Second, it is often difficult to get favorable legal action on discrimination complaints. The administrative agencies that deal with discrimination typically have limited legal powers and inadequate staffing. Discrimination in such decisions as hiring of employees and housing rentals is seldom easy to prove in court. As a result, people who bring discrimination cases to court have a low rate of success, considerably lower than plaintiffs in most other areas of law.[28]

Perhaps most important, seeking to redress discrimination entails cost, and these costs are especially high when the action extends to litigation. Some costs are monetary, such as paying a lawyer who will not take a case on a purely contingent basis. Other costs are psychological. To press a discrimination claim is to become involved in a conflict, to be identified as a complainer, and to live with uncertainty. Such problems are most serious when people complain of discrimination by other people with whom they must continue to deal, such as employers and school administrators. In these cases, to put it mildly, a lawsuit can lead to strained relations. A successful lawsuit hardly solves such problems. Indeed, the atmosphere at a workplace usually becomes too unpleasant for successful litigants to remain. Anticipating these costs of litigation, most people simply live with their grievance or go elsewhere.

Despite all these difficulties, people bring a large number of lawsuits to court, and some people file discrimination cases even though their cases are weak. Collectively, these lawsuits have considerable impact. But those cases are only a fraction of the ones that could be brought.

Personal Injuries Any incident that produces a significant physical injury or costly property damage might seem likely to go to court. For one thing, the injured party and the potential defendant (often another driver or the manufacturer of a product) are generally strangers. Thus the personal costs and risks of litigation are greatly reduced. Further, most people know they have legal remedies for personal injuries.

Lawyers are more readily available than they are in some other fields of law. A potential plaintiff who has a strong case involving a substantial amount of money can nearly always find a lawyer who is willing to take the case on a contingent fee basis. Advertising by attorneys helps to publicize remedies and identifies lawyers who might take a case. And lawyers increasingly make direct contact with people who have been involved in accidents.

Indeed, a serious physical injury is more likely to result in a lawsuit than is a perception of discrimination. Yet in this field as well, suits are filed in only a very small proportion of the cases that could have gone to court—according to two studies, 2 to 4 percent.[29]

Different sources of injuries vary in the paths that lead potential plaintiffs to litigate or to avoid litigation. Because defective products can injure large numbers of people, product liability suits sometimes are brought as class actions by lawyers who act as entrepreneurs in putting together a class of plaintiffs. In those situations, few if any of the class members made decisions to litigate on their own. Two other sources of injuries, auto accidents and medical malpractice, illustrate two different processes that keep most cases out of court.

Auto accidents are by far the largest source of potential and actual lawsuits over personal injuries. After accidents occur, at least a large minority of people who suffer significant physical injuries or property losses make claims against the party they see as responsible.[30] But auto accident claims ordinarily are resolved before a lawsuit is filed.

The potential defendant in these cases is the party that allegedly caused the injury, but any settlement or court judgment would ordinarily be paid by that party's insurance company. Thus the claim quickly becomes one against the insurance company, which takes over for its client in handling the case. Insurance companies generally want to settle claims quickly, in part because they prefer to reach an agreement before the injured person hires an attorney. Insurance companies frequently succeed in securing early agreements, largely because people who have suffered injuries or property damage also want to settle their cases quickly. These settlements usually involve payments to the injured party, although the insurance adjuster sometimes convinces an injured person to accept the lack of a payment and take no further action.

If the two sides do not reach an easy settlement and the injured party remains dissatisfied, more often than not that party will hire an attorney. In one study of bodily injury claims, 55 percent of all injured people eventually used a lawyer.[31] Although this step escalates the conflict to a degree, it also facilitates a settlement. The lawyers who represent injured parties are usually experienced in personal injury cases. Indeed, they are often specialists in that area. On the other side, the insurance company's adjusters or attorneys are also specialists. Thus, as in plea bargaining, the two sides share an understanding of how to negotiate these cases and a sense of the kinds of settlements that are usually reached in common types of cases.

Another similarity with plea bargaining is in the motivations for settling cases. For one thing, both sides want to avoid the risks of a trial—in which an insurance company might be required to pay high damages or an injured party might lose and collect nothing. And both insurance companies and lawyers who represent injured parties want to avoid spending the time that is required to take cases to trial.

In a substantial minority of cases, the lawyer for the injured party eventually files suit, and serious negotiations may not occur until the scheduled trial date is close. But the two sides can usually reach a settlement at some point, for the same reasons that lead to settlement prior to filing a lawsuit. In cases based on bodily injuries in auto accidents, a study found that 18 percent of all claims led to lawsuits, but only 1 percent of the claims actually went to trial—and half of those were settled before a verdict.[32] The cases that do go to trial tend to involve conditions that make negotiated settlements unattractive or difficult to achieve.[33] For instance, if damages are serious but the liability issue seems favorable to the defendant, both sides may prefer a trial to a small cash payment from the insurer.

Medical malpractice differs from auto accidents in that only a small minority of the people who have been injured by negligent medical treatment even file a claim with the doctor's insurance company—about 3 percent, according to two studies—and lawsuits are even less common. These studies also found that most malpractice claims are made by people who were *not* the victims of medical negligence, though many of these people did suffer significant injuries through medical care.[34]

The relative infrequency of claims for medical malpractice seems to reflect several conditions. Patients blame doctors for bad outcomes less often than drivers blame other drivers for accidents. One reason is that patients generally have some kind of relationship with the doctors who treat them, and those relationships in themselves discourage malpractice claims if patients view them positively.[35] Malpractice cases are difficult to win in court, so it can be difficult to win settlements from insurance companies. In turn, lawyers are often reluctant to take malpractice cases.

Thus medical malpractice operates differently from auto accidents. In auto accident cases, the relative rarity of litigation reflects primarily the effectiveness of negotiation in settling legal claims out of court. In malpractice, it reflects primarily the infrequency of claims. The results—at least for use of the courts—are similar.

The Business World   Even more than individuals, businesses frequently find themselves in situations in which they could engage in litigation with each other. Legal issues arise in direct interactions between businesses such as contracts to supply products. A retailer might sue a manufacturer for failure to provide a product as specified; a manufacturer might sue a retailer for failure to pay the money due for a product. Legal issues also arise between competitors. A business might sue another business in the same industry for infringement of a patent or violation of the antitrust laws.

The proportions of potential cases between businesses that actually become lawsuits and that result in trials are uncertain. However, two general patterns are clear. First, litigation between businesses is a common event. A study of state litigation in Rhode Island found that over a two-year period, firms in several sectors of the economy were parties to cases against other businesses at a rate of more than one lawsuit per ten companies. In the financial sector the rate was more than four per ten companies. These rates would have been even higher if federal cases had been included.[36] Second, even such a high rate of litigation represents only a small proportion of the situations in which a business has a basis for a lawsuit against another business.

In one respect, the tendency for businesses to avoid litigation with other businesses may be surprising: large and medium-sized businesses could bear the monetary costs of litigation far more easily than most individuals. But even if those costs are affordable, they are still undesirable. And litigation has other disadvantages. Perhaps the most important is that litigation would jeopardize relationships on which businesses depend. By and large, companies rely on amicable relations with other companies, especially for buying and selling goods and services. Such relations are unlikely to survive a lawsuit, and a firm's readiness to litigate may discourage other businesses from dealing with it. This is especially true of companies that are dependent on their partners, such as car dealers and parts suppliers in their relationships with auto manufacturers.[37]

Another reason for the relatively limited rate of litigation between businesses is the existence of alternative methods to resolve disputes. Close relationships between firms that deal with each other facilitate informal settlements; people in those firms can work out problems because of their mutual trust and their shared understandings about appropriate terms of settlement. When the parties cannot settle disputes by themselves, they can turn for help to other people. The lawyers for two businesses often reach agreements on behalf of their clients. Businesses also make considerable use of *mediation* (in which a mediator helps the parties reach a mutually acceptable resolution of their dispute) and *arbitration* (in which the parties turn a dispute over to an arbitrator who imposes a binding decision on them). Mediation is especially attractive because the parties retain control over the outcome, but both mediation and arbitration usually provide speed, economy, and flexibility that litigation lacks.

Of the disputes between businesses that go to court rather than being resolved in another way, it appears that most involve contractual relationships.[38] Less numerous, but often larger in scale, are cases pitting competitors against each other. Not surprisingly, litigation is more common when the risks are relatively small or the perceived benefits relatively great. If two companies lack a continuing relationship, for instance, one common risk of litigation is irrelevant. And a company may sue another company that owes it a debt if the second company is failing, since the failure means that the two are unlikely to have further dealings with each other. On the benefit side, often the stakes in a dispute are so large that, so long as company officials think victory is likely, litigation will be attractive to them. Sometimes this is true of a small firm whose executives think they are being squeezed out by a larger partner or competitor. Thus a company with one full-time employee sued a very large competitor, charging that the competitor had unlawfully used the design and packaging of an emergency escape ladder that the plaintiff's founders had invented. (The tiny company ultimately won a $17 million settlement after a favorable jury verdict.)[39] And fierce competition between major companies in an industry may lead to litigation, as it has in the battle between Schick and Gillette over the market for electric razors.[40] Another instance of fierce competition, described in Exhibit 7.4, shows that even business litigation can be affected by emotion.

The conditions that affect the use of litigation in the business world result in differences across industries. In an established industry with a stable set of firms, companies typically develop good relations with each other and mechanisms to avoid litigation. But in a new or unstable industry, a great many companies may be struggling for a foothold. Good relations between firms may not exist, and litigation

EXHIBIT 7.4   The Legal Battles Between Amway and Procter & Gamble

Procter & Gamble and Amway are large companies that sell many competing products, such as cleaning products and cosmetics. As one judge put it, there was "a long history of corporate warfare" between the companies. Another said that "recitation of the extensive and hate-filled history between P&G and Amway would take a writing as long as both the Old and New Testaments and involve at least one of the Good Book's more prominent players."

The judge was referring to Satan. Over the years, Procter & Gamble has had to contend with rumors that it was allied with Satan and that its president had actually gone on television to boast of that alliance. After learning that an Amway distributor had broadcast the rumor within Amway's internal communication system, in 1995 Procter & Gamble sued the distributor, Amway itself, and other defendants in federal court in Utah. P&G lost that case on the ground that distribution of the rumor did not constitute a violation of the statute in question.

In 1997 Procter and Gamble brought a second lawsuit against Amway and its distributors, this time in a Texas federal court. P&G again charged the defendants with distribution of the rumor, based on evidence that it had been disseminated in Texas. The company made some additional charges as well. After seven years and a series of court decisions P&G lost this case as well, on the ground that the Utah decision and its affirmance by a court of appeals had resolved the issues.

Meanwhile, Amway brought a lawsuit of its own in a Michigan federal court against the operator of an anti-Amway website, charging that material on the website defamed Amway. It included Procter & Gamble as a defendant, saying that some of what it claimed to be false statements on the website could be attributed to P&G. The defendants won a summary judgment, with the court of appeals ruling in 2003 that the statements on the website were legally protected speech. Its decision ended with a heartfelt plea.

> Amway and P&G have each now prevailed against the other at the appellate level in the federal courts. Although no decision from this Court—or any other, we predict—will end the hatred these two corporate giants harbor for each other, we hope that they will consider the impact of their continuing legal battle on the scarce resources of the courts, and decide to concentrate their creative talents on the more traditional methods of gaining competitive advantage and declare a ceasefire in the judicial arena.

Sources: court decisions. The quotations are from, in order, *Amway Corporation v. The Procter & Gamble Company*, 2001 U.S. Dist. LEXIS 14455, at 3 (W.D. Mich. 2001); *Amway Corporation v. The Procter & Gamble Company*, 346 F.3d 180, 182 (6th Cir. 2003); and the Sixth Circuit decision at 188.

may be attractive as a means to gain a major advantage. Over time, various sectors of the computer industry have fit that description well, and it is not surprising that the industry features a good deal of litigation. But even in the most established and stable industries, there will always be some disputes that cannot be resolved outside of court.

The Incidence of Litigation

In each of the areas surveyed so far, litigation is substantial in absolute numbers but uncommon when compared with the number of potential cases. In this respect, these areas are typical. One study looked at individuals with significant grievances, generally involving $1,000 or more, across a wide range of legal areas. Only 5 percent of these grievances led to the filing of lawsuits, a substantial majority of which were settled out of court.[41] Yet civil suits are hardly rare: more than 20 million civil cases are filed every year.[42] Both the tendency of people to avoid litigation and the large volume of litigation that does occur require explanation.

The Disadvantages of Litigation   The discussion thus far suggests why most potential cases do not go to court: litigation has several features that generally make it unattractive. Three of these features are especially important:

1. Litigation is expensive. The costs required to prepare and try a case make all but the simplest trials unaffordable for most individuals and many organizations, unless a special device such as the contingent fee is operating or people act without attorneys. Even those who can afford litigation would still prefer to avoid its costs.
2. Litigation means that the parties lose control over the outcome. In the hands of a judge or jury, a case might produce a result that is highly unfavorable to one of the parties. As with plea bargaining, it often seems far safer to reach a settlement that is at least palatable to both sides.
3. Litigation creates or exacerbates conflict between the parties. The contest element in trials pits people against each other in a very direct and serious way. For most people, this conflict is unpleasant in itself, and it often has practical consequences as well. If the parties had a relationship before the trial—such as two neighbors or two businesses that deal with each other—it is doubtful the relationship will survive intact.

Taken together, these attributes of litigation create powerful reasons to avoid it. Because people generally recognize at least some of these attributes, most of the time they avoid litigation; those who do litigate, as Sally Engle Merry reported, "usually turn to court reluctantly and only as a last resort."[43]

When Litigation Is Attractive   The fact that so many cases do go to court can be explained in part by conditions that reduce or negate the usual disadvantages of litigation. Under some circumstances, for instance, the monetary costs of litigation are limited. In personal injury cases, the contingent fee makes it possible for many people to afford bringing a lawsuit.[44] The streamlined procedures of small claims courts minimize the costs of bringing a case and arguing it in court.

Similarly, in some situations the element of conflict in litigation is greatly reduced. Most often, there is no relationship that would be damaged by litigation. In the United States, as one scholar said, "litigation tends to be between parties who are strangers."[45] In other instances, the relationship from which litigation arises may have been destroyed before a lawsuit is filed.

Thus, litigation is more likely when its disadvantages are reduced. The same is true when its potential benefits seem especially great. Often these benefits are monetary. Personal injury suits such as those that arise from auto accidents and medical injuries typically reflect judgments by individuals that they are likely to win large amounts of money in pretrial settlements or in court that they could not otherwise obtain. The same is true of businesses whose executives think they can gain a significant advantage over a competitor through a successful lawsuit.

Some people with dubious cases nonetheless file suits in the hope of winning a large sum. They may hope that a company or government will give them a large settlement rather than undergo the costs of contesting the case. Undoubtedly, some of these people do not realize that their cases are dubious.

The perceived benefits of litigation may be symbolic as well as monetary. There are some people for whom the conflict involved in litigation is an attraction rather than a deterrent. In her study of family and neighborhood problems, Merry found people who gained satisfaction from suing acquaintances.

> Some plaintiffs come to use the law as an arena for manipulation and play, a place to
> toy with enemies and to gain strategic successes by pummeling one's opponents with
> legal charges and summonses. . . . Some come to regard the court as entertainment, as
> a place to try out dominance games with others and to see what will happen.[46]

This motivation helps to explain the behavior of the small number of people who file large numbers of cases over time.[47] Two of the lawsuits brought by one litigant were each for one trillion dollars.[48]

Sometimes litigation is attractive for people because they perceive it as a last resort, the only way left to deal with an intolerable situation. This is true of most personal bankruptcies. On the whole, it is true of divorce as well. Divorce is a special case: if one or both partners wish to terminate their marriage officially, they have no alternative but to go to court.

The potential gains from litigation may be political. Such gains range from shaping national policy to influencing the outcome of a presidential election. Political litigation is examined in the next chapter.

Alternatives to Litigation

Whether people go to court depends in part on the availability of alternatives to litigation. Most of the time people do have alternatives. Across all the situations in which people might go to court, several kinds of alternatives exist.

The Array of Alternatives   These alternatives differ in several ways, of which two are especially important. The first is how public they are: to what extent is the issue between the parties opened up to wider participation and scrutiny? The second is the formality of the process by which the issue is handled. These two factors overlap, in that more formal processes tend to be more public as well. Thus, as Figure 7.1 shows, litigation and its major alternatives can be listed in the order of their "publicness" and formality.

Direct negotiation between the parties is the simplest and by far the most common way in which people deal with disputes that might otherwise go to court. Aggrieved

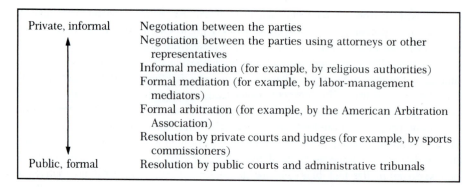

FIGURE 7.1   Litigation and Some Major Alternatives to Litigation

Sources: Adapted from formulations in Marc Galanter, "Why the 'Haves' Come Out Ahead: Speculations on the Limits of Legal Change," *Law & Society Review* 9 (Fall 1974), 124–135; and Austin Sarat and Joel B. Grossman, "Courts and Conflict Resolution: Problems in the Mobilization of Adjudication," *American Political Science Review* 69 (December 1975), 1201–1208.

consumers take their complaints to store managers. A driver whose car has been damaged talks to the owner of the other car and the owner's insurance company. Neighbors who disagree over their property line discuss the problem between themselves.

Negotiation typically becomes more complicated when attorneys represent the parties. The use of lawyers widens the scope of the negotiation, especially for people who do not employ lawyers regularly. Attorneys often introduce an element of legal formality as well. Because they know about law and judges, the way in which a court might respond to the dispute becomes more relevant to negotiation.

Mediation and arbitration have already been mentioned in the context of business disputes, but both are used in other areas as well. Mediation is often informal, as it is when parish priests or other religious authorities help individuals resolve their disputes. Sometimes it is relatively formal, as in the work of professional mediators in negotiations between labor and management.

Arbitration is more formal still, because the arbitrator reaches a decision, one that is sometimes binding on the parties. Arbitration may occur between employers and employees, between two businesses, or between businesses and consumers. One example is the arbitration of disputes between stockbrokers and their customers, conducted by the National Association of Securities Dealers.[49] Most arbitration occurs under agreements that certain kinds of disputes will be arbitrated. The American Arbitration Association, JAMS (formerly Judicial Arbitration and Mediation Services), and other organizations offer arbitration along with other dispute resolution services.

A variant of arbitration is the use of non-governmental courts and judges. Some organizations have their own forums to resolve disputes within the organization. Such forums are common within colleges, sports associations, and religious denominations. For instance, the United Methodist Church has a Judicial Council that serves as the final adjudicator of issues under the rules that govern the Church.[50] In some states, litigants can hire a private judge to reach a decision in lieu of the regular court, and the decision of the private judge—often someone who previously served on a "regular" court—has the same official and binding status as that of the court. One attraction of taking cases to these private judges is their relative privacy, a quality that appealed to Brad Pitt and Jennifer Aniston when they sought to end their marriage.[51]

At the furthest distance from simple two-party negotiation is the resolution of a legal issue in a court or another government tribunal, such as an administrative court in the executive branch. Courts generally reach decisions in a fully public setting on the basis of formal procedures through the application of legal rules. These characteristics distinguish courts at least marginally from all the alternative forums and fundamentally from most.

Growth in the Use of Alternatives   In recent years, interest in alternatives to litigation has burgeoned, often under the heading "alternative dispute resolution," and the actual use of alternatives has grown. This development has several sources, most of them related to the perceived disadvantages of litigation. Alternatives to litigation are widely viewed as cheaper, quicker, and less likely to exacerbate conflict between the parties. The use of alternatives also reduces court caseloads.

Because of these potential benefits, most people in and out of the legal system view the movement toward greater use of alternatives as desirable. But there is some dissent from this view. The most important ground for dissent is the fact that use of alternatives to litigation is not always voluntary. In the contracts of adhesion that were discussed in Exhibit 7.1, businesses often require that consumers and employees give up their right to go to court in disputes that might arise in the future. Most often, such disputes would go to an arbitration system selected by the business. People often do not notice the arbitration requirement that they are accepting, and if they do notice it they are unlikely to refuse a purchase or a credit card or a job on the basis of that requirement. One man who did refuse to accept a law firm's arbitration requirement for its employees was denied a job that he had been offered, and a half dozen years later he lost a challenge to that action in federal court.[52]

Why do companies require their customers and employees to accept arbitration? One reason is the perception that arbitration is less expensive and more efficient than litigation, characteristics that presumably are good for both sides. Yet the decision to rule out litigation is effectively unilateral, made by the party that would be required to defend its actions in court. And the arbitration systems themselves may be one-sided. Often, they are operated by the businesses that are parties to disputes or by the industries of which they are part. In systems where arbitrators are nominally independent, they are often selected by the business parties, giving arbitrators an incentive to rule in favor of those businesses in order to get cases in the future. Consumers or workers may be required to pay high costs to obtain arbitration, thus discouraging them from pursuing their grievances. And some commonly imposed rules such as prohibitions of class actions in arbitration work to the advantage of businesses.

Contract provisions that require arbitration have been challenged in court many times. The Supreme Court has given a broad interpretation to a 1925 federal statute that favors arbitration, turning back challenges to mandatory arbitration in several cases. In contrast, some state courts and lower federal courts have ruled against certain arbitration requirements. For instance, in 2003 a federal court of appeals ruled that AT&T's provisions requiring that its customers take disputes to arbitration violated

California law because customers had no choice but to accept this requirement and because some elements of the arbitration system favored the company.[53] But lower courts have generally enforced mandatory arbitration, and legislatures have done little to limit it. In 2002 and 2003 the California legislature enacted legislation prohibiting mandatory arbitration systems imposed by employers, but Governor Gray Davis vetoed both bills.

Disagreements over mandatory arbitration requirements should not obscure the broader movement toward greater use of alternatives to litigation. Today, as in the past, most individuals and organizations that make use of these alternatives are doing so voluntarily. And in light of all the negative consequences that can result from going to court, it is clear that people often benefit a good deal by using other mechanisms to deal with their disputes and grievances.

However, the dispute about mandatory use of alternative dispute resolution is a good reminder that the choice between litigation and its alternatives is not necessarily neutral. The benefits that result from staying out of court may not accrue equally to the two sides in a dispute, and sometimes one side would be better off in court.

Paths to—and away from—the Courts   By taking the array of potential alternatives into account, we can map out several routes to the courts. When people have a grievance or opportunity that might be litigated, some of them go directly to court. Others employ alternatives, usually starting with those that are least public and formal, and therefore least likely to share the disadvantages of litigation. After one or more alternatives fail to produce a satisfactory result—if, say, the negotiations stall or a mediator suggests an unacceptable solution—these people then go to court.

But a much larger number of people follow paths that do not take them to court. Many people do nothing. Employees who feel they have suffered discrimination or consumers who perceive that a product is defective often simply live with their grievance. Others obtain a satisfactory result through some alternative to litigation, most often negotiation with the other party. Still others accept unsatisfactory outcomes from alternatives rather than taking on litigation with its negative elements. A consumer who finds a merchant unyielding in negotiations and who gets no satisfaction from mediation by the Better Business Bureau may give up at that point. Through a combination of these routes, most possible litigation never occurs.

Government and Litigation

The discussion of litigation thus far has dealt almost entirely with individuals and organizations in the private sector. But government is also a frequent participant in litigation. In 2005, for instance, the federal government was a party—more often than not, a defendant—in about one-fifth of all civil cases filed in federal district court. State governments were also parties in a substantial number of federal cases, primarily cases brought by prison inmates.[54] As repeat players, governments are in a good position to achieve success in litigation. Indeed, the federal government can be considered the ultimate repeat player because of its resources and the large numbers of cases in which it participates.

Like litigation between private parties, most litigation with a government party is routine. But even routine cases involve implementation of public policies such as protection of civil rights and the provision of social security benefits. And some lawsuits by or against government raise broader policy questions. Litigants challenge federal and state legislation under the Constitution. In the current era states frequently act alone or band together to bring lawsuits that attack the practices of businesses such as tobacco companies and prescription drug makers. On issues such as environmental protection, the priorities and positions of the federal government in litigation change from administration to administration in line with the views of the president and attorney general. A similar process occurs at other levels of government. Inevitably, state and federal governments sometimes come into direct conflict in court where their policy views and priorities differ. One example is the lawsuit by Connecticut over the costs of carrying out the federal "no child left behind" education law.[55]

Government plays a second and more fundamental role in litigation by establishing the rules that govern use of the courts. Most fundamentally, government policies create and define legal remedies, thereby establishing who can go to court under what circumstances. And where litigation is allowed, government policies make it more or less attractive to people who might file lawsuits. In this way legislatures and courts themselves regulate access to the courts.

This function is illustrated by civil rights. Lawsuits in federal court for violations of rights were rare until the 1960s, because there were few legal protections for civil rights. But in 2005, as a result of action by Congress and the Supreme Court, there were more than fifty thousand federal civil rights cases.[56] First, a 1961 decision by the Court interpreted an 1871 statute broadly, making it a good vehicle for lawsuits challenging violations of rights by state and local government officials.[57] Then Title 7 of the Civil Rights Act of 1964 allowed people to bring lawsuits against private parties and organizations for discrimination in employment. Amendments to Title 7 and new civil rights laws expanded the areas in which cases could be brought and increased the attractiveness of litigation. For instance, the Americans with Disabilities Act of 1990 allowed lawsuits in many situations for discrimination on the basis of disability.[58] Two laws had effects across the whole field of civil rights: a 1991 statute that allowed plaintiffs to win monetary damages in Title 7 cases and a 1976 statute that allowed attorneys who win civil rights cases to receive money for their fees from the losing side.

The growth in civil rights cases is an especially clear example of the impact of government. But in every legal field, legislation and court rulings largely determine the volume and content of litigation. Court decisions on mandatory arbitration underline the wide range of government policies that affect the use of litigation. Even a law that seems innocuous on its face can have considerable impact. One example is a 2005 federal statute that moved most large class-action suits from state to federal court. That provision was actually intended to reduce the chances of success for class-action cases brought on behalf of consumers.[59]

As this example underlines, government policies that affect litigation often work to the advantage of some segments of society and the disadvantage of others. Inevitably, the interest groups that represent the various segments of society work to shape the law in ways that make it easier for those they represent to use the courts and harder for their opponents to do so. For instance, a 2005 federal law was designed to discourage individuals from filing for bankruptcy by making the terms of bankruptcy less favorable to them. The law was finally enacted after a long battle between coalitions of interest groups on each side, with banks and credit card companies seeking the legislation and consumer groups opposing it. And there has been a long and fierce war between competing interest groups over the legal rules that govern tort law, a war discussed in Exhibit 7.5.

Thus, who goes to court and their chances of success when they get there are based fundamentally on decisions by the three branches of government. In this sense, everything that the courts do in civil cases is rooted in politics.

Litigation and American Culture Today

At the beginning of this section, I discussed a common image of Americans as a litigious people who have become more litigious in recent years, thereby precipitating a "litigation explosion." We can now return to the question of how accurate that image is.

To a considerable extent, the image is based on anecdotal evidence. Seemingly outrageous lawsuits are compiled in books and regularly reported in forums such as Chuck Shepherd's newspaper feature, "News of the Weird."[60] New types of litigation such as lawsuits against fast-food restaurants for contributing to obesity strike many people as indications of excessive litigiousness. Yet it is clear that people in the United States generally avoid opportunities to go to court rather than seizing them. As a result, the number of civil cases is a very small fraction of what it could be if Americans undertook litigation whenever they had a possible case. This fact suggests that today's Americans are not highly litigious.

Even so, it might be the case that Americans are more inclined to sue than they were in the past and that they are more litigious than people in other countries. The perceptions of a litigation explosion can be tested by examining trends in the volume of civil cases. Federal courts hear only a small proportion of all cases, but comprehensive data on their caseloads are available. There was sharp growth in the numbers of civil cases filed in the federal district courts between the mid-1970s and mid-1980s, but those numbers have been stable since then.[61] More limited data on the states suggest that state courts experienced their own sharp growth in civil litigation around the same time as the federal courts but that there has also been a leveling off in recent years. For the states that have appropriate data, the number of civil cases filed in state courts rose 18 percent between 1994 and 2003, a significant increase but not much greater than the growth in population.[62] Many of those who speak of a litigation explosion focus on tort cases. It appears that there was very substantial growth in tort cases in some recent periods. In a set of fifteen states, for instance, the number of cases filed in the tort field increased nearly 50 percent between 1985 and 1996. However, that increase was followed by a decline of nearly 20 percent between 1996 and 2003.[63]

As noted earlier, in both federal and state courts the proportion of cases going to trial has declined considerably. As a result, to take one comparison, the number of trials in state civil cases was slightly lower in 2002 than it had been in 1976.[64] If litigation means taking cases to trial, there has been nothing resembling a litigation explosion.

Some scholars have sought to provide a broader perspective by looking at litigation trends over the course of U.S. history. They have found a tendency for litigation per capita to rise over time, but the increases generally have been moderate, and

EXHIBIT 7.5   The Battle over "Tort Reform"

Legal rules in tort law were devised primarily by state supreme courts, and in the early twentieth century those rules generally favored defendants—primarily businesses and professionals such as medical doctors. But state supreme courts began to make the legal rules more favorable to plaintiffs, and this process accelerated after World War II. Groups representing defendants and insurance companies increasingly perceived that these changes in the law had contributed to rapid growth in the number of lawsuits and the amount of damages that plaintiffs were winning in court.

Under the label of "tort reform," these groups mounted what became a large-scale effort to reverse many of the changes in state tort rules. They argued that the existing rules resulted in considerable harm to manufacturers and physicians, among others, and ultimately damaged state economies. This effort aroused opposition from interest groups that favor broad rights to sue for torts; the most important of these groups was lawyers who represent personal injury plaintiffs. Both sides have lobbied actively and made substantial campaign contributions to influence state legislators, and they also seek to shape public opinion through vehicles such as newspaper ads.

The results have been mixed. However, the groups that favor tort reform have enjoyed considerable success in changing legal rules. One reason is the effectiveness of the business community as an interest group. Another is that its message about the harmful effects of lawsuits is consistent with a widely held view among legislators and other people. Disagreement about tort reform largely follows partisan and ideological lines, so increasing Republican strength in the federal government and many state governments in the 1990s favored advocates of changes in the law.

State tort reform legislation is frequently challenged on the ground that it violates provisions of state constitutions, such as provisions that guarantee people access to the courts. State courts have often ruled in favor of these challenges. In response, business groups have increased their involvement in judicial elections, and their efforts have helped produce more sympathetic supreme courts in states such as Alabama, Michigan, and Ohio. These groups have also sought federal tort legislation that would preempt unfavorable state laws and thus block certain kinds of litigation in state court. They have had some success in this effort, and in the George W. Bush administration several agencies wrote regulations to preempt state laws on matters such as drug labeling and standards for automobile roofs.

The successes of the tort reform movement undoubtedly have discouraged lawyers from bringing some kinds of lawsuits and increased the success of defendants in tort cases. The authors of one study argue that even without formal changes in the law, the supporters of tort reform have had considerable impact in Texas by changing the attitudes of jurors. If so, this result almost surely has occurred elsewhere as well.

Sources: Newspaper and journal articles. The study noted in the last paragraph is Stephen Daniels and Joanne Martin, "The Strange Success of Tort Reform," *Emory Law Journal* 53 (Summer 2004), 1225–1262.

some courts had higher rates in some past periods than in recent years.[65] Summarizing these studies, one writer concluded that the thesis of "the country's growing legal dementia . . . could be true except it overlooks one salient point: It used to be worse."[66] Though not entirely conclusive, this research indicates that Americans have not developed a new inclination to litigate in the current era.

It is difficult to determine whether Americans are more litigious than people in other countries. Comparable data on litigation are not readily available, and differences among countries might reflect government policies rather than just citizens' willingness to go to court. For instance, the low rate of litigation in Japan appears to result from a complex interaction between cultural values and government policies that affect use of the courts.[67] Robert Kagan concluded from a careful analysis of evidence that the United States stands out for the extent of "adversarial legalism," a term referring to "policymaking, policy implementation, and dispute resolution by means of lawyer-dominated litigation." In Kagan's view, the most important source of adversarial legalism source is not a litigious public but the fragmentation of government power.[68] The evidence in his study is important, but in combination with other evidence it does not resolve the question of whether Americans are unusually prone to litigate.

On the whole, the views that people express about comparisons between the United States and other countries and about a litigation explosion in the United States depend less on the realities of litigation than on self-interest and ideological positions. On one side, people in the business community want to encourage a negative attitude toward litigation against businesses in the general public (including potential jurors) and among government officials. For this reason they argue that Americans—and especially lawyers—are too eager to go to court, that there has been a litigation explosion, and that this explosion has done great damage to American society. In this effort, business groups have been supported by political conservatives. They have had considerable success in shaping the perceptions of citizens and government officials, making especially good use of true stories and urban legends about outrageous lawsuits. On the other side, lawyers who represent individual plaintiffs in lawsuits against businesses argue that Americans are not unusually litigious and that litigation has not mushroomed. Groups representing consumers and workers take a similar position on behalf of their members, and they are joined by political liberals. These groups have been on the defensive, and they have largely lost the battle over public opinion.[69] That battle aside, however, one matter seems clear: whether or not there is more litigation in the United States than desirable, Americans as a whole have a stronger inclination to stay away from the courts than to use them.

THE LITIGATION PROCESS

Whatever we conclude about the propensity of Americans to litigate, a great many lawsuits are actually filed in court. Like criminal cases, civil cases can take many different paths; to a great extent, the paths that cases take vary among fields of law.[70] This section focuses on three major types of cases that generally follow different routes; the routes are summarized in Exhibit 7.6.

EXHIBIT 7.6   Paths Through Court for Three Types of Civil Cases

	Personal Injury	**Debt Collection**	**Divorce**
Pretrial Stage			
Typical length of time	Lengthy	Brief	Moderate
Incidence of settlements between parties	Most cases	Some cases	Most cases
Trial Stage			
Typical length of time	Relatively lengthy	Quite brief	Quite brief
Incidence of uncontested trials	Few cases	Most cases, resulting from defaults by defendants	Most cases, resulting from agreements between parties
Post-Trial Stage			
Noncompliance with judgments	Moderately common	Very common	Very common

Source: Based in part on David M. Engel and Eric H. Steele, "Civil Cases and Society: Process and Order in the Civil Justice System," *American Bar Foundation Research Journal*, Spring 1979, 311–317.

Pretrial Settlement and Full Trials: Personal Injuries

In some types of civil cases, the parties are in conflict, but they generally try to reach a settlement before trial and usually succeed. Cases in which the parties do not reach a settlement typically go to full-scale trials, often before juries. The largest category of such cases is personal injury suits.[71] Injury cases arise from a wide range of situations, but a majority of potential and actual cases involve auto accidents. More than 90 percent of personal injury cases are brought by individuals. In most cases the defendants are other individuals, but businesses frequently are defendants.[72] In either case, as noted earlier, an insurance company is usually responsible for paying any judgment against the defendant, and for that reason it takes charge of the defendant's case.

The filing of a personal injury case may reflect the inability of the two sides to reach an early settlement. But the filing more often is a punctuation of negotiations, an indication of seriousness by the lawyer for the injured party. Most suits eventually are settled out of court. Because of such settlements and other methods of pretrial disposition such as dismissals, verdicts by judges or juries are unusual. A study of the seventy-five largest counties in the U.S. found that three-quarters of the tort lawsuits were settled between the parties and only 3 percent were resolved through a verdict after trial.[73] In 2005, 4 percent of the personal injury cases in California were resolved after trial, and 1 percent of the federal cases in this field were resolved during or after trial.[74]

In most respects, negotiation after the filing of lawsuits is similar to earlier negotiation. There is a long period between filing and trial in most civil courts, so the act of filing usually brings no urgency to the negotiations. As the trial date comes closer, lawyers concentrate more on efforts to reach a settlement. As Herbert Kritzer has pointed out, the prospect of trial not only shapes the terms of settlement but helps to make settlement possible.[75]

The filing of a lawsuit gives the parties additional means to test and challenge each other's positions. For example, lawyers use discovery to learn about the content and strength of the other party's case, and what they learn can affect the bargaining power of the two sides. Frequently, filing also brings the court into the settlement process. Judges in civil cases play an active role in encouraging settlements, primarily during pretrial conferences. These direct efforts are supplemented by broader mechanisms to encourage settlements. One example is a federal rule that gives plaintiffs an incentive to accept settlement offers by assessing court costs against a plaintiff who rejects a formal offer and then does no better at trial.[76]

Typically, negotiations are neither long nor complex.[77] The plaintiff's lawyer makes a case in writing for the defendant's lawyer to consider, there are a few rounds of bargaining in writing or on the phone (face-to-face negotiation is unusual), and a settlement is reached. The brevity of negotiations and the relative ease with which settlements are reached reflect lawyers' experience and their incentives to spend limited time on most cases.

In the cases that go to trial, the formality and length of trials vary a great deal. Bench trials and jury trials are both common. In civil cases, like criminal cases, some observers perceive substantial differences between the behavior of judges and juries. It is widely believed that civil juries are more favorable to plaintiffs than judges are. This tendency, it is suggested, arises from sympathy for victims of injuries, hostility toward business, and a kind of "Robin Hood" thinking in which jurors transfer money from wealthy businesses to needy individuals.[78] A set of studies by sociologist Valerie Hans, which included interviews of jurors, surveys of the public, and experiments, showed that this conception of jurors' attitudes is largely wrong. To take one example, "the belief that jurors are universally compassionate to injured plaintiffs is simplistic. . . . Jurors often show doubts about, and sometimes even hostility toward, injured plaintiffs."[79] In fact, the available evidence suggests that, overall, juries differ little from judges in their support for plaintiffs. One study, which took into account differences in the kinds of cases decided by judges and juries, found that judges were more likely to rule in favor of plaintiffs. Juries tended to give more money to successful plaintiffs, but this second difference was less dramatic than many people think.[80]

The limitations of criminal trials as a mechanism to reach the truth were examined in Chapter 6. These weaknesses are also relevant to civil trials, including those in personal injury cases. In some respects, the weaknesses are more serious on the civil side. For instance, the period of time from a personal injury to a trial is usually far longer than the period from a criminal offense to a trial. That difference is consequential, because the recollections of witnesses deteriorate with time. In such areas as product liability, civil cases can involve issues of technical complexity that create special problems of understanding for both judges and juries.

Winning a sum of money at trial does not guarantee that the plaintiff will actually receive that money. After a jury verdict, a judge can reduce the plaintiff's recovery or overturn the verdict altogether. An appellate court can do the same thing, and the prospect of appeal may lead a plaintiff to accept a lesser amount of money in a post-trial settlement. Even after a case has reached a final outcome, plaintiffs may face considerable difficulty in collecting their winnings. Individual defendants often have limited assets. When that is true, plaintiffs seldom can collect money beyond the level of the individual's insurance coverage—if the individual does have coverage. And even business defendants may not pay the amount they owe. Taxi companies in New York City, for instance, use a variety of tactics to avoid paying money they are assessed in lawsuits for auto accidents.[81] And after the families of Ron Goldman and Nicole Brown Simpson won $33.5 million from O.J. Simpson in a lawsuit for wrongful death in 1997, Simpson vowed not to pay any of that money. By the beginning of 2007, Simpson in fact had paid little or none of what he owed.[82]

For all these reasons, plaintiffs as a group do considerably less well in the final outcome than they do in the jury verdict.[83] This is especially true of those who win the largest amounts. In a study of one hundred jury verdicts of 1 million dollars or more, two-thirds of the verdicts were reduced or overturned by trial or appellate judges, many were settled for reduced amounts, and only a few plaintiffs received the full amount they won at trial. To take one example, in 1999 the plaintiffs in a class action suit against State Farm Insurance were awarded a little more than $1 billion in an Illinois lawsuit for breach of contract and consumer fraud. Six years later, the Illinois Supreme Court reversed the trial court's decisions in the case, so the plaintiffs were left with nothing.[84]

Some personal injury cases and sets of related cases have large numbers of plaintiffs.[85] These cases can result from major accidents such as airline crashes. Most of the largest cases involve injuries allegedly caused by products such as prescription drugs, medical devices, asbestos, and tobacco. Large numbers of similar individual claims are sometimes bound together in class action suits or consolidated by courts. In other instances, cases are formally separate but informally lumped together. These cases can be difficult for lawyers and judges to handle. For instance, settlement negotiations tend to be difficult when many lawyers are involved and the monetary stakes are high. In cases that are not settled out of court, trials are likely to be long and complex.

Brief Trials and Defendant Defaults: Debt Collection

Civil cases involving small amounts of money typically go through pretrial stages quickly, with a small proportion of settlements and little court involvement. Most trials are abbreviated and relatively informal, and many defendants lose by default because they fail to take the required actions before trial or fail to appear at the trial. Many of these cases go to small claims courts, which process cases quickly through fairly simple procedures.

Most cases of this type fall in the general category of debt collection, in which businesses seek to recover money from individuals or seek another remedy such as eviction of a tenant. Debt collection actions are quite common, one of the largest categories of civil court cases. Dockets in many small claims courts consist primarily of actions by businesses to collect debts from individuals. Although small claims courts were created to facilitate litigation by individuals, they have also provided attractive forums for business creditors.[86]

Defendants often lose their cases by default because they fail to appear in court or to file an answer to the complaint. Defendants may not receive a summons informing them of the case and the court date, and at least in one period, this apparently was quite common in New York City. Debtors who do receive a summons may not understand what is required of them, may fear going to court, or may feel that no effective defense is possible. These conditions reflect the low proportions of defendants with attorneys and the high proportions with low incomes and limited education.[87]

The defendant's failure to file an answer to the complaint allows the plaintiff to win a default judgment. Cases can be resolved without full trials in several other ways. Some defendants who have filed answers nonetheless lose default judgments because they do not appear for the trial. The creditor may win a summary judgment if the defendant's answer is judged to be inadequate, which is likely if the defendant has drafted that answer without a lawyer's help. Some debtors contact their creditors and reach a settlement prior to trial.

Faced with heavy caseloads, judges often make active efforts to avoid trials. Increasingly, courts that hear debt collection cases divert these cases either to mandatory or to voluntary arbitration systems. Some judges pressure litigants who appear for trial to reach settlements instead. In the small claims court in Washington, D.C., according to a reporter, "Defendants with the temerity to show up are quickly shuffled outside to negotiate a payment plan or make some kind of deal—mediation encouraged by the court."[88]

Some cases do go to contested trials, although the proportion is fairly small. In a study of Chicago, Detroit, and New York, that proportion was estimated to be as low as 1 percent.[89] Jury trials are quite uncommon. Non-jury trials usually are informal, and they typically require only part of a court day. All this is especially true of small claims courts, in which the frequent absence of attorneys further speeds proceedings. Exhibit 7.7 describes the speed with which cases are processed in Chicago's Eviction Court as well as other features of that court's work.

Victorious plaintiffs often find it difficult to collect judgments against defendants in debt collection cases. Many debtors lack the money to pay a judgment readily, and some are unwilling to pay even if they can do so. Creditors then must resort to formal mechanisms to recover what they are owed. One common action is garnishment of wages from debtors who are employed. Despite the use of these mechanisms, many judgments simply cannot be collected. In one study of Iowa small claims courts, only 28 percent of the businesses that won cases against individuals collected all the money they were awarded, and 61 percent collected none at all.[90]

Court Ratification of Pretrial Settlements: Divorce

Divorce is an unusual type of litigation, in that people who wish to terminate a marriage officially must file a case in court, and they will be granted a divorce only if they meet a state's criteria. Until the 1960s, states allowed a divorce only if the spouse who sought it could show "fault" as defined by statute. Every state has eliminated that requirement. The no-fault grounds include irretrievable breakdown of the marriage, irreconcilable differences between the spouses, and living separately for a specified period of time.

EXHIBIT 7.7   Eviction Court in Chicago

One branch of the trial court in Chicago is called the "forcible entry and detainer court," using a legal term for eviction, but it is generally referred to as "eviction court." Landlords in Illinois who seek to evict tenants—most often for non-payment of rent—must obtain a court order to do so, and the law sets out a set of procedures to be followed in eviction cases. In 2002 a set of law students observed 763 cases in Chicago's eviction courts. They could not observe the cases that were resolved out of court, but their findings illuminate the workings of the eviction courts. It should be noted that the study was sponsored and the results reported by a pro-tenant organization.

Frequently, one or both parties failed to appear for their hearings. Landlords were absent in 17 percent of the cases, tenants 44 percent. If only the landlord appeared, the case would proceed without the tenant; if only the tenant appeared, the case was often (but not always) dismissed.

About half the time, the appearance for the landlord was made by an attorney; tenants had lawyers in about 5 percent of the cases. Tenants seldom presented any defense against eviction except when they were prompted by the judge. Under the law, tenants could seek a jury trial or a continuance in the eviction proceeding, but in the great majority of cases they did neither.

From judges' perspective, these cases were generally quite simple: the tenant had failed to pay rent that was due, any defense offered by the tenant was inadequate under the law, and the only question was how long the tenant should be given before eviction. As a result, trials seldom took long. The average court time per case was one minute and forty-four seconds.

Source: Lawyers' Committee for Better Housing, *No Time for Justice: A Study of Chicago's Eviction Court* (Chicago: Lawyers' Committee for Better Housing, 2003).

Each state has adopted one or more of those three grounds. About half the states retain the traditional fault-based grounds as well. But a study of two states found that lawyers avoid bringing cases on those grounds because, as one lawyer put it, "courts aren't particularly interested in hearing any fault grounds."[91] If only one of the spouses seeks a divorce, the other may have the right to contest it, but the no-fault grounds make it difficult to oppose a divorce petition successfully. If the spouses agree to obtain a divorce, under some circumstances in some states they need not actually appear in court.

Aside from granting a divorce, the courts must deal with the economic issues of property division and alimony. Where children are involved, their custody and financial support must also be determined. Judges approve or disapprove agreements between the spouses on these issues and adjudicate cases in which no agreement is reached. (Georgia and Texas allow juries to decide some issues in divorce cases.)

It may be difficult for the parties to reach an out-of-court settlement, because divorce and the issues associated with it often carry large concrete and emotional stakes. But the wife and husband generally find it advantageous to settle their own dispute rather than suffer the risks and other costs of going to court. One study found that 10 percent of the divorce cases in a Virginia county and 5 percent in a Wisconsin county went to trial.[92] It is uncommon for judges to disapprove agreements between the parties. In a sample of three hundred Wisconsin cases, judges refused to approve the couple's agreement in only one instance.[93] Indeed, the judge's scrutiny of an agreement is usually perfunctory.

In part because of this limited scrutiny, expectations of what would happen if a case went to court do not fully govern settlements. This is especially true when there seems little chance that a case actually will be contested in court. As a result, other factors such as the bargaining skills of the two sides are important.

In the small minority of cases that do go to trial, the law gives judges a great deal of discretion over alimony and child custody. Inevitably, their decisions about these issues are influenced by their personal values on such matters as the relative fitness of mothers and fathers as parents. Judges are also affected by the terms of the settlements they approve in uncontested cases, which help set their expectations about how they should decide cases.[94] Thus, as in other areas of law, out-of-court settlements and judges' decisions shape each other.

Noncompliance with court decrees in divorce cases is a common problem. Parents frequently violate agreements concerning custody and visitation rights, and "child stealing" to overcome court judgments has become a highly visible phenomenon. A large proportion of people who are required to pay alimony or child support meet that obligation only in part or not at all, and noncompliance becomes more common over the years after a divorce. Of the parents who were required to pay child support in 2003, 45 percent paid the full amount required, 31 percent part of that amount, and 24 percent none at all. Altogether, 69 percent of the amount due was paid.[95]

Traditionally, courts and other government agencies did little to secure compliance with the terms of divorce decrees. But these efforts have increased considerably in recent years. This is especially true of child support. In the 1980s and 1990s, Congress enacted four statutes with provisions to improve compliance with child support orders. One of these statutes mandated that states deduct child support payments directly from wages and forward the sums to custodial parents. In addition, most states now allow suspension of drivers' licenses for parents who have failed to pay child support.[96] These and other mechanisms to improve compliance have had some effect. But they have not come close to eliminating noncompliance, in part because they are not fully enforced.

Both noncompliance with court orders and other problems can create conflicts between the former spouses after a divorce is granted. These conflicts frequently lead one or both parties to seek court action. One New Hampshire divorce spawned more than twenty lawsuits between the ex-spouses. Prior to the divorce, as it happens, they had collaborated on a legal text on divorce and other issues in family law.[97] Divorce illustrates especially well the reality that legal decrees may not fully resolve the problems that brought people to court.

WINNERS AND LOSERS

In civil cases, trial courts allocate gains and losses to a great many people, and the possibility of court action affects a much larger number of allocations outside of court. Marc Galanter's argument that "the 'haves' come out ahead"—that those who come to court with more resources than their opponents tend to prevail—provides a good structure for examination of winners and losers in three fields of law.

Personal Injuries

In most fields of law, the cases that courts actually decide are a small sample of the matters that could have gone to court. Since some kinds of matters are more likely to end up in court than others, these cases are also unrepresentative of all potential cases. For that reason, we must be careful about our inferences from court decisions. Still, it is useful to look at what we know about court decisions on personal injuries.

A study of cases in state courts in the nation's seventy-five largest counties in 2001 provides a broad picture of patterns in tort decisions.[98] Overall, the two sides were about equally successful in winning verdicts: plaintiffs won 52 percent of the time. Among the categories with large numbers of cases, the rate of plaintiff success ranged from 61 percent in auto accident cases to 27 percent in medical malpractice. The median amount awarded to successful plaintiffs was $27,000. Although malpractice plaintiffs had the lowest proportion of victories, those who did win received a relatively high median award ($422,000); auto accident plaintiffs had the lowest ($16,000). It is widely believed that plaintiffs who win personal injury cases frequently receive high levels of punitive damages. But such damages were awarded in only 5 percent of the cases that plaintiffs won, and the median amount was $25,000.

A study of jury verdicts in tort cases over time indicates a fairly high level of stability in the outcomes of cases.[99] In Chicago and San Francisco between 1960 and 1999, the proportion of verdicts favoring plaintiffs remained around 50 percent. For plaintiffs who won, the average amount awarded by juries increased a good deal over the four decades. When relevant case characteristics such as medical costs are taken into account, it appears that the average level of damages declined slightly for automobile cases but grew for other cases.

Some commentators argue that the outcomes of personal injury cases are largely random, and it is common to refer to tort suits as a kind of lottery. Juries are also criticized for making awards that diverge from legal rules on the basis of their sympathies toward the parties. The available evidence indicates that there is some truth to these charges. But it also shows that there is a strong systematic element to the outcomes of cases, so that what plaintiffs win at trial is fairly predictable. In particular, verdicts tend to reflect the extent of plaintiffs' injuries.[100]

Some studies have looked more broadly at the outcomes of personal injury claims, whether or not these claims result in trials. Auto accidents, the most common source of personal injury cases, have also been the subject of the most research.

The research on auto accidents that result in injuries to people points to several conclusions.[101] First, most people recover something for their injuries—through a settlement with another party, through other sources such as their own insurance, or both. But at least a substantial minority of people with serious injuries receive nothing from the other party, sometimes because they lose in court.

Second, the law has considerable effect on what people recover, even in the cases that do not go to trial. Where a defendant seems to be legally liable for an accident, the injured party is more likely to receive something in an out-of-court settlement and tends to receive a larger amount. Similarly, people with the greatest expenses for their injuries generally are entitled to recover the most under the law, if the defendant is found liable; they also receive the most when they settle out of court.

Third, even with this pattern of outcomes, in an important sense those with the most serious injuries do least well. People with minor losses frequently recover more money than they lost, thereby gaining some compensation for their non-monetary costs. But the people who are most seriously hurt typically receive only a fraction of their costs from the other party—though other sources of payment reduce this gap somewhat.[102] One reason is that minor claims have nuisance value: it is cheaper for insurance companies to offer generous settlements than to bear the costs of going to court. In contrast, people with more severe losses suffer from the opposite situation: insurance companies can discount their offers in such cases because the injured party wants to avoid the costs and delay that would result from going to court. Besides, the costs of a serious accident may exceed the limits on the defendant's insurance coverage. But this relative disadvantage for those who have suffered serious injuries may be declining.

Fourth, lawyers have conflicting economic effects. Injured parties who are represented by attorneys do better than unrepresented parties, presumably because lawyers are effective in bargaining and in threatening court action. But lawyers' fees take up a significant part of what clients recover, a part that averaged a quarter or more of the settlement in one study.[103]

Patterns of outcomes vary across the states. In part, this variation reflects differences in legal rules. Most important, about one-quarter of the states operate under "no-fault" systems, in which people cannot sue for relatively minor injuries. But outcomes vary even among states that have the same legal rules, in part because of practices that develop over time in particular states.

Overall, according to one study, people injured in auto accidents recover 70 percent of their costs from some source, and about one-third of this total comes from legal claims against other parties. The 70 percent recovery rate was somewhat better than the 62 percent rate for all personal injuries.[104]

Personal injury claims generally pit prosperous insurance companies against individuals of varying incomes. Do insurance companies—the haves—usually come out ahead? Personal injury plaintiffs certainly hold their own in court, and they receive a good deal of money from actual and potential defendants through their insurance companies. But on the whole, payments for personal injury claims leave a considerable gap between the costs that individuals bear for accidents and their compensation for those costs. Even the relatively high rate of recovery for auto accidents means that nearly one-third of all costs are not recovered. Thus the overall picture is mixed and ambiguous, and it is not clear how to evaluate the success of the haves and have-nots.

Debt Collection

As noted in the preceding section, defendants in debt cases frequently fail to protect their rights by making necessary court appearances and taking other required actions. Consequently, creditors win a great many cases without opposition. Even when debtors do contest claims at trial, their creditors usually win.

On the whole, then, creditors do quite well in court. Studies of debt collection cases consistently have found that business creditors achieve very high rates of success—over 95 percent—through favorable judgments in trials or, more often, default judgments.[105] One reporter said that in Los Angeles, "eviction actions are almost always successful," and the study of eviction actions in Chicago that was discussed in Exhibit 7.7 reported that in the cases decided on the merits, "the tenant always lost."[106] In a study of major trial courts in Cleveland, Milwaukee, and Baltimore, Craig Wanner calculated that business creditors as a group recovered more money than what they originally claimed was owed to them. This seemingly impossible result resulted chiefly from court penalties against defendants for such items as interest, late-payment charges, and attorneys' fees.[107] That study may overstate the success of business creditors, but their success is clearly quite substantial.

However, the difficulty of actually collecting what the courts award must be taken into account. Although businesses do better than individuals in this regard, a significant proportion of money awarded to them does not get collected. This slippage is an important exception to the general effectiveness with which businesses use the courts for debt collection.

Business success in debt collection can be read in quite different ways. On the one hand, we might see this success as meaning simply that litigants with very strong cases are able to use the courts effectively to secure their rights. According to this interpretation, consumers and borrowers agree to pay money; they fail to do so; and when creditors turn to the courts, they can enforce debtors' obligations to them. Thus the courts are operating as they should in cases where there is little ambiguity about the law and the facts. Indeed, because of difficulties in collecting what they are awarded in court, businesses as "haves" may do less well than they should.

Alternatively, it can be argued that the courts are not operating in so benign a fashion. From this perspective, business creditors have strong cases partly because they have shaped the law in their favor through lobbying in the legislature and through past advocacy in the courts, partly because they can arrange transactions in a way that leaves debtors with little basis for a defense. Furthermore, some debtors have potentially strong defenses under the law, but they cannot protect their interests in the courts because they lack legal knowledge and access to lawyers and because court personnel are unsympathetic to them. In contrast, creditors develop expertise in using the courts and credibility with judges. And because of their backgrounds and experiences, many judges begin with a predisposition to favor creditors. From this perspective, the haves clearly come out ahead in debt collection cases.

Divorce

One outcome of divorce proceedings is that people who want divorces nearly always get them. Depending on the circumstances, the ease of divorce can favor either or both parties.

A second outcome is that mothers usually receive physical custody of children (that is, children are to live only or primarily with their mothers), perhaps 85 to 90 percent of the time.[108] Although many states now encourage joint legal custody arrangements, under joint custody most children live with their mothers most of the time.[109]

Since custody is contested in only a small proportion of cases, it is difficult to judge what this outcome means in terms of winners and losers. Traditionally, judges gave preference to mothers, especially for younger children. There is some evidence that this preference has declined. But it has not disappeared altogether, and groups representing divorced fathers have lobbied and brought lawsuits to secure more favorable treatment in custody decisions.[110] Because of a perception of judicial favoritism for mothers, even a father who would like to obtain custody might not seek it. But some fathers do not seek custody because they do not want it.

The economics of divorce are also complex. In most instances, if the court transferred no money from one partner to the other, the woman would be at a substantial disadvantage. Even if a woman is employed full-time when the divorce occurs, her income is likely to be lower than that of her husband. Many women have no career at the time of divorce. If they take a full-time job after divorce, the level of pay probably will be low. Those women who have custody of children also bear the costs of their care.

This situation can be alleviated by the payment of alimony and child support. In practice, however, alimony has little impact. Studies in the past have found that alimony was awarded in less than one-quarter of all divorces, it was usually awarded for relatively short periods, and the amounts awarded were generally low.[111] Although more recent information is not available, there is no reason to think that alimony awards have become larger or more common.

In contrast, most divorced women with custody of children are awarded child support. Traditionally, the levels of child support awarded, like the levels of alimony, were low. Further, noncompliance with support orders reduced the actual amounts received. As a result, on average, the money transferred from former husbands to former wives was well below the level needed to compensate for the differences in their earnings from employment and for the costs of raising children. Indeed, a number of studies showed that—at least for the first few years after divorce—former husbands generally ended up in a considerably better economic situation than did former wives.[112]

Since 1980, there has been considerable improvement in the economic status of former wives.[113] One possible reason is changes in the child support system. Spurred by federal rules, many states have increased their efforts to enforce child support orders and have established guidelines for judges that tend to increase the levels of support. However, noncompliance with child support orders has not declined substantially, and the average amounts awarded in child support remain fairly low.[114] Indeed, alimony and child support account for a much smaller proportion of the income received by divorced women today than they did a quarter century ago.

Rather, the improvement in the economic situations of former wives results from other trends. Higher levels of education for women and greater experience in the workforce during marriage have led to higher earnings from employment after divorce. Further, on average, divorced women have fewer children than in the past, reducing their economic needs. But with all these changes, there continues to be a significant difference between the post-divorce situations of former wives and former husbands as groups.

Larger awards of alimony and child support would produce economic equality between the former spouses. Why are they not made? Some observers have argued that no-fault divorce laws were a major cause of this situation, because they reduced the

bargaining leverage and economic rights of women who were "innocent parties" in a divorce. Other observers disagree, and they appear to have the better case.[115] The most fundamental explanation for the absence of larger transfers from former husbands to former wives is that judges are reluctant to require that men pay a large share of their income in alimony and child support, a reluctance that affects negotiated settlements as well.[116]

In most divorces, husbands can be considered the "haves" because of their superior economic situation. Courts reallocate substantial resources from former husbands to former wives, but that reallocation is insufficient to produce economic equality. Thus different criteria for success lead to different judgments about who comes out ahead.

An Overview

The three areas of court activity that I have discussed in this section suggest the difficulty of analyzing success in court and in matters affected by the courts.[117] Depending on how we conceptualize success, we might reach different conclusions about the outcomes for a particular group of litigants. Even in debt collection, where the pattern of outcomes is clearest, creditors' degree of success is ambiguous in its implications.

The outcomes of cases that go to trial are visible and relatively easy to analyze, but they do not tell the whole story. Cases that are settled or dropped before trial and potential cases that never get filed must be taken into account to determine who comes out ahead and behind. And the outcomes for various groups in society depend in part on their ability to file lawsuits and go to court in the first place. For this reason, to take one example, the growing use of contracts in which businesses require consumers and employees to forgo litigation against them is an important development.

Of course, individuals who are clearly have-nots win a great many cases in court and achieve favorable outcomes out of court. Further, less advantaged segments of society have recorded some noteworthy achievements in litigation aimed at changing government policy. In particular, the triumphs of civil rights groups in court are an important part of American history. Thus the examination of political litigation in the next chapter will tell more about the successes of haves and have-nots in court.

CONCLUSIONS

Because civil courts deal with a wide array of cases and issues, it is not easy to generalize about their work. But this chapter has identified some general patterns. Of particular importance are two aspects of the relationship between the courts and government and society as a whole.

First, the business of the courts and the outcomes of court cases reflect the political and social context in which courts operate. For one thing, developments elsewhere in government and society shape court agendas. The emergence of major industries, such as those related to computer hardware and software, leads to new litigation.[118] The number of discrimination cases grew enormously as statutes established new legal rights and people became more aware of those rights.

The enactment of civil rights statutes that allowed people to sue for discrimination illuminates the impact of the other branches of government on litigation. The ability to go to court and the chances of winning there are determined largely by rules that the legislature and executive branch adopt. Groups in society seek rules that favor their own litigation and limit litigation against them. Battles over issues such as tort reform and mandatory arbitration are heated because both sides correctly perceive that the stakes are high. The success of different segments of society in getting what they want from the courts depends heavily on the rules that determine who can go to court and what they must do to win cases.

Of course, that success also depends on the resources that the parties bring to court. It is not entirely clear to what extent "haves" come out ahead in court, but certainly they enjoy advantages over parties with fewer resources. Whatever can be said about the outcomes of debt collection cases, it is undeniable that creditors can navigate more effectively through the court process than debtors can.

Second, the courts have a broad effect on society, an effect illustrated by personal injury law. A very small proportion of injuries become the subject of court trials; the rest are handled elsewhere. Yet the laws that courts apply and the decisions they reach influence the resolution of claims and disputes that never come to court, because a dispute that is not settled outside of court would be resolved on terms imposed by the courts. Although negotiated settlements do not mirror court decisions perfectly, they are shaped by predictions of what would happen if cases went to court. It is through this indirect impact that the courts help to allocate far more gains and losses than the number of trials suggests.

These kinds of links between courts and their environments are not unique to the civil side of the law. As Chapter 6 indicates, the work of criminal courts is also linked to events and forces outside of court. But the ties between trial courts and their environments seem especially close in civil cases. Because of these ties, we can understand what courts do only in the context of the larger society in which they operate.

FOR FURTHER READING

Auletta, Ken. *World War 3.0: Microsoft and Its Enemies.* New York: Random House, 2001.

Burke, Thomas F. *Lawyers, Lawsuits and Legal Rights: The Battle Over Litigation in American Society.* Berkeley: University of California Press, 2002.

Greene, Edie, and Brian H. Bornstein. *Determining Damages: The Psychology of Jury Awards.* Washington, D.C.: American Psychological Association, 2003.

Haltom, William, and Michael McCann. *Distorting the Law: Politics, Media, and the Litigation Crisis.* Chicago: University of Chicago Press, 2004.

Hans, Valerie P. *Business on Trial: The Civil Jury and Corporate Responsibility.* New Haven: Yale University Press, 2000.

Kagan, Robert A. *Adversarial Legalism: The American Way of Law.* Cambridge, Mass.: Harvard University Press, 2002.

Kritzer, Herbert M., and Susan Silbey, eds. *In Litigation: Do the "Haves" Still Come Out Ahead?* Stanford: Stanford University Press, 2003.

Merry, Sally Engle. *Getting Justice and Getting Even: Legal Consciousness Among Working-Class Americans.* Chicago: University of Chicago Press, 1990.

Online Study Center Go to college.hmco.com/PIC/baum6e for ACE practice test questions and additional resources.

NOTES

1. Robert H. Mnookin and Lewis Kornhauser, "Bargaining in the Shadow of the Law: The Case of Divorce," *Yale Law Journal* 88 (April 1979), 950–997.
2. See William M. Tabb and Elaine W. Shoben, *Remedies in a Nutshell* (St. Paul, Minn.: Thomson/West 2005), ch.1.
3. Kenneth E. Scott, "Two Models of the Civil Process," *Stanford Law Review* 27 (February 1975), 937–950.
4. On compulsive gambling, see *Merrill v. Trump*, 320 F.3d 729 (7th Cir. 2003). On terrorist attacks, see *In re September 11 Litigation*, 280 F. Supp. 2d 279 (S.D.N.Y. 2003), and Lief H. Carter and Thomas F. Burke, *Reason in Law*, updated 7th ed. (New York: Pearson Longman, 2007), 64–67.
5. See Richard Y. Schauffler, Robert C. LaFountain, Neal B. Kauder, and Shauna M. Strickland, *Examining the Work of State Courts, 2004* (Williamsburg, Va.: National Center for State Courts, 2005), 21–40.
6. Administrative Office of the United States Courts, *Judicial Business of the United States Courts: Report of the Director (2005)* (Washington, D.C.: Administrative Office of the U.S. Courts, n.d.), 182, 245.
7. Marc Galanter, "Why the 'Haves' Come Out Ahead: Speculations on the Limits of Legal Change," *Law & Society Review* 9 (Fall 1974), 95–160; Herbert M. Kritzer and Susan Silbey, eds., *In Litigation: Do the "Haves" Still Come Out Ahead?* (Stanford: Stanford University Press, 2003).
8. Galanter, "Why the 'Haves' Come Out Ahead," 97.
9. Ibid., 97–124.
10. David Hechler, "Allstate Found Liable for Abuse of Process," *National Law Journal*, October 22, 2001, A15, A18; *Crackel v. Allstate Insurance Company*, 92 P.3d 882 (Ariz. Ct. App. 2004).
11. Richard Lempert, "A Classic at 25: Reflections on Galanter's 'Haves' Article and Work It Has Inspired," *Law & Society Review* 33 (1999), 1099–1112. See Brian J. Glenn, "The Varied and Abundant Progeny," in Kritzer and Silbey, *In Litigation*, 371–419.
12. See Mary Kay Kane, *Civil Procedure in a Nutshell*, 5th ed. (St. Paul: Thomson/West, 2003).
13. Reynolds Holding, "Discovery, It Turns Out, Is the Better Part of Judgments," *San Francisco Chronicle*, October 11, 1998, 3.
14. Administrative Office of the U.S. Courts, *Judicial Business (2005)*, 182.
15. Stephen B. Burbank, "Keeping Our Ambition Under Control: The Limits of Data and Inference in Searching for the Causes and Consequences of Vanishing Trials in Federal Court," *Journal of Empirical Legal Studies* 1 (November 2004), 574–575.
16. Brian J. Ostrom, Shauna M. Strickland, and Paul L. Hannaford-Agor, "Examining Trial Trends in State Courts: 1976–2002," *Journal of Empirical Legal Studies* 1 (November 2004), 775–782.
17. Marc Galanter, "The Vanishing Trial: An Examination of Trials and Related Matters in Federal and State Courts," *Journal of Empirical Legal Studies* 1 (November 2004), 459–570.

18. See the Symposium in the *Journal of Empirical Legal Studies* 1 (November 2004), 459–984; and Marc Galanter, "The Hundred-Year Decline of Trials and the Thirty Years War," *Stanford Law Review* 57 (April 2005), 1255–1274.

19. *Delaventura v. Columbia Acorn Trust*, 417 F. Supp. 2d 147, 150 (D. Mass. 2006).

20. Administrative Office of the United States Courts, *Judicial Business of the United States Courts (2005)*, 204; Administrative Office of the Illinois Courts, *Annual Report of the Illinois Courts: Statistical Summary 2003* (Springfield: Administrative Office of the Illinois Courts, n.d.), 55.

21. Jonathan Groner, "23 Years Add Up in Fight Over $14,500," *Legal Times*, August 23, 2004, 1, 8.

22. Stuart Taylor, Jr., and Evan Thomas, "Civil Wars," *Newsweek*, December 15, 2003, 44.

23. Bayless Manning, "Hyperlexis: Our National Disease," *Northwestern University Law Review* 71 (January–February 1977), 772.

24. Gail Russell Chaddock, "Emerging Supporter of Harriet Miers: Businesses," *Christian Science Monitor*, October 12, 2005, 4.

25. See Walter K. Olson, *The Excuse Factory: How Employment Law Is Paralyzing the American Workplace* (New York: Free Press, 1997).

26. Marika F. X. Litras, *Civil Rights Complaints in U.S. District Courts, 2000* (Washington, D.C.: U.S. Justice Department, Bureau of Justice Statistics, 2002), 1; Administrative Office of the U.S. Courts, *Judicial Business (2005)*, 159.

27. Herbert M. Kritzer, Neil Vidmar, and W. A. Bogart, "To Confront or Not to Confront: Measuring Claiming Rates in Discrimination Grievances," *Law & Society Review* 25 (1991), 883; Randall Samborn, "Many Americans Find Bias at Work," *National Law Journal*, July 16, 1990, 1; K.A. Dixon, Duke Storen, and Carl E. Van Horn, *A Workplace Divided: How Americans View Discrimination and Race on the Job* (New Brunswick, N.J.: John J. Heldrich Center for Workforce Development, 2002), 11–15; Laura Beth Nielsen and Robert L. Nelson, "Rights Realized? An Empirical Analysis of Employment Discrimination Litigation as a Claiming System," *Wisconsin Law Review* (2005), 680–707.

28. Kevin M. Clermont and Stewart J. Schwab, "How Employment Discrimination Cases Fare in Federal Court," *Journal of Empirical Legal Studies* 1 (July 2004), 429–458.

29. Richard E. Miller and Austin Sarat, "Grievances, Claims, and Disputes: Assessing the Adversary Culture," *Law & Society Review* 15 (1980–81), 544; Deborah R. Hensler et al., *Compensation for Accidental Injuries in the United States* (Santa Monica, Calif.: Rand Corporation, 1991), 122.

30. This discussion of auto accident cases draws from Miller and Sarat, "Grievances, Claims, and Disputes"; Hensler et al., *Compensation for Accidental Injuries*; All-Industry Research Advisory Council, *Compensation for Automobile Injuries in the United States* (Oak Brook, Ill.: AIRAC, 1989); and H. Laurence Ross, *Settled Out of Court: The Social Process of Insurance Claims Adjustment*, rev. 2d ed. (New York: Aldine, 1980).

31. All-Industry Research Advisory Council, *Compensation for Automobile Injuries*, 115.

32. Ibid., 115.

33. Ross, *Settled Out of Court*, 215–224.

34. Paul C. Weiler et al., *A Measure of Malpractice: Medical Injury, Malpractice Litigation, and Patient Compensation* (Cambridge: Harvard University Press, 1993), 61–76; David M. Studdert et al., "Negligent Care and Malpractice Claiming Behavior in Utah and Colorado," *Medical Care* (March 2000), 250–260. See also Stephen Daniels and Joanne Martin, *Civil Juries and the Politics of Reform* (Evanston, Ill.: Northwestern University Press, 1995), 117–119; Frank A. Sloan and Chee Ruey Hsieh, "Injury, Liability, and the Decision to File a Medical Malpractice Claim," *Law & Society Review* 29 (1995), 413–435; and David M. Studdert et al., "Claims, Errors, and Compensation Payments in Medical Malpractice Litigation," *New England Journal of Medicine* 354 (May 11, 2006), 2024–2033.

35. See Nalini Ambady et al., "Surgeons' Tone of Voice: A Clue to Malpractice History," *Surgery* 132 (July 2002), 5–9.

36. Ross E. Cheit and Jacob E. Gersen, "When Businesses Sue Each Other: An Empirical Study of State Court Litigation," *Law and Social Inquiry* 25 (2000), 803.

37. Lane Kenworthy, Stewart Macauley, and Joel Rogers, "'The More Things Change . . .':

Business Litigation and Governance in the American Automobile Industry," *Law and Social Inquiry* 21 (1996), 631–678.

38. Cheit and Gersen, "When Businesses Sue Each Other."
39. *X-It Products, L.L.C. v. Walter Kidde Portable Equipment, Inc.*, 227 F. Supp. 2d 494 (E.D. Va. 2002); June D. Bell, "Tiny Company Lands Big Settlement," *National Law Journal*, October 21, 2002.
40. *Schick Manufacturing, Inc. v. The Gillette Company*, 372 F. Supp. 2d 273 (D. Conn. 2005); *The Gillette Company v. Schick Manufacturing, Inc.*, 2005 U.S. Dist. LEXIS 34122 (D. Conn. 2005).
41. Miller and Sarat, "Grievances, Claims, and Disputes," 544; Joel B. Grossman, Herbert M. Kritzer, Kristin Bumiller, Austin Sarat, Stephen McDougal, and Richard Miller, "Dimensions of Institutional Participation: Who Uses the Courts and How?" *Journal of Politics* 44 (February 1982), 105.
42. Schauffler et al., *Examining the Work of State Courts, 2004*, 14.
43. Sally Engle Merry, *Getting Justice and Getting Even: Legal Consciousness Among Working-Class Americans* (Chicago: University of Chicago Press, 1990), 3.
44. See Herbert M. Kritzer, *Risks, Reputations, and Rewards: Contingency Fee Legal Practice in the United States* (Stanford: Stanford University Press, 2004).
45. Marc Galanter, "Reading the Landscape of Disputes: What We Know and Don't Know (and Think We Know) About Our Allegedly Contentious and Litigious Society," *UCLA Law Review* 31 (October 1983), 24.
46. Merry, *Getting Justice and Getting Even*, 142–143.
47. Ken Garcia, "Patty Sue Just Won't Go Away," *San Francisco Chronicle*, December 10, 2002, A21.
48. Sarah Treffinger, "Rocky River Sues Woman Who Sued for Trillions," *Cleveland Plain Dealer*, September 13, 2000, 1B; Sarah Treffinger, "Judge Sets Limits for Woman He Finds Files Suit Much Too Often," *Cleveland Plain Dealer*, August 15, 2001, B2.
49. Janet Kidd Stewart and Kathy Bergan, "A Bull Market in Complaints," *Chicago Tribune*, June 3, 2001, sec. 5, 1, 6.
50. See Neela Banerjee, "Methodist Court Removes an Openly Lesbian Minister," *New York Times*, November 1, 2005, A14.
51. Amanda Bronstad, "'Private Judges' Alter Legal Landscape," *National Law Journal*, April 10, 2006, 1, 20; Rodney Ho, "Celebrity Couple Wants No Limelight on Divorce," *Atlanta Journal-Constitution*, August 27, 2005, 2E.
52. Steven Greenhouse, "Case Challenges Employees' Waiving Right to Sue," *New York Times*, May 5, 2003, A19; *Equal Employment Opportunity Commission v. Luce, Forward, Hamilton & Scripps*, 345 F.3d 742 (9th Cir. 2003).
53. *Ting v. AT&T*, 319 F.3d 1126 (9th Cir. 2003).
54. Administrative Office of the United States Courts, *Judicial Business of the United States Courts (2005)*, 158–160.
55. Sam Dillon, "Connecticut to Sue U.S., Saying 'Left Behind' Law Leaves the State in Debt," *New York Times*, April 6, 2005, A21.
56. Administrative Office of the U.S. Courts, *Judicial Business of the United States Courts (2005)*, 159. This number is larger than the number shown in Exhibit 2.2 because it includes civil rights suits by prisoners.
57. *Monroe v. Pape*, 365 U.S. 167 (1961).
58. See Thomas F. Burke, *Lawyers, Lawsuits, and Legal Rights: The Battle Over Litigation in American Society* (Berkeley: University of California Press, 2002).
59. See John F. Harris, "Victory for Bush on Suits," *Washington Post*, February 18, 2005, A1.
60. One book is Matt Silverman, *Loony Lawsuits* (New York: Barnes & Noble, 2003).
61. See the data in Exhibit 2.2, in Chapter 2 of this book.
62. Schauffler et al., *Examining the Work of State Courts, 2004*, 23. These figures do not include domestic relations cases.
63. National Center for State Courts, "Tort Filings in 15 States, 1985–2003" (http://www.ncsconline.org/D_Research/csp/CSP_Main_Page.html).

64. Ostrom, Strickland, and Hannaford-Agor, "Examining Trial Trends in State Courts," 776.

65. Wayne McIntosh, "150 Years of Litigation and Dispute Settlement: A Court Tale," *Law & Society Review* 15 (1980–1981), 823–848; Lawrence M. Friedman and Robert V. Percival, "A Tale of Two Courts: Litigation in Alameda and San Benito Counties," *Law & Society Review* 10 (Winter 1976), 267–301; Stephen Daniels, "Caseload Dynamics and the Nature of Change: The Civil Business of Trial Courts in Four Illinois Counties," *Law & Society Review* 24 (1990), 299–320.

66. William Mullen, "U.S. Seeks a Cure to Legal Dilemma," *Chicago Tribune*, July 26, 1991, sec. 1, 1.

67. See V. Lee Hamilton and Joseph Sanders, *Everyday Justice: Responsibility and the Individual in Japan and the United States* (New Haven, Conn.: Yale University Press, 1992), 186–202.

68. Robert A. Kagan, *Adversarial Legalism: The American Way of Law* (Cambridge, Mass.: Harvard University Press, 2002). The quotation is from p. 3. See also Herbert M. Kritzer, "American Adversarialism," *Law & Society Review* 38 (2004), 349–383.

69. William Haltom and Michael McCann, *Distorting the Law: Politics, Media, and the Litigation Crisis* (Chicago: University of Chicago Press, 2004).

70. David M. Engel and Eric H. Steele, "Civil Cases and Society: Process and Order in the Civil Justice System," *American Bar Foundation Research Journal*, Spring 1979, 307–311.

71. This discussion is based in part on Herbert M. Kritzer, *Let's Make a Deal: Understanding the Negotiation Process in Ordinary Litigation* (Madison: University of Wisconsin Press, 1991); Kritzer, *Risks, Reputations, and Rewards*; and Miller and Sarat, "Grievances, Claims, and Disputes."

72. Steven K. Smith, Carol J. DeFrances, and Patrick A. Langan, *Tort Cases in Large Counties* (Washington, D.C.: U.S. Department of Justice, Bureau of Justice Statistics, 1995), 2, 4, 5.

73. Ibid., 3.

74. Administrative Office of the United States Courts, *Judicial Business of the United States Courts (2005)*, 182–184; Judicial Council of California, *2006 Court Statistics Report* (San Francisco: Judicial Council of California, 2006), 89, 91.

75. Kritzer, *Let's Make a Deal*, 130.

76. Federal Rules of Civil Procedure, Rule 68.

77. Kritzer, *Let's Make a Deal*, 32, 38, 65; Kritzer, *Risks, Reputations, and Rewards*, ch. 5.

78. Valerie P. Hans, *Business on Trial: The Civil Jury and Corporate Responsibility* (New Haven: Yale University Press, 2000).

79. Ibid., 23.

80. Eric Helland and Alexander Tabarrok, "Runaway Judges? Selection Effects and the Jury," *Journal of Law, Economics, and Organization* 16 (October 2000), 306–333.

81. Christopher Drew and Andy Newman, "Taxi Owners Deftly Dodge Claims of Accident Victims," *New York Times*, May 24, 1998, 1, 23.

82. J. Michael Kennedy, "Simpson's Advance is Frozen," *Los Angeles Times*, January 5, 2007, B4.

83. See Myron Levin, "Coverage of Big Awards for Plaintiffs Distorts View of Legal System," *Los Angeles Times*, August 15, 2005, C1.

84. "Verdicts Revisited," *National Law Journal,* September 28, 1998, C1–C12; *Avery v. State Farm Mutual Automobile Insurance Company*, 835 N.E.2d 801 (Ill. 2005).

85. See Deborah R. Hensler, "Revisiting the Monster: New Myths and Realities of Class Action and Other Large Scale Litigation," *Duke Journal of Comparative & International Law* 11 (2001), 179–213.

86. John A. Goerdt, *Small Claims and Traffic Courts: Case Management Procedures, Case Characteristics, and Outcomes in 12 Urban Jurisdictions* (Williamsburg, Va.: National Center for State Courts, 1992), 47; Bruce Zucker and Monica Her, "The People's Court Examined: A Legal and Empirical Analysis of the Small Claims Court System," *University of San Francisco Law Review* 37 (Winter 2003), 341.

87. David Caplovitz, *Consumers in Trouble: A Study of Debtors in Default* (New York: Free

Press, 1974); Erik Larson, "Case Characteristics and Defendant Tenant Default in a Housing Court," *Journal of Empirical Legal Studies* 3 (March 2006), 121–144.

88. Doug Struck, "In a 'People's Court' of Quirky Cases, Even Patience Is Tried," *Washington Post*, July 14, 1997, A1.

89. Caplovitz, *Consumers in Trouble*, 220.

90. Project, "The Iowa Small Claims Court: An Empirical Analysis," *Iowa Law Review* 75 (January 1990), 521.

91. Lynn Mather, Craig A. McEwen, and Richard J. Maiman, *Divorce Lawyers at Work: Varieties of Professionalism in Practice* (New York: Oxford University Press, 2001), 120.

92. Margaret F. Brinig and Michael V. Alexeev, "Trading at Divorce: Preferences, Legal Rules and Transactions Costs," *Ohio State Journal on Dispute Resolution* 8 (1993), 294.

93. Marygold S. Melli, Howard S. Erlanger, and Elizabeth Chambliss, "The Process of Negotiation: An Exploratory Investigation in the Context of No-Fault Divorce," *Rutgers Law Review* 40 (Summer 1988), 1145.

94. Ibid., 1147.

95. Timothy S. Grail, "Custodial Mothers and Fathers and Their Child Support: 2003," *Current Population Reports P60-230*, U.S. Census Bureau (July 2006), 7–8.

96. Charles Babington, "Md. Targets Child-Support Delinquents," *Washington Post*, May 1, 1996, D3.

97. Ken Ringle, "Unamicable Partners," *Washington Post*, March 15, 1999, C1, C7.

98. Thomas H. Cohen, *Tort Trials and Verdicts in Large Counties, 2001* (Washington, D.C.: U.S. Department of Justice, Bureau of Justice Statistics, 2004).

99. Seth A. Seabury, Nicholas M. Pace, and Robert T. Reville, "Forty Years of Civil Jury Verdicts," *Journal of Empirical Legal Studies* 1 (March 2004), 1–25.

100. Edie Greene and Brian H. Bornstein, *Determining Damages: The Psychology of Jury Awards* (Washington, D.C.: American Psychological Association, 2003).

101. This discussion is based on several studies, including U.S. Department of Transportation, *Economic Consequences of Automobile Accident Injuries* (Washington, D.C.: Government Printing Office, 1970); Hensler et al., *Compensation for Accidental Injuries*; All-Industry Research Advisory Council, *Compensation for Automobile Injuries*; and Insurance Research Council, *Auto Injury Insurance Claims: Countrywide Patterns in Treatment, Cost, and Compensation* (Malvern, Pa.: Insurance Research Council, 2003).

102. See All-Industry Research Advisory Council, *Compensation for Automobile Injuries*, 31, 129.

103. See James S. Kakalik and Nicholas M. Pace, *Costs and Compensation Paid in Tort Litigation* (Santa Monica, Calif: Rand Corporation, 1986).

104. Hensler et al., *Compensation for Accidental Injuries*, 105–108.

105. Caplovitz, *Consumers in Trouble*, 221; Goerdt, *Small Claims and Traffic Courts*, 51–52.

106. Richard Marosi, "Dubious Evictions Become an Issue as Vacancy Rates Fall," *Los Angeles Times*, January 7, 2001, 3; Lawyers' Committee for Better Housing, *No Time for Justice: A Study of Chicago's Eviction Court* (Chicago: Lawyers' Committee for Better Housing, 2003), 16.

107. Craig Wanner, "A Harvest of Profits: Exploring the Symbiotic Relationship Between Urban Civil Trial Courts and the Business Community" (paper presented at the 1973 meeting of the American Political Science Association in New Orleans, Louisiana).

108. Maria Cancian and Daniel R. Meyer, "Who Gets Custody?" *Demography* 35 (May 1998), 147–157. On custody decisions generally, see Eleanor E. Maccoby and Robert H. Mnookin, *Dividing the Child: Social and Legal Dilemmas of Custody* (Cambridge: Harvard University Press, 1992), 98–114.

109. See Marsha Garrison, "Good Intentions Gone Awry: The Impact of New York's Equitable Distribution Law on Divorce Outcomes," *Brooklyn Law Review* 57 (Fall 1991), 717.

110. See Dee McAree, "Broad Campaign Aimed at Altering Custody Laws," *National Law Journal*, October 25, 2004, 4.

111. Gordon H. Lester, "Child Support and Alimony, 1987," *Current Population Reports P23–167*, U.S. Census Bureau (June 1990), 8, 11; Garrison, "Good Intentions Gone Awry," 697–699.

112. Suzanne Bianchi and Edith McArthur, *Family Disruption and Economic Hardship: The Short-Run Picture for Children*, U.S. Bureau of the Census, Current Population Reports, Series P-70, no. 23 (Washington, D.C.: Government Printing Office, 1991); Barbara R. Rowe and Jean M. Lown, "The Economics of Divorce and Remarriage for Rural Utah Families," *Journal of Contemporary Law* 16 (March 1990), 322–325; Richard R. Peterson, "A Re-Evaluation of the Economic Consequences of Divorce," *American Sociological Review* 61 (June 1996), 528–536; Suzanne M. Bianchi, Lekha Subaiya, and Joan R. Kahn, "The Gender Gap in the Economic Well-Being of Nonresident Fathers and Custodial Mothers," *Demography* 36 (May 1999), 195–203.
113. The discussion in this paragraph and the next are based on Matthew McKeever and Nicholas H. Wolfinger, "Reexamining the Economic Costs of Marital Disruption for Women," *Social Science Quarterly* 82 (March 2001), 202–217; and Matthew McKeever and Nicolas H. Wolfinger, "Shifting Fortunes in a Changing Economy: Trends in the Economic Well-Being of Divorced Women," in *Fragile Families and the Marriage Agenda*, ed. Lori Kowaleski-Jones and Nicholas H. Wolfinger (New York: Springer, 2006), 127–157.
114. Grail, "Custodial Mothers and Fathers," 3.
115. Herbert Jacob, "Faulting No-Fault," *American Bar Foundation Research Journal* (Fall 1986), 773–780; Stephen D. Sugarman, "Dividing Financial Interests on Divorce," in *Divorce Reform at the Crossroads*, ed. Stephen D. Sugarman and Herma Hill Kay (New Haven: Yale University Press, 1991), 130–165.
116. See Marsha Garrison, "How Do Judges Decide Divorce Cases? An Empirical Analysis of Discretionary Decision Making," *North Carolina Law Review* 74 (January 1996), 473–475.
117. Lempert, "A Classic at 25," 1110–1111.
118. See Ken Auletta, *World War 3.0: Microsoft and Its Enemies* (New York: Random House, 2001).

8

Appellate Courts: The Process

Of all the cases that are filed in court, only a small fraction go beyond the trial level. In those quantitative terms, then, appellate courts would seem considerably less important than trial courts. But a simple count of cases understates the role of appellate courts. In resolving the cases they hear, appellate judges help determine the decisions of trial judges in a much larger number of cases. And the legal rulings made by appellate courts shape public policy on issues that range from compensation for personal injuries to presidential power.

The final two chapters of this book focus on appellate courts. This chapter examines matters of process: how cases flow to and through appellate courts, how and why courts reach their decisions. Chapter 9 considers appellate courts as policymakers, discussing the policies they produce and the impact of those policies.

Trial and appellate courts are closely linked. Cases move back and forth between the two sets of courts, which apply the same body of law in deciding them. Yet in some respects the appellate process differs fundamentally from the trial process. Indeed, as suggested in Chapter 1, in important respects trial and appellate courts each resemble some nonjudicial institutions more closely than they resemble each other.

In this context, it is important to distinguish between first-level and second-level appellate courts. First-level courts stand directly above trial courts and review their decisions. Second-level courts stand above the first-level courts and review *their* decisions. Eleven states have only a single appellate court, usually called a supreme court, that serves as a first-level court. The remaining states and the federal system each have one or more intermediate appellate courts (most often called courts of appeals) as first-level courts and a supreme court that is the state's second-level court.

It is second-level appellate courts that differ most sharply from trial courts. The stately pace of proceedings in second-level courts symbolizes the attention that their judges give to individual cases, in contrast with the routine and rapid processing of individual cases that often occurs in trial courts. First-level appellate courts stand between trial courts and second-level appellate courts in this respect. Growing caseload pressures have increased their resemblance to trial courts. In response to the greater volume of appellate litigation, there is more emphasis on processing cases, and some cases are handled in a fairly routine fashion. In turn, these procedural changes have affected the outcomes of cases and subtly changed intermediate appellate courts as institutions.

AN OVERVIEW OF APPELLATE COURTS

Consideration of appellate courts can begin with some general matters: the purposes that underlie appellate courts, their business, their major participants, and their procedures for handling appeals.

The Purposes of Appeal

Appellate courts exist, and dissatisfied litigants are permitted to appeal, primarily to serve two purposes.

First, appellate courts can correct errors in application of the law to individual litigants. Because individual judges and juries can err, review of their judgments seems necessary so that their mistakes do not cause injustice to litigants. That is why losing parties in trial courts generally have the right to one appeal.

Appellate courts enjoy some advantages in reaching the right result under the law. An appellate court can have the assistance of extensive written briefs and oral arguments in reaching its decisions, and it can take weeks or months to make a judgment. And because appellate decisions are made by multiple judges rather than a single one, the chance of an erroneous decision is reduced.

A second purpose of appellate courts is to increase the clarity and consistency of the law. These qualities are important because they give people and their attorneys greater certainty about the legal consequences of their actions—whether a contract will be declared valid if it is challenged or whether a corporate merger might be disapproved under the antitrust laws. Clarity and consistency also serve the goal of equal justice by helping to ensure that the law is applied in the same fashion to different cases.

One way that appellate courts reduce ambiguity and inconsistency is by resolving conflicting interpretations of the law. If federal district judges in the Seventh Circuit interpret a civil rights statute in different ways, the Court of Appeals for the Seventh Circuit can adopt a single interpretation for them to follow. Even in the absence of a conflict, an appellate court can overturn what its members see as a lower court's mistaken interpretation of a legal provision. By correcting interpretations of the law and the law's application to specific cases, appellate courts supervise trial courts and keep them on what appellate judges see as the right path.

In the systems that have both first-level and second-level courts, their primary purposes differ. Courts of appeals directly review trial court decisions, so they do most of the error correction. As the head of a whole court system, the supreme court concentrates on developing and clarifying the law. This is one major distinction between the two sets of courts.

The Business of Appellate Courts

Because of the general rule that litigants are entitled to an appeal, we would expect the mix of cases in appellate courts to mirror the mix in trial courts. To a considerable extent, this is true. One result is that appellate courts, like trial courts, hear a wide range of cases. But there are some differences as well.

First, the jurisdiction of appellate courts differs from that of trial courts in important respects. Appeals from some administrative agencies go directly to appellate courts, bypassing the trial level entirely. In most states, appeals from minor trial courts go first to major trial courts, and few of these cases ever get to appellate courts. Prosecutors cannot appeal acquittals in trial courts.

The discretionary jurisdiction of second-level appellate courts puts them in a special position. To varying degrees, these courts can choose which cases they will hear and decide from those that litigants bring to them. With this discretion, their judges can choose to hear some kinds of cases rather than others. At the extreme, a state supreme court might turn away a whole category of cases.

Third, litigants in different kinds of cases are not equally likely to appeal. To take one obvious example, criminal defendants who have been given long prison sentences appeal at higher rates than most other types of litigants. Patterns of appeals and the use of discretionary jurisdiction are examined in the next two sections.

Finally, the content of cases is often transformed at the appellate level. The factual questions that dominate most trials are largely irrelevant to appellate courts, which generally accept the conclusions of trial judges and juries about facts. Instead, appeals from trial decisions usually emphasize issues of legal interpretation. Ordinarily, such issues must be raised at the trial level in order to be considered on appeal, but they usually receive much more attention in appellate courts. As a result, a case in which the trial focused on whether the defendant was the person who robbed a store may be transformed on appeal into a case about whether the police followed the proper procedures in searching the defendant's car. Broad legal issues tend to receive even greater emphasis as cases move up to second-level appellate courts.

By no means do all appeals come after trials. Many result from pretrial rulings, and in some states a criminal defendant who pled guilty can appeal the sentence or procedures used in the case. According to one study, only one-quarter of the cases decided by the Arizona court of appeals in Phoenix resulted from trials.[1]

The Participants

Cases on appeal involve a narrower range of participants than do trials. Judges are the central figures, and attorneys play integral roles as well. Other participants are important because they affect what judges and lawyers do: law clerks influence judges, and the parties to cases influence their attorneys.

Judges   In appellate courts, far more than in trial courts, judges are the key participants. A high proportion of cases that come to an appellate court are ultimately decided by the court—by judges—rather than resolved outside of court. And while judges are influenced by other participants in the courts, they have greater freedom to take their own course than do trial judges.

Yet in one respect individual appellate judges are less important than trial judges. Acting alone, trial judges can put their individual stamp on courtroom proceedings and decisions. Because appellate courts decide cases collectively, the power of any single judge is diluted. Unlike trial judges, an appellate judge must have the support of colleagues to make law and policy.

Law Clerks   In appellate courts, as in many trial courts, judges are assisted by attorneys who serve as law clerks.[2] (Law clerks are different from court clerks, who help to administer and manage courts.) Many appellate courts also have central staffs of law clerks who serve the court as a whole. Members of these staffs are sometimes called staff attorneys.

Most law clerks are recent law school graduates who take their positions for a relatively short period, often only a year. Many of these short-term clerks are high-ranking graduates of prestigious law schools. Some clerks, especially those on central staffs, serve for longer periods.

The number of law clerks has grown with the caseloads of appellate courts. In the federal court system, Supreme Court justices can now hire four personal law clerks each, and court of appeals judges are allowed three. Central staffs of clerks now exist in every federal court of appeals and in many state appellate courts.

Caseload growth has also led judges to give clerks more responsibility. One example is the role of central staff attorneys in many intermediate appellate courts. These law clerks categorize cases and perform preliminary work in those deemed to be relatively simple and straightforward—preliminary work that often extends to proposing decisions and opinions to the judges. Judges differ in the tasks they give the clerks who serve them directly, but they typically delegate functions as important as drafting opinions. A legal scholar and federal court of appeals judge has said that "probably more than half the written output of the [Supreme] Court is clerk-authored."[3]

Delegation of responsibility always carries with it a certain amount of power. Without question, then, law clerks have substantial impact on the work of their courts. But there is considerable disagreement about the extent of that impact. Most law clerks for the Supreme Court describe their role as minor and their power as limited, but a former law clerk for Justice Harry Blackmun depicted the Court's clerks as engaged in ideological battles that helped to determine the Court's positions in cases.[4]

Whatever may be the law clerks' power, delegation of responsibility in appellate courts is probably more limited than in most other government organizations. It appears that appellate judges still do their own work more than do cabinet secretaries and members of Congress.

Attorneys   Many appeals are brought *pro se*, that is, without an attorney. It is not surprising that in 2005, nearly 90 percent of all appeals by prisoners to the federal courts of appeals in civil cases were pro se. It may be surprising that more than one-quarter of all appeals in other civil cases were pro se.[5] Still, lawyers predominate in the cases that appellate judges consider fully, and it is rare for non-lawyers to represent themselves in arguments before supreme courts.

The attorneys who handle appeals are a mixture of appellate specialists and non-specialists. Many of the specialists work for government. Appellate specialists in the U.S. Department of Justice undertake some litigation for the federal government in the courts of appeals and most of the government's legal work in the Supreme Court, and some states have similar appellate specialists. Some states operate public defenders' offices that handle only appeals. In the private sector, some lawyers for interest groups do a good deal of appellate litigation, and there is a growing number of attorneys in law firms who specialize in appellate work. Indeed, some lawyers spend a large share of their time on Supreme Court litigation.

But it is the usual practice in the private sector and common in the public sector for a lawyer who has tried a case to handle it on appeal as well. One result is that a good deal of appellate work is done by lawyers with little experience at that level. Most lawyers who argue cases before the Supreme Court do so only once, and frequently such a lawyer argues a significant case in the Court. This was true of Neal Katyal, who won the 2006 case in which the Court ruled against the president's establishment of military commissions to try suspected terrorists at Guantanamo Bay.[6] Such successes aside, the inexperience shared by many appellate lawyers is often reflected in their work. Appellate judges sometimes complain about the limited competence of the lawyers who argue before them, focusing chiefly on the nonspecialists. Anyone who watches several oral arguments in an appellate court is likely to be struck by the weaknesses of some advocates.

At the appellate level, as in trial courts, attorneys play crucial roles in developing and presenting cases. But their roles differ considerably between the two levels. Appellate lawyers do much less negotiation to settle cases than do trial lawyers. And rather than orchestrate the presentation of evidence at trial, they offer legal arguments directly through written *briefs* (detailed presentations of their line of reasoning in the case) and through oral argument.

Parties   Every case on appeal includes at least one *appellant*, the party that brought the appeal, and one or more *appellees*, the other side in the case. The parties to appellate cases, like the cases themselves, are diverse. But two types of parties predominate: governments and criminal defendants and prisoners. Among the cases that came to the federal courts of appeals in 2005, the federal government was a party in about half, and state governments were parties in more than 20 percent. And two-thirds of the cases had criminal defendants or prisoners as parties.[7] Of course, since government acts as prosecutor or jailer, these two patterns are linked.

Some kinds of parties are likely to appear as appellants and others as appellees. A study of the federal courts of appeals found that individuals are usually appellants, largely because so many appeals are brought by criminal defendants and prisoners who lost at trial. In contrast, governments are usually appellees. Businesses appear in the two roles at about the same rate, reflecting their mixed success in the district courts.[8]

The parties that are represented by attorneys do not participate directly in appellate court proceedings. Their roles vary considerably. At one end of the continuum, some parties supervise their attorneys closely. At the other end, some are distant spectators as their lawyers develop and carry out strategies in appellate court.

A Summary of Appellate Court Procedures

Like trial procedures, appellate procedures vary among courts and types of cases. The most important distinction is between a traditional system of full appellate procedure and a collection of procedures that depart from it, chiefly by abbreviating the traditional process.[9]

The Traditional System   The traditional system of appellate procedure has two versions. One applies when a case falls under mandatory jurisdiction, under which a court must decide a case. The other applies when a case falls under discretionary jurisdiction, so that a court can choose whether or not to accept a case for decision. Because first-level appellate courts have mostly mandatory jurisdiction and second-level courts mostly discretionary jurisdiction, they generally use different versions of the traditional procedure. As Exhibit 8.1 shows, however, these two versions have much in common.

Where a court's jurisdiction is mandatory, the process begins when one side (or, occasionally, both sides) decides to appeal a lower-court verdict or another ruling. The party who files an appeal generally is required to have the transcript of the trial proceedings and other parts of the record of the case prepared and transmitted to the appellate court.

The appellant submits a written brief arguing in favor of that party's position. This brief generally focuses on legal issues, alleging errors by the lower court as a basis for overturning its decision. In opposition, the appellee submits a brief supporting the lower-court decision and taking issue with the appellant's contentions. The appellant may then submit a reply brief.

In a case falling under a court's discretionary jurisdiction, these early stages take a somewhat different and more extended form. The process begins when the party that is dissatisfied with a lower-court decision, the *petitioner*, asks the appellate court to call up the case and hear it. This petition takes different legal forms in different courts. In

EXHIBIT 8.1   Typical Stages of Processing in Appellate Courts (Traditional Procedures)

Mandatory Jurisdiction	Discretionary Jurisdiction
a. Filing of an appeal and brief by the appellant	a. Filing of a petition for a hearing by the petitioner
b. Submission of a brief by the appellee	b. Submission of a brief in opposition to this petition by the respondent
c. Submission of a reply brief by the appellant	c. Court decision on whether to grant a hearing
	d. Submission of additional briefs by the parties

1. Prehearing conference (in some courts)
2. Court rulings on motions by the parties (such rulings may also come at other points)
3. Oral argument by the attorneys before the court
4. Court conference to reach a tentative decision
5. Writing of opinion(s) and continuing discussion of the case
6. Announcement of the decision and opinion(s)
7. Further action by the lower court in response to the appellate decision (in many cases)

the Supreme Court, a petitioner asks the Court to issue a *writ of certiorari* to the court that last decided the case; if the writ is issued, it requires that the record of the case be sent up to the Supreme Court. The petitioner submits a brief in support of the request for a hearing, which is accompanied by the record of the case. The other party, the *respondent*, may then submit a brief in opposition to the request.

After receiving these materials, the court considers and rules on the petition. Most supreme courts require a majority vote to accept a case. But the U.S. Supreme Court requires slightly less than a majority (four of nine justices), and a number of states have similar rules.[10] The Virginia Supreme Court sits in panels of three to screen requests for hearings, and only a single vote is required to accept a case. One Virginia justice has described her first session to consider requests for hearings. When cases came up, the other two justices invited the newcomer to speak first. For each of the first three cases, she indicated that the request for a hearing had some merit, only to find that the other justices quickly moved on to the next case. Finally she asked why her colleagues were not speaking. "Don't you know the rule?" one asked. "If one judge feels there's an interesting issue, we grant and move on to the next case."[11]

If a court rejects a petition, it reaches no decision in the case and simply allows the lower court to make its ruling final. But if the petition is accepted, the case is called up for decision. The parties then submit additional briefs on the merits of the case.

From this point on, cases under mandatory and discretionary jurisdiction are treated in the same way. Some cases drop out of first-level appellate courts because the parties settle, and courts such as the Michigan Court of Appeals make active efforts to encourage settlements.[12] Other cases are dropped by the appellant or dismissed by the court. Through these two processes, many appeals are resolved by something other than a decision on the merits. In 2005, this was true of about half the cases in the intermediate appellate courts of Illinois and the federal courts of appeals.[13]

Before a court holds a hearing on a case, it may need to rule on motions by the parties. Among the subjects of these motions are the release of prisoners while their appeals are pending, permission for indigent parties to proceed without paying court fees, and exceptions to the court's procedural rules.

An appellate hearing takes the form of oral argument, in which the attorneys for the two sides make presentations that highlight and supplement their briefs. The judges may interrupt these presentations to ask questions, and in some courts such interruptions are frequent. The length of the oral argument varies, but one common practice is to divide an hour equally between the two sides.

After the hearing, the judges meet in conference to consider the case and reach a tentative decision. Their choice is whether to uphold, or *affirm*, the lower-court decision, or to overturn it either completely or in part. In general, a court *reverses* a decision when it overturns the decision completely, and it *modifies* a decision by overturning the decision in part. The court might, for example, uphold a verdict for a personal injury plaintiff but rule that the damages awarded by the trial court were too high. A court may also *vacate*, or make void, a lower-court decision. The Supreme Court sometimes uses this procedure when a recent change in the law calls into question the validity of a lower-court decision.

At some point, usually after the conference but sometimes earlier, one judge is assigned to write the opinion that will describe the court's decision and the reasoning on which that decision is based. This opinion has several purposes: to justify the decision to the parties and any other audience; to instruct the lower court on what to do if it must reconsider the case; and to announce the rules of law on which this decision was based and that lower courts must follow in relevant future cases.

The assigned judge works to produce a draft opinion for consideration by the other judges, whose comments may cause the opinion to be modified in minor or major ways. Meanwhile, other judges may be writing and circulating alternative opinions, which reach a different result from the assigned opinion or offer different rationales for the same result. Whether or not there are multiple opinions, judges may engage in a process of compromise and bargaining. The heart of this process is an effort by opinion writers to gain the support of colleagues through the way they word their opinions. As Supreme Court justice Sandra Day O'Connor told a colleague in one case, "If you could see your way to incorporating this modification in your circulating draft I would be pleased to join" the opinion.[14]

The process of decision ends when each judge takes a final position. The court's decision is then announced, and the opinion supported by the majority is issued on the court's behalf. In the Supreme Court, unlike most other courts, decisions are announced by the justices in court. Judges who disagree with the court's decision in the case, in that they favored a different outcome for the parties, may cast dissenting votes. If a vote in a state supreme court is announced as 5–2, the two are justices who dissented from the decision.

When judges dissent, one or more usually write *dissenting opinions*, in which they explain their differences with the majority. Other dissenters may sign on to a judge's dissenting opinion. Such opinions have no direct impact on the law, but they allow judges to express their views and perhaps influence future court decisions.

Judges can also write *concurring opinions*. One type of concurring opinion (sometimes called "special") expresses agreement with the court's decision, its treatment of the parties, but disagrees with the rules of law that the court uses to justify its decision. Because the long-term impact of an appellate decision lies chiefly in the rules of law that it announces, the disagreement expressed in concurring opinions often is as significant as the disagreement in dissenting opinions. Another type of concurring opinion (sometimes called "regular") agrees with both the decision and the rules of law in the court's opinion but expresses the judge's individual views about some matter—perhaps an interpretation of the court's opinion or a point of disagreement with a dissenting opinion.

Occasionally, because of disagreement about the rationale, no opinion gains the support of a majority of judges. In this situation, there is a decision but no authoritative interpretation of the legal issues in the case. In one 2006 decision of the Supreme Court, summarized in Exhibit 8.2, there was a majority for only part of the primary opinion, and the Court fragmented in so many ways that it was very difficult for a lower-court judge or any other reader to ascertain the Court's collective views.

What happens after an appellate court decision depends primarily on the content of the decision. If the court affirms the lower court's decision, it notifies the lower court that it can make its ruling final. If the court overturns the lower-court decision in some way, it may make a final disposition of the case itself or direct the lower court to reach a particular final decision. Frequently, however, an appellate court that has reversed,

EXHIBIT 8.2   The Supreme Court Fails to Reach Consensus on a Decision

---

"KENNEDY, J., announced the judgment of the Court and delivered the opinion of the Court with respect to Parts II-A and III, in which STEVENS, SOUTER, GINSBURG, AND BREYER, JJ., joined, an opinion with respect to Parts I and IV, in which ROBERTS, C. J., and ALITO, J., joined, an opinion with respect to Parts II-B and II-C, and an opinion with respect to Part II-D, in which SOUTER and GINSBURG, JJ., joined. STEVENS, J., filed an opinion concurring in part and dissenting in part, in which BREYER, J., joined as to Parts I and II. SOUTER, J., filed an opinion concurring in part and dissenting in part, in which GINSBURG, J., joined. BREYER, J., filed an opinion concurring in part and dissenting in part. ROBERTS, C. J., filed an opinion concurring in part, concurring in the judgment in part, and dissenting in part, in which ALITO, J., joined. SCALIA, J., filed an opinion concurring in the judgment in part and dissenting in part, in which THOMAS, J., joined, and in which ROBERTS, C. J., and ALITO, J., joined as to Part III."

Source: The Supreme Court's syllabus in *League of United Latin American Citizens v. Perry*, 165 L. Ed. 2d 609 (2006).

---

modified, or vacated a decision sends the case back (*remands* it) to the lower court for further consideration in light of the appellate court decision and opinion. The lower court then has at least some freedom to resolve the case as its judges see fit.

Alternative Procedures   Many appellate courts follow this traditional set of procedures closely in at least a portion of their cases. But there have always been deviations from this model, primarily as means to expedite the disposition of cases and to reduce judges' workloads. These deviations have become far more common since the 1960s. In first-level courts today, cases that follow the traditional system in all respects are a distinct minority. Most of the alternative procedures can be placed in three categories.

The first concerns opportunities for the parties to make their case. Most courts have reduced the length of oral argument or, for some cases, eliminated it altogether. In 2005, the federal courts of appeals held oral argument in only 30 percent of the cases they decided on the merits.[15] In many state appellate courts, the proportion is even lower. At the extreme, the Hawaii Supreme Court tried to deal with caseload pressures by scheduling oral arguments only in cases of "extraordinary complexity or importance," and in the years from 1996 through 2001 it held an average of two oral arguments a year.[16] Courts with discretionary jurisdiction sometimes decide cases solely on the basis of the petition for hearing and the brief in opposition, dispensing both with further briefing and with oral argument.

The second category concerns the decision-making process. Judges sometimes dispense with conferences to consider cases collectively, and a few courts announce some of their decisions immediately after oral argument. Some courts assign a case to a single judge at an early point, and in these cases other judges largely defer to the

assigned judge. An even more radical departure is delegation to nonjudges. As noted earlier, many courts give central staff attorneys major responsibilities for some decisions.

The final category concerns the court's opinion. A court may simply announce
its disposition of a case without issuing an opinion. Alternatively, the court may issue
an opinion that is relatively brief—sometimes so brief that it is essentially no opinion
at all. And an opinion of any sort can be designated as *per curiam*, "by the court,"
rather than being signed by a single judge. A somewhat different practice is issuing
an opinion but directing that it not be published. In many courts, the rules of law in an
unpublished opinion cannot be cited by lawyers as precedent, but in 2006 the federal
courts adopted a new rule allowing lawyers to cite unpublished opinions.

These practices for opinions are common. In most intermediate courts, publication of opinions is the exception to the rule. In 2005, for instance, the California Courts
of Appeal published less than 10 percent of their opinions, the federal courts of appeals
20 percent. And most of the federal court of appeals opinions were *per curiam*.[17] These
alternatives to full, published opinions are popular because they save judges' time.
Even a full opinion is less time-consuming if its writer does not have to worry about
its being used as precedent, and an unsigned opinion does not put direct responsibility
on the judge who wrote it.

Often, multiple categories of alternative procedures are used in combination. In
some courts, for instance, certain cases are decided without oral argument, are given
tentative decisions by central staff attorneys, and are handed down with brief unpublished per curiam opinions that are written primarily by staff attorneys. Many appellate
courts have created two tracks, with some cases handled under a system that resembles the traditional one and others given more limited consideration and treatment.
The process of assigning cases to one track or the other is discussed in the section on
screening of cases.

APPEALS

With a few exceptions, cases come to appellate courts because one or more of the parties take cases there. Thus, the work of appellate courts is based on the composition
of appeals and petitions for hearings. For the sake of simplicity, I refer to all cases as
appeals in the discussion that follows.

The Decision to Appeal

In many respects, opting to appeal is like going to court in the first place. In both instances, people who are not entirely satisfied with their situation—in this case, an unfavorable court ruling—must decide whether to accept the situation or seek redress.

But there are differences between the two decisions. Perhaps most important, appealing an adverse decision is less momentous than the original decision to litigate: the
case is already in the court system, and the parties have already experienced the disadvantages of going to court. This difference helps to explain why a higher proportion
of potential cases are filed and why cases are less likely to be settled out of court at the
appellate level. In a study of civil cases in the state courts of large counties, 14 percent

of the verdicts in trial courts were appealed,[18] and the rate of appeal in criminal cases undoubtedly is much higher.

Decisions to appeal, like decisions to go to court initially, are based on many factors. But three considerations seem to be especially important: the degree of dissatisfaction with the lower-court decision, the chances of success on appeal, and the monetary cost.

Dissatisfaction with a Decision   Almost nobody is happy to lose a court case. Yet the intensity of the loser's unhappiness can vary a good deal, depending chiefly on how much has been lost. A criminal defendant who was granted probation and one who was sentenced to death usually have very different feelings about their defeats. Similarly, the amount of money a civil defendant has lost in a trial verdict or that a losing plaintiff had sought conditions their reactions. In state courts in large counties, for instance, cases in which the plaintiff was awarded more than a million dollars are far more likely to be appealed by the defendant than are cases with smaller awards.[19]

This unsurprising pattern has significant effects on the work of appellate courts. First, even the courts that must hear all appeals deal disproportionately with cases that have relatively large stakes. Second, minor trial courts, whose cases involve relatively small stakes, generally are subject to little appellate scrutiny. Finally, since the average case at the federal level involves bigger stakes, the rate of appeal there is higher than in state courts.

Chances of Success   In any appellate court, the odds are against a successful appeal. But the odds vary from case to case, and people appeal most often in situations where they see the chances of victory as relatively great.

Litigants typically lack the experience needed to estimate the chances of a favorable outcome with some accuracy. Thus people who are represented by lawyers often rely heavily on their lawyers in deciding whether an appeal is promising. Lawyers' perceptions of the prospects for success are heavily influenced by past decisions, and in this way appellate courts affect decisions whether to bring appeals. For instance, lawyers for plaintiffs who lose personal injury suits at trial find appeals more attractive in states where appellate courts have shown sympathy for the positions of injured parties. Courts sometimes offer more specific invitations to potential litigants, indicating in opinions that they would look favorably on cases raising a particular legal claim.

Many appeals are brought even though the chances of success seem slim. Sometimes litigants or their attorneys simply miscalculate, and unrepresented litigants are especially prone to make such mistakes. In some cases the stakes are so large that an appeal is attractive regardless of the likely outcome. Some litigants want to use every possible opportunity to express their grievance and to seek what they see as justice.[20]

In some cases, the appellant can win even by losing. For example, a corporation that lost in trial court and that was ordered to pay damages to the other party often gains by delaying the time when the damages actually must be paid. Appeals also can be used as a weapon to wear down opponents who have fewer resources for continued litigation. This is one reason that plaintiffs who have won large amounts against businesses at trial often accept lesser amounts of money in settlements after those businesses file appeals.

Financial Costs   As noted earlier, appeals generally are expensive. It is costly to pay a filing fee and prepare a trial record. If an appellant uses a lawyer, attorneys' fees are typically quite substantial. The remand of a case after a successful appeal frequently results in a new trial, exacting additional costs from the appellant.

As a result, at least in civil cases, individuals and institutions with the most resources are the most likely to appeal. In the absence of special arrangements such as a contingent fee or legal aid, a nonwealthy litigant whose funds have already been depleted by the costs of a trial is often reluctant to undergo the additional expense of an appeal. In contrast, litigants who are in a stronger financial position can bring an appeal if the potential gains from a successful appeal or from delay are sufficient.

Personal financial resources have much less impact on criminal appeals. Most people convicted of serious crimes are indigent. As a result of Supreme Court rulings, the costs of a first appeal ordinarily are waived for indigent defendants. Second-level courts typically allow indigent people to petition for hearings without paying the usual fees and costs for preparing the necessary materials.

As a result, in one important respect, criminal defendants have greater freedom to appeal than do large corporations. As suggested earlier, a defendant who has received a heavy sentence may see little reason not to appeal, whatever the chances of victory: a victory would bring enormous benefits, and there is little cost to trying. Not surprisingly, then, a high proportion of criminal defendants appeal from defeats at trial—a far higher proportion than the proportion of litigants who lose civil cases.

Appeals by Governments

In deciding whether to bring appeals, government officials consider the same factors as do other litigants. But their choices operate somewhat differently from those of other litigants. Most distinctive is the federal government.[21]

The federal government is probably the best example of the "repeat player" in litigation that Marc Galanter has described,[22] and this is especially true at the appellate level. Because of the large and continuing flow of cases, in any given field of law the government has a great many cases that it could appeal. Decisions to appeal are centralized: government cases generally cannot be filed in the courts of appeals or the Supreme Court without the authorization of the solicitor general's office within the Justice Department. Lawyers in that office can take a long-term view, with a focus more on achieving rules of law that favor the government's interests than on winning individual cases. Put another way, they have the capacity to act strategically.

One example of strategic action is the use of selective appeals to help shape the law. The government sometimes forgoes an appeal in a tax case because the court of appeals to which the appeal would go seems unfavorable to the position of the Internal Revenue Service. Instead, it waits for a case in a circuit whose court of appeals seems likely to be more sympathetic.

Another example of strategy is the rationing of petitions for hearings in the Supreme Court. The solicitor general's office is far more selective than other litigants in asking for hearings. This restraint allows the government generally to take only its strongest cases to the Court. One benefit is that the justices expect government petitions to be meritorious.

The federal government's repeat player status also allows its attorneys to develop expertise in handling appeals. In the Supreme Court, the preponderance of the government's legal work is handled by the small staff of attorneys in the solicitor general's office. Those lawyers gain a good deal of experience in writing briefs and arguing cases before the Court—experience that few other attorneys can match.

The skill that they develop through this experience, combined with the government's ability to act strategically, helps to produce an impressive rate of success for the federal government both in getting the Court to accept its cases and in winning cases that the Court does hear. The government does especially well in the case selection process. In its 2004 term, the Court accepted ten of the nineteen cases that the solicitor general asked it to hear, a 53 percent success rate. In contrast, other litigants had a 1 percent success rate.[23]

On the whole, state and local governments lack the full set of advantages held by the federal government in appellate courts. Some state governments lack centralized control over appeals. Local governments may have too few cases to act strategically and to develop experience in their attorneys. Financial constraints on appeals also may be more severe at the state and local levels. But many of the larger state and local governments share enough similarities with the federal government to distinguish them from most private litigants in the ways they operate in appellate courts.

Political Litigation

When people file lawsuits or appeal unfavorable decisions, they are usually acting for themselves alone. People file divorce cases because they want to end their marriages. Individuals sue for personal injuries, and businesses and governments bring debt collection actions, in order to recover money. Such cases can be considered *ordinary litigation.*

Some cases take a different form, in that people act on a broader goal: at least one of their aims is to influence the political process or government policy. And because of this broader goal, litigants and their lawyers are often joined as participants by political interest groups. This kind of case can be labeled *political litigation.* Cases with an element of political litigation are relatively rare in trial courts. Such cases are more common at the appellate level, because political litigation is more likely to result in appeals and because cases sometimes become political only when they reach appellate courts. For that reason political litigation is best discussed in the context of appellate courts.

A case may involve a mix of ordinary and political motives. One example is challenges to affirmative action programs in school admissions. The plaintiff is likely to care primarily about gaining admission, but the plaintiff's lawyers probably want both to win admission for their client and to limit the use of affirmative action in general. And for interest groups that support the plaintiff (and that may provide the plaintiff's lawyers), that broad policy goal motivates their participation in the case.

A distinction should be made between two types of political cases. The first involves what can be called the *classic* form of political litigation: cases are brought with the goal of winning a favorable ruling on an issue of legal policy, preferably from the Supreme Court. This kind of litigation is typified by the campaign of the NAACP

Legal Defense Fund against racial segregation of public school systems, a campaign that culminated in the Supreme Court's decision in *Brown v. Board of Education.*[24]

In the second type, cases are brought for *tactical* purposes, to gain some kind of advantage in a political conflict. Those who bring a case may seek simply to win, without regard for the level of court at which the case is resolved or the legal grounds on which it is decided. Or they may not even care about the outcome of the case, seeking only to gain an advantageous delay. This kind of litigation is typified by the flurry of lawsuits brought by the presidential candidates and their supporters in Florida after the 2000 election. Ultimately, the Supreme Court resolved the election with an interpretation of the Equal Protection Clause of the Fourteenth Amendment that ensured victory for George W. Bush. But Bush's lawyers had raised the equal protection argument as an afterthought, and they would have been equally happy to win a ruling that prevented further recounts of the Florida votes on some other ground or in some other court.[25]

Interest Groups and Classic Political Litigation

Individuals and lawyers can act on their own to bring and carry forward litigation that is aimed at shaping legal policy. But interest groups are frequently involved in this classic form of political litigation, because they have an incentive to participate and because their resources and expertise often make political cases possible. Sustained litigation campaigns, such as the effort to overcome school segregation, are nearly impossible without interest group involvement. Thus this form of political litigation is best understood from the perspective of interest groups.

Interest groups can take three kinds of roles in litigation. The first is direct sponsorship of cases. A group with a general or specific policy goal can look for potential clients whose cases can be used to advance that goal. Thus, local chapters of the American Civil Liberties Union (ACLU) take complaints from individuals that their civil liberties have been violated and use some of those complaints as vehicles for lawsuits.

In the second role, groups locate a case that is already in the courts, and they belatedly sponsor or support one side. After a criminal defendant has been convicted at trial, for instance, the NAACP Legal Defense Fund may learn that the case involves a challenge to racial discrimination in the selection of jurors. It might then offer to finance any appeals. This financing gives the Legal Defense Fund an opportunity to shape the case in ways that serve its own goals.

A group can play a third, more limited, role in a case by submitting an *amicus curiae* ("friend of the court") brief to the court. An amicus brief is aimed at influencing the court's decision by offering arguments on one side or for a position that neither side takes. This is the most common form of interest group involvement in litigation, because it is less expensive and easier to arrange than sponsorship. Amicus briefs are submitted in the great majority of cases heard by the Supreme Court, and in most cases there are several briefs.

Interest groups vary considerably in how frequently they litigate. One reason is that the courts are more relevant to some groups than to others. Courts can do little for a farm organization that seeks increased crop subsidies, but they can do a great deal for an insurance group that seeks favorable rules on liability for personal injuries. Another reason is that at a given time some groups see the courts as more sympathetic to their positions than the other branches, while other groups perceive the legislature or executive branch as more friendly. But nearly every major interest group participates in litigation at least occasionally.

The number of interest groups that participate in litigation and the level of their activity have burgeoned over the past few decades, so cases with major implications for policy increasingly involve battles between competing groups. This development is reflected in the increased numbers of amicus briefs submitted by groups in the Supreme Court and in lower courts.[26] One source of this change is simply that there are more interest groups. Another is that more groups recognize that litigation can help achieve their policy goals.

The most prominent examples of groups that litigate extensively are the ACLU and the NAACP Legal Defense Fund. The Legal Defense Fund, created in 1939, has achieved considerable success in advancing civil rights through lawsuits. Initially focusing on constitutional challenges to discrimination in voting and education, the Fund now pursues litigation on a range of constitutional and statutory issues relating to racial discrimination. The ACLU, founded in 1920, is a large membership group with state affiliates and local chapters. Its litigation covers a wide array of civil liberties issues, but it has given some emphasis to First Amendment issues involving freedom of expression and government policies toward religion. In recent years it has challenged some Bush administration policies relating to terrorism, arguing that they violate constitutional rights.

These two groups provided models for other groups. Partly because the courts were seen as relatively sympathetic to liberal positions, in the 1960s and 1970s most of the groups actively involved in litigation had liberal policy goals. Later, groups with conservative goals developed a larger presence in the courts. One reason for this development was a perceived need to counter the efforts of liberal groups. Another was the growing conservatism of the federal courts, a result of appointments by Republican presidents from Nixon to George W. Bush. The diversity of the groups that are actively involved in litigation is illustrated by the examples in Exhibit 8.3.

Interest groups affect the courts most clearly by bringing cases to them that would not get to court without the initiative or assistance of groups. It is more difficult to assess the influence of interest groups on the decisions that courts reach. Groups potentially can influence courts through the quality of their arguments, which may affect judges' perceptions of issues. For example, an amicus brief may suggest to a court a basis for its decision that might otherwise have gone unnoticed. There is some evidence that the quality of lawyers' presentation in oral argument affects the chances of success for their clients in the Supreme Court. If this is true, experienced lawyers who work with interest groups may enjoy an advantage in the cases they argue.[27] But judges often have strong views about the kinds of issues that interest groups bring to them, so there are limits to how much they can be persuaded by those groups. As one scholar concluded about political litigation in the Supreme Court, "the reasoning and outcome of Court decisions often seem to be a byproduct of events that no litigant can predict nor control."[28]

Tactical Political Litigation   People and organizations may use political litigation for a variety of tactical purposes. As illustrated by the Florida cases brought after

EXHIBIT 8.3   Some Interest Groups That Are Active in the Courts

American Center for Law and Justice   The ACLJ was founded in 1990 by Reverend Pat Robertson's Christian Coalition to litigate on behalf of conservative Christian values. It was modeled in part on the ACLU, reflecting a view that a counterbalance to that organization was needed. The ACLJ has a wide range of concerns, among them religious activities at schools and the rights of antiabortion protesters. In 2003 chief counsel Jay Sekulow argued before the Supreme Court in cases involving federal regulation of campaign finance (which affects religious groups) and state college scholarships for the study of theology. The ACLJ has achieved considerable success in advancing its legal positions in the courts.

Public Citizen Litigation Group   Consumer advocate Ralph Nader helped create this organization in 1972 as a "public interest law firm." The group litigates on many issues, including the rights of consumers and workers, access to government documents, and Internet free speech. Its most visible activity has been a series of challenges to federal laws on the ground that they breached the Constitution's separation of powers among the three branches. These challenges have resulted in major Supreme Court decisions on congressional vetoes of administrative rules, the Gramm-Rudman-Hollings budget deficit reduction law, and guidelines for sentencing by federal judges.

Center for Individual Rights   CIR was founded in 1989 as a conservative counterpart of liberal public interest law firms. Its litigation activity deals with a range of issues, but much of its work has involved challenges to affirmative action programs of several types. CIR sponsored two cases challenging affirmative action programs for admission of students to the University of Michigan. The Supreme Court decided the cases in 2003, upholding a program at the law school and striking down one for undergraduates.

Center for Constitutional Rights   The Center was founded in 1966 to litigate on behalf of human rights concerns. Its agenda has included issues of racial equality in the United States and international human rights. It has brought cases on behalf of people accused of terrorism, and it represented a prisoner at Guantanamo Bay in *Rasul v. Bush* (2004). In that case the Supreme Court ruled that federal courts had jurisdiction to consider challenges to the detention of foreign nationals at Guantanamo.

Sources: newspaper reports; group websites; court cases and decisions.

the 2000 election, one purpose is to gain an electoral advantage. In 2004, unlike 2000, an array of lawsuits was brought *before* the election, primarily on requirements for people to vote.[29] The 2006 elections brought additional lawsuits over the right to vote. Redistricting of legislative seats is another subject of lawsuits. When one political party in a state draws seats in a way that gives it an advantage, people associated with the other party sometimes challenge the redistricting on constitutional grounds. In an episode described in Exhibit 8.4, a bitter battle over redistricting in Texas resulted in lawsuits that were ultimately resolved by the Supreme Court in 2006.

EXHIBIT 8.4   The Battle over Texas Congressional Districts in the Courts

In 1991 the Democratic party controlled the process of drawing congressional districts in Texas, and the legislature adopted a districting plan that was highly favorable to Democratic candidates. Republican voters brought a lawsuit challenging the districting as a partisan gerrymander, but they lost in federal district court. After the 2000 census control of Texas government was divided between the parties, and no redistricting plan could be enacted. Required to act in the face of this deadlock, a federal district court adopted a plan that largely followed the lines of the 1991 plan and retained the Democrats' advantage.

In 2003 the Republican party gained full control of the legislature and governorship. Although it was quite unusual to redistrict seats in Congress in the middle of a decade, Republicans drew up a new plan that would reverse the Democratic advantage. The chief architect of this effort was Tom DeLay, Majority Leader of the U.S. House. The plan was adopted after considerable maneuvering in the legislature, including the mass exodus of Democrats in the Texas House to Oklahoma and a later exodus of Senate Democrats to New Mexico to prevent a legislative quorum and thus block a vote on the redistricting plan.

Several individuals and groups filed lawsuits in federal court to challenge the Republican redistricting. A three-judge district court ruled against the challenge, but the Supreme Court asked the district court to reconsider the case in light of a new Supreme Court decision on political gerrymandering. The district court reached the same conclusion in a second decision. In June 2006 the Supreme Court ruled that, with one small exception, the redistricting plan was constitutionally acceptable.

The Supreme Court ruling ensured that the congressional districts in Texas would continue to favor the Republicans at least through the 2010 election. The ruling also opened the door to mid-decade redistricting in other states when one of the parties wins control of state government. But the legal issues in redistricting were not fully resolved. In all likelihood, the spate of lawsuits over legislative districts that occurs early in each decade will now be followed by additional lawsuits in later years.

Sources: League of United Latin American Citizens v. Perry, 165 L. Ed. 2d 609 (2006); newspaper articles.

A related category consists of lawsuits aimed at weakening political opponents outside the election context. Opponents of President Clinton brought a number of lawsuits that were intended partly to embarrass him and expose wrongdoing in his administration.[30] The most damaging, the lawsuit brought by Paula Corbin Jones, originated as ordinary litigation: Jones's effort to protect her reputation after publicity about her encounter with Clinton. But after she replaced her original lawyers with attorneys who had a political agenda, her lawsuit became a mechanism to attack Clinton and ultimately brought about his impeachment.[31]

One category of tactical litigation has acquired a label of its own, Strategic Lawsuits Against Public Participation or "SLAPPs."[32] These lawsuits, typically for libel or slander, are brought to punish people for expressing themselves on public issues and, more important, to deter such expressions in the future. SLAPPs are brought most often by a business with a stake in a government decision against people who oppose the business on that issue. People who seek to block land developments on environmental grounds are one target of such suits.[33] The term SLAPP is usually limited to lawsuits that have little chance of success in court, but these lawsuits often achieve their objectives by imposing legal costs on the defendants and frightening them into ending their involvement in the issue in question. As one federal judge said, "That a plaintiff's suit ultimately fails after trial is little solace to a defendant crushed by the sheer expense of litigation."[34] A less political version of SLAPPs is lawsuits brought against people for criticizing a company or its products. For instance, lawsuits have been brought against several "gripe sites" that were set up on the Internet to express dissatisfaction (often in vitriolic terms) with particular companies, primarily suits for trademark infringement.[35]

SLAPPs illustrate the use of government policy to influence the use of litigation. In response to publicity about SLAPPs, a majority of the states have enacted legislation to deter their use by allowing for quick dismissal of meritless cases, allowing defendants to recover their legal costs from plaintiffs, or both. These laws appear to have some of their desired impact. Ironically, however, the California legislature amended its anti-SLAPP law because businesses were using it to attack "public interest" lawsuits against them.[36]

Some lawsuits look a bit like classic political litigation, in that they are brought to challenge some government policy, but they have a different purpose. That purpose is not to win an authoritative legal ruling but rather to block a specific action. Environmental groups may sue to prevent the building of a dam, or homeowners may challenge the approval of new housing in their area. Those litigants are satisfied if their suit prevents a project from going forward, whether this result occurs through a court decision or simply through delay. Ultimately, then, these lawsuits are tactical in their purposes.

SCREENING CASES

Inevitably, the numbers of cases that come to appellate courts grow over time. As more cases come to trial courts, more decisions of those courts are appealed. Further, at least over the past few decades, the proportion of decisions by trial courts that generate appeals has grown. For both these reasons, to take one example, the numbers of cases brought to the federal courts of appeals grew from about 3800 in 1960 to about 68,000 in 2005.[37]

As caseloads grow, at some point appellate judges come to feel they cannot give full attention to each case without creating an intolerable backlog. Legislatures and courts have responded by adopting systems under which some cases receive full judicial consideration while others receive more limited consideration.

These screening systems take two quite different forms. One involves the exercise of discretionary jurisdiction, under which some cases are given no decision on the merits at all. This form is found primarily in second-level appellate courts. In the other form, which predominates in first-level courts, some cases that must be decided on the merits under mandatory jurisdiction are handled with expedited procedures.

Discretionary Jurisdiction

The discretionary jurisdiction held by some appellate courts is linked to the creation of appellate systems with two levels. Most supreme courts began as the only full appellate courts in their systems. Because of the belief that litigants are entitled to one appeal, most jurisdiction was mandatory. But as a supreme court's caseload grew and became burdensome, its justices sought relief. The legislature responded by creating an intermediate appellate court and giving the supreme court discretionary jurisdiction over a large share of the cases that come to it. As caseloads continued to grow, some supreme courts were given discretionary jurisdiction over a broader set of cases.

Under discretionary jurisdiction, a court can simply deny a hearing in any case that it chooses, thereby allowing the lower-court decision to become final. A court's refusal to hear a case cannot be appealed elsewhere. (However, the U.S. Supreme Court can agree to hear a case that a state supreme court has refused to hear, and it occasionally does so.) Thus courts with broad discretionary jurisdiction hold an impressive power to set their agendas as they see fit.

They can use this power to keep control of their caseloads. In general, courts that receive many mandatory cases take fewer discretionary cases, and those that receive larger numbers of petitions for hearings accept smaller proportions of petitions. In the 1970s, Supreme Court justices complained that they were overwhelmed by the rapidly growing numbers of petitions for hearings, and there were even proposals to create a new court to assist the Court with its work. But the Court took care of the workload problem by itself, primarily by raising its standards for acceptance of cases. This change in standards was apparent during the years after William Rehnquist became chief justice in 1986, when the Court cut the number of cases it heard by about half. The Court has maintained that smaller number since then.[38]

Screening Procedures   Courts use a variety of procedures in deciding on requests for hearings. In general, the courts that receive the largest volume of cases have developed the most elaborate screening procedures.

The U.S. Supreme Court receives more petitions than any other court, currently more than seven thousand each year. To deal with these petitions, it has created a two-stage screening process. In the first stage, the Court identifies cases that seem to deserve closer scrutiny by putting them on its *discuss list*. Petitions for certiorari that fail to reach this list are denied without collective consideration.

The chief justice is primarily responsible for creating the discuss list, but another justice can add cases to it. In practice, at this stage the justices delegate to law clerks most of the work of evaluating petitions, and most justices personally read only a small portion of the petitions and supporting materials. As of 2007, all but one of the justices (John Paul Stevens is the exception) pool their law clerks so that a single clerk summarizes a particular petition for all the justices who participate in the pool. Later, a justice's own clerks do additional work on the petitions.

A small proportion of cases, perhaps one in eight, reach the discuss list.[39] The justices vote in conference on whether to hear these cases, usually without much discussion. Four votes from the nine justices are necessary to accept a case.

State supreme courts vary a good deal in their screening procedures. The procedures used by the California Supreme Court resemble those in the U.S. Supreme Court in some respects. Typically, an attorney on the court's central staff prepares a memorandum on each petition for a hearing and makes a recommendation for the court's action. The attorney assigns the petition to the "A" list if the recommendation is to accept the case or take some other positive action, or if the petition seems to merit further scrutiny. Other petitions are assigned to the "B" list. Petitions on the A list are considered by the justices at a conference, while petitions on the B list are automatically denied unless a justice asks that they be put aside for further consideration. A majority vote (four of seven justices) is required to accept a case.[40]

Screening Criteria   Many considerations influence court decisions whether to accept cases. In broad terms, judges are motivated both by perceptions of their court's responsibilities and by policy goals. More specifically, several criteria appear to be important.

One is the significance of the legal issues involved in a case. A supreme court can do the most to make the law clear and consistent, and its members can best advance their policy goals, by selecting cases with broad legal and practical significance. It usually makes little sense to accept a tort case with a narrow issue related to the facts of that case, an issue that may never arise again. But it makes a great deal of sense to accept a tort case that involves general requirements for the safety of products, requirements that will be relevant to any product liability case in the future. Many petitions for hearings can be denied almost automatically because the narrowness of their issues is self-evident. This does not mean that all significant cases are accepted, but those with the greatest potential impact have the best chance to gain a hearing.

Another important criterion is conflict or uncertainty in the law. Conflict can arise when two lower courts interpret a legal provision differently or when a lower court seems to depart from an interpretation by its supreme court. In practice, judges give high priority to resolving conflict and uncertainty. But as the numbers of laws and lower-court decisions proliferate, so too does the volume of legal conflicts and uncertainties. As a result, at least some supreme courts are unable to accept all the cases in which the law needs to be clarified. Still, a conflict or uncertainty on a significant issue, such as the meaning of a major tax provision or a basic principle of divorce law, is very likely to gain consideration.

An impression that the lower court has made an error in the decision under review often impels supreme court justices to accept certain cases. Though correcting errors is not the primary purpose of second-level courts, justices feel better about allowing a lower-court decision to stand if they agree with that decision. As a result, courts with discretionary jurisdiction reverse lower courts in a much higher percentage of their decisions than do courts with mandatory jurisdiction. Of course, different justices may not agree on whether a lower court erred, and their judgments are colored by their ideological predispositions. To take one example, liberals are more inclined to accept cases brought by criminal defendants than are conservatives.

Judges' policy preferences operate in a more complicated way when they act on their predictions about what would happen if their court accepted a case. If a justice thinks that the lower court interpreted the law incorrectly but that the supreme court would still affirm the lower court, the justice might prefer to leave the decision standing rather than give it supreme court approval. This practice is so common on the U.S. Supreme Court that it has a standard label: "defensive denials."[41] By the same token, justices may reach out to accept cases when they expect that the Court would reach a decision they favor.[42]

A court may also turn aside a case if its members think that the case would be problematical in other ways. In 2002 the New Jersey Supreme Court refused to hear a case in which the ACLU sought disclosure of the identities of prisoners held in county jails at the behest of the federal government after the terrorist attacks in 2001.[43] Some of the justices may have wanted to avoid involvement in a highly controversial matter. Perhaps that motive came into play when the Florida Supreme Court in 2005 decided (by a 4–3 vote) not to hear a case in which political commentator Rush Limbaugh sought to prevent the use of his medical records that had been seized in an investigation of possible violations of drug laws.[44]

As this discussion suggests, judges frequently disagree about whether a case should be heard. In the Supreme Court, a great many cases are accepted with only four or five votes, and occasionally justices are so unhappy with decisions to deny hearings that they announce their dissents from those decisions. In turn, these disagreements indicate that the agendas of courts with discretionary jurisdiction reflect the goals and perspectives of their justices at any given time. As a court's membership changes, so will its case-screening decisions.

Screening of Mandatory Cases

When judges on supreme courts find their caseloads burdensome, they can seek discretionary jurisdiction. But judges on intermediate courts lack that option: their jurisdiction will remain mandatory. They can request additional judges, but legislators are unlikely to provide enough judges to keep up with growth in the number of cases. As a result, it has become common to speak of a "crisis of volume" in first-level appellate courts.[45] The long-term growth in caseloads is sometimes accompanied by sharp increases in the short run, such as the flood of immigration cases that have come to some federal courts of appeals in recent years.[46]

Courts have adopted a variety of measures to deal with the pressures that result from caseload growth. Most important, they have made staffing and procedural changes that allow them to dispose of cases with smaller expenditures of judicial time. The key changes are the creation of central staffs and the regular use of abbreviated alternatives to traditional procedures. In most courts, the two innovations go together: central staff members screen cases to determine which will receive abbreviated consideration, and they do much of the work in the cases that are given abbreviated consideration. In courts that regularly use abbreviated procedures, those procedures can become the rule rather than the exception.

Case Screening and the Use of Abbreviated Procedures   Different courts screen cases and abbreviate their consideration in different ways.[47] But certain patterns exist, in part because courts have copied practices from each other. The approach taken by most courts follows the general lines of the following model:

1. After the court receives the full set of written materials in a case, these materials go to its central staff. Either the chief staff attorney or another member of the staff then reviews each case and decides tentatively whether it should receive full court consideration or more limited treatment. Cases assigned to the limited-treatment category are the ones that are thought to be easy to decide, usually because the appellant seems to have a weak case. Cases to be given full consideration are sent to a panel of judges (typically, three judges) for a decision; in most courts, the panel usually holds oral argument in these cases. The cases designated for abbreviated treatment are retained within the central staff for further work.

2. A staff attorney examines more fully each case that has been retained. At this point, the staff member may decide that the case actually requires full consideration by judges. Ordinarily, however, the staff member proceeds to write a memorandum on the case, usually with a recommendation as to how it should be decided. In many courts, the staff member also writes a proposed opinion for the court.

3. The cases that the staff has considered are assigned to a court panel, often a special "screening" panel, and the case materials are forwarded there as well. The judges on the panel review each case. If any judge feels that oral argument is necessary, it can then be scheduled. Otherwise the panel considers the case and reaches a decision on the basis of the written materials. This decision is issued with an opinion, usually a brief per curiam opinion that is based on the staff attorney's work. This opinion generally goes unpublished.

The Impact of Case Screening and Abbreviated Procedures   Courts screen mandatory cases and employ abbreviated procedures so they can improve their efficiency. By deciding a high proportion of cases with less of its judges' time, a court can dispose of more cases with the same number of judges. But changes in the ways that courts process cases can also affect the quality and content of their decisions.

As advocates of the new procedures argue, preparatory work by staff attorneys might improve the quality of decision making by providing judges with a better basis for their decisions. Yet staff work on cases might have the opposite effect, causing judges to rely too heavily on the summary material on cases that staff attorneys provide and on their suggested decisions. Two legal scholars with experience on appellate courts perceived "a substantial risk that central staff case processing may lead to premature judgment based upon information inaccurately filtered by staff."[48] Indeed, a study of the Michigan Court of Appeals found that judges' decisions agreed with central staff recommendations a high proportion of the time. But it is possible that most cases retained by the staff have obvious outcomes, so that agreement between staff and judges is inevitable.[49]

If staff screening and work on cases affect the outcomes of cases, the most likely consequence is that it works against appellants. Most cases to which courts give abbreviated consideration are put in this category because staff members perceive that the appellant's case is weak. It may be difficult to overcome this presumption, especially in the absence of oral argument. In effect, then, abbreviated procedures might weaken the right of appeal. It is uncertain whether this effect occurs: the available evidence, taken from the federal courts of appeals, is old, limited, and ambiguous.[50] But it is quite plausible that procedural changes in first-level courts have affected patterns of

EXHIBIT 8.5   A Court Discourages Oral Argument

In 1990 a division of one of the California Courts of Appeal established a system under which lawyers were sent drafts of the court's opinion prior to oral argument as a means to focus the argument on issues that concerned the court. As the system developed, it came to include a procedure under which lawyers in some cases were strongly encouraged to waive their right to oral argument. According to the notice sent to lawyers in those cases, "The court has determined that . . . oral argument will not aid the decision-making process" and that "the tentative opinion should be filed as the final opinion without oral argument in the interests of a quicker resolution of the appeal and the conservation of scarce judicial resources." Lawyers were also told that if they requested oral argument they "may not repeat arguments made in counsel's briefs" and "sanctions may be imposed for noncompliance with this notice."

In 2004 the California Supreme Court determined that the notice used by the court of appeal division was improper. "By suggesting the Court of Appeal already has decided the case without oral argument and that oral argument, if requested, would have no impact on its decision, the oral argument waiver notice here has the potential to improperly discourage the exercise of the right to present oral argument on appeal." The supreme court was also concerned with the possibility of sanctions for repeating arguments from the briefs, especially because the general rule in California is that courts need not consider points that lawyers raise for the first time at oral argument.

It appears that the supreme court was concerned primarily with the appearance that the court of appeal had reached its decision prior to oral argument. As the justices may have recognized, there is no way to prevent judges from making up their minds early. But for judges to announce that they had done so, and to foreclose any efforts to change their minds, created an impression that the supreme court found to be disturbing.

Sources: Thomas E. Hollenhorst, "Tentative Opinions: An Analysis of Their Benefit in the Appellate Court of California," *Santa Clara Law Review* 36 (1995), 1–38; *People v. Pena*, 83 P.3d 506 (Calif. Sup. Ct. 2004). The quotations are from the supreme court's opinion at pages 509 and 514, respectively.

case outcomes. This is one example of a more general point: structural and procedural changes adopted for seemingly neutral reasons such as efficiency can affect the substance of what courts do.

Aside from their impact on the quality and content of courts' work, abbreviated procedures may affect perceptions of that work. By emphasizing efficiency, courts may give litigants and lawyers the impression that they are not getting full consideration of their cases. A California practice described in Exhibit 8.5 illustrates this possibility.

DECISION MAKING

Whether its jurisdiction is chiefly mandatory or discretionary, the heart of an appellate court's work is its decisions in the cases it hears. These decisions produce victories and defeats for individual litigants. More important, they establish rules of law that influence future court cases and activity elsewhere in government and society. For this reason, explanation of appellate court decisions is one of the central issues in the study of courts.

Perspectives on Decision Making: An Overview

The explanations for court behavior presented in Chapter 1 suggest that appellate court decisions can be understood from several perspectives: the legal perspective, which views decisions as the product of legal rules; the personal perspective, which explains decisions in terms of the judges themselves; and the environmental perspective, which emphasizes influences from the larger society. The relevance of each perspective differs somewhat between first-level and second-level appellate courts.

   First-Level Courts   Because first-level courts have mandatory jurisdiction, they must decide both "easy" and "difficult" cases. Judges on these courts frequently express the view that most of their cases are easy to decide because the merits clearly lie on one side. Legal scholar and Supreme Court justice Benjamin Cardozo long ago concluded that perhaps 90 percent of appeals in first-level courts could be decided only one way, and judges more recently have offered similar judgments.[51]

   When judges speak of easy cases, for the most part they are referring to appeals that have little merit, so that affirmance is the obvious result. The chief judge of the federal Eighth Circuit Court of Appeals in St. Louis estimated that about one-quarter of all appeals his court receives are "frivolous."[52] A judge on a California court of appeal commented that "if 90 per cent of this stuff were in the United States Post Office, it would be classified as junk mail."[53]

   In effect, these judges are saying that the law is the dominant element in the courts' decision making: most of the time, only one result can be justified under the law. This belief makes judges more comfortable about delegating responsibility over seemingly easy cases to central staffs. It also helps to explain the low rates of dissent in most first-level appellate courts: in a high proportion of these cases, it would be difficult for judges to disagree about the result.

   In some cases, probably more than most judges recognize, the decision is not so clear-cut. In these cases, judges must exercise discretion. In doing so, they are seldom subject to much external pressure. Most first-level courts are intermediate courts, less visible to the public than the courts above or below them. Especially at the state level, intermediate courts typically receive little attention and thus limited scrutiny from the mass media and interest groups.

   Certainly these courts are influenced by their environments, but the influence is primarily indirect and fairly subtle. Because external pressures are fairly weak, judges' personal characteristics are especially important in shaping their judgments within the constraints of the law. And because appellate decisions are made by groups of judges, their interaction helps to determine how individual predilections translate into collective decisions.

   Second-Level Courts   Second-level courts usually have some mandatory jurisdiction. As a result, they decide some relatively easy cases. But their jurisdiction is mainly discretionary. Because there would be little reason to hear cases with obvious results, the cases that a court selects generally involve more difficult and uncertain questions. Thus existing legal rules constrain second-level courts to only a limited degree. Indeed, cases often require that courts establish new rules in order to clarify ambiguities and fill in gaps in the law.

Of course, the law is relevant to decisions in these courts. The state of the law often pushes a court toward some results and away from others. This legal influence is one reason why the nine justices on the U.S. Supreme Court make a good many unanimous decisions even though they hold widely varying views about the issues they address. At the same time, the frequency of dissent in the Supreme Court and in many state supreme courts reflects the difficulty of most of the legal questions they resolve.

The relationship between supreme courts and their political environment is complicated. Because they are the highest courts in their systems, supreme courts receive greater attention than the intermediate courts below them. Interest groups often participate in cases before them, and legislators pay considerable attention to their work. Indeed, external scrutiny of supreme courts and their decisions seems to be growing. Thus justices on supreme courts feel more direct pressure than intermediate appellate judges. Yet most of what supreme courts do gets little attention, and (with the exception of the U.S. Supreme Court) they typically get little news coverage.[54] And even when supreme court justices receive intense scrutiny, they are usually less vulnerable to external pressures than are legislators and chief executives.

Thus the law and the environment leave judges on second-level courts with considerable freedom to take the directions they wish in their decisions. As a consequence, perhaps more than in any other courts, judicial decisions are the product of judges' values and other personal characteristics and of their interactions with colleagues. For this reason, explanations of decisions by supreme courts must focus chiefly on their justices.

The impact of the law needs to be kept in mind, especially in the "easy" cases that come to first-level courts. The rest of this section looks more closely at the other factors that shape appellate court decisions: judges' policy preferences, group processes, and the political and social environment.

Policy Preferences

In June 2006, In the last week of its 2005 term, the Supreme Court decided *Kansas v. Marsh*. In that case the Kansas Supreme Court had held that its state's death penalty law was unconstitutional. The Supreme Court reversed that decision, upholding the Kansas law. The Supreme Court's decision was by a 5–4 vote. The majority opinion by Justice Clarence Thomas was joined by Chief Justice John Roberts and by Antonin Scalia, Samuel Alito, and Anthony Kennedy. The dissenters were David Souter, John Paul Stevens, Ruth Bader Ginsburg, and Stephen Breyer.

That lineup of justices was neither unusual nor surprising. Of the justices who sat on the Court in 2006, the four dissenters in *Marsh* were the most likely to support claims by criminal defendants that their procedural rights had been violated. Those four justices were also the most likely to support civil liberties claims in general. When the Court reached decisions by a 5–4 vote, most often these were the four dissenters.

Among the five members of the majority in *Marsh*, Justice Kennedy supported civil liberties claims most often. Indeed, he was regarded as the Court's "swing vote," the justice whose position often determined whether the Court reached a decision favoring or opposing civil liberties claims. As the Court began its new term in October 2006, commentators frequently referred to Kennedy's pivotal position on issues such as abortion.

Preferences, Ideology, and Decisions   The pattern of justices' positions on civil liberties claims can be understood in ideological terms. Support for broader interpretations of legal protections for liberties is usually characterized as liberal, support for narrower interpretations as conservative. Indeed, most of the policy issues that the Supreme Court and other appellate courts address can be characterized as conflicts between more liberal and more conservative positions. Thus, we can describe the votes that judges cast and the opinions they write in terms of their positions on a liberal-conservative continuum. Figure 8.1 shows where the Supreme Court justices who served in 2006 would fall along that continuum on the basis of their votes on civil liberties cases in the 2005 term.

Why do some justices take conservative positions much more often than others? The single best explanation for differences in the justices' responses to the same cases is their personal attitudes toward the policy issues in those cases. External pressures and the law can move the whole Court in one direction or the other, but disagreements among the justices stem chiefly from their preferences about policy.

One type of evidence for this explanation is the similarity between the positions that justices take on policy issues before they reach the Court and the positions they take on the Court. Reflecting this similarity, one study found a strong correlation between perceptions of justices' ideological positions when they were appointed to the Court and the frequency with which they supported civil liberties claims in cases.[55] Further, the views that justices express away from the Court typically are consistent with the positions they take in cases. Among the current justices, Clarence Thomas and Antonin Scalia are especially willing to offer their views about social issues in speeches and other forums, and those views are as conservative as the opinions they write on the Court. Finally, the justices who are relatively liberal in one field of judicial policy tend to be relatively liberal in other fields as well. That ideological consistency

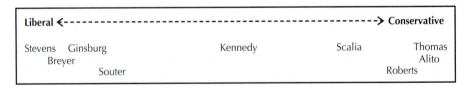

FIGURE 8.1   Positions of the 2006 Supreme Court Justices on a Liberal-Conservative Continuum in Civil Liberties Cases

Note: The places of the justices on the continuum and the width of the distances between them are based on the proportions of liberal and conservative votes cast by each justice in civil liberties cases in the 2005 term of the Court. (Alito's place is based on a comparison between him and other justices in the cases in which he participated.) These proportions were calculated from data in the Supreme Court Database, compiled by Harold Spaeth (available at http://www.as.uky.edu/polisci/ulmerproject/sctdata.htm).

across areas in which the legal issues are quite different is difficult to explain except as a result of the justices' policy preferences.

The ideological element in the justices' behavior should not be exaggerated. Some issues that come to the Court, such as disputes between states over their borders, do not have much ideological content. Further, the ideological tenor of justices' policy preferences sometimes differs across issues. A justice who is generally a strong conservative may have liberal views on a particular issue. This is especially true of economic issues, on which justices' attitudes seem to be considerably more complex than they once were.

More fundamentally, justices' choices do not always follow from their policy preferences. Even justices who have expressed strong views on particular issues sometimes take positions that seem to deviate from these views. Such deviations may result from their reading of the law, an interest in achieving unanimity, or forces outside the Court. All this being true, however, justices' policy preferences exert a powerful impact—perhaps the most fundamental impact—on their choices as decision makers.

Justices' policy preferences often change marginally over time, and they sometimes change substantially. After Harry Blackmun joined the Court in 1970, he established a strongly conservative record. But his views gradually changed, and by the time of his 1994 retirement he had become considerably more liberal. On the whole, however, justices' preferences and thus their record on the Court are fairly stable. In turn, this stability gives predictability to the Court's divisions. At the beginning of the Court's 2006 term, it was easy to predict that, to take one example, Justice Souter would cast far more liberal votes during that term than Justice Thomas.

Because of their power to select cases, most other second-level courts are similar to the Supreme Court in the importance of justices' policy preferences for their decisions. Just as commentators are accustomed to describing Supreme Court justices in ideological terms, observers of supreme courts in states such as California and Texas do the same. Because first-level courts hear so many cases with seemingly obvious results or narrow technical issues, ideology does not play as prominent a role across the full range of decisions in those courts. As a federal court of appeals judge wrote, "A large proportion of our cases (particularly administrative law cases) have no apparent ideology to support or reject at all."[56] But the minority of cases in which ideology is relevant tend to be the most consequential and thus the most visible. For this reason, ideological divisions among judges on federal courts of appeals are well known.

Because judges' preferences are so important to their choices, the membership of a court has considerable impact on the content of its decisions. One implication is that differences among courts in their policy positions are largely the product of differences in the mixes of judges on those courts. The twelve federal courts of appeals all apply the same body of law. But they vary in the balance of liberals and conservatives among their members, and as a result they also differ in the ideological tenor of their decisions. For instance, in recent years the Fourth Circuit in the South Atlantic region has been distinctly more conservative than the Ninth Circuit on the West Coast.[57]

By the same token, change in a court's membership over time can affect its positions on legal issues. If judges with liberal views succeed judges with more conservative views, a court is likely to shift to the left. A court may even reverse its position on the same issue, as illustrated by the episode in Exhibit 8.6.

EXHIBIT 8.6   The Illinois Supreme Court Disapproves a Search and Then Approves It

In 1998 an Illinois state trooper stopped a car driven by Roy Caballes for driving 71 miles per hours on an interstate highway with a speed limit of 65. Hearing the trooper's call to his dispatcher, another trooper appeared on the scene with a drug-sniffing dog. The dog "alerted" at the car trunk, the trooper searched the trunk, and he found a substantial amount of marijuana. Caballes was charged with trafficking in marijuana and was sentenced to twelve years in prison. He appealed his conviction, and the case reached the Illinois Supreme Court.

The circumstances of the stop and search were somewhat unusual. Among other things, as a member of the U.S. Supreme Court later noted, it was a "remarkable fact that the police pulled over a car for going 71 miles an hour on I-80." But when the Illinois Supreme Court reviewed the case in 2003, it focused on a different aspect of the search: whether the trooper had had sufficient basis for use of the drug-detection dog. By a 4–3 vote the court ruled that there was not a sufficient basis under the Constitution, and it overturned Caballes's conviction.

The state asked the U.S. Supreme Court to hear the case, the Court agreed, and by a 6–2 vote it overturned the state supreme court decision in 2005. The Supreme Court interpreted the Fourth and Fourteenth Amendments to allow the dog sniff under the circumstances involved in this case. The case was then remanded to the Illinois Supreme Court for reconsideration. When it reheard the case, the court addressed an issue that it had not needed to decide in 2003: if the search did not violate the U.S. Constitution, did it violate the Illinois Constitution? By a 4–3 vote, the court ruled in 2006 that the search was acceptable under the state constitution as well.

The two decisions by the Illinois Supreme Court were not inconsistent, because they involved different constitutions. One of the justices could have interpreted the U.S. Constitution to disallow the search while later interpreting the state constitution to allow it. But that is not what happened. One of the justices who had voted to disallow the search in 2003 left the court in 2004, and his successor Lloyd Karmeier voted to allow the search in 2006. With each of the other six justices taking the same positions in the two cases, the new justice created a new majority, and Caballes would have to serve his sentence.

Sources: People v. Caballes, 802 N.E.2d 202 (Ill. Sup. Ct. 2003); *Illinois v. Caballes*, 543 U.S. 405 (2005); *People v. Caballes*, 851 N.E.2d 26 (Ill. Sup. Ct. 2006). The quotation is from Justice Souter's dissenting opinion in the U.S. Supreme Court decision at p. 414.

Court Policies and the Selection of Judges   If the membership of a court is so important to its positions on legal policies, this means that the people who select judges have considerable power to influence the courts' direction. Presidents and governors are in the best positions to shape the courts' membership and policies. Presidents nominate federal judges, and governors choose a high proportion of state judges through regular and interim appointments. Given enough opportunities, sufficient care, and some good luck, a chief executive can change a court's policies quite substantially.

Certainly, this has been true of the Supreme Court. In the 1960s, the Court took highly liberal positions on a range of legal issues. Since 1969, however, twelve of the fourteen appointments to the Court have been made by Republican presidents. Not all of these twelve justices proved to be highly conservative, but collectively they have moved the Court considerably to the right on issues ranging from labor law to criminal justice.

Presidents have similar effects on the lower federal courts. Simply by choosing judges from their own party, presidents shift the federal courts of appeals to the left or right.[58] The controversies over appointments to the courts of appeals by Bill Clinton and George W. Bush reflect a growing awareness of this impact, which is symbolized by a Sixth Circuit decision in a 2004 death penalty case. Sitting en banc, with all its judges, the court upheld a conviction and death sentence by an 8–7 vote. Every justice in the majority was appointed by a Republican president, every dissenter by a Democratic president.[59]

Governors affect the ideological positions of state courts in the same ways. Their impact seems to have grown because governors as a group are paying more attention to the policy views of their appointees than they did in the past. For example, some recent Republican governors have used appointments to make their supreme courts more conservative on economic issues, civil liberties, or both. One example is John Engler, who served as governor of Michigan from 1991 to 2003.

In the states that elect judges, the voters and those who campaign for judicial candidates help determine the ideological balance of appellate courts. In states such as Alabama and Ohio, business groups have done much to secure the election of conservative supreme court justices and thereby secure judicial policies that are more favorable to their interests. In one of the most expensive judicial contests ever, a contest described in Exhibit 4.5, these groups helped a Republican candidate win a pivotal seat on the Illinois Supreme Court. As Exhibit 8.6 describes, that justice—Lloyd Karmeier—also shifted the court's position on at least one issue in criminal justice. When a governor uses interim appointments to change a court's policies, the voters can reinforce or blunt this strategy with their reactions to the governor's choices in subsequent elections.

Group Processes

In the image of appellate courts that most observers share, what might be called the standard image, judges work closely with each other on cases, discussing and arguing about the issues, drafting and redrafting opinions, until the court reaches its collective judgment. Thus group processes are integral to the court's choices.

This image reflects two incentives that judges have to work together. One is the desire to reach consensus. Judges want to produce an opinion that can be accepted by at least a majority, so that the court issues an authoritative statement of legal principles. Judges have an interest in achieving even greater consensus—ideally, unanimity on the outcome of the case and the court's opinion—because unanimity may give their decisions greater authority.

Another incentive may be even more powerful. Based on their reading of the law or their policy preferences, judges reach conclusions about the outcome and legal rules that are most desirable in a particular case. When they have strong feelings about a case, they have a strong incentive to try to win their colleagues' support for their positions.

Group Processes in Practice   Powerful as these incentives can be, what might be called the group element in appellate court decisions is not as strong as the standard image suggests. For one thing, the strength of judges' views about cases gives them an incentive to influence colleagues, but it also creates resistance to influence. When a court comes to a case involving product liability or criminal procedure, its members may not be open to persuasion. Judges who recognize this reality might see little point in trying to shift their colleagues' positions.

Even more important is time pressure. Most appellate courts have more to do than their members can handle comfortably. Thus judges may find it very difficult to work at length with colleagues in order to produce a true group product.

Because these conditions differ among courts, so does the importance of group processes. On the whole, the group element is stronger in second-level courts. Discretionary jurisdiction reduces time pressures on judges, and the average case is likely to seem more important to judges than the average case in a first-level court. Moreover, most second-level courts decide every case with the same full set of judges, who come to know each other well through regular interaction.

The Supreme Court is an example. It is true that the Court diverges from the standard image of appellate courts in important ways. Cases are discussed only briefly in the Court's conference, and communication about cases is generally in writing rather than face-to-face. But the justices use their questions and comments at oral argument to present their views to their colleagues. And once the Court reaches a tentative decision at the conference, the justices interact a good deal through draft opinions and memos. In some cases their interactions are extensive and intense. The importance of these interactions is indicated by frequent changes in the language of opinions and occasional shifts in the majority between the Court's tentative vote on a case and its final decision.[60]

In contrast, first-level courts often depart fundamentally from the standard image of appellate courts. Judges on many of these courts work under great time pressure, pressure reflected in the delegation of responsibilities to central staffs in many courts. In courts with constantly shifting three-judge panels, such as large federal courts of appeals, it is difficult for any set of three judges to develop the sorts of relationships and routines that facilitate effective group decision making. And because many cases seem both unimportant and "easy," judges have less reason to discuss cases and argue about them.

One frequent result is deference to a single judge. In many courts, a case is assigned to one judge early in the decision process, with the implicit understanding that this judge will take primary responsibility for the decision. The other judges pay less attention to the case and generally defer to the assigned judge's view. As a result, the court's decision sometimes depends largely on the random assignment of a case to one judge rather than another.

Even in a court that does not use early assignment procedures, judges may be reluctant to disagree with the position of the colleague who writes the opinion in a case because it would be time-consuming to express that disagreement in writing. Several judges on one federal court of appeals reported that they limited their dissents to cases in which they disagreed strongly with the majority—when they felt what one judge called "outrage"—primarily because of a lack of time.[61]

Whether or not judges on a first-level court strongly defer to the judge who was assigned the opinion, the low stakes and the lack of disagreement among judges that characterize most cases limit their interaction in the decision process. According to one judge on a federal court of appeals, "After conference, usually all you get is a draft disposition . . . and maybe a memo or two. In a great bulk of cases, it is a memo or two after conference, and it's over."[62] But some cases interest judges more and produce greater disagreement, and in those cases there is more interplay among the judges who are deciding the case.

Beyond the difference between first-level and second-level courts, a court's traditions and mode of operation may affect the group element in decisions. To take one example, patterns of interaction differ between courts in which the judges do their work in the same city and those in which they are spread across a state or a federal circuit.

On the whole, group processes are not nearly as important as judges' individual attitudes and perspectives. Even in the Supreme Court, justices' votes on the outcome of cases typically stay the same over the course of the decision process, and most of the Court's opinions look similar in final form to the way they looked in their initial draft. Still, the group element sometimes makes a critical difference for court decisions: the language of opinions changes in important ways, a minority becomes a majority.

Influence of Individual Judges   In the group processes that shape decisions, we can expect some judges to exert more influence than others. One source of special influence is a judge's formal position. Each court has a chief judge or chief justice who holds certain powers within the court. Especially where the position is permanent rather than rotating among judges, it may also carry a degree of prestige. On appellate courts that divide into panels, the most senior judge on each panel generally acts as a kind of temporary chief who directs the panel's work.

Of the powers that chief judges hold, among the most important is presiding over conference discussions of cases. The conference leader can formulate the alternatives to be considered and channel the discussion of those alternatives, thereby helping to move the court in a particular direction. Also useful is the power to designate who will write the court's opinion. On most appellate courts, assignment of opinions generally is random. But in some courts the chief judge assigns opinions. (In a few of these courts, including the U.S. Supreme Court, chief justices assign opinions only when they were part of the majority in the court's initial vote on a case.) By assigning an opinion to an ideological ally or writing the opinion personally, the chief judge can help to secure a desired rationale for the decision. On the Supreme Court, chief justices routinely adopt this strategy while also taking into account the need to distribute the workload of opinion writing among justices.[63]

The influence of a chief judge depends not only on formal powers but also on leadership skills and the inclinations of other judges. Some chief justices of the Supreme Court have exerted considerable influence over the Court's direction, while others have played much more limited roles. It seems clear, for instance, that William Rehnquist (1986–2005) was more influential than his predecessor, Warren Burger (1969–1986), and early signs are that John Roberts will also be an effective chief justice. As chief judge of the federal court of appeals for the District of Columbia, Harry Edwards brought considerable peace to a court that had a long history of battles along ideological lines. (Supreme Court Justice Felix Frankfurter had once referred to the court as "a collectivity of fighting cats.")[64]

Of course, judges who lack the chief's formal position can also have a disproportionate influence on their colleagues—an influence often stemming from extraordinary legal or persuasive skills. On the Supreme Court, Sandra Day O'Connor (1981–2006) appeared to exert considerable influence, in part because of the skills she gained as a state legislator and participant in politics.[65] In contrast, some judges exert relatively little influence over their colleagues, because they make only a minimal effort to sway other judges or because of their situations or personal traits.

But the small size of appellate courts and panels produces a considerable equality of influence. Simply casting one vote out of nine provides a good deal of leverage in itself, and one out of three provides even more. On any court, then, influence is likely to operate in all directions.

Interpersonal Relationships   The potential for bad feelings among judges exists on any appellate court. Judges often have strong feelings about the cases they decide, and disagreements about decisions can turn into bad feelings. Over time, as judges interact with each other, frictions and even enmity may develop. Despite these sources of conflict, on many courts judges manage to maintain good relations with each other. But on other courts, conflict reaches a high level.

The state of the relationships within a court is usually difficult to discern from outside the court. Frequent disagreement in cases does not necessarily reflect or produce conflict among the judges who disagree. Even when judges' opinions direct heated language toward their colleagues, the writer and target may get along perfectly well.

Occasionally, however, the conflict within a court is so intense that it becomes visible even to outsiders. At various times, for instance, there have been poor relations among justices on the state supreme courts of Nevada, Ohio, Pennsylvania, and Washington.

In Mississippi, conflicts among the state's supreme court justices culminated in an effort by five colleagues to secure the suspension of Justice Chuck McRae from the court in 2003. The state Commission on Judicial Performance ultimately decided not to recommend suspension of Justice McRae, concluding that some of his colleagues had "substantially contributed to the overall disruptive condition of the court." Public hearings before the commission featured charges and countercharges by the justices of bad behavior by their colleagues, including an account of an exchange in which two justices offered to engage in fisticuffs.[66]

Not surprisingly, conflicts within courts often fall along ideological lines. Certainly this is the case with the federal court of appeals for the Sixth Circuit in Cincinnati, which has featured heated conflicts between liberals and conservatives in recent years. One conflict, involving an allegation that the court's chief judge had delayed the decision in a major affirmative action case to secure the result he wanted, was described in Exhibit 2.5. The court's liberals and conservatives have also fought over the handling of cases involving the death penalty, with each side accusing the other of acting inappropriately. One conservative's dissent from a stay of execution asserted that prisoners "could file a hot dog menu, and the en banc court might use that as a legal basis to stay their execution. The truth may be that for _this_ prisoner, a majority of the active members of *this* court would grant a stay based on a hot dog menu." In other cases, the court's liberals charged that the court's procedural rules had been manipulated or violated in order to allow executions. The language in two 2006 decisions involving police searches and election rules makes it clear that bitterness between the ideological camps has not disappeared.[67]

Aside from their effects on a court's image, bad relations among judges are likely to affect its functioning. Surely the Mississippi Supreme Court or the Sixth Circuit would operate more effectively if all their judges felt good will toward each other.

The Court's Environment

In a sense, everything that courts do can be traced to external forces. Even judges' policy preferences reflect social influences over the course of their lives. Here I am concerned with more direct influences from a court's environment. Though judges enjoy some insulation from the rest of government and society, the world around them still affects their decisions.

The Legal Environment   Appellate courts are part of a legal community that includes lawyers and other courts. One effect of the legal community is to reinforce the influence of legal rules and legal considerations on judges. This community exerts other kinds of influences as well.

Judges are obliged to follow legal rules established by courts above them, but they also pay attention to the positions of other courts. The opinions of state and federal appellate courts constitute a body of doctrine from which judges on any court can draw ideas. Like legislators and administrators, judges look to their counterparts elsewhere for solutions to policy problems. When the Oregon Supreme Court faces a contract issue that is new to it, its members will be interested in how other state supreme courts have dealt with the same issue. If several courts have addressed an issue and the weight of judicial opinion lies primarily on one side, that weight may sway another court that faces the issue. This is especially true of the federal courts of appeals, because disagreements among the circuits create a conflict in federal law. As one judge said, "If the circuits are split, then I'm on my own, but if they've only gone in one direction, I'll generally go along. It would have to be an off-the-wall position for me to disagree."[68] Opinions by individual judges who are well regarded may exert considerable influence on other courts. One example is Judge Richard Posner of the federal court of appeals for the Seventh Circuit in Chicago.[69]

Lawyers can also influence a court's judgments. Of course, the lawyers who argue cases affect specific decisions through their arguments. Lawyers' advocacy can have broader effects as well. The litigation campaigns of interest groups and the skill of some of the lawyers who represent these groups have shaped judicial policy on issues ranging from school desegregation to environmental regulation.

Judges may also be influenced by the general pattern of opinion within the bar on social and political issues. Law school and legal practice shape the attitudes of people who later become judges, and judges continue to interact with lawyers and read what lawyers are saying about legal issues. As a result, judges are drawn toward prevailing opinions within the bar. Traditionally, the predominant viewpoint of the legal profession was conservative, but in recent years that viewpoint has become more liberal. Indeed, some conservatives think that the liberalism of the legal profession has combined with other forces to move Supreme Court justices "leftward," as one commentator put it. "That is how you get the applause of the American Bar Association, good ink in the liberal press, acclaim in the elite law schools and invitations to tony Georgetown parties."[70]

The Political Environment   Judges are part of the legal community, but they are also part of the political system. Depending on their perspective and their situation, judges' choices might be influenced by the public or the other branches of government.

The most obvious source of influence is judges' interest in remaining judges. State supreme court justices who face the voters periodically may be reluctant to make decisions that might arouse electoral opposition. Of all the issues that might present dangers for elected judges, the death penalty stands out. One judge on a federal court of appeals reported that "I have spoken with judges who must stand for election, and I have heard them say that they cannot afford to reverse capital convictions in cases that engender heated community passions."[71] Beyond capital punishment, judges may avoid making other decisions that could be used by electoral opponents to label them as "soft on crime."

Other issues may present dangers as well. The supreme courts of four states— Hawaii, Massachusetts, New Jersey, and Vermont—have reached decisions which required that their state allow civil unions or marriage for same-sex couples. (The Hawaii decision was overturned by a state constitutional amendment.) It is probably no coincidence that these four states are all among the minority of states in which supreme court justices do not go before the voters. Justices who do face elections are likely to feel less freedom to take controversial positions on such issues.

Whether or not they are elected, judges have good reason to pay attention to the legislature and chief executive.[72] The other branches of government affect appellate courts in several ways: they determine court budgets, they adopt legislation relating to judges' working conditions, they can overturn or limit court decisions, and they help determine whether decisions are enforced. In some states they decide whether judges win additional terms. In the federal system and most states, the chief executive helps determine whether judges on intermediate courts win promotions to the supreme court.

Judges might modify their positions in cases in order to reduce the chances that their decisions will be overturned by the other branches. More important, they want to avoid attacks on their court as an institution, and this is an era in which policymakers at both the federal and state levels frequently threaten attacks. In all likelihood, members of appellate courts make most of their decisions without taking the other branches into account. But like the voters, legislators and chief executives may loom large in judges' minds when a potential decision could trigger an adverse reaction. Following a period of tensions between the California Supreme Court and the state legislature, one law professor said that the court's chief justice "has gone out of his way to avoid displeasing the Legislature" with decisions in order to secure favorable treatment of the court's budget requests.[73] A 2004 decision of the Louisiana Supreme Court, described in Exhibit 8.7, may illustrate such sensitivity to the other branches.

EXHIBIT 8.7   The Louisiana Supreme Court Rules Against the Oyster Farmers

Beginning early in the twentieth century, the federal government and the state of Louisiana worked to contain flooding and achieve other ends by controlling the flow of the Mississippi River. Some projects were aimed at manipulating the salinity of coastal waters to improve oyster production. One project, undertaken in 1988, enhanced restoration of a portion of the Louisiana coast. It also improved oyster production in some areas, but it greatly reduced production in an area in which oyster farmers leased water lands from the state. In 1994 those farmers sued the federal government in federal court and brought a class-action suit against Louisiana in state court.

The farmers lost the federal suit. But they won their state lawsuit before a jury, which awarded them $1.3 billion from the state government. With dissents, the state court of appeals affirmed that award in 2003. Attention then shifted to the Louisiana Supreme Court, which agreed to hear the case.

State officials made their interest in the case clear, predicting that both the state's credit rating and its efforts to restore the coastline would be severely damaged if the jury award stood. Several state and local government agencies submitted amicus briefs to the supreme court in which they argued that the award should be overturned. Governor Kathleen Blanco issued a statement refusing to settle the lawsuit with the oyster farmers and asking the supreme court to "reverse the court rulings that provided for these outrageous judgments."

Indeed, the court did reverse those rulings unanimously in November 2004. In a sweeping decision, the court ruled that the terms of oyster farmers' leases from the state and a time limit on bringing lawsuits ruled out any damages for any farmers. The court also gave a broad interpretation to the state's power to protect its coast, thereby limiting the threat of lawsuits against the state in the future. It is impossible to know whether the state government's expression of strong concern about the case had any influence on the justices. But in light of that strong concern, one legal scholar in New Orleans said that "the pressure on the court was like that on the U.S. Supreme Court after 9/11."

Sources: Avenal v. Department of Natural Resources, 858 So. 2d 697 (La. App. Ct. 2003); *Avenal v. State of Louisiana*, 886 So. 2d 1085 (La. Sup Ct. 2004); newspaper articles. The quotations are from, respectively, Jeffrey Meitrodt, "Blanco Rejects Oyster Settlement," *New Orleans Times-Picayune*, June 16, 2004, 2; and Dee McAree, "Louisiana Dodges a $1.3B Bullet," *National Law Journal*, November 1, 2004, 5.

The clearest evidence that appellate courts are influenced by their environments comes from instances in which a court reverses its decision in a specific case after receiving strong criticism for that decision. In 2005, for instance, a panel of the federal court of appeals for the Fifth Circuit in the South refused to allow a defendant to challenge a death sentence on the basis of a favorable Supreme Court decision, because his lawyer had missed a filing deadline. After the decision was condemned in several newspaper editorials, three months later two of the three judges on the panel changed their positions and allowed the defendant's challenge.[74]

In another instance, judges may have been responding to criticism, but perhaps they simply reacted to new information about the potential impact of their decision.

In 2001 a panel of the Ninth Circuit court of appeals on the West Coast ruled that an airline pilot could use the federal Wiretap Act to sue a superior who gained access to the pilot's website under false pretenses. State and federal prosecutors protested that the court's decision would make it more difficult for them to investigate child molesters who used the Internet to communicate with potential victims. The court withdrew its decision and then, with one judge dissenting, issued a new decision that reversed its position on the Wiretap Act.[75]

Another reversal is less ambiguous. In 2004 the Delaware Supreme Court interpreted a state statute to require the release on parole of certain prisoners who were serving life sentences. State legislators responded with considerable anger, and they quickly and unanimously enacted a law that declared the supreme court's decision "null and void." The supreme court then announced that it would reconsider the case. Five months after its original decision, the court issued a new decision. In that decision, it held in strong terms that the legislature's effort to overturn that decision was unconstitutional on multiple grounds. Having done that, the court then reversed the decision itself, saying that it "shall have no force or effect." The original decision had been unanimous; the reversal was also unanimous. It appeared that while defending their prerogatives as an independent branch of government, the justices decided that it would be a good idea to retreat from the source of legislative anger.[76]

It should be emphasized that external pressures do not always move appellate courts. Indeed, judges often demonstrate considerable independence when they feel those pressures. Even in criminal justice, the field in which pressures tend to be strongest, many state supreme courts have used their state constitutions to expand the rights of criminal defendants. For that matter, some justices have voted to overturn large numbers of death sentences despite the political risks involved in doing so. The Supreme Court has adopted some policies that were highly unpopular in Congress and in the nation as a whole, such as its prohibition of laws that punish flag burning. The Court has also risked confrontations with the other branches over decisions that provided procedural rights for suspected terrorists.[77]

The strongest external forces on the courts are likely to be the most subtle and the least visible. Most important, currents of opinion in the legal and political communities rule out some possible policies and influence judges' choices among other policies. Changing attitudes toward issues such as crime, drugs, and gender roles inevitably are reflected in decisions that judges make about those issues. In this sense, the environments of courts are similar to the state of the law these courts apply. Each directs appellate judges toward some decisions rather than others, but both leave considerable room for judges to put their own stamp on the decisions they reach.

CONCLUSIONS

This chapter has examined the processes by which the agendas of appellate courts are set and by which they reach decisions on the cases they hear. The discussions of these subjects point to some conclusions about the forces that shape these courts.

First, judges have a great deal of control over what their courts do. Appellate judges largely set their own agendas, accepting some cases for full decisions and relegating others to more limited scrutiny or rejecting them altogether. And in the cases they decide fully, judges have a good deal of leeway to reach the judgments that they see as most desirable.

At the same time, the work of appellate courts is influenced by people outside the courts. While judges can set their own agendas, they start with the cases that are brought to them. The growing volume of political litigation has helped involve judges in conflicts over politics and policy. Further, the political and legal environment has both a direct and indirect impact on judges' choices as decision makers.

Finally, the growing volume of all appeals has created case pressures that have powerful effects. Judges increasingly delegate control over screening of cases to law clerks and central staff attorneys. In first-level courts, judges have given these subordinates important roles in the process of reaching decisions in some cases. This delegation has allowed judges to focus their efforts on the cases that seem to deserve the most judicial attention. In doing so, however, they have changed the character of their courts.

FOR FURTHER READING

Baker, Thomas E. *Rationing Justice on Appeal: The Problems of the U.S. Courts of Appeals.* St. Paul: West Publishing, 1994.

Biskupic, Joan. *Sandra Day O'Connor: How the First Woman on the Supreme Court Became Its Most Influential Justice.* New York: HarperCollins, 2005.

Cohen, Jonathan Matthew. *Inside Appellate Courts: The Impact of Court Organization on Judicial Decision Making in the United States Courts of Appeals.* Ann Arbor: University of Michigan Press, 2001.

Greenhouse, Linda. *Becoming Justice Blackmun: Harry Blackmun's Supreme Court Journey.* New York: Times Books, 2005.

Hettinger, Virginia A., Stefanie A. Lindquist, and Wendy L. Martinek. *Judging on a Collegial Court: Influences on Federal Appellate Decision Making.* Charlottesville: University of Virginia Press, 2006.

Johnson, Timothy R. *Oral Arguments and Decision Making on the United States Supreme Court.* Albany: State University of New York Press, 2004.

Klein, David E. *Making Law in the United States Courts of Appeals.* New York: Cambridge University Press, 2002.

Langer, Laura. *Judicial Review in State Supreme Courts: A Comparative Study.* Albany: State University of New York Press, 2002.

Maltzman, Forrest, James F. Spriggs II, and Paul J. Wahlbeck. *Crafting Law on the Supreme Court: The Collegial Game.* New York: Cambridge University Press, 2000.

Pacelle, Richard L., Jr. *Between Law and Politics: The Solicitor General and the Structuring of Race, Gender, and Reproductive Rights Litigation.* College Station: Texas A & M Press, 2003.

Segal, Jeffrey A., and Harold J. Spaeth. *The Supreme Court and the Attitudinal Model Revisited.* New York: Cambridge University Press, 2002.

Songer, Donald R., Reginald S. Sheehan, and Susan B. Haire. *Continuity and Change on the United States Courts of Appeals.* Ann Arbor: University of Michigan Press, 2000.

Online Study Center   Go to college.hmco.com/PIC/baum6e for ACE practice
test questions and additional resources.

NOTES

1. Joy A. Chapper and Roger A. Hanson, *Intermediate Appellate Courts: Improving Case Processing* (Williamsburg, Va.: National Center for State Courts, 1990), 6–7.
2. On law clerks generally, see Nadine J. Wichern, "A Court of Clerks, Not of Men: Serving Justice in the Media Age," *DePaul Law Review* 49 (Winter 1999), 621–671. Law clerks in the Supreme Court are discussed in Todd C. Peppers, *Courtiers of the Marble Palace: The Rise and Influence of the Supreme Court Law Clerk* (Stanford, Calif.: Stanford University Press, 2006); and Artemus Ward and David L. Weiden, *Sorcerers' Apprentices: 100 Years of Law Clerks at the United States Supreme Court* (New York: New York University Press, 2006). Law clerks in the federal courts of appeals are discussed in Jonathan Matthew Cohen, *Inside Appellate Courts: The Impact of Court Organization on Judicial Decision Making in the United States Courts of Appeals* (Ann Arbor: University of Michigan Press, 2002), 87–117.
3. Richard A. Posner, "The Courthouse Mice," *New Republic*, June 5–12, 2006, 33.
4. Edward Lazarus, *Closed Chambers: The First Eyewitness Account of the Epic Struggles Inside the Supreme Court* (New York: Times Books, 1998). See David J. Garrow, "Acolytes in Arms," *Green Bag* 9 (Summer 2006), 420.
5. Administrative Office of the United States Courts, *Judicial Business of the United States Courts: Report of the Director (2005)* (Washington, D.C.: Administrative Office of the United States Courts, n.d.), 43.
6. *Hamdan v. Rumsfeld*, 165 L. Ed. 2d 723 (2006). See T. R. Goldman, "Katyal's Crusade," *Legal Times*, July 31, 2006, 1, 17.
7. Administrative Office of the U.S. Courts, *Judicial Business (2005)*, 106–110.
8. Donald R. Songer, Reginald S. Sheehan, and Susan B. Haire, *Continuity and Change on the United States Courts of Appeals* (Ann Arbor: University of Michigan Press, 2000), 85.
9. See Daniel John Meador and Jordana Simone Bernstein, *Appellate Courts in the United States* (St. Paul: West Publishing, 1994), 70–88. Appellate procedures are catalogued in Carol R. Flango and David B. Rottman, *Appellate Court Procedures* (Williamsburg, Va.: National Center for State Courts, 1998).
10. Flango and Rottman, *Appellate Court Procedures*, 111–115.
11. From a presentation by Justice Elizabeth B. Lacy at the University of Virginia, March 7, 2001, as reported by David Klein.
12. Jeremy L. Fetty, "Pre-Argument Settlement at the Michigan Court of Appeals: A Secret Too Well Kept," *Journal of Appellate Practice and Process* 7 (Fall 2005), 317–333.
13. *Annual Report of the Illinois Courts: Statistical Summary 2005* (Springfield: Administrative Office of the Illinois Courts, n.d.), 138; Administrative Office of the U.S. Courts, *Judicial Business (2005)*, 126.
14. Forrest Maltzman, James F. Spriggs II, and Paul J. Wahlbeck, *Crafting Law on the Supreme Court: The Collegial Game* (New York: Cambridge University Press, 2000), 65.
15. Administrative Office of the U.S. Courts, *Judicial Business (2005)*, 40.
16. "Quiet! Justices at Work," *National Law Journal*, September 26, 1994, A10; Lynda Arakawa, "High Court Keeps Low Profile," *Honolulu Advertiser*, November 25, 2003.
17. Judicial Council of California, *2006 Court Statistics Report* (San Francisco: Judicial Council of California, 2006), 29; Administrative Office of the U.S. Courts, *Judicial Business (2005)*, 42.
18. Thomas H. Cohen, *Appeals from General Civil Trials in 46 Large Counties, 2001–2005* (Washington, D.C.: Bureau of Justice Statistics, U.S. Department of Justice, 2006), 1.
19. Thomas H. Cohen and Steven K. Smith, *Civil Trial Cases and Verdicts in Large Counties,*

2001 (Washington, D.C.: Bureau of Justice Statistics, U.S. Department of Justice, 2004), 5; Cohen, *Appeals From General Civil Trials*, 7.

20. See Scott Barclay, "Posner's Economic Model and the Decision to Appeal," *Justice System Journal* 19 (1997), 77–99.

21. See Richard L. Pacelle, Jr., *Between Law and Politics: The Solicitor General and the Structuring of Race, Gender, and Reproductive Rights Litigation* (College Station: Texas A & M Press, 2003).

22. Marc Galanter, "Why the 'Haves' Come Out Ahead: Speculations on the Limits of Legal Change," *Law & Society Review* 9 (Fall 1974), 97–125.

23. These data are from a statistical report compiled by the Office of the Solicitor General, U.S. Department of Justice.

24. *Brown v. Board of Education*, 347 U.S. 483 (1954). See Richard Kluger, *Simple Justice: The History of Brown v. Board of Education and Black America's Search for Equality* (New York: Knopf, 1976).

25. Jeffrey Toobin, *Too Close to Call: The Thirty-Six-Day Battle to Decide the 2000 Election* (New York: Random House, 2001). The decision was *Bush v. Gore*, 531 U.S. 98 (2000).

26. See Sarah F. Corbally, Donald C. Bross, and Victor E. Flango, "Filing of Amicus Curiae Briefs in State Courts of Last Resort: 1960–2000," *Justice System Journal* 25 (2004), 39–56.

27. Timothy R. Johnson, Paul J. Wahlbeck, and James F. Spriggs II, "The Influence of Oral Arguments on the U.S. Supreme Court," *American Political Science Review* 100 (February 2006), 99–113.

28. Neal Devins, "Better Lucky than Good," *The Green Bag* 8 (Autumn 2004), 41.

29. Henry Weinstein, "Election Suits Are Filed Early and Often," *Los Angeles Times*, October 28, 2004, A17.

30. David Segal, "Pursuing Clinton Suits Him Just Fine," *Washington Post*, May 30, 1998, A1, A7.

31. Jeffrey Toobin, *A Vast Conspiracy: The Real Story of the Sex Scandal That Nearly Brought Down a President* (New York: Touchstone Books, 1999).

32. George W. Pring and Penelope Canan, *SLAPPs: Getting Sued for Speaking Out* (Philadelphia: Temple University Press, 1996), 3.

33. One possible example of this type of SLAPP is described in Henry Weinstein, "Builder Sues Forest Service Workers Under RICO Act," *Los Angeles Times*, December 20, 2004, A1.

34. *Suzuki Motor Corp. v. Consumers Union of United States*, 330 F.3d 1110, 1115 (9th Cir. 2003).

35. Tresa Baldas, "The Cost of Griping on the Web: Lawsuits," *National Law Journal*, November 29, 2004, 1, 22.

36. See *Blanchard v. DirecTV, Inc.*, 20 Cal. Rptr. 3d 384 (Calif. Ct. App. 2d Dist. 2004).

37. Songer, Sheehan, and Haire, *Continuity and Change on the United States Courts of Appeals*, 15; Administrative Office of the U.S. Courts, *Judicial Business (2005)*, 101. The sources of caseload growth are discussed in Richard A. Posner, *The Federal Courts: Challenge and Reform* (Cambridge: Harvard University Press, 1996), 53–79, 110–121.

38. See David M. O'Brien, "A Diminished Plenary Docket: A Legacy of the Rehnquist Court," *Judicature* 89 (November–December 2005), 134–137, 182.

39. See Ruth Bader Ginsburg, "Remarks for American Law Institute Annual Dinner May 19, 1994," *Saint Louis University Law Journal* 38 (Summer 1994), 884.

40. California Supreme Court, *Internal Operating Practices and Procedures of the California Supreme Court* (revised 2003 and 2004) (http://www.courtinfo.ca.gov/courts/supreme/documents/sc082504.pdf).

41. H. W. Perry, Jr., *Deciding to Decide: Agenda Setting in the United States Supreme Court* (Cambridge: Harvard University Press, 1991), 198–207.

42. Sara C. Benesh, Saul Brenner, and Harold J. Spaeth, "Aggressive Grants by Affirm-Minded Justices," *American Politics Research* 30 (May 2002), 219–234.

43. *American Civil Liberties Union v. County of Hudson*, 799 A.2d 629 (Superior Ct. of N.J., App. Div. 2002), 803 A.2d 1162 (N.J. Sup. Ct. 2002).

44. *Limbaugh v. State*, 887 So. 2d 387 (Fla. Ct. App. 2004), 903 So. 2d 189 (Fla. Sup. Ct. 2005).
45. Mark I. Levy, "Appellate Overload," *National Law Journal*, May 22, 2006, 15.
46. Solomon Moore and Ann M. Simmons, "Immigration Pleas Crushing Federal Appellate Courts," *Los Angeles Times*, May 2, 2005, A1.
47. See Symposium, "Expedited Appeals in Selected State Appellate Courts," *Journal of Appellate Practice and Process* 4 (Spring 2002), 191–302.
48. Robert S. Thompson and John B. Oakley, "From Information to Opinion in Appellate Courts: How Funny Things Happen on the Way Through the Forum," *Arizona State Law Journal* (1986), 41.
49. Mary Lou Stow and Harold J. Spaeth, "Centralized Research Staff: Is There a Monster in the Judicial Closet?" *Judicature* 75 (December–January 1992), 216–221; David J. Brown, "Facing the Monster in the Judicial Closet: Rebutting a Presumption of Sloth," *Judicature* 75 (April–May 1992), 291–293.
50. Charles R. Haworth, "Screening and Summary Procedures in the United States Courts of Appeals," *Washington University Law Quarterly* (Spring 1973), 309–319; Jerry Goldman, "Appellate Justice Economized: Screening and Its Effect on Outcomes and Legitimacy," in *Restructuring Justice: The Innovations of the Ninth Circuit and the Future of the Federal Courts*, ed. Arthur D. Hellman (Ithaca, N.Y.: Cornell University Press, 1990), 136–162.
51. Benjamin N. Cardozo, *The Growth of the Law* (New Haven, Conn.: Yale University Press, 1924), 60. See also Harry T. Edwards, "The Judicial Function and the Elusive Goal of Principled Decisionmaking," *Wisconsin Law Review*, 1991, 856–858; and Frank M. Coffin, *On Appeal: Courts, Lawyering, and Judging* (New York: W.W. Norton, 1994), 275.
52. Douglas O. Linder, "How Judges Judge: A Study of Disagreement on the United States Court of Appeals for the Eighth Circuit," *Arkansas Law Review* 38 (Summer 1985), 498 n. 72.
53. John T. Wold, "Going Through the Motions: The Monotony of Appellate Court Decisionmaking," *Judicature* 62 (August 1978), 61–62.
54. William Haltom, *Reporting on the Courts: How the Mass Media Cover Judicial Actions* (Chicago: Nelson-Hall, 1998), ch. 3.
55. Jeffrey A. Segal and Albert D. Cover, "Ideological Values and the Votes of U.S. Supreme Court Justices," *American Political Science Review* 83 (June 1989), 557–565; Jeffrey A. Segal and Harold J. Spaeth, *The Supreme Court and the Attitudinal Model Revisited* (New York: Cambridge University Press, 2002), 320–324.
56. Patricia M. Wald, "A Response to Tiller and Cross," *Columbia Law Review* 99 (January 1999), 237.
57. See Deborah Sontag, "The Intellectual Heart of Conservative America," *New York Times Magazine*, March 9, 2003, 38–45, 54, 65, 77, 80.
58. Ashlyn Kuersten and Donald Songer, "Presidential Success Through Appointments to the United States Courts of Appeals," *American Politics Research* 31 (March 2003), 107–137.
59. *House v. Bell*, 386 F.3d 668 (6th Cir. 2004). See John Brummett, "Judges Who Kill and Judges Who Don't," *Arkansas News Bureau*, October 25, 2004.
60. Forrest Maltzman, James F. Spriggs II, and Paul J. Wahlbeck, *Crafting Law on the Supreme Court: The Collegial Game* (New York: Cambridge University Press, 2000).
61. Linder, "How Judges Judge," 484–486.
62. Cohen, *Inside Appellate Courts*, 137.
63. See Forrest Maltzman and Paul J. Wahlbeck, "A Conditional Model of Opinion Assignment on the Supreme Court," *Political Research Quarterly* 57 (December 2004), 551–563.
64. Lily Henning, "The Edwards Treatment," *Legal Times*, November 21, 2005, 1, 10, 12. The quotation is from Jeffrey Brandon Morris, *Calmly to Poise the Scales of Justice: A History of the Courts of the District of Columbia Circuit* (Durham, N.C.: Carolina Academic Press, 2001), 197.
65. Joan Biskupic, *Sandra Day O'Connor: How the First Woman on the Supreme Court Became Its Most Influential Justice* (New York: HarperCollins, 2005).

66. This account is based on newspaper reports. The quotation is from Matt Volz, "Commission Won't Recommend McRae's Suspension," Associated Press State & Local News Wire, October 31, 2003.

67. The quotation is from *In re Byrd*, 269 F.3d 578, 582 (6th Cir. 2001). The 2006 decisions were *United States v. McClain*, 444 F.3d 537 (6th Cir. 2006), and *Stewart v. Blackwell*, 444 F.3d 843 (6th Cir. 2006). The conflicts within the court are discussed in Adam Liptak, "Order Lacking on a Court: U.S. Appellate Judges in Cincinnati Spar in Public," *New York Times*, August 12, 2003, A10.

68. David E. Klein, *Making Law in the United States Courts of Appeals* (New York: Cambridge University Press, 2002), 90.

69. See David E. Klein and Darby Morrisroe, "The Prestige and Influence of Individual Judges on the U.S. Courts of Appeals," *Journal of Legal Studies* 28 (1999), 371–392.

70. Thomas Sowell, "Justice Kennedy Goes Soft on Crime," *Columbus Dispatch*, August 13, 2003, A11.

71. Quoted in *Congressional Record*, vol. 142 (daily edition), H12262 (October 2, 1996).

72. See Laura Langer, *Judicial Review in State Supreme Courts: A Comparative Study* (Albany: State University of New York Press, 2002).

73. Bob Egelko, "Supreme Court Tackles Same-Sex Marriage," *San Francisco Chronicle*, May 23, 2004, E6.

74. *In re: Wilson*, 433 F.3d 451 (5th Cir. 2005), 442 F.3d 872 (5th Cir. 2006); Adam Liptak, "Facing Death, His I.Q. Low, Man Wins Rare About-Face," *New York Times*, March 15, 2006, A21.

75. *Konop v. Hawaiian Airlines, Inc.*, 236 F.3d 1035 (9th Cir. 2001), 302 F.3d 868 (9th Cir. 2002); Bob Egelko, "Appeals Court Overturns Own Web Site Ruling," *San Francisco Chronicle*, August 28, 2002, A4.

76. *Evans v. State*, 2004 Del. LEXIS 545 (Del. Sup. Ct. 2004), 872 A.2d 539 (Del. Sup. Ct. 2005); Esteban Parra, "Top Court to Revisit Sentencing," *Wilmington News Journal*, February 5, 2005. The quotations are from the statute, 10 Del. Code sec. 5402 (2006), and from p. 558 of the 2005 supreme court decision.

77. The flag-burning decisions were *Texas v. Johnson*, 491 U.S. 397 (1989); and *United States v. Eichman*, 496 U.S. 310 (1990). The decisions on the rights of suspected terrorists were *Hamdi v. Rumsfeld*, 542 U.S. 507 (2004); *Rasul v. Bush*, 542 U.S. 466 (2004); and *Hamdan v. Rumsfeld*, 165 L. Ed. 2d 723 (2006).

9

Appellate Courts:
Policy and Impact

T rial courts make policy mostly through the accumulation of narrow decisions that affect specific litigants. In appellate courts, policymaking is often more direct and more visible. When they determine who can bring personal injury suits or define the power of Congress, appellate courts establish broad legal rules whose impact can go far beyond the litigants in the cases before them. When people speak of the power of courts in national life, they are referring chiefly to appellate courts.

This chapter examines appellate courts as policymakers. The first part of the chapter focuses on what they do, the content of their decisions. The second part examines what happens after appellate courts act, the impact of their policies elsewhere in government and in society as a whole. Together, those two inquiries provide a picture of the roles that appellate courts play in government and society.

APPELLATE COURT DECISIONS AS POLICIES

Appellate court decisions have two components, corresponding to the two functions that were discussed in Chapter 8. The first is a review of how the lower court treated the parties to the case, a review that is important primarily to those parties. The second is a judgment about the principles of law that apply to the case. I will discuss the review of lower courts briefly and then turn to several aspects of the second component: the content of courts' agendas, the ideological direction of their policies, and the extent of their activism in policymaking.

Review of Lower-Court Decisions

When they review lower-court decisions, most of the time appellate courts leave those decisions standing. First-level appellate courts review trial courts directly, and in the great majority of cases they affirm the decisions that are appealed to them. Rates of affirmance and reversal can be calculated in different ways, but studies of federal and state courts show that by any calculations, at least two-thirds of the time first-level courts fully affirm the trial-court decisions they review rather than "disturbing" them through modification or reversal. And a high proportion of the disturbances are modifications such as reducing a jury's award to a tort plaintiff while leaving the verdict standing.[1]

Several forces help to produce these low disturbance rates. Widely accepted legal doctrines give a strong presumption of validity to trial court decisions. One such doctrine and its interpretation are described in Exhibit 9.1. This presumption is strengthened in practice by the experience of appellate judges, who learn that most cases are suitable for affirmance. And frequent reversals would exacerbate conflict between trial and appellate judges and increase appellate caseloads by encouraging appeals.

The rates at which trial-court decisions are reversed vary among types of cases. They also vary with the identities of those who bring appeals. In civil cases, the federal courts of appeals overturn verdicts in favor of plaintiffs at a higher rate than they overturn verdicts for defendants. This pattern is especially strong in fields in which plaintiffs are typically individuals and defendants are typically organizations, such as torts and civil rights. The authors of one study surmised that judges on the courts of appeals are trying to correct for what they perceive as a pro-plaintiff tendency on the part of trial judges and juries.[2]

Unlike first-level appellate courts, those at the second level disturb lower-court decisions in a high proportion of the cases they decide. In its 2005 term, the U.S. Supreme Court affirmed the lower court in only 28 percent of its decisions on the merits of cases. But that figure is deceptive because Supreme Court justices and judges on other second-level courts are inclined to accept cases in which they think that the lower court erred in its decision. If we take into account all the cases the Court refused to hear in its 2005 term, it left lower court decisions standing about 98 percent of the time.[3]

EXHIBIT 9.1   The "Clearly Erroneous" Standard for Review of Trial Court Decisions

Under the Federal Rules of Civil Procedure, findings about the facts of cases in district courts "shall not be set aside unless clearly erroneous." The "clearly erroneous" standard has been widely applied to criminal cases as well. One federal court of appeals described how it interpreted that standard:

> Under the clearly-erroneous standard, we cannot meddle with a prior decision of this or a lower court simply because we have doubts about its wisdom or think we would have reached a different result. To be clearly erroneous, a decision must strike us as more than just maybe or probably wrong; it must, as one member of this court recently stated during oral argument, strike us as wrong with the force of a five-week-old, unrefrigerated dead fish.

The last part of that formulation—what might be called the fish rule—has been widely quoted by courts of appeals. This does not mean that appellate judges always defer to the findings of trial courts, and at times they seem eager to second-guess those findings. But on the whole, they give a strong burden of proof to appellants who argue that a judge or jury got the facts wrong.

Sources: The quotation is from *Parts and Electric Motors, Inc. v. Sterling Electric, Inc.*, 866 F.2d 228, 233 (7th Cir. 1988). One recent decision that quoted from this opinion is *Prete v. Bradbury*, 438 F.3d 949, 968 n. 23 (9th Cir. 2006).

When an appellate court does modify or reverse a decision it reviews, most of the time it remands the case to the lower court for reconsideration. In a study of five state courts, three-quarters of the criminal defendants who had their convictions overturned faced the possibility of a new trial rather than having their cases dismissed.[4] It is common for litigants who win their appeals to lose again after their cases go back to trial court. One famous example is Ernesto Miranda, whose victory in the Supreme Court produced new rules for police questioning but who lost again when his case was retried.

Through one route or another, then, the result of most appeals is that the lower court's original decision becomes final. When we take into account the high proportion of decisions that are not appealed in the first place, lower courts have a great deal of autonomy. In this sense, then, appellate courts intervene rather little in the work of the courts below them.

But this is only one aspect of the relationship between higher and lower courts. Even though appellate courts overturn relatively few decisions, the opinions they write influence what the courts below them do in a much larger number of cases. For example, one state supreme court decision on liability rules in auto accident cases can shape hundreds of trial court decisions.

Appellate Court Agendas

The potential impact of courts on the rest of government and society is determined, first of all, by the types of issues they address. We can begin to sketch out the roles of appellate courts in policymaking by examining the sets of cases they hear and decide with opinions—their agendas. The more work that a court does in a particular field, the greater its potential to shape public policy in that field. As suggested in Chapter 8, the agendas of appellate courts reflect rules of jurisdiction, patterns of litigation and appeals, and judges' choices of cases in which to write opinions. The 2006 agendas of three appellate courts at different levels are summarized in Exhibit 9.2.

The agendas of state supreme courts reflect the diverse work of state courts at all levels. But as the example of Kansas illustrates, state supreme courts focus far more on public law—cases that arise from government policy in a fairly direct way—than do the trial courts below them. The large portion of the agenda devoted to criminal cases reflects several conditions, including the incentives of defendants who have received heavy sentences to take their cases to the highest level, the substantial number of unresolved issues involving criminal procedure, and the mandatory jurisdiction of supreme courts over death sentences.

Kansas is part of the federal Tenth Circuit, which also includes much of the Mountain West. As the Tenth Circuit illustrates, the agendas of federal courts of appeals show both similarities to the agendas of state supreme courts and differences from them. The courts of appeals concentrate on public law even more than do the state appellate courts. The higher proportion of cases resulting from economic regulation reflects the broad sweep of regulation by the federal government. The proportion of criminal cases in the Tenth Circuit was nearly as high as it was in the Kansas Supreme Court. Criminal cases in the courts of appeals arise from both prosecutions for federal crimes and habeas corpus cases in which state prisoners challenge their convictions.

EXHIBIT 9.2   Subject Matter of Cases Decided with Published Opinions in 2006, Selected Appellate Courts, in Percentages

Category of Cases	Kansas Supreme Court	Federal Court of Appeals, Tenth Circuit	U.S. Supreme Court
Private law			
Debt and contract	8%	6%	6%
Torts	9	5	6
Family and estates	1	0	1
Public law			
Criminal	64	51	36
Civil liberties	2	16	20
Regulation of economy	3	13	16
Other	12	9	16

Notes: Cases are coded on the basis of their original subject matter, which may differ from the issues that a court addresses on appeal. All cases stemming from criminal prosecutions, including those involving prisoners, are in the "criminal" category. Many cases would have fit into other categories if different coding rules had been used. For this reason, the percentages should be viewed as showing only general patterns in the three courts' agendas.

  Kansas cases are from January–June 2006, 10th Circuit cases from January–April 2006, and Supreme Court cases from the 2005 term (October 2005–June 2006).

The agenda of the U.S. Supreme Court is distinctive. The Court's specialization in public law is even greater than Exhibit 9.2 suggests, because most of the private law cases it hears involve questions about government power and procedure by the time they reach the Court. For instance, the one case in the "family and estates" category concerned the jurisdiction of federal courts to hear disputes over estates. As it happened, this highly technical case received widespread publicity because it involved the claim of a young celebrity (Anna Nicole Smith) to hundreds of millions of dollars from the estate of the husband whom she had married when he was eighty-nine years old, one year before his death.[5] The Court is something of a civil liberties specialist. Along with the cases in the civil liberties category, most of the criminal cases it hears involve civil liberties issues.

The agendas of appellate courts, like those of trial courts, evolve over time. The federal courts of appeals illustrate this evolution.[6] Criminal law has become more prominent with the expansion of state prisoners' rights to challenge their convictions in federal court and with the growing role of the federal government in criminal justice. The share of these agendas that is devoted to civil liberties has also grown, largely because of new legal protections of rights by Congress and the Supreme Court. There has been a corresponding decline in the portion of the agenda devoted to economic matters, especially those in which government plays no direct role. Thus the work of the courts of appeals today is somewhat different from what it was half a century ago.

Appellate courts address a broad range of issues, but there are some important areas of public policy in which they are largely inactive. The outstanding example is foreign policy, which state courts barely touch and in which federal courts make relatively few decisions. Even in fields where they are active, the courts may not deal with the most fundamental issues. In economic regulation, for instance, courts focus primarily on the details of regulatory policy rather than on the general form and scope of regulation.

Ideological Patterns in Appellate Court Policy

In the areas on which appellate courts focus their attention, the content of their policies is most easily summarized in ideological terms: the distribution of liberal and conservative policies. At any given time, the courts' policies are diverse ideologically, but this does not mean they are random. For most of American history, by the current definition of liberal and conservative positions, appellate courts as a whole were fairly conservative in their policies. In contrast, their policies over the last seventy years have been quite mixed in ideological terms.

The traditional conservatism of appellate courts was best reflected in economic policies. Federal and state courts addressed a wide range of legal issues affecting the interests of economically powerful groups, and the dominant theme in their decisions was support for those interests.

The U.S. Supreme Court did much to protect property rights and the freedom of business enterprises from restrictions by state and federal governments. As legislation to regulate and restrict business practices grew in the early twentieth century, the Court frequently struck laws down as unconstitutional. Ultimately, the Court overturned much of President Franklin Roosevelt's New Deal economic program in the 1930s.

The economic policies of state courts also had a conservative tone, although scholars disagree about the strength of this tone.[7] As the industrial economy developed, state courts did much to protect the business sector from threats to its economic well-being. For instance, they adopted a set of rules for personal injury law that favored businesses over injured individuals.

This conservative tone to appellate court policy is not difficult to understand. Judges came primarily from economically advantaged sectors of society and were imbued with the values of those sectors. They were trained in a legal profession in which conservative values predominated, and they often embarked on legal careers that involved service to business enterprises. Further, the most skilled advocates in court generally represented businesses and other institutions with conservative goals. Because of all these forces, perhaps it was inevitable that judicial policy was more conservative than liberal.

In the period from the 1940s to the present, taken as a whole, judicial policies have been relatively liberal in comparison with earlier periods. Across a range of issues, the courts have given significant support to the interests of relatively weak groups in society, groups that possess far fewer social and economic resources and far less conventional political power than the business interests that courts tended to favor in the past. But the content of judicial policies has varied considerably over time and across courts.

The Supreme Court became increasingly liberal in the first half of that period. Beginning in 1937, the Court quickly abandoned its earlier support for business interests that sought protection from government regulation. More slowly, in a process that culminated in the 1960s, it began to provide support for the civil liberties of relatively powerless groups in American society. It extended the constitutional rights of criminal defendants from federal to state proceedings and established new controls on police investigations and trial procedures. It required the desegregation of southern public schools and protected the rights of racial minority groups in other areas of life. It strengthened freedom of expression both for the mass media and for people who express their views through vehicles such as pamphlets and marches.

The Court has moderated its liberalism since the 1970s. In the current period it generally favors business interests in fields such as labor relations and environmental law. It has narrowed the rights of criminal defendants, and it has been less inclined to expand civil liberties in any area. It has also set some limits on congressional power to protect civil liberties. Still, the Court has maintained considerable support for individual liberties. And despite some hints of a new direction, the Court has continued to accept active government regulation of the economy in most respects.

To a degree, the federal courts of appeals have taken the same ideological path as the Supreme Court. But the positions of the courts of appeals have differed considerably from court to court.[8] The stances of the various courts of appeals are shaped by the political views that predominate in their regions, but this influence is far from total. The Fifth Circuit championed racial equality under the law during the 1950s and 1960s despite the pressures against civil rights in that region.

Early in the twentieth century, state supreme courts began to move away from their long-standing support for business in tort law by expanding rights to recover compensation for personal injuries. This trend gained momentum as courts increasingly eliminated old rules that had favored defendants. Most dramatically, in the 1960s and 1970s, supreme courts largely eliminated the requirement that people who are injured by defective products must prove that the manufacturer was negligent. In the past two decades, the movement to expand the rights of injured people has slowed considerably. Indeed, some state courts have become considerably more favorable to the interests of tort defendants.[9] But for the most part the revolution in personal injury law remains intact.

State courts have taken decidedly mixed positions in civil liberties. In the 1950s and 1960s, some supreme courts openly resisted the Supreme Court's expansions of individual liberties, interpreting the Court's decisions narrowly. Since the 1970s, as the Supreme Court itself has narrowed some liberties, some state courts have accepted this direction enthusiastically. But others, especially in the West and Northeast, have undertaken their own expansions of liberties by finding independent sources of protections in their state constitutions.[10] These expansions have been especially common in criminal justice. For instance, many state courts have gone further than the Supreme Court to exclude evidence that law enforcement officers had seized illegally.[11] State courts have broadened protections of liberties in other areas, ranging from freedom of expression to sex discrimination.

The relative liberalism of appellate courts since the 1930s is more difficult to explain than was their traditional conservatism. Undoubtedly, this liberalism has roots in a changing pattern of social values. Support by the general public and political leaders for government regulation of business enterprises increased during the twentieth century. Meanwhile, some civil liberties—especially those related to equality—gained more support. This change in values has been reflected in judges' own attitudes and in the litigation and arguments that come to appellate courts.

Another source of this ideological change is the kinds of people who become judges. Like judges in the past, most current judges come from families with high status. But there are more exceptions today. As a result, the attitudes of judges on economic issues are less likely to be conservative.

More directly, on the whole the people who select judges in the current period are themselves more liberal than they were in earlier periods. At the federal level, liberal Democratic presidents have sought out appellate judges who shared their liberalism. Franklin Roosevelt's appointments turned the Supreme Court away from its traditional economic conservatism, and appointments by Kennedy and Johnson in the 1960s helped solidify its commitment to civil liberties. Roosevelt, Johnson, and Jimmy Carter all used their appointments to move the lower federal courts in a liberal direction. At the state level, growing Democratic strength in the North from the 1930s on brought more liberal governors into office, and these governors influenced the direction of state appellate courts with their own appointments.

To some extent, this shift to greater liberalism reinforced itself. The courts' support for civil liberties encouraged interest groups to bring new cases, seeking further expansions of liberties. When the Supreme Court in the 1960s played a strong role in expanding civil liberties, many lawyers gained an appreciation for that role, and those who reached the bench themselves sought to maintain it. As the changes in tort law demonstrate especially well, a trend in judicial policy tends to gain a certain momentum of its own.

The partial reversal of this liberal trend in recent years reflects events outside the courts. The success of Republican presidential candidates from 1968 through 1988 brought more conservatives into the federal courts, with an inevitable impact on judicial policy. This trend has been reinforced by George W. Bush's judicial appointments. In part because of campaigns by interest groups, fears about negative effects of expanded rights for injured people became widespread, and these fears undoubtedly influenced state court decisions in tort law.[12]

Of course, future directions in appellate court policies will reflect further developments in their political environments, developments as broad as trends in social thinking and as specific as the outcomes of presidential and gubernatorial elections. Observers of the courts tend to view their current tendencies as permanent, but the policy shifts that have occurred in the current era should remind us that the ideological stance of the courts is always subject to change.

Judicial Activism

Observers of the courts and judges themselves frequently speak of *judicial activism*. It is not always clear what they mean by the term. Activism can refer to a wide range of actions by courts. And because judicial activism has a negative connotation, suggesting that judges have acted in an illegitimate way, people often use the term simply to denounce court decisions and lines of judicial policy with which they disagree. Members of Congress regularly do so. "Basically," according to one scholar, "judicial activism is what the other guy does that you don't like."[13] This reality is illustrated by reactions to the battle over Florida's electoral votes in the 2000 presidential election. Supporters of George W. Bush denounced the Florida Supreme Court for what they saw as activism that favored the prospects of Al Gore, while Gore's supporters denounced the U.S. Supreme Court for what they perceived as activist decisions that ensured Bush's victory.

Thinking About Activism   Yet activism does have real meaning, and its most important aspect concerns participation in public policymaking. Judges cannot avoid making policy, which is inherent in their work. But they have some control over the *extent* of their involvement in policymaking. In deciding cases, judges often face a choice between alternatives that would enhance their court's impact on the content of government policy and those that would limit its impact. A court might decide a tort case on the basis of a narrow rule, or it might announce a broad rule that affects a whole class of tort cases. If a statute is challenged under the Constitution, a court can uphold the statute or overturn it. When judges choose to increase their impact in these and other respects, their policies can be called activist.

When courts engage in activism, they may do so in support of either liberal or conservative policies. In any era, the ideological pattern of activism will be mixed, but the relative strength of liberal and conservative activism will reflect the ideological tenor of judicial policy as a whole. The most prominent activism of the relatively conservative federal courts in the early twentieth century involved overturning of laws that restricted business practices. The more liberal courts that followed were most activist in support of individual liberties for groups such as political dissenters, members of racial minority groups, and criminal defendants.

Leaving aside its negative connotation, is judicial activism undesirable? Many people think that it is, on several grounds. Most important, they perceive activism as illegitimate because the courts are relatively free from popular control and accountability—especially the federal courts, whose judges are appointed for life. In this view, policy should be made by elected legislators and chief executives, not by the courts. In contrast, defenders of activism view the courts' freedom from popular control as a virtue rather than a weakness, because that freedom allows the courts to protect important but unpopular values such as certain civil liberties. This debate is impossible to resolve definitively. In any event, most people react to activism not in terms of its benefits and costs in the abstract but in terms of its ideological content at a given time.

Judicial Activism Today   While it is inevitable that courts engage in a good deal of activism, the level of that activism can vary over time. It appears that this level has been unusually high in the past few decades. One measure of activism is the number of laws that the Supreme Court declares unconstitutional. From 1960 through 2005, by one count, the Court struck down 88 federal statutes and 598 state and local laws.[14] The number of federal laws overturned in that period constitutes more than half of the total for the Court's entire history.

These figures reflect the Supreme Court's involvement in a wide range of important policy questions. Some examples will underline the extent of that involvement:

- The Court has been a central participant in public policy on race. In decisions over the past half century, the Court has established rules about when school segregation is unconstitutional and what action is required when it is. It has shaped the meaning of federal statutes that prohibit discrimination in voting, employment, and other areas. Its decisions have determined when affirmative action is legally acceptable.

- In *Roe v. Wade* (1973), the Court intervened in the developing debate over abortion law with a ruling that effectively struck down the laws of at least forty-six states. Since then the Court has handed down a series of decisions on abortion issues that range from the legality of restrictions on government funding for abortion to the legality of restrictions on protests at clinics that perform abortions.

- Partially reviving a role that it played in an earlier era, since the mid-1990s the Court has closely scrutinized the use of federal power under the Constitution to regulate state governments and the private sector. The Court has struck down several federal laws and limited the reach of others on a range of issues that include gun control, labor relations, and religious freedom.

- The Court intervenes in the political process as well. Most important, a series of decisions since 1976 has severely limited government regulation of campaign finance, thus making it impossible to maintain a comprehensive system of regulation. Of course, the Court dramatically intervened in politics after the 2000 election.

Judicial activism extends well beyond the Supreme Court, as suggested by the examples of activist decisions in Exhibit 9.3. Like the Supreme Court, the lower federal courts often overrule policies of the federal government on the grounds that they are inconsistent with statutes or the Constitution. One example is a series of recent rulings in which federal judges in the West have held that the federal government was failing to carry out its duties under environmental laws.[15] And federal district judges frequently intervene in the governance of public institutions such as schools, prisons, and mental institutions by holding that existing conditions are unconstitutional and then supervising the task of reforming them.

In state supreme courts, the increased use of state constitutions as independent protections for civil liberties has brought about a significant expansion in the courts' roles. Perhaps the most striking example is the series of supreme court rulings on school funding. In 1973, the U.S. Supreme Court ruled that systems based on local property taxes did not violate the equal protection clause of the Fourteenth Amendment even though those systems produced substantial differences in funding levels across school districts within a state.[16] Litigants had already begun to challenge these funding systems under state constitutions, and after 1973 they focused solely on state-level challenges. More often than not, courts have upheld their states' funding systems, but supreme courts in more than one-third of the states have struck down their systems—in several states, multiple times.[17] The amounts of money involved are often quite large. In New York, where the state's highest court had not yet ruled on school funding, a trial judge in 2005 held that the state must increase its spending on New York City schools by several billion dollars a year, specifying the amounts.[18]

EXHIBIT 9.3   Some Examples of Activist Decisions in 2005 and 2006

- The Washington state supreme court ruled that a change in federal law had the effect of eliminating the state's estate tax. Its decision required the state to refund about $150 million in back taxes and cost it about $140 million a year in future taxes.
- In an opinion that ran more than seventeen hundred pages, a federal district judge in Washington, D.C. denounced the tobacco industry for what she saw as deceptive marketing practices and ordered major changes in those practices.
- A federal district judge in Maryland held that a state law requiring large employers to pay at least a minimum percentage of their payrolls for employee health insurance was invalid because it conflicted with the federal law that regulates employee benefit programs.
- The federal court of appeals in D.C. invalidated a rule adopted by the federal Securities and Exchange Commission to regulate "hedge funds," a sector of the investment market that includes more than $1 trillion in assets.
- A Montana trial judge ruled that three proposed initiatives could not go before the state's voters because of the way that signatures had been gathered to put the measures on the ballot. The state supreme court affirmed his decision.

Sources: Newspaper stories; court decisions.

If activism is at a relatively high level today, what accounts for that increase? To a degree, it simply reflects the policy goals of judges. This is most often true of judges whose commitment to civil liberties leads them to invalidate policies of the other branches, but other judges act on their disagreement with affirmative action or federal regulation of state governments. The Supreme Court helps to foster activism in the lower courts through its own example, as the Court did with its expansions of civil liberties during the 1950s and 1960s. By the same token, lower courts set examples for each other. It is easier for a federal district judge to order major prison reforms when a dozen judges in other districts have already done so.

The high level of activism also reflects forces outside the courts. Perhaps its most fundamental source is the growth in government action at all levels. Because government policies now touch people more often and more deeply than in past eras, it is inevitable that more questions about the legal validity of government action arise. Today the Supreme Court strikes down more laws than it did in the past, but there are more laws on the books now. For example, the *United States Code*, the compilation of federal statutes, has grown enormously over the years.

There also has been growth in interest group litigation to challenge government action. Interest groups cannot force activism on a reluctant court, but they can facilitate activism by providing opportunities and constructing arguments for it. Groups such as the American Civil Liberties Union have played a critical role in bringing civil liberties cases to court, just as groups such as the Sierra Club have done on environmental issues. For their part, courts have encouraged interest groups and others to challenge government action through decisions that responded favorably to such challenges.

Judicial activism, like so much about the courts, results from an interaction between judges and the larger society in which they work.

THE IMPACT OF APPELLATE COURT POLICIES

Whatever their level of activism may be, appellate courts make a good deal of public policy. By doing so, they might exert considerable impact on the rest of government and American society.

The impact that courts actually achieve depends heavily on how other people and organizations respond to court decisions. To take one example, the federal courts of appeals and the Supreme Court have made a long series of decisions interpreting the federal laws against employment discrimination. Those decisions have established important new rules about who can sue for discrimination and what they must prove to win their cases. The actual effect of those rules depends on a wide range of choices by people in government and the private sector: whether Congress allows the rulings to stand, how judges and juries apply them to specific cases, whether individuals file lawsuits, and the extent to which employers change their practices. And similar processes occur in other fields of judicial policy.

Implementation by Lower Courts and Administrators

Among all the people who shape the impact of appellate court policies, the most direct roles are played by lower-court judges and administrators. When a court rules on a legal issue, the courts and administrative bodies below it are responsible for applying that ruling in the same case and in other cases and situations. Such administrative bodies include all the agencies in the executive branch of government, ranging from federal regulatory commissions to police departments and school systems.

The Implementation Record   In responding to decisions by appellate courts, lower-court judges and administrators have choices to make. Most fundamentally, they must decide how fully they will put those decisions into effect. Their responses to appellate court decisions differ a great deal.

Most of the time, judges and administrators comply fully with the legal rules that appellate courts lay down. This compliance typically receives little attention, because it is undramatic and accords with people's expectations. But it merits some emphasis, because it suggests that appellate courts have considerable capacity to shape the choices of officials who stand below them in the legal hierarchy.

At the other end of the spectrum, some officials simply fail to follow rulings that apply to them, even in the same case in which the ruling was handed down. In 2000, a Kansas City federal judge ordered that a prisoner be released from prison; two years later, a letter from the prisoner informed him that the release had never occurred.[19] That noncompliance may have been inadvertent. But in another case, law enforcement officials in California sought to avoid releasing a prisoner after his conviction was overturned. One of their means to this end—transferring the prisoner to a county jail because county officials were not covered by a court order to release him—was of questionable legitimacy.[20] Nor do judges always carry out the orders of higher courts faithfully. In one case, a New Jersey judge responded to an order that he reduce a verdict of $3 million or have a new trial on the amount of damages by reducing the verdict to $2,999,999.99.[21]

This variation in compliance with appellate court policies can be illustrated by examining two areas of policy in which courts have issued broad legal rules that must be applied by judges and administrators. The first area is criminal procedure. State and federal appellate courts frequently issue rulings that prescribe procedures for trial judges, prosecutors, and law enforcement agencies to follow. The Supreme Court, for instance, has made major decisions on issues such as police searches, questioning of suspects, and selection of jurors. Some state supreme courts have gone even further than the Supreme Court in regulating police practices.

Compliance with these rulings is far from complete. Even though evidence that is obtained illegally cannot be used in court, it is common for police officers to engage in searches that violate legal rules or to question suspects in ways that do not fully accord with the *Miranda* rules established by the Supreme Court.[22] Despite a series of rulings by the Court and other courts since 1986, prosecutors sometimes use challenges to dismiss prospective jurors on the basis of their race.[23] For their part, trial judges do not always enforce rules for police and prosecutors, and judges have engaged in their own noncompliance with rules on matters such as providing lawyers to misdemeanor defendants who are indigent.[24]

At the same time, rulings by appellate courts have secured considerable change in the behavior of people in the criminal justice system. Perhaps the most sweeping effects have been on police investigation of crimes. If searches and questioning of suspects do not always follow court-made rules, the practices followed by local law enforcement agencies are quite different from what they were before appellate courts began to impose major restrictions on those practices.

The second area is school religious activities.[25] Over the past half century, federal courts have limited religious observances in public schools in several ways. Especially important were decisions by the Supreme Court in 1962 and 1963 that prohibited schools from engaging in organized prayer or Bible reading exercises, decisions that the Court has reiterated and extended since then. A great many schools eliminated observances that the courts struck down, even though these observances were often deeply rooted in local tradition. But many other schools maintained these practices despite their illegality.

Indeed, it appears that noncompliance with the Supreme Court's original rulings has increased since the 1990s. Meanwhile, its 1992 restriction on prayers at graduation ceremonies and its 2000 decision prohibiting student-led prayers at football games have encountered their own resistance.[26] "There are communities largely of one faith," one commentator said, "and despite all the court rulings and Supreme Court decisions, they continue to promote one faith" in their public schools.[27] Altogether, the extent of resistance to the Court's rulings is striking.

How can we account for imperfections in the implementation process? What causes variation in responses to appellate court rulings? Several factors are relevant.

Attitudes Toward Policy   When judges and administrators respond to an appellate court decision, they often have strong attitudes about the policy embodied in that decision. One kind of attitude is their *policy preferences*, their views about the desirability of a policy in itself. Another is how they think a policy will affect their *self-interest*. Not surprisingly, these attitudes are the most powerful forces that determine how officials implement a court policy.

The policy preferences of judges and administrators affect their implementation of decisions in a straightforward way. If asked to carry out an appellate court decision with which they agree, they can be expected to do so with alacrity. Their response will be less enthusiastic if they strongly disagree with a decision.

It follows that the implementation of appellate court decisions has an ideological dimension. In the federal courts of appeals, for instance, liberal judges on the Ninth Circuit have balked at some of the conservative policies adopted by the Supreme Court in recent years. For their part, conservative judges on the Fifth Circuit have resisted some of the Court's decisions that favor the rights of criminal defendants.

Appellate court rulings can affect the self-interest of judges and administrators in several ways. These rulings may threaten or reinforce practices that officials find advantageous. Or they may ask elected officials to take positions that are highly popular or unpopular with their constituents.

These two attitudes go far to explain responses of judges and administrators to appellate court decisions on criminal procedure and school religious observances. Many teachers and school administrators strongly favor prayer as part of the school day and extracurricular activity. There is often very strong community support for religious observances in school. Thus it is not surprising that noncompliance with the Supreme Court rulings has been widespread.

The incentives to balk at decisions that expand the rights of criminal defendants may be even stronger. Most people who work in the criminal justice system believe that such decisions represent bad public policy. Further, expanded procedural rights make their work more difficult. For trial judges, full compliance with decisions that favor defendants can consume considerable time and resources, and such compliance may have negative political consequences in light of the strong public support for tough stances toward defendants.

The same explanations account for the most significant example of noncompliance in the recent past, the near-absence of school desegregation in the Deep South in the first decade after *Brown v. Board of Education*. Most decision makers in that region thought that school segregation was desirable. Further, school administrators, state officials, and even federal district judges felt strong political and social pressure to maintain segregation. Under the circumstances, compliance with *Brown* was not an attractive option.

Any court decision that requires major changes in policy is likely to conflict with the policy preferences or self-interest of many judges and administrators. One reason is that people and organizations left on their own choose the policies that accord with their preferences and self-interest. Hence, when an appellate court intervenes to demand a change, it is usually demanding that officials do what they find less desirable. Perhaps just as important, officials tend to resist any major change that is imposed on them because it is easier to continue doing things the same way than to adopt new routines.

In light of all this, why do major court decisions receive as much positive response as they do? For one thing, the judges and administrators who are responsible for carrying these decisions out are not always strongly opposed to them. The border states desegregated their schools more quickly than the Deep South largely because their school officials were not as strongly opposed to the idea of desegregation. Police officers gradually learned that literal compliance with *Miranda* did not make their job much more difficult, because most suspects are willing to answer questions despite hearing the prescribed warnings. And two other factors, discussed next, work in favor of compliance.

Judicial Authority   One of the factors that can foster compliance is acceptance of appellate court *authority,* the right of those courts to bind legal subordinates with their rulings. It appears that most public officials accept an obligation to follow the legal rules that are laid down by courts above them as part of their general obligation to obey the law. Lawyers are directly imbued with this duty through their training. Because most judges are lawyers and because they themselves benefit from judicial authority, judges are especially willing to accept the authority of higher courts.

The impact of court authority can be seen in the responses to some unpopular decisions. To take one example, a great many teachers and school administrators have eliminated religious observances that they personally favored. This willingness to follow the courts' lead despite disagreement with their decisions stems chiefly from acceptance of the obligation to do what courts ask. The impact of authority is sometimes quite explicit, when judges proclaim their willingness to apply a higher-court precedent despite their disapproval of the policy expressed in that precedent. In 2003, for instance, a federal court of appeals judge said that a long prison sentence that had been imposed under a "three-strikes" law was "unconscionable and unconstitutional," but he also said that he would affirm the sentence because of a relevant Supreme Court decision.[28]

Although judicial authority may be strong, it is not absolute, and a public official's disagreement with the substance of a policy may outweigh the authority of the court that issued the policy. Such intense disagreement is most likely to arise on issues that arouse strong feelings, such as abortion and the death penalty. More important, officials can often reconcile their acceptance of a court's authority with evasion of its ruling. They may, for instance, seize upon the ambiguity in an appellate court opinion to avoid following its spirit. This was the response of many federal district judges to *Brown v. Board of Education*, in which the Supreme Court required that schools be desegregated "with all deliberate speed."[29] Judges who opposed desegregation interpreted this language as allowing them to delay the initiation of desegregation for many years, so long as they could point to any practical difficulties.

Sanctions   If appellate courts encounter resistance to their rulings, we might expect them to employ *sanctions,* penalties designed to force compliance. Appellate courts do possess sanctions they can employ against disobedient judges and administrators. But these sanctions are fairly weak in comparison with those in most other organizations. The Supreme Court, for instance, cannot fire a district judge who refuses to follow its decisions.

For lower-court judges, the most common sanction is reversal of decisions that fail to follow an applicable ruling. Judges do not like to have their decisions reversed because this suggests that they have erred, and a judge who is frequently reversed may be perceived as incompetent. Hence judges have an incentive to apply appellate court rulings properly to the cases they decide.

Yet reversal has limited practical consequences—usually only the requirement that a judge rehear a case. Thus, judges may be willing to accept reversals as the cost of taking the course they prefer. One Cincinnati judge continued the practice of expunging (in effect, erasing) convictions for serious violent offenses despite a state law to the contrary and more than a dozen reversals by a state court of appeals.[30] And a federal district judge in California re-imposed a relatively lenient sentence twice after reversals of that sentence. The third time that it heard the case, the court of appeals allowed the sentence on the basis of the Supreme Court's recent decision striking down the mandatory federal sentencing guidelines. For a dissenting judge on the court of appeals, this was just an "excuse": "faced with the district judge's obdurate refusal to comply in any serious way with our mandate, we have given up."[31] In any event, reversals do not always follow disobedient decisions, in part because such decisions might not be appealed and reviewed.

For administrative bodies, having to defend a policy in court and becoming subject to a court order that requires a change in policies can constitute significant sanctions. If a school continues to hold prayer exercises despite the Supreme Court's decisions, an unhappy parent can file suit and secure an order against such practices. The monetary costs of going to court and the embarrassment of an adverse court order can deter noncompliance. But like reversal, this is not a very powerful set of sanctions. One reason is that someone with legal standing must go to court to seek an order requiring compliance with a decision, and frequently no one does so. Thus many school districts can continue religious observances that the Supreme Court prohibited because no lawsuit has ever been filed against them.

For administrative bodies that depend more directly on the courts, judges have a stronger sanction: the refusal to give needed support to agency policies. Some regulatory agencies, such as the National Labor Relations Board, require court enforcement of their rulings. Less directly, police departments are dependent on courts to convict the defendants they arrest. Thus noncompliant behavior that jeopardizes enforcement of agency rulings or conviction of defendants carries real costs. For instance, police officers want to follow court requirements for obtaining evidence so that their evidence will not be ruled inadmissible in court. But achieving a conviction is not always of great importance to individual police officers, who are judged chiefly on their ability to make "good arrests" rather than on the convictions of people they arrest. For this reason, they may be willing to jeopardize a conviction by violating judicial rules.

Faced with what they see as noncompliance, appellate courts can take stronger measures. For one thing, they can try to embarrass noncompliant officials by rebuking them. Some federal courts of appeals have strongly criticized immigration judges in the Justice Department, primarily for decisions that deny applications for political asylum.[32] But such rebukes may have limited effect if officials have strong reasons to adhere to their ways of doing things, as is true of immigration judges.

When administrators violate a direct court order, they or their governments may be cited for contempt of court and given a monetary penalty. Though judges are usually reluctant to use such a strong sanction, they occasionally rule that governments or their personnel are in contempt. The use of the contempt power figured in a long battle between a federal district judge and the executive branch over trust funds it held on behalf of Indian tribes, a battle described in Exhibit 9.4.

EXHIBIT 9.4   Judge Lamberth, the Court of Appeals, and the Executive Branch

As part of the federal government's complex policies toward Indian tribes and their members, the government holds certain lands in a trust for individual members. As one court opinion put it, "the federal government has failed time and again" to carry out its duties as trustee properly. In response to this record, in 1996 five individuals brought a class-action lawsuit on behalf of all beneficiaries of the trust, challenging its handling by the Interior and Treasury departments.

The case was assigned to Judge Royce Lamberth of the federal district court for the District of Columbia. Once he was immersed in the case, Judge Lamberth expressed considerable unhappiness with both the historical mismanagement of the trust and what he perceived as the failure of current federal officials to meet their responsibilities to the trust and to his court. Over the years he handed down several decisions designed to overcome these problems by ordering changes in the government's practices and supervising its handling of the trust accounts. In 1999 he held that the Secretary of the Treasury, the Secretary of the Interior, and an Assistant Secretary of the Interior in the Clinton administration were in contempt of court for failure to provide certain documents. Three years later he ruled that the Secretary of the Interior and one of her Assistant Secretaries in the George W. Bush administration were in contempt. His opinions criticized the executive branch in unusually strong terms.

Judge Lamberth's rulings were regularly appealed to the court of appeals for the D.C. circuit. The judges who heard those appeals agreed with Lamberth that the government had not met its responsibilities, but in several decisions they held that he had gone too far in his rulings and reversed those rulings. This interaction culminated in a 2006 decision by the court of appeals. In that decision the court reversed two orders that Lamberth had issued to the Interior Department, one of them requiring that every mailing it sent to beneficiaries of the trust include a notice that any of the information in the mailing "may be unreliable." Citing the history of the case and Lamberth's scathing criticism of the executive branch, the court of appeals asked the chief judge of the district court to reassign the case to a different judge.

In the same opinion the court of appeals added a warning to the executive branch: "the government must remember that although it regularly prevails on appeal, our many decisions in no way change the fact that it remains in breach of its trust responsibilities. In its capacity as trustee and as representative of all Americans, the government has an obligation to rise above its deplorable record and help fashion an effective remedy." The court of appeals had overcome what its judges saw as Judge Lamberth's straying from the proper course under the law. But neither the court of appeals nor Judge Lamberth had overcome what both saw as the failure of the executive branch to do what was required under the law.

Sources: Court decisions. The quotations are from, in order, *Cobell v. Norton*, 240 F.3d 1081, 1086 (D.C. Cir. 2001); *Cobell v. Norton*, 229 F.R.D. 5, 22 (D.D.C. 2005); and *Cobell v. Kempthorne*, 455 F.3d 317, 335 (D.C. Cir. 2006).

Taken together, the sanctions that appellate courts can employ are significant but quite imperfect. Lower-court judges and administrators often have strong reasons to balk at appellate court policies. Although the authority of appellate courts and their sanctions do overcome some resistance, they are not strong enough to produce perfect compliance. As a result, the policies of appellate courts—like other government policies—often run into implementation problems.

Responses by the Legislative and Executive Branches

Legislatures and chief executives have considerable power to shape the impact of court decisions. Unlike lower-court judges and administrators, they can directly overturn decisions with which they disagree. They also hold power over courts as institutions.

Responding to Statutory Interpretations   The primary business of appellate courts is interpretation of statutes, the laws that legislatures enact. Most of these interpretations are uncontroversial. But some statutory decisions arouse opposition from legislators or officials in the executive branch. These opponents can use a straightforward remedy: adoption of new legislation that overrides the offending court decision. In this sense, the legislature is "the ultimate appeals court."[33]

Bills to undertake such overrides are introduced quite often in Congress. Like other legislation, most of these bills fall by the wayside at some point, but many are enacted. Indeed, one study found that more than 5 percent of the Supreme Court's statutory decisions from the late 1970s to the late 1980s eventually were overturned by Congress.[34] Although no comparable figures are available on state legislatures, it is clear that they also override statutory decisions with some frequency.

More often than not, efforts to overturn statutory decisions stem from the unhappiness of interest groups with those decisions. In 2005, for instance, a federal court of appeals struck down some regulations of the Agriculture Department on the ground that they were inconsistent with the Organic Foods Production Act of 1990. The decision thereby prohibited the use of synthetic substances in processing of food that was labeled "organic." Large food producers, which used synthetic substances in food processing but wanted the marketing advantage of the "organic" label, sought an override of the decision. Later in 2005, they achieved their goal when Congress included an override in the annual appropriations bill for the Agriculture Department.[35] The executive branch can be thought of as an interest group, one that has special influence in Congress, and some overrides result from initiatives by the president or administrative agencies. One prominent example was the overrides of two Supreme Court decisions on the rights of suspected terrorists, described in Exhibit 9.5.

Occasionally, legislators act in response to their own outrage at a court decision or what they perceive as their constituents' outrage. In September 2003, a federal district judge ruled that the Federal Trade Commission did not have the authority to establish a "do-not-call" registry for people to block commercial solicitations by phone. The decision aroused widespread unhappiness, and the other branches reacted with unusual speed: six days after the decision, President Bush signed into law a bill authorizing the do-not-call registry.[36] In California, a state supreme court decision that upheld a prenuptial agreement and thus limited what baseball player Barry Bonds

EXHIBIT 9.5   Overriding the Supreme Court on the Rights of Guantanamo Prisoners

In 2002 the United States began to house suspected terrorists in a prison at the Guantanamo Bay Naval Base in Cuba. The detention and treatment of these suspects raised several legal questions. One question was whether inmates at Guantanamo could challenge their detention by seeking writs of habeas corpus. In *Rasul v. Bush* (2004), the Supreme Court ruled that federal courts had jurisdiction to hear such challenges.

President George W. Bush then sought legislation to overturn the *Rasul* decision. After considerable debate, Congress enacted the Detainee Treatment Act of 2005, which barred habeas corpus suits by detainees at Guantanamo. The language of the statute did not make explicit whether it applied to cases that had already been initiated when the statute was enacted. The Bush administration argued that the law barred such pending cases, but in *Hamdan v. Rumsfeld* (2006), the Supreme Court ruled against the administration on that issue. In *Hamdan* the Court also held that there was no legal basis for the military commissions that the Defense Department had set up to try some of the Guantanamo prisoners.

President Bush once again asked Congress to reverse the Supreme Court, and Congress responded with the Military Commissions Act of 2006. This statute effectively nullified the two major rulings in *Hamdan* by barring habeas corpus actions that were pending when it was enacted and by providing legislative authorization for military commissions. Some commentators argued that the prohibition on habeas corpus lawsuits was unconstitutional. That argument was certain to be raised in federal court, so the interplay between the courts and the other branches over the Guantanamo prisoners would continue.

Sources: Supreme Court decisions, statutes, newspaper articles.

owed to his former wife helped to spur legislation that added new conditions under which prenuptial agreements would be unenforceable.[37]

Those whose court victories have been snatched away by legislatures sometimes challenge the new statutes on the ground that they violate a constitutional provision. In a bitter post-divorce battle, the former wife was imprisoned for contempt of court in the District of Columbia for refusing court-mandated visitation by her former husband with their daughter. Members of Congress who sympathized with the mother secured enactment of a 1989 law that freed her from prison. She then took the daughter to live in New Zealand, beyond the reach of the court that had ordered visitation. When she sought to return to the U.S., Congress in 1996 passed a second provision that was named after the mother and that was written in a way that would prevent the father from having visitation. The mother and daughter then came home. The father challenged this provision on multiple grounds. In 2003 a federal court of appeals struck down the law under the constitutional provision that prohibits bills of attainder—acts of Congress aimed at punishing individuals—because of the effects of the congressional action on the father's reputation.[38]

Legislative overrides of statutory decisions are only one aspect of the process through which the statutory law develops. In fields such as criminal law and environmental protection, each branch helps to shape and reshape public policy through a series of actions and decisions. Legislation, implementation by the executive branch, and judicial interpretations modify and build on each other, creating a body of law that reflects the initiatives of all three branches.

Responding to Constitutional Interpretations   Ordinarily, a court decision that overturns a statute on constitutional grounds can itself be overturned only by a constitutional amendment. The federal and state constitutions have intentionally been made difficult to amend. Under the usual procedures, amendment of the United States Constitution requires the agreement of two-thirds of each house of Congress and three-quarters of the state legislatures. Since the Bill of Rights was adopted in 1791, only seventeen amendments have survived this process. State constitutions are usually amended through another two-stage process, which involves a proposal by the legislature and its ratification by the voters. This process is less cumbersome than its federal counterpart, but it is still difficult. In some states, however, the voters can amend their constitution unilaterally by approving an initiative measure.

At both the state and federal levels, constitutional amendments have been used to overturn court decisions. Four amendments to the federal Constitution clearly were aimed at overturning Supreme Court decisions, and five others also might be put in that category. The most recent such amendment was the Twenty-sixth, which nullified a 1970 decision that limited congressional power to lower the legal voting age.[39] In the states, several constitutional amendments have been adopted in recent years to overturn court decisions. The most common subject has been criminal justice issues. In 2004, for instance, Hawaii voters voted for three measures overturning state supreme court decisions that had been favorable to criminal defendants.[40]

Especially at the federal level, most efforts to overturn decisions through constitutional amendments fail even when the decisions in question are highly unpopular. In response to the liberal activism of the Supreme Court since the 1950s, members of Congress have introduced dozens of amendments designed to overturn particular decisions, yet only on flag burning have such resolutions received the necessary two-thirds majority in either house of Congress. The House has provided that majority in every two-year Congress since 1995, and in 2006 one of the flag-burning measures failed by only a single vote in the Senate.

Under some circumstances, a legislature can negate or limit the effect of a constitutional decision through statutory action. When the Supreme Court struck down state death penalty laws in *Furman v. Georgia* (1972), its ambiguous decision seemed to indicate that redrafted versions of those laws would be constitutionally acceptable if they established clearer standards for imposing the death penalty. In response, most states did redraft their statutes, and the Court upheld some of the new statutes in 1976.[41] As a result, any state legislature that wanted to impose the death penalty simply had to follow the models that the Court accepted.

Other statutory responses have been in more direct conflict with the court decisions in question. After *Brown v. Board of Education*, for example, southern states adopted a variety of laws to prevent desegregation, most of which were clearly unconstitutional and were struck down by federal courts. State legislatures have also enacted statutes that directly contravened Supreme Court decisions on school prayer and abortion.

Influencing the Implementation Process In several ways, legislatures and chief executives can help determine how court decisions are put into practice. First, they may influence the behavior of implementers by taking positions on controversial decisions. For example, the strong and active opposition of some southern governors to school desegregation contributed to the lack of meaningful desegregation in the Deep South during the decade after *Brown v. Board of Education.*

Second, the legislature and executive can provide—or fail to provide—tangible help in achieving effective implementation. After a decade of inaction in the Deep South, Congress in 1964 gave the executive branch the power to withhold federal funds from school districts that refused to desegregate. The Johnson administration used this power with some vigor, and the result was that real desegregation finally began in that region.

Finally, some court decisions require compliance by legislatures or chief executives themselves. Perhaps the most famous example was the Supreme Court decision in *United States v. Nixon* (1974), which required that President Nixon turn over tape recordings of his conversations to a federal court. After some hesitation, Nixon complied, even though material in the recordings forced his resignation. President Clinton was faced with a series of federal court orders in the investigations of his conduct by independent counsel Kenneth Starr and in other legal proceedings. Clinton complied with those orders by turning over evidence and providing his own testimony, even though that testimony ultimately resulted in his impeachment. His compliance, like that of Nixon and other presidents, reflects a perception that the president's legitimacy would be seriously damaged by a refusal to obey court rulings.

In recent years, state legislatures have frequently been faced with court rulings that required them to make major changes in public institutions. In many states, federal judges have ordered improvements in prisons and mental hospitals, and several state supreme courts have ordered changes in state systems for the funding of public schools. Legislators have good reasons to try to carry out these orders. Most important, if they fail to do so, courts may take more drastic action, such as requiring that a prison be closed. But budgetary constraints may make effective implementation of a sweeping decision very difficult, and legislators often resent court rulings that require institutional change.

As a result of these conflicting considerations, the record of legislative action in response to those decisions is mixed. For instance, state legislatures have responded very differently to court decisions that require fundamental changes in school funding systems. At one end of the spectrum, the Kentucky legislature responded enthusiastically to a 1989 state supreme court decision that struck down the state's funding system. At the other end, the New Jersey Supreme Court battled with the state legislature for twenty-five years over changes in school funding mandated by the court. In Ohio the legislature engaged in only minimal compliance with the rulings of the state supreme court on school funding, and the court ultimately chose to retreat from confrontation with the other branches.[42]

By no means do all issues of legislative compliance involve momentous policy questions. Exhibit 9.6 describes a long-running battle over use of a local beach in Connecticut.

EXHIBIT 9.6   Winning Access to the Beaches of Greenwich

Greenwich is an affluent town of about sixty thousand people in Connecticut. In 1977 the town enacted an ordinance that allowed only town residents and their guests into public beaches. Responding to a lawsuit by a nonresident, in 2001 the state supreme court ruled that the residents-only law violated provisions of both the federal and state constitutions.

The town chose to comply with the decision in literal terms, but it did not exactly welcome nonresidents to its beaches. Early in 2002 the Greenwich Board of Selectmen approved a fee of $308 for a nonresident adult for a summer season pass to its beaches and an additional fee of $100 for parking. (Residents paid $20 for a season pass and nothing for parking.)

Stung by criticism, town officials then took a harder line, announcing that the pass requirement would apply to all city parks. But they later retreated a bit, establishing a new fee structure that charged $10 per person for a day's pass to the city's beaches plus a $20 parking fee. With modifications, this policy was maintained in future years. In 2006 a lawsuit from another nonresident was pending, one that charged Greenwich with "willful and wanton contempt" of the 2001 decision. That July an out-of-town reporter rode his bicycle to the gate to the park and beach that had been the subject of the supreme court's decision. He was informed that he needed to go to the civic center two miles away to pay his daily fee. A clerk there sold him a day pass. "They don't really want you here," she explained.

Sources: Leydon v. Town of Greenwich, 777 A.2d 552 (Conn. Sup. Ct. 2001); newspaper articles. The quotations are from Rick Green, "Greenwich Freezes Out an Outsider," *Hartford Courant*, July 11, 2006, B1.

Attacking the Courts as Institutions   The policies that legislatures and chief executives adopt in response to court decisions are only one part of their relationship with courts. Another element of that relationship derives from the power of the other branches over court jurisdiction, budgets, and staffing. If they are unhappy with court policies, officials in the other branches can use these powers to attack the courts, either to limit what the courts can do as policymakers or simply to exact a measure of revenge. And whether or not they actually use their powers against the courts, public officials can threaten their use explicitly or implicitly.

At the federal level, the president and Congress frequently threaten to take action against the courts, but such an attack is seldom carried out. Since the 1950s, for instance, a multitude of bills have been introduced in Congress to remove the jurisdiction of the Supreme Court or of all federal courts over such areas as abortion and school busing. A few of these bills have passed one house of Congress, but none have been enacted.[43] Nor has anything come of occasional threats to impeach judges whose decisions displeased members of Congress. Even so, strong and sometimes vitriolic criticism from Congress concerns judges. In the past few years, several Supreme Court justices have expressed their concern about this criticism, and Sandra Day O'Connor has spoken several times about it before and since her retirement from the Court. In one 2005 speech she said that "in our country today, we're seeing efforts to prevent an independent judiciary."[44]

In the states, serious conflicts between courts and the other branches are far from rare. Such conflicts have arisen in states such as Colorado, Connecticut, and New Hampshire in recent years. The conflicts have been especially heated in Massachusetts, the result of state supreme court decisions on issues such as same-sex marriage and state funding of political campaigns.[45]

Perhaps nowhere have the battles between branches been as fierce as they are in Florida. Since the Republican party gained control of the legislature and the governorship in 1999, ideological differences between the courts and the other branches have produced a series of conflicts over the death penalty, school vouchers, and other issues. When decisions by the Florida Supreme Court and some lower courts temporarily threatened the election of George W. Bush as president in 2000, Republican legislators and Governor Jeb Bush denounced the decisions. Various proposals have been put forward to give the other branches greater control over the courts, and in 2001 the legislature did change the law so that the governor could select all members of the commissions that nominate appellate judges. One battle ultimately extended to the federal government as well. That episode, described in Exhibit 9.7, underlines the tensions that currently exist between the judicial branch and the other branches of government.

As much as some judges decry hostility from the other branches today, things were worse in some states during the early nineteenth century. One legislature reportedly expressed its displeasure with a decision of the state supreme court by reducing the justices' annual salaries to twenty-five cents.[46] The Kentucky legislature went even further in the 1820s. Unhappy with decisions that had struck down two statutes, some legislators sought to remove all the judges on the Kentucky Court of Appeals. After they failed to obtain the necessary two-thirds majority to achieve the judges' removal, they acted by a simple majority to abolish the court and create a replacement for it. The old court refused to disband, and litigants and trial judges had to decide which court to pay attention to. At one point, the governor prepared to use military force to prevent the old court from recovering its papers that had gone to the new court. The conflict was settled after two years when the legislature rescinded its establishment of the new court.[47]

The Courts and the Other Branches: The General Relationship

The other branches of government frequently override court decisions that interpret statutes, and they sometimes override the courts' interpretations of constitutions or take action that limits their impact. Legislators and chief executives sometimes denounce the courts and threaten measures that would affect them directly, such as the removal of jurisdiction or the impeachment of judges. Occasionally, they follow through on those threats.

Still, the other branches use their powers against courts and court decisions less often than we might expect. This is especially true at the federal level. Congress and the president have vast powers to undo court decisions through legislation and the proposal of constitutional amendments and equally vast powers to attack the courts as institutions. Why have they not used these powers more extensively?

EXHIBIT 9.7 The Battle over Terri Schiavo

In 1990 a Florida woman named Theresa (Terri) Schiavo, twenty-six years old, suffered a heart attack. She never regained consciousness but continued to live in what one court characterized as "a permanent or persistent vegetative state." In 1998 Schiavo's husband Michael sought to end the procedures that maintained Terri's life. Her parents, the Schindlers, opposed that step, and a fierce conflict between them and Michael developed.

A state trial court authorized the step that Michael Schiavo sought, and a court of appeal affirmed its judgment in 2001, on the basis of the judges' best judgment of what Terri Schiavo would have wanted. The Schindlers challenged that ruling in a new legal action, but the trial court and court of appeal ruled against them. In 2003, after additional court proceedings, the procedures that maintained Terri Schiavo's life were terminated.

But legislators and Governor Jeb Bush strongly opposed that action. Legislation was quickly enacted to require that the life-sustaining procedures be reinstated, and under this legislation Governor Bush signed an executive order that brought about immediate reinstatement. Michael Schiavo challenged the legislation, and all three levels of Florida courts held that it was unconstitutional. In 2005 the Supreme Court decided not to hear the case.

At that point President George W. Bush and conservatives in Congress sought federal legislation to preserve Terri Schiavo's life. After some debate, a law was enacted that allowed the Schindlers to bring a federal lawsuit to reinstate the life-sustaining procedures. The Schindlers did bring a lawsuit, but a federal district court and court of appeals ruled against their motion to require that the procedures be reinstated, and the Supreme Court once again refused to hear the case. Further efforts were made in federal and state court to reverse that result, but these were rejected, and Terri Schiavo died.

The judges who ruled against the Schindlers had received strong criticism, and the criticism escalated after Terri Schiavo's death. House Majority Leader Tom DeLay denounced in strong terms the federal judges whom he viewed as having ignored the will of Congress, saying that "the time will come for the men responsible for this to answer for their behavior." After polls showed widespread disapproval of the federal government's intervention in the case, Congress took no action against the judiciary. But the episode was one more source of tension between courts and the other branches, both in Florida and at the national level.

Sources: court decisions, newspaper stories. The quotations are from *In re Guardianship of Schiavo*, 780 So. 2d 176, 177 (Fla. Ct. App. 2001), and Carl Hulse and David D. Kirkpatrick, "Even Death Does Not Quiet Harsh Political Fight," *New York Times*, April 1, 2005, A1.

One reason is the sheer difficulty of such action. On controversial matters—and direct action against a court or its judges is almost always controversial—it is usually difficult to get past the many potential roadblocks in the legislative process. Because constitutional amendments require more than simple legislative majorities, they are relatively difficult to adopt.

Another reason is the tinge of illegitimacy that is attached to many forms of anti-court action, especially attacks on the courts as institutions. Even the adoption of constitutional amendments may seem illegitimate if the provisions to be amended are themselves regarded as sacrosanct. Amendments to overturn Supreme Court decisions that expanded civil liberties have the appearance of cutting into the Bill of Rights, and such a step would bother many members of Congress a good deal. This is part of the reason that none of the many resolutions to undo the civil libertarian decisions of the past half century with a constitutional amendment has yet been approved by Congress and sent to the state legislatures.

The courts themselves sometimes deter action against them by the other branches. Faced with heavy criticism, judges may retreat from unpopular policies or avoid creating new provocations. The general doctrine that courts should avoid declaring laws unconstitutional when possible helps to limit tensions with legislators.

Though these factors reduce conflict between branches, they hardly eliminate it. As noted earlier, we are now in a period when officials in the legislative and executive branches are especially prone to criticize courts and judges in strong terms. And such conflict aside, in a routine and undramatic way legislators and chief executives frequently take actions that fully or partially reverse court rulings. The other branches of government have considerable impact on the courts and on the policies they make.

The Impact of the Courts on Society

The most important impact that any government institution can have is on society as a whole—on people's behavior as individuals and on social institutions such as the family and the economy. The courts have been given credit, or blame, for a wide range of effects on society:

- Some commentators argue that state court decisions expanding the right to sue for personal injuries have resulted in enormous economic costs for businesses. These commentators also argue that much-needed products and services are unavailable because of increased fears of lawsuits on the part of business leaders and professionals such as doctors.
- Since the 1960s, conservatives have criticized the Supreme Court and other courts on the ground that their expansions of the rights of criminal defendants have seriously weakened the effectiveness of the criminal justice system. Similarly, some people have concluded that court decisions expanding the legal rights of public school students have, as one commentator put it, "threatened the ability of public schools to socialize youth for productive roles in society."[48] On the other hand, some liberals believe that these and other decisions have improved American society by effectively expanding the rights and liberties of Americans.
- Supreme Court decisions, especially those on abortion and school prayer, have been cited as powerful stimuli for the emergence of the religious right as a major political movement. By the same token, Supreme Court decisions in support of racial equality are often credited with helping to spur the civil rights revolution in the 1950s and 1960s and improving the status of African American citizens since that time.

- Religious leader Pat Robertson has asserted that the "ill-conceived decisions" of the Supreme Court, "more than any other cultural phenomenon, have shredded the moral fabric of this nation."[49] For his part, Supreme Court justice Clarence Thomas has argued that the "rights revolution" fostered by the courts has produced "a culture that declined to curb the excesses of self-indulgence" and "has affected the ideal of personal responsibility."[50]

If most of these assertions and others like them are accurate, courts make a great deal of difference for American society.

Limits on the Impact of Courts   When commentators claim that courts have had powerful effects, good or bad, their logic is often quite reasonable. Still, these claims should be viewed with some skepticism, because court decisions are only one of many influences on social behavior and social institutions.

First, policymakers in the other branches also act on issues that courts address, and their actions can narrow or even negate court-made policies. *Brown v. Board of Education* did not produce much desegregation in the Deep South for a decade because school administrators and other officials resisted the Supreme Court's ruling. When desegregation did occur later, the most direct cause was enforcement actions by Congress and the Johnson administration.

More broadly, judicial policies in any field coexist with policies of the other branches of government. Those policies have their own impact, and effects that are ascribed to courts actually may result from legislative and executive action. Thus much of the great increase in legal abortion rates during the 1970s resulted from statutes enacted by state legislatures before *Roe v. Wade*.[51] A tremendous array of government policies might influence the education and behavior of young people, and it is the other branches rather than the courts that operate the schools.

Second, forces other than government policies shape society in powerful ways. The capacity of government to do either good or ill is constrained by more fundamental influences on individual behavior and the structure of society. Racial discrimination has proved at least moderately resistant to government action, in part because it is deeply rooted in some people's perceptions and attitudes. Government has an impact on American culture, but so do family socialization, the mass media, and other influences. Courts are limited by these conditions just as the other branches are.

Two somewhat different examples of potential impact illustrate these limits on the courts' impact.

The Status of Women   Until the 1960s, courts generally ratified and accentuated the inequalities between women and men that were established by other institutions in society. The Supreme Court, for instance, upheld state laws that excluded women from the legal profession, restricted other employment opportunities, and prevented women from voting.

In the last four decades, courts have largely reversed that traditional position. Through interpretations of the federal and state constitutions, courts have issued a great many decisions that demand equal treatment of women and men by government. This wave of court decisions has overturned a large number of laws and legal rules that put women at a disadvantage, including provisions that limited the rights of women in marriage and laws that treated female criminal defendants in special ways. These decisions have also speeded the elimination of other laws that discriminate by sex and made still other laws unenforceable.

During the same period, the status of women in American society has changed dramatically. One of many examples is the growing representation of women in such professions as law and medicine. To what extent are the courts responsible for these changes? On the whole, it appears that they have played only a minor part.[52] One reason is that the judiciary as a whole has not been fully committed to eradicating sex discrimination in the law. But even a stronger commitment would have had only limited effects when compared with other forces. Changes in the status and roles of women reflect a general social revolution in American society, a revolution that has been spurred chiefly by changes in matters such as women's educational attainments rather than by government action. To the extent that government has encouraged this revolution, legislatures and chief executives have done more than appellate courts, primarily because they are better situated to take actions that can have a major impact.

Employment provides a good illustration of these general points. The concentration of women in certain occupations and the relatively low wages of the average female worker result from a wide range of conditions, including the education and socialization of girls, the disproportionate role of women in caring for children, and discrimination by employers. Recent improvements in the employment status of women also derive from several sources. Government policies certainly have played a part in achieving these improvements. But the courts did not and could not initiate those policies: the constitutional requirements of equality that courts interpret do not apply to the private sector, and courts cannot establish detailed rules and enforcement schemes even for discrimination in government employment. Rather, legislation against employment discrimination such as the Civil Rights Act of 1964 and its implementation by the executive branch have been the key government actions. Courts have made some important interpretations of antidiscrimination laws on issues such as sexual harassment. Yet the effects of their decisions appear to be quite limited in comparison with action by the other branches and with social change in society as a whole.

The Incidence of Crime   Over the past half century, state and federal appellate courts have expanded the procedural rights of criminal defendants in several areas. The Supreme Court of the 1960s played the most visible part in this development. Among other things, the Court required that indigent defendants in any serious case be provided with attorneys, that suspects be warned of their rights prior to police questioning, and that evidence seized illegally by the police be excluded from use in court. Since the 1970s, the Court has been less supportive of defendants' rights, but it has maintained substantial protections for those rights. Supreme courts in many states have participated in the expansion of rights, sometimes going beyond the Supreme Court in this respect.

Almost from the beginning, these expansions of defendants' rights were blamed for contributing to the problem of crime. As a candidate for president in 1968, Richard Nixon frequently said that "some of our courts have gone too far in weakening the peace forces as against the criminal forces."[53] Three decades later, a legal scholar and future federal judge referred to "*Miranda*'s countless victims" and "the human suffering *Miranda* inflicts" by preventing confessions.[54] Other political candidates and scholars, among other people, have voiced similar sentiments.

How might court decisions affect the incidence of crime? As critics see it, appellate court decisions make it more difficult to obtain and use needed evidence against criminals, thus reducing the likelihood that they will be apprehended and convicted. One effect is that people who would otherwise be imprisoned are left free to commit additional crimes. Further, as people who are contemplating criminal acts become aware that their chances of conviction and punishment have decreased, they are more willing to commit such offenses.

This analysis cannot be evaluated with confidence because the information we have is both limited and conflicting, but some very tentative judgments are possible. The first issue is the effect of expanded defendants' rights on conviction rates. It is not clear how many convictions are "lost" because illegally seized evidence is ruled out or because suspects are read their *Miranda* rights and then decide not to talk with the police, and there is heated disagreement among scholars about the *Miranda* issue.[55] But the studies that have been done suggest that a fairly small proportion of potential convictions are lost as a result of restrictions on questioning of suspects and on searches and seizures of evidence.[56]

Of course, these small proportions translate into sizable numbers of cases. Thus it might be true that court decisions expanding the rights of criminal defendants have led to many additional crimes by people who otherwise would have been incarcerated. But if appellate courts have the massive impact that some people ascribe to them, this impact must be considerably broader, extending to calculations by people who are considering whether to commit crimes: large numbers of people would choose to commit crimes because they perceive that the chances of conviction have declined. Rational calculations appear to play a part in many, if not most, decisions to commit crimes. But emotional and moral factors are involved as well. Even if a significant reduction in the likelihood of conviction has resulted from rulings of appellate courts, it is not clear that such a reduction would be sufficient to change many decisions whether to engage in crime.

In any event, policymakers who participate in the criminal justice system on a day-to-day basis almost surely affect conviction rates a good deal more than do appellate courts. Police officers, prosecutors, and trial judges have more direct control over what happens in specific cases. They also put appellate court policies into effect, reshaping and sometimes weakening these policies in the process. Legislatures have considerable impact through their funding of the criminal justice system. Thus the numbers of people who are apprehended and punished for crimes and the deterrent impact of the criminal justice system on people who are contemplating criminal activity are affected primarily by institutions other than appellate courts.

The impact of court decisions that expand the rights of criminal defendants remains uncertain. But there are reasons to question the judgment that these decisions have a major impact on the incidence of crime.

The Impact That Courts Do Have   The examples of crime and women's status underline the need for caution about ascribing massive effects to court decisions.

These examples also show why it is difficult to ascertain the impact of the courts on society: their policies coexist with other forces that affect the same phenomena, and in that situation it is usually quite difficult to isolate the courts' effects. Thus, we should not overestimate the impact of court decisions or assume that we can pinpoint that impact. Even so, the courts can and do help to shape society. Their impact operates in several ways.

First, court decisions have direct effects. If judges and juries are sympathetic to injured individuals and thus prone to transfer money from businesses to those individuals, the transfers in themselves affect the resources of these two groups.

Second, courts affect social behavior by changing people's incentives and opportunities. Thus expansion of the right to sue for personal injuries may have increased the economic incentives for individuals and lawyers to bring lawsuits. In turn, the growing volume of lawsuits may have increased the financial risk of making products that are subject to lawsuits for personal injuries, thereby leading manufacturers to stop making those products. Similarly, people may be more willing to assert their right to free speech if court decisions reduce the chances that they will be punished for doing so.

The kind of impact is especially visible in the economic arena. Interpretations of the antitrust laws by the federal courts since the 1970s have reduced the legal barriers to mergers, thereby reinforcing more basic sources of the trend toward larger and fewer companies in particular industries. A 1938 Supreme Court decision allowed employers to hire permanent replacements for striking workers, and the belated use of this power by companies in the 1980s and 1990s was one reason for the weakening of the labor movement.[57]

Finally, courts can help to trigger broader social change by influencing people's thinking and the structures in which they operate. It is important not to overstate the contribution of the courts to changes in the status and roles of African American citizens.[58] Courts certainly have not been the primary source of those changes. As with women's rights, the most important sources were outside government. Moreover, much of the government policy supporting racial equality came from the legislature (such as prohibitions of employment discrimination) or was initiated by the courts but became effective only when the other branches of government acted (such as school desegregation and protection of the right to vote in the Deep South).

Yet courts almost surely facilitated change in race relations. Although court decisions were insufficient to desegregate southern schools without congressional help, they did make desegregation possible. Perhaps more important, *Brown v. Board of Education* and other decisions were significant symbols; they declared that government support for discrimination was constitutionally unacceptable and encouraged other efforts to achieve racial equality. Once the civil rights movement became active, the Supreme Court took extraordinary steps to protect it, striking down convictions of people arrested in demonstrations and overturning state laws that were intended to cripple civil rights organizations. The Court's decisions were neither necessary to sustain the movement nor sufficient to protect it from harassment, but they probably helped to strengthen it.

The second and third mechanisms for court impact have both operated in the area of abortion. The impact of the Supreme Court's 1973 decision in *Roe v. Wade* is often exaggerated because people do not take into account the changes in social attitudes and legislative policies that preceded *Roe*. Yet the Court greatly speeded up the process of legal change with its original decision and with later rulings that limited state regulation of abortion. Thus the Court's decisions were one of the forces that produced large increases in the numbers of legal abortions.

Politically, *Roe v. Wade* became a focal point for the debate over abortion. Political movements often grow in response to unfavorable developments, and *Roe* provided a strong impetus for growth in the pro-life movement. And court decisions on social issues such as abortion have served as a basis for mobilization of conservative groups since the 1970s, an impact reflected in the continuing criticisms of the courts—sometimes vitriolic—by conservative political leaders.

That criticism is a reminder of another function of court decisions. Whether or not they have a significant impact on social behavior, rulings by the courts stand as symbols, sometimes as pronouncements of constitutional values. This is one reason that decisions with almost no practical effect can still arouse strong emotions, as has been true of the Supreme Court's rulings on flag burning. If the courts' impact on society is often exaggerated, the function of their decisions as symbols helps to explain that exaggeration.

CONCLUSIONS

This chapter has examined the roles of appellate courts as policymakers. The discussion of these roles has highlighted some general lessons that run through the book as a whole. Three lessons are especially important.

First, the actions that courts take reflect a complex set of factors. The factor with the most direct effects is the qualities of the people who serve as judges. Their values, their self-interest, and their personalities largely determine the choices they make on the bench. Thus, it makes considerable difference which people become judges. In turn, this means that those who select judges—presidents, governors, voters, and others—have considerable impact on the courts. To a great extent, the shifts in the policies of the federal courts over the last century can be explained by the appointment decisions of a series of presidents.

Of course, judges are not the only decision makers in the courts. At the trial level, jurors are regular participants in decision making. For their part, attorneys have a great deal to do with what happens to cases. When judges do decide cases, they are subject to an array of influences from their political, social, and legal environment. Those influences can be as specific as the fear that a decision might threaten a judge's re-election or as diffuse as changes in public attitudes that affect judges' own perceptions of an issue. The most fundamental influence is the language of the laws that courts are called upon to interpret, language created chiefly by legislatures. Thus, judges are not entirely autonomous when they choose what to do.

Second, the work of the courts depends on the cases that come to them. This means that lawyers make a good deal of difference, since their advice to clients and their own choices help to determine which cases go to court and which are appealed. On the criminal side of the law, police officers are important in creating potential cases through their decisions whether to arrest suspects.

For the same reason, ordinary people shape the courts' work. What courts do is largely a product of the millions of decisions made each year by people about whether to take their problems and opportunities to court: to seek the collection of a debt, the termination of a marriage, or compensation for an injury. In this way, the willingness of people to litigate in general and in specific situations basically sets the agendas of the courts.

Third, the power of courts over the other branches of government and over society as a whole is substantial but limited. Without question, the courts make a great deal of difference. They influence the political process, the content of government policies, and the lives of individuals. Everything from the custody of children to the outcomes of elections is sometimes resolved by courts.

At the same time, the courts' impact is channeled by a variety of forces. Administrators and legislators help to determine what actually happens to a Supreme Court decision. The long-term impact of court decisions on school prayer or abortion results from a series of responses by government officials and private citizens. Because of those responses, a decision often has narrower effects than its wording would suggest.

These lessons point to the most general conclusion of this book: the courts are closely linked with the rest of government and society. There is a tendency to view the courts as distinct and isolated, separate from the political process that operates in the other branches of government. The reality is quite different. The cases that come to court, what courts do with those cases, and the effects of their choices all involve the same kind of complex process that affects legislatures and the executive branch. Thus, the courts are very much a part of American government and society.

FOR FURTHER READING

Bell, Derrick. *Silent Covenants: Brown v. Board of Education and the Unfulfilled Hopes for Racial Reform.* New York: Oxford University Press, 2004.

Canon, Bradley C., and Charles A. Johnson. *Judicial Policies: Implementation and Impact,* 2nd ed. Washington, D.C.: CQ Press, 1999.

Ely, James W., Jr. *Railroads and American Law.* Lawrence: University Press of Kansas, 2002.

Epp, Charles R. *The Rights Revolution: Lawyers, Activists, and Supreme Courts in Comparative Perspective.* Chicago: University of Chicago Press, 1998.

Leo, Richard A., and George C. Thomas III, eds. *The Miranda Debate: Law, Justice, and Policing.* Boston: Northeastern University Press, 1998.

McCann, Michael W. *Rights at Work: Pay Equity Reform and the Politics of Legal Mobilization.* Chicago: University of Chicago Press, 1994.

Pacelle, Richard L., Jr. *The Transformation of the Supreme Court's Agenda from the New Deal to the Reagan Administration.* Boulder, Colo.: Westview Press, 1991.

Reed, Douglas S. *On Equal Terms: The Constitutional Politics of Educational Opportunity.* Princeton, N.J.: Princeton University Press, 2001.

Rosenberg, Gerald N. *The Hollow Hope: Can Courts Bring About Social Change?* Chicago: University of Chicago Press, 1991.

White, Welsh S. *Miranda's Waning Protections: Police Interrogation Practices after Dickerson.* Ann Arbor: University of Michigan Press, 2001.

Online Study Center Go to college.hmco.com/PIC/baum6e for ACE practice test questions and additional resources.

NOTES

1. Theodore Eisenberg, "Appeal Rates and Outcomes in Tried and Nontried Cases: Further Exploration of Anti-Plaintiff Appellate Outcomes," *Journal of Empirical Legal Studies* 1 (November 2004), 663–667; Lynne Liberato and Kent Rutter, "Reasons for Reversal in the Texas Courts of Appeals," *South Texas Law Review* 44 (2003), 436–454; Thomas H. Cohen, *Appeals from General Civil Trials in 46 Large Counties, 2001–2005* (Washington, D.C.: U.S. Department of Justice, Bureau of Justice Statistics, 2006), 1, 4.
2. Kevin M. Clermont and Theodore Eisenberg, "Plaintiphobia in the Appellate Courts: Civil Rights Really Do Differ from Negotiable Instruments," *University of Illinois Law Review* 2002 (2002), 971. See also Eisenberg, "Appeal Rates and Outcomes."
3. The proportion of affirmances is based on analysis of the Supreme Court Database, created by Harold Spaeth (available at http://www.as.uky.edu/polisci/ulmerproject/sctdata.htm). The 2 percent disturbance rate treats as disturbances the actions in which the Court sends cases back to lower courts for reconsideration without hearing arguments or writing opinions.
4. Joy A. Chapper and Roger A. Hanson, *Understanding Reversible Error in Criminal Appeals* (Williamsburg, Va.: National Center for State Courts, 1989), 34–35.
5. *Marshall v. Marshall*, 164 L. Ed. 2d 480 (2006). See David Savage, "Justices Side with Ex-Model, Keeping Alive Her Estate Claim," *Los Angeles Times*, May 2, 2006, A4.
6. This discussion is based primarily on Donald R. Songer, Reginald S. Sheehan, and Susan B. Haire, *Continuity and Change on the United States Courts of Appeals* (Ann Arbor: University of Michigan Press, 2000), 47–70.
7. See, for instance, Stanton Wheeler, Bliss Cartwright, Robert A. Kagan, and Lawrence M. Friedman, "Do the 'Haves' Come Out Ahead? Winning and Losing in State Supreme Courts, 1870–1970," *Law & Society Review* 21 (1987), 403–445; Peter Karsten, *Heart versus Head: Judge-Made Law in Nineteenth-Century America* (Chapel Hill: University of North Carolina Press, 1997); and James W. Ely, Jr., *Railroads and American Law* (Lawrence: University Press of Kansas, 2002).
8. Songer, Sheehan, and Haire, *Continuity and Change on the Courts of Appeals*, 119–128.
9. James A. Henderson, Jr., and Theodore Eisenberg, "The Quiet Revolution in Products Liability: An Empirical Study of Legal Change," *UCLA Law Review* 37 (February 1990), 479–553; Theodore Eisenberg and James A. Henderson, Jr., "Inside the Quiet Revolution in Products Liability," *UCLA Law Review* 39 (April 1992), 731–810.
10. Barry Latzer, "The Hidden Conservatism of the State Court 'Revolution,'" *Judicature* 74 (December–January 1991), 190–197; G. Alan Tarr, "The Past and Future of the New Judicial Federalism," *Publius* 24 (Spring 1994), 63–79.
11. Wayne R. LaFave, *Search and Seizure: A Treatise on the Fourth Amendment*, 4th ed. (St. Paul, Minn.: Thomson/West, 2004), vol. 1, 68 n.45.
12. William Haltom and Michael McCann, *Distorting the Law: Politics, Media, and the Litigation Crisis* (Chicago: University of Chicago Press, 2004).
13. Richard Willing, "'Activist' Label Actively Applied," *USA Today*, March 10, 1997, 3A (quoting Joel Grossman). See Keenan D. Kmiec, "The Origin and Current Meanings of 'Judicial Activism'," *California Law Review* 92 (October 2004), 1441–1477.
14. These figures are taken from Lawrence Baum, *The Supreme Court*, 9th ed. (Washington, D.C.: CQ Press, 2007), 165, 168.
15. Blaine Harden, "Bush Policy Irks Judges in West," *Washington Post*, October 6, 2006, A3.
16. *San Antonio Independent School District v. Rodriguez*, 411 U.S. 1 (1973).
17. See Karen Swenson, "School Finance Reform Litigation: Why Are Some State Supreme Courts Activist and Others Restrained?" *Albany Law Review* 63 (2000), 1147–1182.

18. Greg Winter, "Judge Orders Billions More in Aid for New York City Schools," *New York Times*, February 15, 2005, A19.

19. "Prisoner's Release Comes After Wait of Two Years," *Washington Post*, June 4, 2002, A11.

20. Henry Weinstein, "Judges Want a Convicted Killer Freed; D.A. Unmoved," *Los Angeles Times*, January 29, 2004, A1; Henry Weinstein, "Inmate Finally Freed as D.A. Backs Off," *Los Angeles Times*, April 3, 2004, A1.

21. *Tomaino v. Burman*, 834 A.2d 1095 (N.J. Super. Ct., App. Div. 2003).

22. See Jon B. Gould and Stephen D. Mastrofski, "Suspect Searches: Assessing Police Behavior Under the U.S. Constitution," *Criminology and Public Policy* 3 (2004): 901–948, and Welsh S. White, *Miranda's Waning Protections: Police Interrogation Practices after Dickerson* (Ann Arbor: University of Michigan Press, 2001).

23. Leonard Post, "A Loaded Box of Stereotypes," *National Law Journal*, April 25, 2005, 1, 18; Holly Becka, Steve McGonigle, Tim Wyatt, and Jennifer LaFleur, "Judges Rarely Detect Jury Selection Bias," *Dallas Morning News*, August 23, 2005, 1A, 10A, 11A.

24. See Steve Bogira, *Courtroom 302: A Year Behind the Scenes in an American Criminal Courthouse* (New York: Alfred A. Knopf, 2005), 16–17, 67, 157–158, 261.

25. Martha M. McCarthy, "Much Ado over Graduation Prayer," *Phi Delta Kappan* 75 (October 1993), 120–125; Kevin T. McGuire, "Schools, Religious Establishments, and the U.S. Supreme Court: An Examination of Policy Compliance" (paper presented at the annual meeting of the Midwest Political Science Association, Chicago, April 2005).

26. See Mark Singer, "God and Football," *The New Yorker*, September 25, 2000, 38–42.

27. Neela Banerjee, "Families Challenging Religious Influence in Delaware Schools," *New York Times*, July 29, 2006, A8.

28. *Wallace v. Castro*, 65 Fed. Appx. 618, 619 (9th Cir. 2003).

29. *Brown v. Board of Education*, 349 U.S. 294, 301 (1955).

30. *State of Ohio v. Pitts*, 2003 Ohio App. LEXIS 1656 (Ohio Ct. App. 2003).

31. *United States v. Menyweather*, 431 F.3d 692, 705 (9th Cir. 2005).

32. See *Benslimane v. Gonzales*, 430 F.3d 828 (7th Cir. 2005).

33. Bill McAllister, "535, the Ultimate Appeals Court," *Washington Post*, December 11, 1997, A25.

34. Lori Hausegger and Lawrence Baum, "Behind the Scenes: The Supreme Court and Congress in Statutory Interpretation," in *Great Theatre: The American Congress in the 1990s*, ed. Herbert F. Weisberg and Samuel C. Patterson (New York: Cambridge University Press, 1998), 228.

35. The decision was *Harvey v. Veneman*, 396 F.3d 28 (1st Cir. 2005). The statute was the Agriculture, Rural Development, Food and Drug Administration, and Related Agencies Appropriations Act, 2006, Public Law 109-97 (2005); the override was contained in Section 797. See "An Organic Drift" (editorial), *New York Times*, November 4, 2005, A26.

36. The decision was *U.S. Security v. Federal Trade Commission*, 282 F. Supp. 2d 1285 (W.D. Okla. 2003). The statute was Public Law 108-82 (2003).

37. The decision was *In re Marriage of Bonds*, 5 P.3d 815 (Calif. Sup. Ct. 2000). The statute was California Family Code sec. 1615, amended 2001. See "Prenuptial Contract Bill Goes to Davis," *San Jose Mercury News*, August 28, 2001.

38. *Foretich v. United States*, 359 F.3d 1198 (D.C. Cir. 2003). The history of this conflict is described in the court's opinion.

39. *Oregon v. Mitchell*, 400 U.S. 112 (1970).

40. Jaymes Song, "Isle Ballot Measures Shake Up Legal Arena," *Honolulu Star-Bulletin*, December 20, 2004.

41. *Gregg v. Georgia*, 428 U.S. 153 (1976).

42. William Celis III, "Kentucky Begins Drive to Revitalize Its Schools," *New York Times*, September 26, 1990, B6; Russell S. Harrison and G. Alan Tarr, "School Finance and Inequality in New Jersey," in *Constitutional Politics in the States: Contemporary Controversies and Historical Patterns,* ed. G. Alan Tarr (Westport, Conn.: Greenwood Press, 1996), 178–201; *Abbott v. Burke*, 710 A.2d 480 (N.J. Sup. Ct. 1998); *State ex rel. State of Ohio v. Lewis*, 789 N.E.2d 195 (Ohio Sup. Ct. 2003).

43. Lauren C. Bell and Kevin M. Scott, "Policy Statements or Symbolic Politics? Explaining Congressional Court-Limiting Attempts," *Judicature* 89 (January–February 2006), 196–201.

44. Andrew Cohen, "Lady Justice Rises," CBSNews.com, July 25, 2005.

45. Mark C. Miller, "Court-Legislative Conflict in Massachusetts," *Judicature* 88 (September–October 2004), 97–99.

46. Evan Haynes, *The Selection and Tenure of Judges* (Newark, N.J.: National Conference of Judicial Councils, 1944), 95.

47. Theodore W. Ruger, " 'A Question Which Convulses a Nation': The Early Republic's Greatest Debate About the Judicial Review Power," *Harvard Law Review* 117 (January 2004), 827–897.

48. Richard Arum, *Judging School Discipline: The Crisis of Moral Authority* (Cambridge, Mass.: Harvard University Press, 2003), 188.

49. Pat Robertson, *Courting Disaster: How the Supreme Court is Usurping the Power of Congress and the People* (Nashville: Integrity Publishers, 2004), xxiv.

50. "Thomas Critiques the 'Rights Revolution,' " *Legal Times*, May 23, 1994, 23.

51. See Matthew E. Wetstein, "The Abortion Rate Paradox: The Impact of National Policy Change on Abortion Rates," *Social Science Quarterly* 76 (September 1995), 607–618.

52. See Gerald N. Rosenberg, *The Hollow Hope: Can Courts Bring About Social Change?* (Chicago: University of Chicago Press, 1991), 202–246.

53. Donald Grier Stephenson, Jr., *Campaigns and the Court: The U.S. Supreme Court in Presidential Elections* (New York: Columbia University Press, 1999), 181.

54. Paul G. Cassell, "Miranda's 'Negligible' Effect on Law Enforcement: Some Skeptical Observations," *Harvard Journal of Law & Public Policy* 20 (Winter 1997), 345. The decision was *Miranda v. Arizona*, 384 U.S. 436 (1966).

55. See, for instance, Paul G. Cassell, "*Miranda*'s Social Costs: An Empirical Assessment," *Northwestern University Law Review* 90 (Winter 1996), 387–499, and George C. Thomas III and Richard A. Leo, "The Effects of Miranda v. Arizona: 'Embedded' in Our National Culture?" *Crime and Justice* 2002 (2002), 203–266.

56. On *Miranda*, see the studies cited in the two preceding notes. Evidence on searches and seizures is presented in Thomas Y. Davies, "A Hard Look at What We Know (and Still Need to Learn) About the 'Costs' of the Exclusionary Rule: The NIJ Study and Other Studies of 'Lost' Arrests," *American Bar Foundation Research Journal* 1983 (Summer 1983), 611–690; and Peter F. Nardulli, "The Societal Costs of the Exclusionary Rule Revisited," *University of Illinois Law Review* 1987 (Spring 1987), 223–239.

57. Fredrick Kunkle, "Many Strikers Outmatched," *Washington Post*, October 23, 2000, B1, B5; Steven Greenhouse, "Strikes Decrease to a 50-Year Low," *New York Times*, January 29, 1996, A1, A10. The decision was *National Labor Relations Board v. Mackay Radio & Telegraph Co.*, 304 U.S. 333 (1938).

58. Rosenberg, *The Hollow Hope*, 39–169; Derrick Bell, *Silent Covenants: Brown v. Board of Education and the Unfulfilled Hopes for Racial Reform* (New York: Oxford University Press, 2004).

Index of Cases

In citations of court decisions, the first number is the volume of the court reports in which the decision is found, the designation of the court reports (such as "U.S." for the United States Reports) follows that number, and the second number is the first page of the decision. The year of the decision is in parentheses; except for the Supreme Court or where the name of the reporter indicates which court decided the case, the designation of that court is indicated before the year. A state name (such as "Mass.") indicates a state supreme court; a state name preceded by a district (such as "N.D. Fla.") indicates a federal district court; a circuit number (such as "9th Cir.") indicates a federal court of appeals.

Index

Abbott, Karen, 148
Abortion
  as court concern and subject of litigation, 1
  implementation and impact of court decisions, 297, 304, 307, 308, 311, 312
  judicial policies, 292
Abraham, Henry J., 120
Abramoff, Jack, 183
Abramowicz, Michael, 131
Acevedo, Roland, 197
Administration of courts, *see* Federal courts; State courts
Administrative agencies. *See also specific federal agencies*
  appeals from agency decisions, 245
  compared with courts, 6
  implementation of court decisions, 294–300
Administrative courts, 6
African Americans. *See also* Racial discrimination
  as judges, 126, 127
  as lawyers, 59, 60, 64
Agriculture Department, U.S., 300
Aguirre, Mike, 67
Alabama
  courts, 145, 223
  judges, 145
  lawyers, 75
  selection of judges, 108, 111, 271
Alaska
  courts, 174
  judges, 152
  lawyers, 152, 153, 174
Albonetti, Celesta, 195
Alexeev, Michael V., 241
Alito, Samuel, 14, 97–99, 267, 268
Allstate Corporation, 204
Alschuler, Albert W., 196
Alternative dispute resolution, 219, 220
Ambady, Nalini, 238
American Arbitration Association, 218

American Association for Retired Persons (AARP), 77
American Bar Association (ABA), 56, 57, 71, 75, 86, 100, 144, 276
American Center for Law and Justice (ACLJ), 258
American Civil Liberties Union (ACLU), 256, 257, 263, 293
American Judicature Society, 94
American Telephone and Telegraph Company (AT&T), 219
Americans with Disabilities Act (ADA), 221
Amestoy, Jeffrey, 50
Amicus curiae briefs, 256, 257
Amon, Elizabeth, 92
Amway Corporation, 215
Amy, Marc T., 148
Aniston, Jennifer, 219
Appellate courts. *See also* Federal courts; State courts; *specific states*
  agendas and business, 244, 245, 260, 263, 286–288
  appeals, 252–260
  central staffs, 246, 252, 264
  compared with trial courts, 5, 8, 9, 133, 134, 243, 245
  decision making, 265–278
  functions and purposes, 7, 8, 244
  impact of policies, 294–312
  participants, 245–247
  policies, 288–294
  procedures, 247–252
  review of lower court decisions, 284–286
  screening of appeals, 260–265
Appointment of judges, *see* Judicial selection
Arakawa, Lynda, 123, 280
Arbitration, 6, 214, 218–220
Argetsinger, Amy, 198
Arizona
  lawyers, 58
  selection of judges, 115